Strategies and Techniques
of Child Study

Strategies and Techniques of Child Study

Edited by

ROSS VASTA

Department of Psychology
State University of New York
College at Brockport
Brockport, New York

Foreword by

PAUL H. MUSSEN

ACADEMIC PRESS 1982
A Subsidiary of Harcourt Brace Jovanovich, Publishers
New York London Toronto Sydney San Francisco

ACADEMIC PRESS, INC.
111 Fifth Avenue, New York, New York 10003

United Kingdom Edition published by
ACADEMIC PRESS, INC. (LONDON) LTD.
24/28 Oval Road, London NW1 7DX

Library of Congress Cataloging in Publication Data
Main entry under title:

Strategies and techniques of child study.

    Includes index.
    1. Child psychology--Methodology. 2. Child
psychology--Research. I. Vasta, Ross.
BF722.S77 1981   155.4'01'8   81-15072
ISBN 0-12-715080-3   AACR2
ISBN 0-12-715082-X (pbk.)

PRINTED IN THE UNITED STATES OF AMERICA

82 83 84 85   9 8 7 6 5 4 3 2 1

For Jamie

Contents

1   Child Study: Looking toward the Eighties   1

ROSS VASTA

2   Infancy   13

TIFFANY FIELD

11 Working with Children 325

PENELOPE H. BROOKS and EARLINE D. KENDALL

List of Contributors

Numbers in parentheses indicate the pages on which the authors' contributions begin.

JEFFREY BISANZ (209), Department of Psychology, University of Alberta, Edmonton, Alberta, Canada T6G 2EL

PENELOPE H. BROOKS (325), George Peabody College for Teachers, Vanderbilt University, Nashville, Tennessee 37203

JILL G. deVILLIERS (117), Department of Psychology, Smith College, Northampton, Massachusetts 01063

PETER A. deVILLIERS (117), Department of Psychology, Smith College, Northampton, Massachusetts 01063

BEVERLY I. FAGOT (273), Department of Psychology, University of Oregon, Eugene, Oregon 97403

TIFFANY FIELD (13), Departments of Pediatrics and Psychology, Mailman Center for Child Development, University of Miami, Miami, Florida 33101

ANN M. FRODI (49), Department of Psychology, University of Rochester, Rochester, New York 14627

JOAN E. GRUSEC (245), Department of Psychology, University of Toronto, Toronto, Ontario, Canada M5S 1A1

ROBERT KAIL (209), Department of Psychological Sciences, Purdue University, West Lafayette, Indiana 47907

EARLINE D. KENDALL (325), George Peabody College for Teachers, Vanderbilt University, Nashville, Tennessee 37203

MICHAEL E. LAMB (49), Department of Psychology, University of Utah, Salt Lake City, Utah 84112

SCOTT A. MILLER (161), Department of Psychology, University of Florida, Gainesville, Florida 32611

HARRIET L. RHEINGOLD (305), Department of Psychology, University of North Carolina at Chapel Hill, Chapel Hill, North Carolina 27514

DANIEL W. SMOTHERGILL (83), Department of Psychology, Syracuse University, Syracuse, New York 13210

ROSS A. THOMPSON* (49), Department of Psychology, University of Michigan, Ann Arbor, Michigan 48109

ROSS VASTA† (1), Department of Psychology, State University of New York College at Brockport, Brockport, New York 14420

* *Present address:* Department of Psychology, University of Nebraska, Lincoln, Nebraska 68588

† *Present address:* Department of Applied Behavioral Sciences, University of California, Davis, Davis, California 95616

Foreword

Interest and activity in the field of child study has burgeoned in the last 20 years. The scope and definition of the field have expanded enormously, new areas of research have emerged, and traditional issues have been conceptualized in novel ways; analyses of problems have become more profound and more subtle; the urgent need to investigate socially relevant problems systematically is generally recognized; and naturalistic studies are more prominent than they were in the past.

As is always true in science, advances are based to a great extent on improvements in old research methods and on the introduction of better, more adequate techniques and strategies. This volume, edited by Ross Vasta, describes the most significant recent approaches and innovative methods in child study, especially those that have emerged in the last 20 years. However, it should not be regarded as a simple revision or updating of the *Handbook of Research Methods in Child Development* that I edited over 20 years ago, for it differs radically in organization and content from that earlier, now outdated, book. The contrasts between the two books—too numerous to delineate here—attest to the vast improvement in the caliber of research as well as to the vigor and sophistication of the field today. The evidence of change and progress in the last 20 years is impressive.

Nine chapters of this volume deal with topics that now receive major research attention. These chapters, written by experts in the field, describe the newest and most valid methods used in research in particular aspects of development, evaluating their advantages and shortcomings in concrete, practical terms. Many of these techniques—experimental, observational, and statistical—which permit more rigorous, more valid, and more reliable studies, did not even exist (or existed only in very primitive forms) 20 years ago—for example, video equipment and videotaping, microanalysis, telemetry, computer devices for automated recording and analysis, time-lag correlations, path analysis, and multivariate analyses.

But this book offers much more than descriptions and evaluations of a broad array of modern research methods. Its pages contain a wealth of research wisdom, basic principles, advice, goals, ideals, and caveats. The reader is stimulated to *think* about basic issues of research: the conceptualization of problems, design of research, choice of methods to be used, and ethical questions that might arise. Methods per se cannot direct research plans; on the contrary, the ways in which problems are formulated determine the most appropriate strategies and methods to be used.

The contributors also communicate attitudes and orientations that foster the development of the best research climates. They urge researchers to act as creative problem solvers, applying the greatest possible ingenuity and imagination not only to the invention of special techniques but also to devising new research paradigms. Researchers are warned to draw conclusions cautiously, relying on multiple methods, multiple samples, and multiple testing, together with converging findings, rather than on the analyses of a single set of data. In elaborating methods of studying specific topics, the authors focus attention on the interactive nature of development, the complex relationships among antecedent and outcome (effect) variables. As they make clear, findings on one particular facet of development—say, language acquisition—must be placed in the contexts of other aspects of development—such as thinking and personality—and of social and historical settings.

In brief, the book addresses a broad range of general and specific issues clearly and in depth, sensibly balancing "how to" directions and basic principles of research. Students just beginning their research careers will find it a welcome introduction and guide, and experienced researchers will gain a rich and useful source of new information and new ideas.

PAUL H. MUSSEN

Department of Psychology and Institute of Human Development
University of California, Berkeley

Preface

In 1960 Paul Mussen edited the *Handbook of Research Methods in Child Development*. This now classic work, for the first time, organized research approaches in all areas of child behavior and development and presented them together in a single volume. The text has since served as a unique reference work for developmental and child psychologists.

The present volume will function, in part, to update many of the topics covered in the *Handbook*. It differs, however, in both level and scope.

The text is designed primarily for use by graduate-level students in training as child researchers. It also may be of value to some advanced undergraduates. Although not designed expressly for professional researchers, its value for them may be in describing methodological approaches in areas lying outside their principal fields of expertise.

This volume also is considerably less ambitious than the earlier volume (the *Handbook* was more than 1000 pages). Hence, the limited length will permit it to be used as a textbook, serving primarily a pedagogical rather than a resource function.

An introductory chapter provides an overview of child development research, emphasizing the movement toward ecologically valid methods. Chapters 2-9 are organized topically, with a major researcher in each area providing coverage of current methods, research problems, and emerging trends. Chapter 10 is a discussion of ethical considerations of research with children and the ever-increasing constraints they place on research methodology. Finally, Chapter 11 relates practical problems encountered when working with children, and offers a number of potential solutions and useful tips.

An overriding theme of the text is that high-quality, productive research often involves methods reflecting considerable creativity and ingenuity. As such, the book goes beyond a simple enumeration of research techniques to a more general consideration of methodological strategies and the problem solving required for their development.

For assistance in preparing a text of this sort, I must acknowledge the contributions of many individuals. I am particularly indebted to each of the contributors, whose confidence and continued support made the project possible. I also wish to thank Susan Marie Heiman and Barbara Miles Duffy for help in preparing the index material. Finally, I am grateful to the Department of Psychology at Brockport for providing an accommodating and fertile environment in which to pursue this task.

1

Child Study:
Looking toward the Eighties

ROSS VASTA

When discussing the progress that has occurred in child psychology (or, for that matter, in any field of science), we typically focus on increases in substantive knowledge, perhaps occasionally also acknowledging the guiding role of insightful theorizing. Milestones of progress are marked by such events as the discovery of a wide-ranging or counterintuitive phenomenon, or the development of a conceptual model that synthesizes previously disparate sets of data. Too often, advances in research methodology remain unheralded as a most important element in the evolution of a science. But it is the thesis of this text that it frequently falls on progress in research strategies or methods to move a theoretical issue from the stage of armchair debate to the point of empirical resolution, and that some advances in research methods represent as major a contribution as does any set of data or conceptual reformulation.

Others, in particular Kuhn (1970), have also noted the important role of changing methodology as the basis for scientific evolution. Kuhn's thesis is that at any given moment a particular field of science may be dominated by a generally accepted research paradigm. This paradigm, in essence, defines the "world view" of the field at that moment and establishes the framework within which most research is conducted. Only when the prevailing paradigm is abandoned and replaced, however, does revolution (and presumably, major advances in knowledge) become possible.

Child psychology is not easily characterized by any small number of such paradigms, perhaps owing to its comparatively recent beginnings. Instead, a number of dramatically different theoretical views and research approaches currently coexist. These include, for example, Skinnerian-based learning analyses, biologically oriented ethological views, Piagetian-type cognitive approaches, and computer-like information processing models.

1

STRATEGIES AND TECHNIQUES
OF CHILD STUDY

Consistent with Kuhn's position, however, the research paradigms corresponding to each of these theoretical positions often reflect assumptions inherent in the particular world view. The "arbitrary" nature of responses studied by Skinnerian theorists, the unobtrusive manner of ethological observational methods, or the clinical, probing quality of Piagetian assessment techniques, each is predicated on the researcher's larger conceptual view of the organism.

Progress in developmental psychology, therefore, does not currently appear to be constrained by a few limiting paradigms, at least not to the extent that is true in other areas of science. Rather, child psychologists remain comparatively free to approach research questions or issues with whatever scientific methods they choose, constrained only by their ingenuity and imagination. It is perhaps in this freedom that dramatic advances in our understanding of developmental processes may lie for the very near future.

Kuhn's analysis, however, is not entirely without relevance to research with children. But the sorts of changes required to move the field to a new plateau may involve simply a redirecting of our current efforts, rather than any major restructuring of our world view. Moreover, progress in research methodology may be an integral part of such a change in focus. To best pursue that issue, it is useful first to examine our current state of methodology.

CONTEMPORARY RESEARCH

The modern study of child psychology is rooted in the methods of science as they have developed principally during the past century. Inherent in this approach are a concern for rigorous objectivity, an emphasis on observable events and behaviors, and an acknowledgment of the need for agreed-upon rules of scientific evidence and a common language for professional communication.

Until recently, virtually all research could be classified approximately into two general categories. *Laboratory-experimental* research typically requires that the child be studied under highly structured conditions that can be carefully described and precisely replicated. This approach is designed to generate causative statements regarding the effects of specific variables on specific behaviors. In the *naturalistic-observational* approach, structure is sacrificed for realism. The research is conducted in the field or naturally occuring context of the behavior of interest. Here, a noninterventionist approach permits only correlational descriptions of variables, with the direction of causation remaining unspecifiable.

These classes of methodologies offer such different approaches to the investigation of any question or issue that their simultaneous acceptance by the scientific community may appear difficult to reconcile. But the coexistence of these approaches simply reflects the fact that multiple criteria exist for the evaluation of scientific research. And because each approach is more successful in satisfying some portion of these criteria, it offers advantages not found in the other.

The criteria conventionally used to evaluate the adequacy of research in psychology were developed some years ago (Campbell & Stanley, 1963). But, they remain valid today, despite the major changes in methodology that have since occurred.[1]

Internal Validity

The great majority of research investigations in child development have been, and continue to be, of the laboratory–experimental variety. The essence of this approach is the demonstration of cause–effect relationships by systematically varying some aspect of the environment (independent variable) and observing corresponding changes in some aspect of the child's behavior (dependent variable). The careful and repeated demonstration of such covariation permits the researcher to conclude that a functional relationship exists between the two classes of variables—that is, one causes the other.

In any experimental situation, many other variables may potentially be responsible for the observed changes in the dependent measure. Such alternative causes must either be eliminated or examined in the experiment, using various methodological, design, or statistical techniques. The certainty with which the researcher can ultimately conclude that changes in the behavior resulted from changes in the manipulated variable (and not from other sources) is referred to as the *internal validity* of the experiment.

Although each experiment possesses a unique array of variables offering potential alternative interpretations, a number of common classes of competing explanations can be described. In their early work, Campbell and Stanley offered eight frequent threats to internal validity. It is perhaps a sign of the increasing sophistication of research methodology that more re-

---

[1] More recent writings have expanded these criteria to include *statistical conclusion validity* and *construct validity* (Cook & Campbell, 1976). This wider classification does not alter the essence of the present chapter, and so the original criteria were retained for simplicity.

cent writings have included as many as fourteen (Cook & Campbell, 1976). Some of these factors are presented in Table 1.1.

External Validity

Whereas internal validity is concerned with our ability to reach unambiguous conclusions as to the cause–effect relationships under investigation, external validity moves beyond the specific experimental situation to our ability to generalize these findings. To what degree do the relationships one has identified in a particular study continue to hold true in other set-

TABLE 1.1
Threats to Internal Validity

History—Any environmental event that occurs between a pretest and posttest, other than the experimental variable, offers a competing explanation for pre- to postbehavior change.

Maturation—Biological or physiological changes (e.g., growth, fatigue, motor development) that occur between the pre- and postmeasurements may obscure the influence of the manipulated variable.

Testing—Repeated measurement or test taking may itself produce changes in behavior in addition to those that would otherwise be produced in the experiment.

Instrumentation—Any change in the measuring instrument (e.g., calibration of timers, accuracy of observers, validity of tests) may produce a change in response scores over time that is independent of treatment effects.

Statistical regression—Individuals scoring very high or very low on a pretest can be predicted, by probability alone, to display less extreme scores on a posttest, independent of any intervening treatment manipulation.

Selection—Any unplanned initial differences between groups of subjects may compete with the manipulated variable as an explanation for differences in the groups' behavior.

Mortality—If subjects are lost from the experiment for any reason, and the degree of loss differs over the various treatment groups, selection problems may result that distort posttest findings.

Selection-maturation interaction—In some research designs, selection involves intact, rather than randomly assigned, groups (e.g., males, good readers, high-risk babies) whose maturation during the pre- to postinterval may not be equivalent, confounding any between-group treatment manipulation.

Diffusion of treatment—If subjects in the different treatment groups can communicate with one another, the planned manipulation may be reduced, decreasing artificially the likelihood of between-group differences.

Compensatory equalization of treatment—When one treatment is viewed as potentially useful or desirable, individuals outside of the experimental situation (e.g., teachers, parents) may inappropriately provide similar experiences for the other subjects.

Compensatory rivalry/resentful demoralization—When assignment to different treatment groups is known, subjects in untreated or nonoptimal groups may alter their behavior in reaction to their group affiliation, either by spuriously inflating or depressing the behavior under study.

TABLE 1.2
Threats to External Validity

Testing sensitization—Pretesting subjects to determine their initial level of a behavior may change their sensitivity to the experimental variable and thus inappropriately alter posttest performance of the behavior.

Treatment-treatment interaction—If a subject is exposed to more than one treatment condition, performance on the second treatment may be affected by the previous exposure to the first treatment.

Selection-treatment interaction—If the procedures used in recruiting subjects for an experiment tend to favor or discourage certain groups, the treatment effects may not be generalizable to the larger population.

Setting-treatment interaction—The effects of a manipulated variable that are demonstrated in an experimental setting may not hold true in other settings.

History-treatment interaction—When the demonstration of an experimental effect coincides with an unrelated environmental event (e.g., studying children on the day before Christmas vacation), the generalizability of the effect may be in doubt.

tings, at other times, or with other subjects (Bracht & Glass, 1968)? Frequent threats to external validity are outlined in Table 1.2.

Contemporary investigators have selected their research methods to satisfy more or less these two forms of criteria. But, our traditional paradigms have been notably deficient in adequately satisfying both—hence the continued existence of two apparently disparate research approaches. This situation, however, appears to be changing markedly.

CHILD RESEARCH IN THE 1980s

Child psychology may be on the threshold of a new era. A retrospective view suggests that the discipline has progressed rapidly in this century. The 1920s and 1930s were marked by a relatively naive empiricism, in which researchers investigated many different areas and collected large stores of data with little theoretical direction. The pendulum swung considerably in the other direction during the 1940s and 1950s, when empiricism gave way to the building of grand theories and macroanalyses of child behavior and development. Perhaps the most important contribution of the 1960s was the rise of experimental child psychology. As a result of improved research techniques, many of the more rigorous laboratory methods in use with adults and lower animal species were applied to children and, increasingly, to infants and newborns.

The decade just passed is less easy to characterize, but certainly one major feature has been the abandoning of strong, exclusive, theoretical camps. With a new generation of psychologists has come a greater synthesis of ideas drawn from earlier schools of thought. Most clearly, the nature–nurture debate, along with its corollary controversies between heredity and environment and maturation versus learning, is all but gone as a global issue. These questions have been replaced by an increased interest in the operation of specific processes and mechanisms or in the interaction of innate and acquired factors. This change has been led, in large part, by an increasing attempt to develop theories so that they explain *typical* child development, rather than simply the behavior of the child as a laboratory subject.

As we move into the 1980s, then, what lies ahead? If the 1960s marked the application of rigorous laboratory methods to child study, and the 1970s witnessed a growing concern for "natural processes," the 1980s promise to be the decade when we move rigorous methodology out of the laboratory to join our theoretical focus on the real world.

The Ecological Movement

Traditionally, laboratory–experimental research permitted the investigator to take great care in insuring the internal validity of the experiment. Extraneous or competing sources of variability could be carefully monitored and rigorously controlled to provide a comparatively high degree of certainty in the ultimate cause–effect conclusions.

But the inordinate structure and sterility of the laboratory offered obvious concerns regarding the study's generalizability. Do relationships demonstrated under these conditions also hold true in the natural environment? Bronfenbrenner (1979) has been one of the leading critics of traditional laboratory research, arguing that: "The emphasis on rigor has led to experiments that are elegantly designed but often limited in scope. This limitation derives from the fact that many of these experiments involve situations that are unfamiliar, artificial, and short-lived, and call for unusual behaviors that are difficult to generalize to other settings [p. 18]."

McCall (1977), too, has argued cogently that both our theoretical and research efforts must move beyond the laboratory walls: "What value is our knowledge if it is not relevant to real children growing up in real families and in real neighborhoods . . . the process of development as it naturally transpires in children growing up in actual life circumstances has been largely ignored [p. 334]."

Such concerns, moreover, have not been restricted to developmental researchers. Similar statements, for example, can be found among researchers in the social (Ellsworth, 1977; Ring, 1967), comparative (Miller, 1977), and environmental (Proshansky, 1976) areas, as well.

The essence of these positions is that we must begin to consider an additional criterion when evaluating the adequacy of a research effort—its *ecological validity*. That is, to what extent do the principles or processes revealed in the laboratory continue to operate in a similar fashion in the organism's more typical environment? And to what extent are important processes that occur in the natural setting overlooked or de-emphasized in our experimental work (Gibbs, 1979; Wicker, 1979)?

The concern for authenticity, of course, is neither new nor restricted to only a small group of investigators. Over the years, even the most die-hard laboratory researchers have never professed an interest in studying processes that are unrelated or antithetical to those occurring in the natural environment. But the requirements of strict experimental control often left the investigator with little alternative other than to retain a high degree of structure. Put simply, child researchers have been aware of the preferred settings in which to conduct their research, but they have not had methods adequate to the task. What makes the current call for naturalism of greater significance, however, is that we may finally be acquiring the tools and tactics to make such an approach viable.

SOURCES OF ECOLOGICAL PROGRESS

If, as we suggest, child study is moving into a new era, it is because advances in our research methodology are leading the way. In terms of our earlier discussion, we have begun to increase markedly the external and ecological validity of our studies without the usual trade-off of internal validity requirements.

Illustrations of this movement will appear many times in this volume. In the areas of early social development (Chapter 3), language acquisition (Chapter 5), and sex role development (Chapter 9), in particular, a considerable degree of success in examining natural processes has already been achieved. The types of methodological advances necessary to increase ecological validity, of course, will vary with the subject area. But several general categories of improvements can be identified that have played a major role in adding rigor to a wide range of naturalistic research.

Observational Methods

As ecological concerns have pressed child study into field settings, the collection of observational data has gained increasing importance. Such methods often are nonmanipulative and always are as unobtrusive as possible, in an effort to capture the uncontaminated essence of the behaviors of interest.

But a traditional shortcoming of this approach is that data collected by a human observer, rather than by a machine, are potentially very imprecise. In addition to physical (e.g., reaction time), physiological (e.g., fatigue), and processing (e.g., coding and scanning) deficits, the human is also vulnerable to a host of subjective biases and prejudices not occurring in automated apparatus.

In recent years, however, the sophistication of observational methods has increased dramatically. The historical roots of these advances can be traced both to the applied behavior analysis movement of the 1960s (Bijou, Peterson, & Ault, 1968; Kent & Foster, 1977), as well as to researchers operating within the ethological framework (Sackett, 1978).

Three features of modern observational methodology are most clearly responsible for the increased rigor of this approach. First, the observational codes and procedures have themselves become more intricate and detailed. Second, the requirement of statistical reliability between independent observers has permitted some degree of assessment of the validity of observational data and, as such, has increased our confidence in data collected by this method. And finally, the increased focus of research on observational methods has uncovered previously ignored sources of bias and is helping to identify more efficient and reliable procedures (e.g., Kent, O'Leary, Diament, & Dietz, 1974; Mash & McElwee, 1974).

Observational Technology

Paralleling the growing sophistication of observational procedures have been technological advances in observational tools. Of primary importance here has been the increasing use of videotape equipment, as this form of recording has become less expensive and more portable.

The most obvious advantage of video recording is the opportunity it affords the researcher to capture a given event or interaction and reobserve it an infinite number of times. This flexibility permits the investigator to achieve a high degree of interobserver reliability, for example, by focusing attention on only restricted characteristics of the interaction during any single viewing. Moreover, as new research questions arise, or as coding and recording procedures improve, the very same tapes can be reobserved and rescored to provide additional or revised findings.

A second technological step involves automated recording and analysis devices designed for observational study. The best known of these is Datamyte (Electro General Corporation), a solid-state, portable keyboard that allows events to be recorded as they occur and stored in various memory formats. The board also can be interfaced with computer facilities to provide virtually simultaneous data analysis and feedback, including measures of frequency, duration, and conditional probabilities.

Such advances in technological sophistication, however, are not without their pitfalls. In Chapter 3 some of these potential problems (e.g., over-zealous, atheoretical data collection) are considered.

Statistical Techniques

One important goal of the modern scientific method is to identify cause–effect relationships. Traditionally, such conclusions have only been possible by means of experimental manipulation, relegating observational data to descriptive, preliminary, or at best, suggestive status. And because naturalistic research often involves primarily noninterventionist methods, the laboratory has appeared to be the ultimate testing ground for any research hypothesis. Although systematic manipulation remains the more sophisticated method of scientific inquiry, several statistical approaches do allow some degree of causal inference from nonexperimental data. These approaches are not all new, but their application to naturalistic research has increased markedly in recent years.

One of the best examples of these methods involves *time-lagged correlations* and *path analysis.* In essence, these techniques can be used to examine correlations between descriptive data taken at various points in time. By comparing the correlations among several variables at a given point with their intercorrelations over a particular time interval, direction-of-effects conclusions can be inferred. Further description and examples of this approach can be found in Chapters 8 and 9. (See also Rogosa, 1980, for a critique of this method.)

Another statistical technique useful in field-setting research is the *interrupted time-series* design. Often an investigator is interested in the effect of an abrupt environmental change on an ongoing behavior. At times, the manipulation may be introduced experimentally, but often it is simply an unplanned alteration occurring in the natural environment. If enough data are available prior to and following the interruption, it is possible to compare the rates of pre- and postbehavior and determine whether any observed change in the behavior sufficiently coincided with the environmental change to infer a causal relationship. This method is also becoming evident among operant and applied behavior analysis researchers, who have traditionally eschewed the use of conventional statistical techniques (e.g., Jones, Vaught, & Weinrott, 1977).

Additional statistical methods that increase the rigor of naturalistic research include the use of conditional probabilities (Patterson, 1974), multivariate analyses (McCall, 1977), sophisticated longitudinal designs (Wohlwill, 1973), and scaling techniques (see Chapter 6 of this volume).

Ecological Validity and the Laboratory

The categories of advances just described, along with innumerable specific methodological refinements, are rapidly increasing our ability to conduct child research of a very high caliber. Internal and external validity requirements are being concomitantly achieved in areas or on issues not previously amenable to both.

But it would be erroneous to conclude that simply moving our investigations to field settings automatically improves the ecological validity of the research. Nor is it always necessary to leave the laboratory in order to increase the generalizability of our data. Our purpose here is not to suggest that the laboratory will soon become obsolete as a crucible for scientific inquiry. In fact, as we shall see in the chapters to follow, the great bulk of current child study continues to occur within comparatively structured laboratory milieux.

The laboratory only threatens ecological validity to the extent that it spawns findings not applicable to the environment of ultimate interest to the researcher. Indeed, if findings generated in the lab can, in fact, be demonstrated to also hold true in the natural setting, many of the potential threats to generalizability (e.g., rigid structure, sterile surroundings, lack of spontaneity, etc.) then become methodological assets to our ability to draw clear cause–effect conclusions.

It follows then that moving scientific rigor out into the world need not be the only approach to increasing ecological validity. Alternatively, we may achieve the same end by introducing critical elements of the natural environment into the lab. This latter tactic, too, has been occurring with increasing frequency in child research. But, perhaps because this approach often involves more subtle methodological changes, it has been less salient as a research trend. Many examples of such laboratory advances will be evident throughout this volume.

THE CHILD RESEARCHER AS PROBLEM SOLVER

The movement toward more ecologically valid research clearly has gained impetus by progress in research methods. But, in turn, by raising the scientific community's consciousness to such concerns, ever-increasing methodological demands on the researcher are sure to follow. No longer are "highly generalizable" data likely to be viewed as unusually interesting or useful. Soon this characteristic may well become virtually a necessary component of acceptable research, reflected in such areas as journal publication policy, or federal grant funding decisions. Thus the press for better and more innovative techniques of child study appears certain to characterize the coming decade.

But studying children, whether in the lab, the home, or the school, is not a simple matter. A child's limited cognitive abilities often do not permit the application of many of the research techniques used in studying adults. Tasks involving complex instructions or those requiring unusual patience or perseverance, for example, may not be suited to the younger subject and, thus, may not elicit the information of interest. But, unlike the laboratory rat or monkey, a child possesses many more complex capabilities, including a sophisticated receptive and vocal language repertoire and a number of well-developed cognitive, reasoning, and operational skills. Many of the simpler techniques used to study other species would be inadequate to investigate the richness and diversity of children's abilities. In addition, some aspects of research on lower animals could not be applied to the study of children for social or ethical reasons.

This, then, is the challenge of child psychology—to develop methods and techniques that can be successfully used with a young, immature organism but that, nevertheless, can be effective in revealing the growing sophistication of a child's world. In this text, some of the emerging solutions to this task will become apparent, as we examine how child researchers are developing strategies and methods to answer our queries in many areas of child development. Sometimes the solution may lie in a specific technological advance, such as the development of a new instrument or recording device. Often, however, advances in methodology involve simply the creative application of current knowledge and techniques in novel ways to solve longstanding, and often thorny, problems.

In this regard, a major role of the successful child researcher must be that of a creative problem solver. Faced with the task of answering a particular theoretical or applied question, the investigator must select or develop a method that will unambiguously supply the relevant information. There are no rules or formulas that can easily lead the way to such solutions—only the researcher's experience, insight, and resourcefulness.

Unfortunately, science is sometimes viewed as a cold, impersonal business, requiring little sensitivity or imagination. But, when developing research methods, the effective scientist often displays the originality and creativity of an accomplished artist. In the pages that follow, some of this artistry is explored.

REFERENCES

Bijou, S. W., Peterson, R. F., & Ault, M. H. A method to integrate descriptive and experimental field studies at the level of data and empirical concepts. *Journal of Applied Behavior Analysis*, 1968, *1*, 175–191.

Bracht, G. H., & Glass, G. V. The external validity of experiments. *American Educational Research Journal*, 1968, *5*, 437–474.

Bronfenbrenner, U. *The ecology of human development: Experiments by nature and design.* Cambridge, Mass.: Harvard University Press, 1979.

Campbell, D. T., & Stanley, J. C. *Experimental and quasi-experimental designs for research.* Chicago: Rand McNally, 1963.

Cook, T. D., & Campbell, D. T. The design and conduct of quasi-experiments and true experiments in field settings. In M. D. Dunnette (Ed.), *Handbook of industrial and organizational psychology.* Chicago: Rand McNally College Publishing Company, 1976.

Ellsworth, P. C. From abstract ideas to concrete instances: Some guidelines for choosing natural research settings. *American Psychologist*, 1977, *32*, 604–615.

Gibbs, J. C. The meaning of ecologically oriented inquiry in contemporary psychology. *American Psychologist*, 1979, *34*, 127–140.

Jones, R. R., Vaught, R. S., & Weinrott, M. Time-series analysis in operant research. *Journal of Applied Behavior Analysis*, 1977, *10*, 151–166.

Kent, R. N., & Foster, S. L. Direct observational procedures: Methodological issues in naturalistic settings. In A. R. Ciminero, K. S. Calhoun, & H. E. Adams (Eds.), *Handbook of behavioral assessment.* New York: John Wiley & Sons, 1977.

Kent, R. N., O'Leary, K. D., Diament, C., & Dietz, A. Expectation biases in observational evaluation of therapeutic change. *Journal of Consulting and Clinical Psychology*, 1974, *42*, 774–780.

Kuhn, T. S. *The structure of scientific revolutions.* Chicago: University of Chicago Press, 1970.

McCall, R. B. Challenges to a science of developmental psychology. *Child Development*, 1977, *48*, 333–344.

Mash, E. J., & McElwee, J. D. Situational effects on observer accuracy: Behavior predictability, prior experience, and complexity of coding categories. *Child Development*, 1974, *45*, 367–377.

Miller, D. B. Roles of naturalistic observation in comparative psychology. *American Psychologist*, 1977, *32*, 211–219.

Patterson, G. R. A basis for identifying stimuli which control behaviors in natural settings. *Child Development*, 1974, *45*, 900–911.

Proshansky, H. M. Environmental psychology and the real world. *American Psychologist*, 1976, *31*, 303–310.

Ring, K. R. Experimental social psychology: Some sober questions about some frivolous values. *Journal of Experimental Social Psychology*, 1967, *3*, 113–123.

Rogosa, D. A critique of cross-lagged correlation. *Psychological Bulletin*, 1980, *88*, 245–258.

Sackett, G. P. (Ed.). *Observing behavior* (Vols. I and II). Baltimore: University Park Press, 1978.

Wicker, A. W. Ecological Psychology. *American Psychologist*, 1979, *34*, 755–765.

Wohlwill, J. F. *The study of behavioral development.* New York: Academic Press, 1973.

2 | Infancy

TIFFANY FIELD

Infancy, meaning "without language," by its very definition describes the methodological challenge posed for researchers in this field. An entire chapter on infant methodology may therefore seem unnecessary. In addition, some may suggest that, unlike the psychological processes accorded separate chapters in this volume, infancy is not a psychological process but a stage during which psychological processes evolve. Others might argue that the unique methodological problems and the close interdependence of psychological processes during infancy warrant a separate treatment of the area, as if it were a process in its own right. The latter position is assumed for this chapter, and some of the problems are elaborated by providing examples of methodologies used in infant research.

ORIENTATIONS TOWARD INFANCY

The first question an infancy student might ask is why people study infants. Some have viewed the infancy stage as an optimal testing ground for heredity–environment or nature–nurture questions. Others treat it as an embryonic stage of evolving psychological processes. The recent popularity of the field suggests that infants are gradually being viewed as intrinsically interesting and worthy of study even outside the context of circuitous nature–nurture questions and evolving psychological processes.

The development of methodologies specific to infancy has proceeded more slowly than the interest in infants. Methodologies traditionally used in the field have been adapted from animal, child, and adult laboratory studies. *Infancy,* not unlike its parent, *developmental psychology,* inherited a number of experimental psychology paradigms. While experimental rigor

13

STRATEGIES AND TECHNIQUES
OF CHILD STUDY

Copyright © 1982 by Academic Press, Inc.
All rights of reproduction in any form reserved.
ISNB 0-12-715080-3 0-12-715082-X (p)

may accord the field status in the scientific community, some infancy researchers have called for more ecologically meaningful methodologies such as naturalistic observations (Bronfenbrenner, 1977; McCall, 1977; Trevarthen, 1974).

Naturalistic observations of infants such as those recorded in the diaries of Darwin (1877) and Piaget (1952) were instrumental in establishing infancy as an area of study and were inspirational for many laboratory studies in the field. However, the methodology of Darwin and Piaget has not been as widely accepted as a research paradigm, as indicated by Bronfenbrenner's (1977) report that 76% of all developmental investigations have been conducted in the laboratory. Unfortunately, many interesting, spontaneous behaviors of infants, such as their notorious exploration of objects by mouth, their pointing gestures, and their "container" behaviors, to name only a few, probably lend themselves more readily to naturalistic observation than laboratory study. McCall (1977), in a plea for more naturalistic observation research, wrote: "A case can be made that the description of relationships in naturalistic environments while not sufficient to establish that factor X does cause behavior Y, is necessary for such a conclusion. . . . We rarely take the time to keep our experimental hands off a behavior long enough to make descriptive observations in naturalistic settings of the several dimensions and circumstances of the behavior we wish to study [p. 336]."

Thus there are some broad methodological orientations, such as a laboratory approach, that derive from a world view about why we study infancy, such as to answer nature–nurture questions and understand evolving psychological processes. More frequently these orientations have involved investigations of what the infant can do with what we provide him or her rather than what the infant spontaneously does and how he or she does it. Both questions and both laboratory and naturalistic observation approaches are critical to the field.

Another orientation that has guided the field is the search for predictors of later development. The failure to find these has given rise to a theory that there are no developmental continuities, that infancy is discontinuous with later developmental stages and is therefore a less critical stage of development and area of study than previously thought (Kagan, Kearsley, & Zelazo, 1978). As Wolhwill (1973) and others have suggested, the developmental course of individual infants may not be linear or even unidirectional, and there is little reason to expect predictability from this earliest period, given the multitude of interactional events that occur.

Still another orientation bias is the highly specialized focus on psychological processes during infancy. Just as there are those who study, for example, memory in childhood, there are now those who study infant memory. There are problems with transferring a specific process orientation such as memory to the infancy stage since, unlike memory at later stages, it cannot be isolated and studied independently of several other processes, including perceptual, attentional, and physiological processes. Whether an infant is awake and non-fussy, attending, perceiving, processing the information and only finally remembering are processes not very easily separated at the infancy stage.

In addition, that process, again using memory as an example, is rapidly developing, so that infant memory may look very different at 3 than at 6 months. Psychological processes (which by definition occur in time) are rarely longitudinally studied across infancy in the true sense of the term developmental.

In summary, then, some of the methodological challenges posed for the infant researcher are the need to observe the infant's spontaneous behaviors, to study an evolving process in the context of other highly related processes, and to track these longitudinally across infancy. Although the popular laboratory studies may have ecological validity problems, they highlight some of the methodological problems posed by the infants themselves.

METHODOLOGICAL PROBLEMS POSED BY THE INFANT

There are a number of challenges the infant presents as research subject. Among these are an inability to communicate verbally, a limited repertoire of other responses, lability of behavioral state and attention span, and dramatic developmental changes.

Limited Response Repertoire

The primary problem for the infant researcher is the infant's inability to communicate verbally his or her perceptions, thoughts, and feelings and the researcher's inability to remember these experiences in his or her own infancy. In the absence of language, infant researchers have relied on a number of motor and autonomic responses as measures of psychological processes. Among these are simple reflex behaviors such as sucking, and voluntary behaviors such as head turning and visual fixation. In addition, autonomic activity such as heart rate is frequently used as a convergent measure of attentional or processing phenomena.

Sucking and Head Turning. Sucking is a universal activity most infants enjoy. It can be conditioned at a very early stage, with infants sucking more or less vigorously as they learn contingencies between their behaviors and the reinforcers provided. However, there are associated problems with the use of sucking as a dependent measure including: (*a*) many breastfed babies will not suck on a pacifier, even when honey-coated, (*b*) sucking often ceases when an infant's attention is captured (the Bronshtein effect), and (*c*) while pacifiers are frequently used to quiet infants during an experimental procedure, sucking invariably affects other dependent measures. If the infant is preoccupied with sucking, he or she often will not attend to other stimulation (Bruner, 1973). Sucking also confounds the measurement of heart rate owing to its "driving" effect on heart rate. Cardiac accelerations systematically occur at the onset of sucking bursts, and decelerations at the end of bursts, thus confounding any heart rate directional changes to discrete stimulus presentations (Nelson, Clifton, Dowd, & Field, 1978). (See Figure 2.1.)

Head turning is similarly readily conditioned (Papousek, 1967), but must be carefully controlled for directional head turning preferences related to the early tonic neck reflex.

Visual Fixations. These are frequently used as a measure of attention, preference, and habituation and are reliably recorded from corneal reflections either through peepholes proximal to the infant's line of visual regard or via infrared photography (Haith, 1969). While reliable, visual fixation data are often difficult to interpret. For example, preterm infants are frequently noted to show lengthy visual fixations even at the neonatal stage. However, several researchers have anecdotally reported that preterm infants "blankly" stare as if "looking through the stimulus" with very minimal responsive movements of their eyes.

Differential interpretations of visual fixations also arise from some investigators using them as an index of stimulus preference (Fagan, 1972), whereas others use them as an index of habituation (Cohen & Gelber, 1975). Longer visual fixations to a novel stimulus are viewed by some as evidence of preference and the infant having processed a previously presented (the familiar) stimulus. When observed in a habituation paradigm, however, the infants' failure to cease looking at the stimulus over trials is interpreted as a failure to learn.

In addition, visual fixations appear to differ as a function of the nature of the stimulus. Novelty (Hutt, 1970), complexity (Berlyne, 1966; Caron & Caron, 1969), and stimulus movement (Karmel & Maisel, 1975) are among the many stimulus qualities thought to affect visual fixations. When comparing visual fixations to animate and inanimate stimuli, infants often pro-

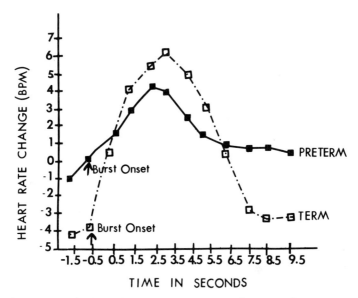

FIGURE 2.1. Temporal relationship between sucking and heart rate (beats per minute) in term and preterm infants, suggesting that heart rate accelerations occur at the onset of sucking bursts and may confound measurement of heart rate directional changes to discrete stimulus presentation if the infant is given a pacifier. This concept also appears in Field *et al.* (1979) and Nelson *et al.* (1978).

long their gaze at inanimate stimuli while alternating their gaze toward and away from an animate stimulus (Brazelton, Koslowski, & Main, 1974; Field, 1979c). In a stimulus preference paradigm the longer fixations at the inanimate stimulus would be interpreted as preference for the inanimate stimulus, and in an habituation paradigm they would be interpreted as their being more difficult to process. Neither interpretation makes good intuitive sense, which illustrates the problem of generalizing interpretations of responses across different stimulus situations.

Heart Rate Activity. Heart rate is the most frequently employed autonomic measure during infancy. Phasic heart rate decelerations have been interpreted as orienting responses, and heart rate accelerations as aversive responses (Graham & Clifton, 1966). Elevated tonic heart rate (heart rate averaged over a situation and compared to baseline) is indicative of an aversive situation, and diminished heart rate of an attentive situation (Field, 1979c).

With advances in telemetry, heart rate is conveniently recorded using a matchbox-size battery, easily applied, disposable electrodes, and a simple portable tape recorder; and the infant is free to move around the room (Sroufe & Waters, 1977). However, the measurement of heart rate without simultaneous recording of other measures known to influence heart rate, such as respiration and muscle potential, is difficult to interpret. But to attach additional electrodes for muscle potential or galvanic skin response and a strain gauge or bellows for respiration and an actometer for limb movements is a lot of paraphernalia for an infant to tolerate. We are left then with heart rate data that may be confounded by movement artifacts (Campos, Emde, Gaensbauer, & Henderson, 1975), fussing (Vaughn & Sroufe, 1979), gaze averting (Field, 1981b), sucking (Nelson *et al.,* 1978), and respiration (Porges, 1979), to name only a few.

Other problems with using heart rate as a dependent measure include potential state-related changes, for example, heart rate being higher during active versus quiet sleep, and higher during active than quiet alert, and the effects of electrode placement, which has been shown during time lapse photography to affect state and is referred to as the "first nap" effect (Anders & Sostek, 1981). Developmental shifts in heart rate activity are also noted, including a frequent failure to observe heart rate deceleration to stimuli presented during the neonatal period, a finding that may relate to immaturity of the cardiovascular system or to overriding state or activity variables.

Autonomic measures are advisably used as convergent measures to provide additional information. Using heart rate without also recording behavior can lead to uninterpretable data, for example, finding accelerations instead of decelerations only because the infant, unknown to the experimenter, was sleeping throughout the stimulus trials.

Other Responses. Other response measures, less frequently used in the laboratory but often recorded during naturalistic observations, include eye widening, smiling, grimacing, laughing, and cooing. While these may more adequately reflect the infants' attentive, arousal, and affective state, their underlying processes may be more difficult to interpret.

Ecologically Meaningful Stimuli

Since stimulus dimension considerations would comprise a volume in itself, only brief mention will be made of stimulus selection. This methodological consideration is critical since the mere elicitation of infant attention and motivation is highly dependent on stimulus attributes such as novelty, complexity, intensity, and temporal features. A less frequently mentioned consideration is the ecological validity or meaningfulness of the stimulus for the infant. Colored paper forms may be less interesting to the infant than dancing colored lights. Many erroneous conclusions about infant capabilities have probably derived from situations in which boring or meaningless stimuli were used. The experimenter may mistakenly attribute the absence of a response to limitations of the infant rather than the stimulus itself.

If infants appear to prefer social visual stimuli, for example, a human face rather than a bull's eye (Fantz, 1966), or social auditory stimuli, for example, the mother's voice versus pure tones (Hutt, Hutt, Lenard, Bernuth, & Muntjewerff, 1968), and animated rather than inanimate stimuli, then perceptual processes may be measured more effectively with these more salient stimuli. While these are more complex and may require more sophisticated measurement techniques, the development of those techniques may be less costly to the experimenter than the subject loss associated with the use of less interesting stimuli.

Developmental Changes in Meaningfulness of Stimuli and Responses

The validity of stimulus dimensions and the reliability of response measures vary widely across the months of infancy. Both the salience of stimuli and the functional significance of responses are affected by shifting state organization, sensorimotor abilities, and developmental agendas of the infant. Changing state organization has been documented for sleep states (Parmelee & Stern, 1972; Thoman, 1975; Wolff, 1966) and for sleep–wake cycles (Dittrichova & Lapachova, 1964), with the most dramatic shifts occurring at stages of rapid physiological change and brain maturation, for example, at 6 and 12 weeks. Changes in sensorimotor abilities have been documented by the naturalistic observations and laboratory replications of Piaget (1952) and by longitudinal data on developmental milestones tapped for infant assessments such as the Bayley scales.

For any behavioral measure used there may be variable responding as a function of how developed that behavior is. Changes in visual perception and information processing abilities, for example, may explain the shifts in visual preferences for regular face stimuli at birth (Goren, Sarty, & Wu, 1975), and scrambled faces at 8 months (Kagan, 1967). If grasping is used as a response measure in a form perception study, variable results may relate to the stage of grasping development more than the stage of form perception.

Similarly, the infant's developmental agenda, for example whether he or she is currently "working on" walking or talking skills, may interfere with the measurement of other processes at that time. A 12-month-old infant preoccuppied with walking may not be amenable to sitting still for an attention task, just as 6-month-old infants are less interested in social interactions since they are preoccupied with object manipulations at that time.

Behavioral State—The Culprit Variable

That an infant subject may fall asleep or go on a crying jag in the middle of an observation is certainly the infant researcher's greatest worry. Given that state is so highly variable, particularly during the early months, investigators usually implore parents to arrive at the lab at the infants' optimal time, and even then, a waiting period is often required.

Some view the time midway between feedings as optimal (Brazelton, 1973), whereas others consider the period immediately prior to a feeding as optimal (Pomerleau-Malcuit & Clifton, 1973). Just prior to a feeding, infants are often more alert but sometimes fussy, whereas immediately after a feeding they may be less fussy but also less alert. A study by Koch (1968) mapped conditioning performance of 5-month-old infants and its temporal relation to sleep and feeding and found, for example, that conditioning performance peaked at approximately 40 minutes following feeding. Unfortunately, parametric studies of this kind have not been very popular among infancy researchers.

Despite investigators' efforts to find their subjects in optimal states, infant attrition rates due to drowsiness or fussiness often approximate 50%. Only researchers who study sleep-related phenomena experience lower attrition rates, although even sleeping infants are often in the wrong sleep state. High attrition rates tend to bias findings since they then represent a self-selected group who tend to be less irritable or more alert. Although reduced subject variability may facilitate the desired effects, generalizability to the larger world of infants is then limited.

Until very recently researchers gave pacifiers to fussy infants. However, sucking activity, as has been noted, often interferes with attentional processes (Bruner, 1973) and affects directional heart rate changes (Lipsitt, Reilly, Butcher, & Greenwood, 1976; Nelson et al., 1978). Infant researchers have also discovered that state can be affected by position of the infant. At birth, for example, infants are more alert in an upright position (Korner & Thoman, 1970), and by 6 months they become extremely fussy when placed in an infant seat (Field, 1981a).

Since infant responses vary as a function of infant state, investigators attempt to observe all infants in a similar state. An approximation of this can be achieved by providing a brief feeding prior to a recording session. In addition, the order of experimental conditions is counterbalanced across subjects to control for gradual state shifts across the session. Irrespective of the paradigm, infant state should be continuously monitored and wherever possible entered as a covariate in analyses, since failure to find treatment effects may relate primarily to nonoptimal state. Finally, sleep–wake cycles and attention span at different ages should dictate the length of testing sessions, and multiple sessions should be scheduled whenever longer test times are required.

In summary, the infant, by virtue of labile state organization and rapidly changing skills and interests, poses a rather large set of methodological problems. Some of these may derive from the constraints imposed on the infant by paradigms extrapolated from animal, child, and adult research and by laboratory manipulations requiring relatively underdeveloped responses to uninteresting stimuli. Despite these problems, infants frequently surprise the researcher by their amazing competence (Appleton, Clifton, & Goldberg, 1975). In the following sections some of the infants' amazing skills will be highlighted by the methodology examples presented. These are drawn from a very few of the classic and even fewer of the recent studies of infant perception, learning, and social development, the most frequently studied areas. Most of the studies feature infants in the age range of birth to 6 months, since these are the most frequently studied age groups.

PERCEPTUAL COMPETENCE

Recently, a number of infant researchers have investigated perceptual abilities as early as the neonatal stage. While several of these studies are published in *Science* as brief reports not yet replicated, they are suggestive of very early perceptual competence. Since the neonate is the most difficult subject to study, some of these studies will be described.

Visual Perception

One of the most readily elicited skills of the newborn is tracking or following a visual stimulus. Most alert newborns readily perform this task during the Brazelton Neonatal Behavior Assessment Scale (Brazelton, 1973). In a more controlled investigation of this ability to perceive and follow a visual stimulus, Goren *et al.* (1975) demonstrated that 9-minute-old newborns turned their eyes and heads to facial stimuli moved across their visual field. Tracking was most reliably elicited by regular and par-

tially scrambled as opposed to scrambled face patterns, suggesting a very
early discrimination and preference for a regular face. While it seems adap-
tive that a newborn may prefer a regular face, the stimuli may have been
confounded by vertical and horizontal placement of face features. Since the
regular and partially scrambled face features lie on the horizontal and the
scrambled face features are distributed vertically, and since vertical scanning is noted to be more difficult for the neonate, the investigators may
have biased their procedure in favor of the regular and partially scrambled
face. (See Figure 2.2.)

Using a visual fixation paradigm neonatal color preferences were recently demonstrated by Jones-Molfese (1977). Neonates showed longer fixations or preference orderings of blue, green, and red acetate stimuli.

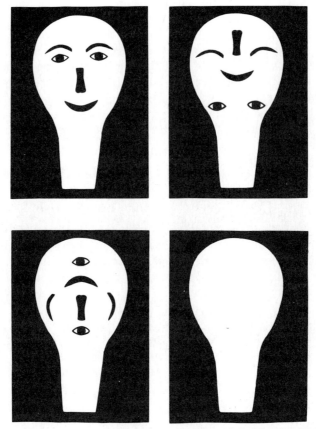

FIGURE 2.2. Face stimuli used by C. C. Goren, M. Sarty, and P. K. Wu, "Visual Following and
Pattern Discrimination of Facelike Stimuli by Newborn Infants," *Pediatrics, 56*(4):
544–549. Copyright American Academy of Pediatrics 1975.

However, while these stimuli were of equivalent brightness, as judged by adults, the infants' preference for blue and green may relate to their being more sensitive to short-wavelength stimuli. The brightness differences may have provided the basis for discrimination, illustrating the problem of extrapolating our knowledge of an adult process to infants.

Several of the more complex neonatal visual perception studies have been conducted by Bower and his colleagues (Bower, 1974). While attempts to replicate Bower's work have suffered from his failure to provide sufficient methodological details, they have nonetheless stimulated a considerable body of early visual perception research. In one study, Bower (1974) investigated whether infants perceive objects as being graspable. Infants wore polarizing goggles that presented the illusion of a graspable object. Infants cried when grasping at the illusion image, suggesting that this was a violation of their perception. Without goggles, infants were presented with two objects, one within and one beyond their reach. The infants made twice as many attempts to reach the proximal object.

Using a shadow-casting device, Bower and his colleagues also investigated whether neonates could perceive an object rotating in such a way that its forward edge appeared about to strike the baby on the nose (Dunkeld & Bower, 1976). This event elicited the same self-defensive behavior that had been observed by Ball and Tronick (1971) with older infants in the face of a rear-projected image moving on a hit-or-miss path toward the infant. These studies solved an interesting methodological problem of providing a stimulus with looming visual effects without the accompanying physical displacement of air, which in itself could cause a defensive reaction. (See Figure 2.3.)

That infants' visual discrimination abilities develop rapidly during the first several weeks is demonstrated by a familiarization–novelty paradigm developed by Fantz and Fagan (Fagan, 1970; Fantz, 1966). Infants are first familiarized with a pair of identical stimuli (usually faces or geometric patterns). The familiar stimulus is then paired with a novel stimulus for 10-second periods, and fixations are recorded. The use of this paradigm with preterm infants suggests that with additional familiarization time they too can make these discriminations (Field, 1980; Rose, 1980). Furthermore, Fagan (1980) has reported data that show correlations between performance on this task at 8 weeks and 4-year IQ test performance. Because of these suggestive data and the adaptability of this paradigm for measuring infant memory (simply by varying the intervals between test trials), it has recently become a popular methodology. The use of still photographs and unidimensional geometric patterns, however, may be outmoded rather quickly, as even neonates are noted to process multidimensional, animated stimuli (Field, Woodson, Greenberg, & Cohen, 1981b).

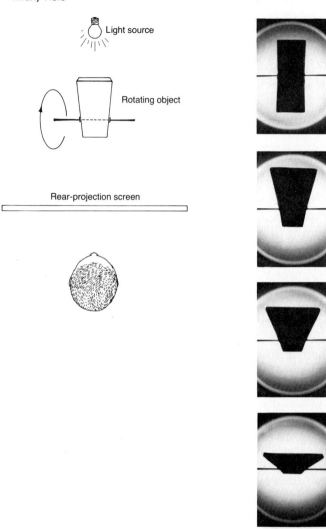

FIGURE 2.3. Shadow-casting device and baby's view of rotating object from *A Primer of Infant Development*, by T. G. R. Bower, W. H. Freeman and Company. Copyright © 1977 (After Dunkeld and Bower, *Perception*, 1980; photos by Jane Dunkeld).

Auditory and Speech Perception

A number of investigators have reported responsivity to auditory stimuli of varying intensities and frequencies at birth (Hutt *et al.,* 1968) and at earlier gestational ages (Eisenberg, 1970). Using an habituation–dishabituation paradigm, Field *et al.* (Field, Dempsey, Hatch, Ting, & Clifton, 1979) presented a 90-db buzzer and rattle to sleeping neonates (term and preterm neonates who had been treated for severe medical complications). Following habituation trials and a dishabituation stimulus (thumping of the bassinette), the original stimulus was reintroduced. Using this paradigm, behavioral habituation–dishabituation (or reduced and then renewed limb movements) was noted for both term and preterm infants. However, cardiac habituation–dishabituation was noted only for term infants. In addition, only the term infants showed differential responsivity (or discrimination) of the same intensity buzzer and rattle stimuli. Since preterm infants were more frequently in active than deep sleep, as is typical of preterm infants, and because autonomic responsivity may be greater in active sleep, their failure to show diminished cardiac responses may have related to state. Another methodologically interesting finding was that the more complex, and perhaps more interesting, rattle stimulus was less readily habituated by either group of neonates.

Several researchers have noted neonates' preference for auditory stimuli in the frequency band of the human voice (Hutt *et al.,* 1968; Kearsley, 1973). Condon and Sander (1974) presented tapes of human voices to neonates and found that they moved their limbs in synchrony with the speech segments. That is, when each frame of the film was superimposed on the audio transcript, distinct limb movements corresponded to the onsets of separate speech segments. A replication attempt with additional controls is currently in progress (Dowd, 1980) since Dowd has speculated that the infants' limb movements may reflect self-synchrony or movements synchronous with speech rhythms rather than speech segments.

Another recent study demonstrated neonates' preference for their own mother's voice (DeCasper & Fifer, 1980). Neonates were presented with audiotapes of their mothers and other mothers reading Dr. Suess's *To Think That I Saw It on Mullberry Street* (certainly an interesting stimulus). Infants sucked on a nonnutritive nipple connected to a pressure transducer which then triggered, via a programmer, the mother's or other mothers' audiotape as a function of the length of the interval between sucking bursts. Depending on their random assignment to groups, infants had to shorten (as compared to baseline) or lengthen their interburst intervals to produce their mother's voice. The effects of response requirements and voice characteristics were controlled by requiring half the infants to respond after short and half after long intervals and by having each maternal voice serve as the nonmaternal voice for another infant. Additional controls were (*a*) reversing the response requirements for half the infants, and (*b*) using a different discriminative stimulus (a 400-Hz tone) for tone and no-tone periods during which a sucking burst might produce the mother's reading of Dr. Seuss. This well-controlled study suggested that infants prefer their own mother's voice and learn to produce her voice by varying their nonnutritive sucking behavior.

The categorical perception of speech sounds like "ba"s and "pa"s, "da"s and "ga"s has been investigated using a number of different methodologies including heart rate changes (Eimas, 1975), high amplitude sucking (Morse, 1972), and a reinforcement paradigm labeled VRISD (visually reinforced infant speech discrimination) in which a dancing, musical bear reinforces head turning in the direction of speech sounds (Eilers, Wilson, & Moore, 1977).

Other Perceptual Abilities

The infants' olfactory and gustatory perceptions have been assessed by similar paradigms. A series of olfactory perception studies conducted by Lipsitt and his colleagues suggest that infants can discriminate very subtle odors, including the components of various mixed odorants (Engen & Lipsitt, 1965; Engen, Lipsitt, & Kaye, 1963). Anise oil or asafetida alone and in combination were separately presented by placing a cotton swab before the infant's nostrils. The newborns were habituated to a given odorant, whereupon another odorant was presented. Using a similar paradigm, MacFarlane (1975) reported neonates' preference for their own mother's versus other mothers' breast pads.

Taste perception has also been noted for newborns (Lipsitt, Kaye, & Bosack, 1966). By reinforcing the infants' sucking response with dextrose solution, Lipsitt and co-workers showed neonatal preference for sweet solutions. Siqueland and Lipsitt (1966), using Papousek's (1967) head-turning paradigm, arranged a series of contingencies such that a head turn to one side following a paired rooting stimulus and tone, or to the other side following a paired rooting stimulus and buzzer, was reinforced by a dextrose solution. The authors labeled the differential responding for dextrose reinforcement an "hedonic" response. Similar paradigms have been used to demonstrate discrimination of tactile stimuli (Field, Dempsey, Ting, Hatch, & Clifton, 1979; Rose, Schmidt, & Bridger, 1976).

Intersensory Integration

Intersensory integration or the coordination of stimuli of different modalities has been demonstrated with increasingly sophisticated methodologies. Wertheimer (1961) observed that his own neonate turned her eyes repeatedly in the direction of a toy cricket sound, an observation that has been confirmed on hundreds of newborns using the Brazelton assessment rattle stimulus. While McGurk and co-workers (McGurk, Turnure, & Creighton, 1977) in a more controlled study with the toy cricket failed to replicate neonatal localizations, they had presented the click sounds for only 3 seconds' duration, an extremely brief period given the neonate's latent and slow head turning responses.

Recent studies in the laboratories of Field (Muir & Field, 1979) and Clifton (Clifton, Morrongiello, Kalig, & Dowd, 1980) have corrected many of the methodological problems of the previous studies, for example, by having the examiner wear earphones to mask the rattle sounds and presenting the sounds via audiotape to eliminate motion and air displacement cues and by blind ratings of the videotaped responses. Even with these controls, neonates demonstrated sound localization.

LEARNING

Two somewhat different orientations to infant learning, the behaviorist and the Piagetian approaches, have evolved.

Behaviorist Orientation

In this orientation, learning is inferred from changes in responses to the stimulation provided, and the processes by which learning is thought to occur include habituation and various forms of conditioning (operant and classical).

Habituation. Habituation is considered the most primitive form of learning. According to Sokolov (1963), an orienting response first occurs to a stimulus, a response characterized by quieting, attentiveness, and heart rate deceleration (Graham & Clifton, 1966). After repeated stimulus presentations the stimulus no longer elicits the orienting reflex, which is then said to have habituated. If a new stimulus is presented, the orienting response is again elicited or the response is dishabituated. While Sokolov and others considered habituation a cortical process, Graham and co-workers (Graham, Leavitt, Strock, & Brown, 1978) recently demonstrated habituation in an anencephalic infant, suggesting that it may be a subcortical process.

Typically infant researchers have presented either a predetermined number of trials or trials to criterion (determined by the infant's reaching a behavioral criterion). Following habituation of the original stimulus, a novel stimulus is then presented, or a startle stimulus is presented followed by a number of trials of the original stimulus. An example of the former procedure is the Engen *et al.* (1963) olfactory study (discussed in the previous section) in which diminished responding to anise oil was followed by the presentation of asafetida or vice versa. An example of the latter approach was the Field *et al.* (1979) study where instead of introducing a novel stimulus following habituation, the authors provided a startle stimulus and then reintroduced the original auditory or tactile stimuli for dishabituation trials. The purpose of dishabituation trials is to ensure that diminished responding is not due to fatigue. Infants may learn not to respond to irrelevant or weak stimuli, although they may continue to respond to salient or strong stimuli.

Operant Conditioning. While habituation is simply the weakening of an unlearned response to stimulation, operant conditioning requires the modification of an old response. Operant or instrumental conditioning involves the contingent presentation or removal of a stimulus that will increase or decrease the rate of behavior. The investigator typically waits for a response that is already in the infant's repertoire, for example, sucking, head turning, or kicking, and then reinforces that response. The infant then learns the relationship between his or her behavior (the operant) and the reinforcer.

Illustrations of this paradigm include the infants learning to alter their sucking rhythms for the Dr. Seuss story (DeCasper & Fifer, 1980) or to modify their sucking behavior (to give a suction or expression component of sucking) to receive a nutrient (Sameroff, 1968). Several other infant responses have been instrumentally conditioned including leg movements (Rovee & Rovee, 1969) and head turning (Watson & Ramey, 1972) to turn a mobile and sucking to produce pictures (Siqueland & DeLucia, 1969).

Classical Conditioning. This learning paradigm involves the pairing of a neutral stimulus (the conditional stimulus or CS) with an unconditional stimulus (US). The US—for example, a rooting stimulus or touching of the cheek—will lead to a UR (unconditional response), or head turning toward the rooting stimulus. If a tone (CS) is sounded prior to the rooting stimulus, it may eventually elicit a CR (conditioned response) or a conditioned head turn to the tone.

Among those who have reportedly succeeded in classically conditioning the neonate are Lipsitt and Kaye (1964), who presented a tone (CS) paired with the insertion of a nipple (US) to condition sucking (UR). The experimental group showed greater amounts of sucking than a control group who were provided the same stimuli which were not paired. Other successful attempts include a temporal conditioning study in which the CS was elapsed time (Stamps, 1977) and studies involving conditioning of heart rate responses (Clifton, 1974; Stamps & Porges, 1975).

The significance of appropriate controls is highlighted by a series of studies in which investigators of different research groups have argued over the conditionability of the Babkin reflex. Some claimed to have conditioned the Babkin reflex or mouth opening elicited by touching the neonate's palm (Cantor, Fischel, & Kaye, 1980; Connolly & Stratton, 1969; Kaye, 1965). The CS used by Kaye involved raising the neonate's arms, whereas Connolly and Stratton used arm raising in one study and a tone in another study. Sostek and several colleagues (Sostek, Sameroff, & Sostek, 1972) noted that neither study had adequately controlled for state changes or had included a group that received the CS and US noncontingently. While Sostek *et al.* failed to condition the Babkin reflex, they did observe heightened responding related to infant state and observed that arm raising (the CS) itself elicited the Babkin in some infants. Sameroff (1971) followed this study with a review in which he concluded that the newborn could not be conditioned. Among the methodological problems suggested by Sameroff were inadequate controls for state instability, habituation to the unconditioned stimulus, finding a neutral stimulus for a newborn for whom most stimulation is novel, and newborn's inability to assimilate stimuli and responses cross-modally. A recent study by Cantor *et al.* (1980) addressed some of these methodological problems by pairing two neutral stimuli (the Babkin reflex as the US and sucking onset as CS) and by providing suitable stimulus and state controls, and successfully conditioned suppression of sucking.

The cumulative data suggest that under some conditions the newborn can be classically conditioned. Kasatkin (1972) has suggested that there is an invariant sequence of conditional stimulus effectiveness that is phylogenetically determined. Older sensory systems (vestibular, cutaneous, gustatory, and olfactory) are more readily conditioned than younger systems (auditory and visual). Phylogenetically older response systems, for example, the autonomic system can be conditioned earlier than the motor system. Motor reflexes are also more likely candidates than voluntary motor behaviors. The data, showing Babkin reflex conditioning (Cantor *et al.*, 1980) and autonomic conditioning (Clifton, 1974; Stamps & Porges, 1975) are consistent with Kasatkin's notion of the older response systems being amenable to conditioning in the very young organism.

Operant and Classical Conditioning Combined. In this procedure a conditional stimulus (e.g., a tone) followed by the unconditioned response (head turning) was reinforced by a nutrient (Papousek, 1967). If neither of these stimuli elicited head turning, the experimenter turned the infant's head and a reinforcer followed. Following a number of correct responses the CS was presented without reinforcement until several consecutive responses were made in the direction not previously reinforced (extinction).

After the infants had learned to respond in one direction to the tone, they were trained to respond in the other direction to a buzzer. Others have used this paradigm to show auditory discriminations of sounds (Siqueland & Lipsitt, 1966) and mothers' voices (DeCasper & Fifer, 1980).

These, then, are only a few of the countless attempts to condition neonates and young infants, many of which are detailed in a number of reviews (Clifton, 1974; Fitzgerald & Porges, 1971; Reese & Porges, 1976; Sameroff, 1971). While modifications of these paradigms, which had previously been used with animals, have yielded more interesting conditions for young infants, it is not clear whether these are the processes whereby infants learn. McCall (1977), for example, raised the question, "Do babies learn by operant conditioning in conventional family environments? [p. 334]"

Learning in Piagetian Terms

Jean Piaget traced the cognitive development of his three infants by observing, experimenting, and sometimes interfering with their activities (Piaget, 1952). According to Piaget, infants during the sensorimotor period (birth to 2 years) learn by two processes, assimilation and accommodation, assimilation being defined as the application of existing skills or responses (schema) to events encountered, and accommodation defined as the modification of schema to incorporate an event or accomplish a task. The infant was then described as passing through an invariant sequence of stages from a reflex stage to a stage entitled the "invention of new means through mental combinations [p. 331]." While the descriptions Piaget provides of his infants' activities during these stages are rich with detail on many processes, most of the laboratory replications have investigated only two of these, object permanence and imitation.

One of the classic object permanence studies involves moving objects behind a screen and observing the infant's search behaviors (Bower, Broughton, & Moore, 1970). Variations on this paradigm have included the object's reappearance sooner than would be expected (trajectory violation) or the appearance of a different object (Moore, Borton, & Darby, 1975) with heart rate recorded as a convergent measure (Goldberg, 1976).

Imitation experiments have been conducted as early as the neonatal stage, providing a model of behaviors already in the infant's repertoire, for example, mouth opening, tongue thrusting, and finger movements (Meltzoff & Moore, 1977) and imitations of facial expressions (Field *et al.,* 1981b). (See Figure 2.4.) Control procedures, including rating of the videotaped imitations by naive coders, were used to ensure against some of the possible experimenter biases. However, the possibility remains that many of these so-called imitations are random behaviors, given the fre-

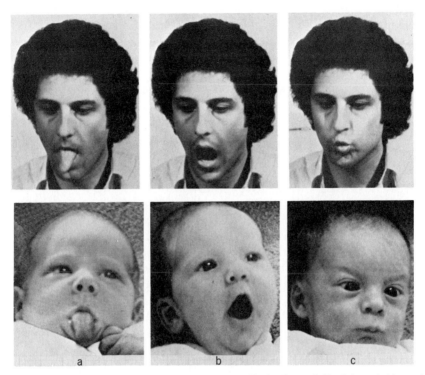

FIGURE 2.4. Examples of imitation taken from "*Imitation of Facial and Manual Gestures by Human Neonates,*" by Andrew N. Meltzoff and M. Keith Moore, *Science, 198*, 75–78. Copyright 1977 by the American Association for the Advancement of Science.

quency with which they normally occur. In addition, a study in which tongue thrusting was also elicited with some regularity to the movement of a pen in front of the neonate's face suggests that the responses made by the infants in the Meltzoff and Moore study may not be pure imitations (Jacobson, 1979).

Many of the object permanence and imitation studies suggest that these phenomena occur sooner than Piaget had noted. They provide an illustration of the contrast between studies oriented toward what infants can do when they are trained in a laboratory situation and what they characteristically do as noted during naturalistic observations.

Another series of studies inspired by Piaget are exploration–play studies. Infants were, for example, placed in a high chair and toys were presented in series (Hutt, 1967; Messer, Kagan, & McCall, 1970). Exploration, play, and habituation were then recorded and analyzed as a function of various stimulus properties such as novelty and complexity. The same kinds of paradigm and measures have also been used for playpen play (Fischer,

1973) and floor play at later ages (Collard, 1968; Goldberg & Lewis, 1969; Rubinstein, 1967). Some of the more interesting findings emerging from these studies were the developmental changes in qualitative aspects of exploration and play, the rhythmic variation of playing and pausing, and the individual differences in tempo of play. However, as frequently happens in infant studies, the results presented focused on the quantitative measures as a function of sex, birth order, social class, parity, or other readily measured demographic variables rather than the qualitative features and developmental processes per se.

SOCIAL BEHAVIOR AND COMMUNICATION SKILLS

A number of different approaches have been taken to the study of social behavior and communication skills in infancy. These can be generally grouped as follows: (*a*) the development of affect, (*b*) social learning, (*c*) attachment, and (*d*) early interactions. Since the methodologies of these areas are very different, they will be discussed separately.

Affect Development

In the area of affect development, the discrimination and production of emotional expressions, typically facial expressions, have been studied by separate research groups.

Discrimination or Decoding of Emotional Expressions. The most common methodologies used in this area are the visual preference and habituation paradigms. Photographs, slides, or live models are used to present those expressions most commonly observed in adults of this and other cultures including joy, sadness, anger, disgust, shame, fear, surprise, and neutral (Ekman & Friesen, 1975; Izard, 1971). In one of the very few studies to date, 4-month-old infants were habituated to slides of the expressions joy, anger, and neutral of a male model (LaBarbera, Izard, Vietze, & Parisi, 1976). Each slide remained visible until the infant fixated it and was removed when the infant looked away after an intertrial interval. Using an increase in fixation time to the new expression as a criterion, investigators observed that infants looked significantly longer at the joy expression.

Another group, investigating different expressions (sad, happy, and surprise) in a different age group (3 months), used an habituation–recovery paradigm (Young-Browne, Rosenfeld, & Horowitz, 1977). The authors claimed to use this paradigm since it was "more sensitive than spontaneous fixation in assessing infant visual discrimination [p. 556].'' The rationale given for the selection of expressions was that toddlers had discriminated them more often than others (Izard, 1971), as had adults (Ekman, 1972). Again a male model was trained to control the particular facial muscles relevant to each expression, and in this case both colored and achromatic slides were used. Both experimental and control groups were included, with the experimental group being given repeated presentations until a behavioral criterion of habituation was met. Based on a comparison of the recovery scores of experimental and control groups, the infants discriminated the surprise from the happy and occasionally from the sad expressions. Since no significant differences were noted for mean looking times at the different expressions, the authors suggested that the habituation–recovery paradigm is a more sensitive procedure than the visual fixation paradigm.

The visual preference methodology was used by Nelson, Morse, and Leavitt (1979) to determine just how sensitive the technique was and to determine whether infants could generalize their discrimination of facial expressions across more than one model. Nelson *et al.* (1979) were concerned that, in both of the studies just described, the authors had failed to examine the infants' ability to notice the invariant features that characterize an expression by demonstrating recognition of expression when it was posed by more than one face. While Nelson *et al.* demonstrated that infants can discriminate happy versus fear expressions across faces of different actors, the discrimination was affected by the order in which the stimuli were presented. These order effects reflected a greater rate of habituation within this testing paradigm to the happy expressions, indicating that facial expression discrimination studies may be affected by differential habituation rates to different expressions. In fact, the more frequent reports of discriminating positive faces (happy, surprise) than negative faces (sad, angry, fearful) may relate to the latters' eliciting defense-like responses, which are generally habituated more slowly. Another implication of this study is that the habituation paradigm, given a correction for differential habituation to positive and negative stimuli, may be more sensitive than the visual preference paradigm for studying early discrimination of facial expressions.

While these studies employed still photographs (a relatively unfamiliar stimulus for infants), infants' discriminations might be facilitated by live expressions viewed in motion. Neonates, for example, can discriminate live happy, sad, and surprised facial expressions (Field *et al.,* 1981b). In addition, since there is some suggestion that children cue on vocal more than facial expressions (Volkmar & Siegel, 1979), the vocal components of emotional expressions may be more salient for infants as well.

Production or Encoding of Emotional Expressions. Most of the studies on infants' production of facial expressions have investigated the reliability of adults' judgments of those expressions. Emde and several colleagues (Emde, Kligman, Reich, & Wade, 1978), for example, filmed infants 2–4 months of age playing with their mothers and strangers. Mothers and nurses then gave free responses and forced choices while viewing slide and motion picture presentations of the expressions. Both types of adult ratings of infant facial expressions could be readily classified within the Izard (1971) list of eight adult expressions (enjoyment, interest, distress, fear, anger, surprise, shame, and disgust) with the addition of only two categories, passive–bored and sleepy. In addition, very high agreement was reported between judgments based on slide and motion picture presentations.

A similar study by Izard and co-workers (Izard, Heubner, Risser, McGinnes, & Dougherty, 1980) demonstrated that reliability can be increased approximately 15% by training raters on an anatomically based facial movement coding system. For this task trained judges had applied facial muscle change criteria in selecting expression stimuli from videotape recordings of 1–9-month-old infants' responses to a variety of incentive events ranging from playful interactions to the pain of inoculations. The training effects reported were approximately equal for emotion labeling (a free-response labeling task), emotion recognition (a selection from a list of nine emotions), or an emotion-matching technique (a visual comparison using simultaneous presentation of adult and infant expressions). These authors also reported a negligible difference in the reliability with which still (slides) and motion (videotape) expressions can be rated.

To determine whether reliable judgments of infant expressions can be made in the absence of contextual information and can be verified by instrumental behaviors, Hiatt, Campos, and Emde (1979) elicited expressions in a peekaboo game and collapsing toy situation (happiness), a toy switch and a vanishing object task (surprise), and the visual cliff and the approach of a stranger (fear). Using forced-choice and confidence ratings of those judgments raters reliably coded happiness and surprise expressions in the absence of contextual information.

Together, these studies suggest that infant facial expressions, previously assumed to be prone to observer bias or subjective interpretation, can be reliably classified using the same coding systems and expression categories that are used with adults. While the discrimination and production studies involved different expressions and infants of different ages, positive expressions were more reliably discriminated and produced than negative expressions. This highlights the need for developmental studies tracing both the emerging discrimination and production skills of the same infants. The only published longitudinal study tracked the development of smiling and laughing as a function of their effective elicitors (Sroufe & Wunsch, 1972). A longitudinal study on the development of both discrimination and production abilities might address questions such as whether discrimination and production abilities develop in parallel or at different rates and whether performance in the two areas are related so that "good" discriminators are also "good" producers (Field & Walden, 1981). The study of different components of the same process by separate groups of investigators has contributed to a very incomplete understanding of the process.

Social Learning

The studies in this area have applied operant procedures to enhance various expressions such as smiling (Brackbill, 1958) and vocalizing (Bloom, 1975; Gewirtz & Gewirtz, 1968; Rheingold, Gewirtz, & Ross, 1959; Weisberg, 1963). These studies combined suggested that any form of social stimulation was effective in increasing the infants' social expressions. They are interesting studies because each remedied a methodological weakness of the previous study. Rheingold et al. (1959) and Gewirtz and Gewirtz (1968) demonstrated that simply saying "tsk tsk tsk," smiling, and patting the infant's belly were effective reinforcers of infant vocalizations. Weisberg (1963) added controls including the provision of noncontingent stimulation and nonsocial reinforcers (door chime) and showed that only the contingent social stimulation effectively increased vocalizations. Schwartz and several colleagues (Schwartz, Rosenberg, & Brackbill, 1970) compared the total and partial stimulation complex and concluded that each was equally effective. Bloom and Esposito (1975) used yoked-control procedures, arguing that they are logically preferable to random presentation of response-independent stimulation (as used by Weisberg) because they allow comparisons to be made between subjects whose experimental experience (except for the response–reinforcer contingency) is entirely equivalent. Using this procedure they noted that response-independent stimulation was equally effective as response-contingent stimulation in increasing the infants' rate of vocalization, suggesting that the previous studies' failure to provide the necessary control had led to "unwarranted confidence in the effects of social operant conditioning." In a separate study, Bloom (1975) also noted that both the response-independent and response-contingent stimulation were effective only when the infants could see the eyes of the adult who delivered the social stimulus.

Given that social reinforcement consistently occurs during adult–infant interactions, it is surprising that these or other researchers have not investigated this phenomenon during naturalistic or spontaneous interactions in a way that is similar to the demonstration of the infant's conditioning the mother by Gewirtz and Boyd (1977).

Stranger Fear and Maternal Attachment

The mother and stranger have played key roles in dozens of studies demonstrating infant attachment. While infants discriminate mothers from strangers as early as 2 weeks of age (Carpenter, 1973), they show a steady increase in negative reactions to strangers across the first 9 months (Bronson, 1972). These negative reactions are highly variable as a function of the age and size of the stranger (infant and midget strangers being less aversive; Brooks & Lewis, 1976) and the way they approach the infant (a loud, rapidly intruding stranger being more aversive; Morgan, 1973). These factors, in addition to individual differences in the amount of prior experience with other adults, may explain the variability of findings in this literature (Weinraub, Brooks, & Lewis, 1977).

The widely used, strange situation procedure includes eight episodes of the infant being alone, with the mother or with strangers, and the latter two joining and leaving the infant at different time intervals over a 30-minute period (Ainsworth & Whittig, 1969). Infants are then classified as A, B, or C babies as a function of their avoidant, enthusiastic, or variable responses to the mother's return.

Methodological problems have been elaborated by Vietze (1980) for the early attachment or "bonding" studies (Klaus & Kennel, 1976) in which infants, given additional contact with their mothers during the postpartum period, are described as "more attached."

Early Interaction Studies

These have a very brief but busy history, and during that period methodologies have changed dramatically as elaborated in several volumes on the subject (Cairns, 1979; Ciba Foundation, 1975; Field, Goldberg, Stern, & Sostek, 1980; Field, Sostek, Leiderman, & Vietze, 1981; Lamb, Suomi, & Stephenson, 1979; Lewis & Rosenblum, 1974; Schaffer, 1977; Stern, 1977). Some of the methodological considerations include the infant's interaction partner, interaction context, and recording and analytic techniques.

Interaction Partner. Literally dozens of early interaction studies have focused on the mother–infant dyad in various contexts (feeding, face-to-face, or floor play) with various agendas (a natural or an interaction in which the mother is given an instruction). In many of these studies the types and amounts of behaviors (gaze patterns, vocalizations, kinesics, games, and rhythmicity) have been noted to vary as a function of demographic variables such as age, sex, birth order, or condition of the infant (normal or at-risk) and age, parity, education, socioeconomic status, or cultural group of the mother. Variables less frequently studied include individual differences (Korner, 1971) such as temperamental differences that are known to affect early interactions (Field, Dempsey, Hallock, & Shuman, 1978) but which are typically assessed by mothers rather than researchers.

While there has been an increasing emphasis on the mother–infant dyad as an interacting unit, most of the studies have focused on mother behaviors and, in general, have revealed that mothers behave in unique ways with their infants—for example, exaggerating facial and vocal expressions, repeating those expressions, and imitating infant behaviors as they constantly monitor the infants' behaviors. Some have viewed these "infantized" behaviors as prewired or unique to the mother.

A methodological advance, father–infant research, suggested that these behaviors were not unique to mothers, since fathers, while more playful, often behaved similarly with infants (Parke & O'Leary, 1975; Yogman, Dixon, Tronick, Adamson, Als, & Brazelton, 1976). A study in which primary and secondary care-giver fathers were compared to mothers suggested that primary care-giver fathers were more like mothers, perhaps because of equivalent experience with their infants (Field, 1978b).

Other new interaction partners include siblings (Lamb, 1978) and infant peers (Field, 1979b; Fogel, 1979). A study that compared infants' interactions with mother, father, siblings, and infant peers suggested that just as the quality and quantity of the stimulation provided varied by interaction partner, so did the infant's attentive and affective behaviors vary (Field, 1980a). The infant's interactions with his mirror image have been investigated (Papousek & Papousek, 1974) by showing infants on TV monitors a mirror image that precluded eye contact and a comparable playback of themselves allowing eye contact. Infants first attended more to the former, a notably salient stimulus (Caron & Caron, 1969; Caron, Caron, Caldwell, & Weiss, 1973; Stern, 1974), and eventually more to the latter, as if discovering the contingency of their own behavior (Field, 1979c). In a similar study, infants were seated face-to-face with a mirror and an infant peer. While attending (and showing more heart rate deceleration) to the former, they emitted more social behaviors to the peer (Field, 1979a).

The differential behavior of the infant as a function of interaction partner is more dramatically illustrated by the presence of multiple interaction partners, for example, the presence of mother and father or a triadic interaction (Pederson, Yarrow, Anderson, & Cain, 1979), a larger family interaction (Field, 1978a), or multiple mothers and peers. Lewis and several colleagues (Lewis, Young, Brooks, & Michalson, 1975), for example, found that in the presence of both peers and mothers infants show more distal behaviors to peers and proximal behaviors to mothers, and Field (1979b) noted fewer negative infant behaviors toward peers when mothers were absent than when they were present.

Other variations of interaction partners involving social animate and inanimate stimuli demonstrate the variability of infant interaction behaviors (Brazelton *et al.,* 1974). The infant's behavior (visual, affective, and cardiac activity) for example, varies as a function of how animated the mother is (spontaneous or slowed down) or how animated the inanimate social stimulus (a still or a talking, head-nodding Raggedy Ann doll) (Field, 1979c). (See Figures 2.5 and 2.6.)

Interaction Context. Observations are typically made of feeding interactions during the early weeks (Field, 1977b; Kaye, 1977; Osofsky & Danzger, 1974), of face-to-face play during the early months (Brazelton *et al.,* 1974; Field, 1977a; Stern, 1974), and of floor play (Field & Ignatoff, 1981; Goldberg, Brachfeld, & DiVitto, 1980) or teaching interactions (Kaye, 1976) during the later months as the infants' interests, abilities, and

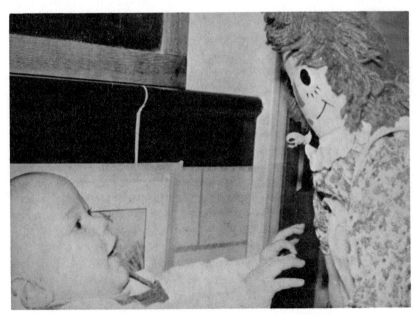

FIGURE 2.5. Infant's response to inanimate social stimulus, a Raggedy Ann doll.

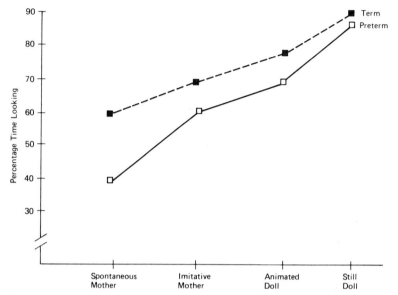

FIGURE 2.6. Looking time to animated and inanimate social stimuli taken from Field (1979c). (Copyright © 1979 by the Society For Research in Child Development, Inc.)

the salient interaction context accordingly shift. The situations are usually spontaneous, although some have investigated manipulations of interactions in which the mother, for example, is given an instruction to remain still-faced (Field, 1981b; Fogel, Diamond, Langhorst, & Demos, 1981; Trevarthen, 1974; Tronick, Als, Adamson, Wise, & Brazelton, 1978) to keep her infant's attention or to imitate her infant's behaviors (Field, 1977a). While some of these manipulations disrupt the infant's interaction behavior (e.g., the still-face and attention-getting manipulations) in the same way that latent responding or interrupting confederates disrupt adult interaction behaviors (Chapple, 1970), others such as the mother's imitations are noted to facilitate more attentiveness and positive affect (Field, 1977a).

Interactions are typically filmed in the home or in a laboratory situation. While some have speculated that the home is an ecologically more natural setting for interactions (Yarrow & Anderson, 1979) and the mother is more active in the lab (Belsky, 1980), others suggest that the mother may feel "more on stage" in her own home. In any case, the laboratory is often made more homelike by those who are concerned about observing interactions in a standardized and more controlled situation.

Recording and Analytic Techniques. Interactions are characteristically recorded using time-sample unit (paper and pencil) or motion picture (film or videotape) techniques. While mothers anecdotally report feeling less observed in the presence of a camera than a live observer, knowing she's being videotaped (versus being unaware of videotaping) contributes to significant increases in her verbal and play behavior (Field & Ignatoff, 1981; Graves & Glick, 1978). Videotaping in the lab usually involves the use of two cameras and a split-screen generator and electronic timer to provide a view of both partners and a time readout on the same screen. This can be achieved in the home with the use of one camera and a mirror set at an angle to one of the partners. (See Figure 2.7.)

The behaviors coded typically include gaze, vocalizations, body movements, facial expressions, and occasionally heart rate. The temporal units vary from broad sampling units (e.g., observing for 10 seconds and then recording the behaviors that occurred during that period on a checklist), to coding in real time, using polygraph or electronic digital recorders as behaviors are viewed live or on videotape, to using special film editors and coding frame-by-frame in fractions of a second.

Depending on the recording technique and the investigator's predilections, macro- or microanalyses are then conducted ranging from rating scales based on the data records, to frequency counts and durations, to more elaborate contingency and sequential analyses (Bakeman, 1977). There has been a recent trend from macro- to microrecording and analytic

FIGURE 2.7. Face-to-face interaction filmed with the use of a mirror and one camera.

techniques, probably related to the increasingly sophisticated instrumentation (e.g., video and electronic recorders) and data manipulation technology available (e.g., time series and spectral analyses). Arguments about
macro or micro, lumping or splitting, objective or subjective behaviors are
found in a number of excellent interaction methodology volumes (Cairns,
1979; Lamb, Suomi, & Stephenson, 1979). While macroanalyses are less
tedious and time-consuming, microanalyses may uncover subtle rhythms
and phenomena, for example, a co-occurrence of behaviors noted by Stern
and his colleagues (Stern, Jaffe, Beebe, & Bennett, 1975) using milliseconds
as a base, which had not been noted by Schaffer *et al.* (1977) using seconds.
However, a recent correlation analysis suggested very high relationships
between fine-grained microanalyzed behaviors and more global behavioral
ratings of the same interactions (Field, 1978c). As Lipsitt (1979) recently
commented, "There's obviously a place for very fine-grained studies with
small categories and microanalysis . . . and a place for people who are still
using rating scales and working with very global kinds of things. . . . Our
problems are not so much with this stage . . . as they are with a later
stage . . . when people start saying we've become too mechanistic, too
precise, too objective and that we've lost sight of the child we started to
study [pp. 221–222]."

To summarize, in a word, since we are out of space, the best way to
learn infancy methodology is to work in the laboratory of a rigorous
methodologist and to observe lots of infants at various times and stages in
several places playing with different things and people. Even without
language infants can tell you a great deal.

REFERENCES

Ainsworth, M. D. S., & Wittig, B. A. Attachment and exploratory behavior of one-year-olds
in a strange situation. In B. M. Foss (Ed.), *Determinants of infant behavior* (Vol. 4). London: Metheuen, 1969.

Anders, T., & Sostek, A. The biosocial importance and environmental sensitivity of infant
sleep/wake behaviors. In K. Bloom (Ed.), *Prospective issues in infant research*. Hillsdale,
N.J.: Lawrence Erlbaum Associates, 1981.

Appleton, T., Clifton, R., & Goldberg, S. The development of behavioral competence in
infancy. In F. D. Horowitz (Ed.), *Review of Child Development Research* (Vol. 4).
Chicago: University of Chicago Press, 1975.

Bakeman, R. Untangling streams of behavior: Sequential analysis of observation data. In
G. P. Sackett & C. C. Haywood (Eds.), *Application of observational methods to the study
of mental retardation*. Baltimore: University Park Press, 1977.

Ball, W., & Tronick, E. Infant responses to impending collision: Optimal and real. *Science,*
1971, *171,* 818–820.

Belsky, J. Mother–infant interaction at home and in the laboratory: A comparative study.
Journal of Genetic Psychology, 1980.

Berlyne, D. E. Curiosity and exploration. *Science,* 1966, *153,* 25–33.

Bloom, K. Social elicitation of infant vocal behavior. *Journal of Experimental Child Psychology,* 1975, *20,* 51–58.

Bloom, K., & Esposito, A. Social conditioning and its proper control procedures. *Journal of Experimental Child Psychology,* 1975, *19,* 209–222.

Bower, T. G. R. *A primer of infant development.* San Francisco: W. H. Freeman, 1977.

Bower, T. G. R. *Development in infancy.* San Francisco: W. H. Freeman, 1974.

Bower, T. G. R., Broughton, J. M., & Moore, M. K. Infant responses to approaching objects: An indicator of response to distal variables. *Perception and psychophysics,* 1970, *9,* 193–196.

Brackbill, Y. Extinction of the smiling response in the infant as a function of reinforcement. *Child Development,* 1958, *29,* 115–124.

Brazelton, T. B. *Neonatal behavioral assessment scale.* London: Spastics International Medical Publications, 1973.

Brazelton, T. B., Koslowski, B., & Main, M. The origins of reciprocity: The early mother-infant interaction. In M. Lewis & L. A. Rosenblum (Eds.), *The effect of the infant on its caregiver.* New York: Wiley, 1974.

Bronfenbrenner, U. Toward an experimental ecology of human development. *American Psychologist,* 1977, *32,* 513–531.

Bronson, G. W. Infants' reactions to unfamiliar persons and novel objects. *Monographs of the Society for Research in Child Development,* 1972, *37* (3, Ser. No. 148).

Brooks, J., & Lewis, M. Infants' responses to strangers. Midget, adult and child. *Child Development,* 1976, *4,* 323–332.

Bruner, J. S. Pacifier-produced visual buffering in human infants. *Developmental Psychobiology,* 1973, *6,* 45–51.

Cairns, R. B. (Ed.). *The analysis of social interactions.* Hillsdale, N.J.: Lawrence Erlbaum Associates, 1979.

Campos, J. J., Emde, R. N., Gaensbauer, T., & Henderson, C. Cardiac and behavioral interrelationships in the reactions of infants to strangers. *Developmental Psychology,* 1975, *11,* 589–601.

Cantor, D., Fischel, J., & Kaye, H. *Conditioned disruption of newborn sucking.* Paper presented at Eastern Psychological Association meetings, Hartford, Conn., April 1980.

Caron, J. A., Caron, R. F. S., Caldwell, R. C., & Weiss, S. S. Infant perception of the structural properties of the face. *Developmental Psychology,* 1973, *9* 1(3), 385–399.

Caron, R. F., & Caron, A. J. Degree of stimulus complexity and habituation of visual fixation in infants. *Psychonomic Sciences,* 1969, *14,* 78–79.

Carpenter, G. C. *Mother-stranger discrimination in the early weeks of life.* Paper presented at the biennial meeting of the Society for Research in Child Development, Philadelphia, April 1973.

Chapple, E. D. Experimental production of transients in human interaction. *Nature,* 1970, *228,* 630–633.

Ciba Foundation Symposium. *Parent-infant interaction.* London: Ciba Foundation, 1975.

Clifton, R. K. Cardiac conditioning and orienting in the infant. In P. A. Obrist, A. H. Black, J. Brener, & L. V. DiCara (Eds.), *Cardiovascular psychophysiology: Current issues in response mechanisms, biofeedback and methodology.* Chicago: Aldine, 1974.

Clifton, R., Morrongiello, B., Kalig, J., & Dowd, J. Developmental changes in auditory localization in infancy. In R. Aslin, J. Alberts, & M. Peterson (Eds.), *Sensory and perceptual development: Influences of genetic and experimental factors.* New York: Academic Press, 1980.

Cohen, L., & Gelber, E. Visual habituation and memory in infancy. In L. B. Cohen & P. H. Salapatek (Eds.), *Infant perception and cognition.* New York: Academic Press, 1975.

Collard, R. R. Social and play responses of first-born and later-born infants in an unfamiliar situation. *Child Development,* 1968, *39,* 325–334.

Condon, W. S., & Sander, L. W. Synchrony demonstrated between movements of the neonate and adult speech. *Child Development,* 1974, *45,* 456–462.

Connolly, K., & Stratton, P. An exploration of some parameters affecting classical conditioning in the neonate. *Child Development,* 1969, *40,* 431–441.

Darwin, C. A biographical sketch of an infant. *Mind,* 1877, *2,* 285–294.

DeCasper, A. J., & Fifer, W. P. Of human bonding: Newborns prefer their mothers' voices. *Science,* 1980, *208,* 1174–1176.

Dittrichova, J., & Lapackova, V. Development of the waking state in young infants. *Child Development,* 1964, *35,* 365–270.

Dowd, J. The temporal organization of spontaneous movements in the human infant (Doctoral dissertation, University of Massachusetts, 1980).

Dunkeld, J., & Bower, T. G. R. *Infant response to impending optical collision.* Unpublished manuscript, University of Edinburgh, 1976.

Eilers, R. E., Wilson, W. R., & Moore, J. M. Developmental changes in speech discrimination in infants. *Journal of Speech and Hearing Research,* 1977, *20,* 766–780.

Eimas, P. Speech perception in early infancy. In L. B. Cohen & P. H. Salapatek (Eds.), *Infant perception and cognition.* New York: Academic Press, 1975.

Eisenberg, R. B. The organization of auditory behavior. *Journal of Speech and Hearing Research,* 1970, *13,* 453–471.

Ekman, P. Universal and cultural differences in facial expressions of emotion. In J. K. Cole (Ed.), *Nebraska symposium on motivation* (Vol. 19). Lincoln: University of Nebraska Press, 1972.

Ekman, P., & Friesen, W. V. *Unmasking the face.* Englewood Cliffs, N.J.: Prentice-Hall, 1975.

Emde, R. N., Kligman, D. H., Reich, J. H., & Wade, T. O. Emotional expression in infancy: I. Initial studies of social signaling and an emergent model. In M. Lewis & L. A. Rosenblum (Eds.), *The development of affect.* New York: Plenum Press, 1978.

Engen, T., & Lipsitt, L. P. Decrement and recovery of responses to olfactory stimuli in the human neonate. *Journal of Comparative and Physiological Psychology,* 1965, *59,* 312–316.

Engen, T., Lipsitt, L. P., & Kaye, H. Olfactory responses and adaptation in the human neonate. *Journal of Comparative and Physiology Psychology,* 1963, *12,* 19.

Fagan, J. F. Memory in the infant. *Journal of Experimental Child Psychology,* 1970, *9,* 217–226.

Fagan, J. F. Infants' recognition memory for faces. *Journal of Experimental Child Psychology,* 1972, *13,* 453–476.

Fagan, J. *Relationships between infant memory performance and later IQ.* Paper presented at the first symposium on Infants Born at Risk, Miami, January 1980.

Fantz, R. L. Pattern discrimination and selective attention as determinants of perceptual development from birth. In A. H. Kidd & J. L. Riviore (Eds.), *Perceptual development in children.* New York: International University Press, 1966.

Field, T. Effects of early separation, interactive deficits in experimental manipulations of infant–mother face-to-face interaction. *Child Development,* 1977, *48,* 763–771. (a)

Field, T. Maternal stimulation during infant feeding. *Developmental Psychology,* 1977, *13,* 539–540. (b)

Field, T. *Family interactions.* Unpublished manuscript, University of Miami, 1978. (a)

Field, T. Interaction behaviors of primary versus secondary caretaker fathers. *Developmental Psychology,* 1978, *14,* 183–184. (b)

Field, T. *Relationships between microanalyses and ratings of interaction behaviors.* Unpublished manuscript, University of Miami, 1978. (c)

Field, T. Differential behavioral and cardiac responses of 3-month-old infants to a mirror and peer. *Infant Behavior and Development,* 1979, *2,* 179–184. (a)

Field, T. Infant behaviors directed toward peers and adults in the presence and absence of mother. *Infant Behavior and Development,* 1979, *2,* 47–54. (b)

Field, T. Visual and cardiac responses to animate and inanimate faces by young term and preterm infants. *Child Development,* 1979, *50,* 188–194. (c)

Field, T. *Visual memory performance in infants who received nonnutritive sucking stimulation in the ICU.* Unpublished manuscript, University of Miami, 1980.

Field, T. Gaze behavior of normal and high-risk infants during early interactions with mothers, fathers, siblings, infant peers, a mirror and doll. *Journal of the American Academy of Child Psychiatry,* 1981. (a)

Field, T. Infant gaze aversion and heart rate during face-to-face interactions. *Infant Behavior and Development,* 1981. (b)

Field, T., & Walden, T. Perception and production of facial expressions. In H. Reese & L. Lipsitt (Eds.), *Advances in child development* (Vol. 16). New York: Academic Press, 1981.

Field, T., Dempsey, J., Hallock, N., & Shuman, H. Mothers' assessments of the behavior of their infants. *Infant Behavior and Development,* 1978, *1,* 156–167.

Field, T., Dempsey, J., Ting, G., Hatch, J., & Clifton, R. Cardiac and behavioral responses to repeated tactile and auditory stimulation by preterm and full-term infants during the neonatal period. *Developmental Psychology,* 1979, *15,* 406–416.

Field, T. M., Goldberg, S., Stern, D., & Sostek, A. M. (Eds.). *High risk infants and children: Adult and peer interactions.* New York: Academic Press, 1980.

Field, T., & Ignatoff, E. Videotaping effects on play and interaction behaviors of low income mothers and their infants. *Journal of Applied Developmental Psychology,* 1981.

Field, T., Sostek, A., Goldberg, S., & Shuman, H. (Eds.). *Infants born at risk.* New York: Spectrum, 1979.

Field, T., Sostek, A., Leiderman, P. H., & Vietze, P. (Eds.). *Culture and early interactions.* Hillsdale, N.J.: Lawrence Erlbaum Associates, 1981. (a)

Field, T., Woodson, R., Greenberg, R., & Cohen, D. *Habituation and imitation of facial expressions by newborn infants.* Unpublished manuscript, University of Miami, 1981. (b)

Fischer, T. *Rhythms of infant play.* Unpublished master's thesis, Tufts University, 1973.

Fitzgerald, H. E., & Porges, S. W. A decade of infant conditioning and learning research. *Merrill-Palmer Quarterly,* 1971, *17,* 79–117.

Fogel, A. Peer vs. mother directed behavior in 1- to 3-month-old infant. *Infant Behavior and Development,* 1979, *2,* 215–226.

Fogel, A., Diamond, G. R., Langhorst, B. H., & Demos, V. Affective and cognitive aspects of the two-month-old's participation in face-to-face interaction with its mother. In E. Tronick (Ed.), *Joint regulation of behavior.* Cambridge, England: Cambridge University Press, 1981.

Gewirtz, J. L., & Boyd, E. F. Experiments on mother–infant interaction underlying mutual attachment acquisition: The infant conditions the mother. In T. Alloway, L. Krames, & P. Pliner (Eds.), *Attachment behavior. Advances in the study of communication and affect* (Vol. 3). New York: Plenum, 1977.

Gewirtz, J., & Gewirtz, H. Visiting and caretaking patterns for kibbutz infants: Age and sex trends. *American Journal of Orthopsychiatry,* 1968, *38,* No. 3.

Goldberg, S. Visual tracking and existence constancy in 5-month-old infants. *Journal of Experimental Child Psychology,* 1976, *22,* 478–491.

Goldberg, S., Brachfeld, S., & DiVitto, B. Feeding, fussing and playing: Parent–infant interaction in the first year as a function of prematurity and prenatal problems. In T. Field, S. Goldberg, D. Stern, & A. Sostek (Eds.), *High risk infants and children: Adult and peer interactions.* New York: Academic Press, 1980.

Goldberg, S., & Lewis, M. Play behaviors in the year-old infant: Early sex differences. *Child Development,* 1969, *40,* 21–31.

Goren, C. C., Sarty, M., & Wu, P. K. Visual following and pattern discrimination of face-like stimuli by newborn infants. *Pediatrics,* 1975, *56* (4), 544–549.

Graham, F. K., & Clifton, R. K. Heart rate change as a component of the orienting response. *Psychological Bulletin,* 1966, *65,* 305–320.

Graham, F. K., Leavitt, L., Strock, B., & Brown, J. Precocious cardiac orienting in a human anencephalic infant. *Science,* 1978, *199,* 322–324.

Graves, Z., & Glick, J. The effect of context on mother–child interaction: A progress report. *The Quarterly Newsletter of the Institute for Comparative Human Development,* 1978, *2,* 41–46.

Haith, M. M. Infrared television recording and measurement of ocular behavior in the human infant. *American Psychologist,* 1969, *24,* 279–283.

Hiatt, S. W., Campos, J. J., & Emde, R. N. Facial patterning and infant emotional expression: Happiness, surprise and fear. *Child Development,* 1979, *50,* 1020–1035.

Hutt, C. Effects of stimulus novelty on manipulatory exploration in an infant. *Journal of Experimental Psychology,* 1967, *8,* 241–247.

Hutt, C. Specific and diversive exploration. In H. W. Reese & L. P. Lipsitt (Eds.), *Advances in child development and behavior* (Vol. 5). New York: Academic Press, 1970.

Hutt, S. J., Hutt, C., Lenard, H. G., Bernuth, H. V., & Muntjewerff, W. J. Auditory responsivity in the human neonate. *Nature,* 1968, *218,* 888–890.

Izard, C. E. *Face of emotion.* New York: Appleton, 1971.

Izard, C. E., Heubner, R. R., Risser, D., McGinnes, G. C., & Dougherty, L. M. The young infants' ability to produce discrete emotion expressions. *Developmental Psychology,* 1980, *16,* 132–140.

Jacobson, S. W. Matching behavior in the young infant. *Child Development,* 1979, *50,* 425–430.

Jones-Molfese, V. J. Responses of neonates to colored stimuli. *Child Development,* 1977, *48,* 1092–1095.

Kagan, J. The growth of the face schema: Theoretical significance and methodological issues. In J. Hellmuth (Ed.), *The exceptional infant* (Vol. 1). Seattle: Bruner/Mazel, 1967.

Kagan, J., Kearsley, R. B., & Zelazo, P. R. *Infancy: Its place in human development.* Cambridge, Mass.: Harvard University Press, 1978.

Karmel, B. Z., & Maisel, E. B. A neuronal activity model for infant visual attention. In L. B. Cohen & P. Salapatek (Eds.), *Infant perception: From sensation to cognition* (Vol. 1). *Basic visual processes.* New York: Academic Press, 1975.

Kasatkin, N. I. First conditioned reflexes and the beginning of the learning process in the human infant. In G. Newton & A. H. Reisen (Eds.), *Advances in psychobiology* (Vol. 1). New York: Wiley, 1972.

Kaye, H. The conditioned Babkin reflex in human newborns. *Psychonomic Science,* 1965, *2,* 287–288.

Kaye, K. Infants' effects upon their mothers' teaching strategies. In J. C. Glidewell (Ed.), *The social context of learning and development.* New York: Gardner Press, 1976.

Kaye, K. Toward the origin of dialogue. In H. R. Schaffer (Ed.), *Studies in mother-infant interaction.* New York: Academic Press, 1977.

Kearsley, R. B. The newborn's response to auditory stimulation: A demonstration of orienting and defensive behavior. *Child Development,* 1973, *44,* 582–590.

Klaus, M., & Kennell, J. *Maternal-infant bonding*. St. Louis: Mosby, 1976.

Koch, J. The change of conditioned orienting reaction in 5-month-old infants through phase shift of partial biorhythms. *Human Development*, 1968, *11*, 124–137.

Korner, A. F. Individual differences at birth: Implications for early experience and later development. *American Journal of Orthopsychiatry*, 1971, *41*, 608–619.

Korner, A. F., & Thoman, E. B. Visual alertness in neonates as evoked by maternal care. *Journal of Experimental Child Psychology*, 1970, *10*, 67–78.

LaBarbera, J. D., Izard, C. E., Vietze, P., & Parisi, S. A. Four- and six-month old infants' visual responses to joy, anger, and neutral expressions. *Child Development*, 1976, *47*, 535–538.

Lamb, M. The development of sibling relationships in infancy: A short-term longitudinal study. *Child Development*, 1978, *49*, 1189–1196.

Lamb, M., Suomi, S. J., & Stephenson, G. R. (Eds.). *Social interaction analysis*. Madison: University of Wisconsin Press, 1979.

Lewis, M., & Rosenblum, L. A. (Eds.). *The effect of the infant on its caregiver*. New York: Wiley, 1974.

Lewis, M., Young, G., Brooks, J., & Michalson, L. The beginning of friendship. In M. Lewis & L. Rosenblum (Eds.), *Friendship and peer relations*. New York: Wiley, 1975.

Lipsitt, L. Comments on chapter by L. J. Yarrow and B. J. Anderson. In E. B. Thoman (Ed.), *Origins of the infants' social responsiveness*. Hillsdale, N.J.: Lawrence Erlbaum Associates, 1979.

Lipsitt, L. P., & Kaye, H. Conditioned sucking in the human newborn. *Psychonomics Sciences*, 1964, *1*, 29–30.

Lipsitt, L. P., Kaye, H., & Bosack, T. N. Enhancement of neonatal sucking through reinforcement. *Journal of Experimental Child Psychology*, 1966, *4*, 163–168.

Lipsitt, L. P., Reilly, B. M., Butcher, M. J., & Greenwood, M. M. The stability and interrelationships of newborn sucking and heart rate. *Developmental Psychobiology*, 1976, *9*, 305–310.

MacFarlane, A. Olfaction in the development of social preference in the human neonate. In *Parent-infant interaction*. London: Ciba Foundation Symposium, 1975.

McCall, R. B. Challenges to a science of developmental psychology. *Child Development*, 1977, *48*, 333–344.

McGurk, H., Turnure, C., & Creighton, S. J. Auditory-visual coordination in neonates. *Child Development*, 1977, *48*, 138–143.

Meltzoff, A. N., & Moore, M. K. Imitation of facial and manual gestures by human neonates. *Science*, 1977, *198*, 75–78.

Messer, S. B., Kagan, J., & McCall, R. B. Fixation time and tempo of play in infants. *Developmental Psychology*, 1970, *3*, 406.

Moore, M. K., Borton, R., & Darby, B. L. *Visual tracking in young infants: Evidence for object identity or object permanence*. Paper presented at the biennial meeting of the Society for Research in Child Development, Denver, April 1975.

Morgan, G. A. *Determinants of infants' reactions to strangers*. Paper presented at the biennial meeting of the Society for Research in Child Development, Philadelphia, April 1973.

Morse, P. A. The discrimination of speech and nonspeech stimuli in early infancy. *Journal of Experimental Child Psychology*, 1972, *3*, 477–492.

Muir, D., & Field, J. Newborn infants orient to sounds. *Child Development*, 1979, *50*, 431–436.

Nelson, C. A., Morse, P. A., & Leavitt, L. A. Recognition of facial expressions by seven-month-old infants. *Child Development*, 1979, *50*, 1239–1242.

Nelson, M., Clifton, R., Dowd, J., & Field, T. Cardiac responding to auditory stimuli in newborn infants: Why pacifiers should not be used when heart rate is the major dependent variable. *Infant Behavior and Development*, 1978, *1*, 277–290.

Osofsky, J. D., & Danzger, B. Relationships between neonatal characteristics and mother–infant interaction. *Developmental Psychology,* 1974, *10,* 124–130.

Papousek, M. Experimental studies of appetitional behavior in human newborns and infants. In H. W. Stevenson, E. M. Hess, & H. L. Rheingold (Eds.), *Early behavior: Comparative and developmental approaches.* New York: Wiley, 1967.

Papousek, H., & Papousek, M. Mirror image and self-recognition in young human infants: I. A new method of experimental analysis. *Developmental Psychobiology,* 1974, *1,* 149–157.

Parke, R. D., & O'Leary, S. Father–mother–infant interaction in the newborn period: Some findings, some observations and some unresolved issues. In K. Riegel & J. Meacham (Eds.), *The developing individual in a changing world* (Vol. 2). *Social and environmental issues.* The Hague: Mouton, 1975.

Parmelee, A. H. Jr., & Stern, E. Development of states in infants. In C. D. Clements, D. D. Purpura, & F. E. Mayer (Eds.), *Sleep and the maturing nervous system.* New York: Academic Press, 1972.

Pederson, F., Yarrow, L., Anderson, B., & Cain, R. Jr. Conceptualization of the father influences in the infancy period. In M. Lewis & L. Rosenblum (Eds.), *The child and its family* (Vol. 2). New York: Plenum, 1979.

Piaget, J. *The origins of intelligence in children.* New York: International Universities Press, 1952.

Pomerleau-Malcuit, A., & Clifton, R. K. Neonatal heart rate response to tactile, auditory and vestibular stimulation in different states. *Child Development,* 1973, *44,* 485–496.

Porges, S. Innovations in fetal heart rate monitoring: The application of spectral analysis for the detection of fetal distress. In T. Field, A. Sostek, S. Goldberg, & H. Shuman (Eds.), *Infants born at risk.* New York: Spectrum, 1979.

Reese, H. W., & Porges, S. W. Development of learning processes. In V. Hamilton & M. D. Vernon (Eds.), *The development of cognitive processes.* New York: Academic Press, 1976.

Rheingold, H. W., Gewirtz, J. L., & Ross, H. W. Social conditioning of vocalizations in the infant. *Journal of Comparative and Physiological Psychology,* 1959, *52,* 68–73.

Rose, S. A. Enhancing visual recognition memory in preterm infants. *Developmental Psychology,* 1980, *16,* 85–92.

Rose, S. A., Schmidt, K., & Bridger, W. M. Cardiac and behavioral responsivity to tactile stimulation in premature and full-term infants. *Developmental Psychology,* 1976, *12,* 311–320.

Rovee, C. K., & Rovee, D. T. Conjugate reinforcement of infant exploration behavior. *Journal of Experimental Child Psychology,* 1969, *8,* 33–39.

Rubenstein, J. Maternal attentiveness and subsequent exploratory behavior in the infant. *Child Development,* 1967, *38,* 1089–1100.

Sameroff, A. The components of sucking in the human newborn. *Journal of Experimental Child Psychology,* 1968, *6,* 607–623.

Sameroff, A. J. Can conditioned responses be established in the newborn infant: 1971? *Developmental Psychology,* 1971, *5,* 1–12.

Schaffer, H. R. Studies in mother-infant interaction. New York: Academic Press, 1977.

Schaffer, H. R., Collis, G. M., & Parsons, G. Vocal interachange and visual regard in verbal and pre-verbal children. In H. R. Schaffer (Ed.), *Studies in mother–infant interaction.* New York: Academic Press, 1977.

Schwartz, A., Rosenberg, D., & Brackbill, Y. An analysis of the components of social reinforcement of infant vocalization. *Psychonomic Science,* 1970, *20,* 323–325.

Siqueland, E. R., & DeLucia, C. A. Visual reinforcement of nonnutritive sucking on human infants. *Science,* 1969, *165,* 1144–1146.

Siqueland, E. R., & Lipsitt, L. P. Conditioned head-turning in human newborns. *Journal of Experimental Child Psychology,* 1966, *3,* 356–376.

Sokolov, Y. N. *Perception and the conditioning reflex.* New York: Macmillan, 1963.

Sostek, A., Sameroff, A. J., & Sostek, A. Evidence for the unconditionability of the Babkin reflex in newborns. *Child Development,* 1972, *43,* 509–519.

Sroufe, A., & Waters, E. Heart rate as a convergent measure in clinical and developmental research. *Merrill-Palmer Quarterly,* 1977, *23,* 1; 3–25.

Sroufe, A., & Wunsch, J. P. The development of laughter in the first year of life. *Child Development,* 1972, *43,* 1326–1344.

Stamps, L. Temporal conditioning of heart rate responses in newborn infants. *Developmental Psychology,* 1977, *13,* 624–629.

Stamps, L. & Porges, S. W. Heart rate conditioning in newborn infants: Relationships among conditionability, heart rate variability and sex. *Developmental Psychology,* 1975, *11,* 424–31.

Stern, D. N. Mother and infant at play. In M. Lewis and J. Rosenblum (Eds.), *The effect of the infant on its caregiver.* New York: Wiley, 1974.

Stern, D. N. *The first relationship.* Cambridge, Mass.: Harvard University, 1977.

Stern, D. N., Jaffe, J., Beebe, B., & Bennett, S. L. Vocalizing in unison and in alternation: Two modes of communication within the mother–infant dyad. *Annals of the New York Academy of Science,* 1975, *263,* 89–100.

Thoman, E. B. Sleep and wake behaviors in neonates: Consistencies and consequences. *Merrill-Palmer Quarterly,* 1975, *21,* 295–314.

Trevarthen, C. Conversations with a two-month-old. *New Scientist,* May 2, 1974, pp. 230–233.

Tronick, E., Als, H., Adamson, L., Wise, S., & Brazelton, T. B. The infants' response to entrapment between contradictory messages in face-to-face interaction. *Journal of Child Psychiatry,* 1978, *17,* 1–13.

Vaughn, B., & Sroufe, A. The temporal relationship between infant heart rate acceleration and crying in an aversive situation. *Child Development,* 1979, *50,* 565–567.

Vietze, P. M. Mother–infant bonding: A review. In N. Kretchmer & J. Brasel (Eds.), *The biology of child development.* New York: Masson Publishing, 1980.

Volkmar, F. R. S., & Siegel, A. E. Young children's responses to discrepant social communications. *Journal of Child Psychology and Psychiatry,* 1979, *20,* 139–149.

Watson, J. S., & Ramey, C. T. Reactions to response-contingent stimulation in early infancy. *Merrill-Palmer Quarterly,* 1972, *18,* 219–228.

Weinraub, M., Brooks, J., & Lewis, M. The social network: A reconsideration of the concept of attachment. *Human Development,* 1977, *20,* 31–47.

Weisberg, P. Social and nonsocial conditioning of infant vocalizations. *Child Development,* 1963, *34,* 377–388.

Wertheimer, M. Psychomotor coordination of auditory and visual space at birth. *Science,* 1961, *134,* 1692.

Wolff, P. H. The courses, controls and organization of behavior in the neonate. *Psychological Issues,* 1966, *5,* 1–99.

Wolhwill, J. F. *The study of behavioral development.* New York: Academic Press, 1973.

Yarrow, L. J., & Anderson, B. J. *Procedures for studying parent–infant interaction: A critique.* Hillsdale, N.J.: Lawrence Erlbaum Associates, 1979.

Yogman, M. W., Dixon, S., Tronick, E., Adamson, L., Als, H., & Brazelton, T. B. *Development of infant social interaction with fathers.* Paper presented at Eastern Psychological Association, New York, April 1976.

Young-Browne, G., Rosenfeld, H. M., & Horowitz, F. D. Infant discrimination of facial expressions. *Child Development,* 1977, *48,* 555–562.

3 Early Social Development

MICHAEL E. LAMB, ROSS A. THOMPSON, AND ANN M. FRODI

Seth, an 8-month-old infant, crawled briskly into his family's living room and stopped only when he was in the middle of the floor. The animated smile that accompanied his entrance dimmed noticeably as he scanned the adult faces surrounding him—some of which he had seen before, others he had not. He continued to look pensively at these people until finally he located the face of his mother, Mary, who had been watching him all along. Simultaneously Seth and Mary broke into broad smiles. Seth scurried over to some toys by his mother's feet.

Adult conversation over the next half-hour was frequently punctuated by the explosive squeals and shrieks, and quieter cooing, of an infant at play. Periodically Seth looked up to catch Mary's eyes. His gaze was frequently reciprocated, and he easily returned to play. As the adult meeting ended, one of the participants, emboldened by his observations of mother–infant exchange of glances and smiles, stooped down to Seth and smiled at him. "How ya doin', big fella?" he asked. Seth looked up at him with a serious expression, and for a moment examined the stranger's face intently. Then he broke down into loud, anguished sobs.

This brief episode represents a typical and quite predictable interaction between an infant, mother, and other adult figures. Such apparently simple social interactions at this very early age have been of considerable interest to psychologists and other developmental researchers. This attention has occurred primarily for two reasons.

Early social development is rather distinct from later social interactions in that the number of significant people in the infant's social world and the variety of the infant's social interactions are both comparatively small. It is possible, therefore, to examine in some detail the nature and formation of these social bonds from the perspectives of both the child and

49

STRATEGIES AND TECHNIQUES
OF CHILD STUDY

the adults. In addition, early social development has been assumed by many developmental theorists to play an important role in the child's later social and personality development. The long-term impact of the mother-infant attachment process, in particular, has attracted a good deal of theoretical and research attention. The importance of these two defining characteristics as research issues will become evident as this chapter proceeds.

The purpose of this chapter, then, is to examine the methods researchers have developed to investigate the child's earliest social behaviors. And it will become quite obvious that, despite their seeming simplicity, such early interactions have required rather complex and sophisticated research techniques.

THE STUDY OF EARLY SOCIAL DEVELOPMENT

During the twentieth century, academic interest in personality development has waxed and waned. Early in this century, the developmental focus of both psychoanalysis and behaviorism combined to make speculations about the development of personality the most popular and lively area within academic psychology. Over the succeeding decades, however, the popularity of this area declined. One reason for this decline was the failure of psychologists to substantiate their speculations with empirical support. Where research was attempted, furthermore, the methods employed were questionable. Case study reports by clinicians were used to buttress psychoanalytic predictions, and parental reports of child and parental behavior provided the empirical support for learning theory and behaviorism. Case study reports and parental reports are both techniques of uncertain reliability, and this undoubtedly hampered researchers' progress. The *coup de grace* was delivered around 1960 when an intensified national concern with the acceleration of intellectual development and the discovery of Piaget by American psychologists provoked a shift of interest from the study of sociopersonality development to the study of cognitive development. Only in the 1970s was interest in social and personality development rekindled.

The field today appears much stronger and healthier than in its earlier heyday. There are two obvious reasons for this newfound strength. First, there exist today better-articulated and more cautious theories than ever before, and these have permitted researchers to ask more focused questions. Second, a diverse array of research techniques are employed in attempts to answer these questions. Thus when case-study reports or parental questionnaires are employed, they supplement information gathered in other ways. Our goal in this chapter is to describe these research techniques and illustrate the types of issues or topics they can be used to address.

Research techniques tend to shift into and out of favor, and recent technological advances have quickened the pace with which new techniques are developed. Differences between new and old techniques are often more apparent than real, however: Once one understands the goals or purposes of certain approaches, new developments and revisions of research techniques are readily comprehensible. For this reason, this chapter emphasizes issues and approaches; the specific techniques described are presented as examples of the ways in which relevant data may be sought. By adopting this strategy, we hope that this chapter will remain useful even after the techniques we describe have been superseded.

Before discussing research approaches, however, we want to describe the theoretical perspective that defines the issues of interest to us. Briefly, we are interested in inborn characteristics, socializing experiences, and the interactions between the two. We begin with the assumption that the way in which each child develops is determined jointly by the child's individual characteristics[1] and the experiences he or she has. These two sources of influence are not independent: Adults behave differently depending on the characteristics (e.g., temperament, gender, appearance) of the children with whom they are interacting, and many of those characteristics themselves change as a consequence of development and experience. Thus in order to explain the processes of early social development, we must learn how various social experiences interact with individual differences among infants to yield a person's characteristic social style and personality. This has led researchers to focus attention on the meshing of caretaker and infant behavior. In the first substantive section of this chapter, we discuss several approaches to the measurement of dyadic interaction. These same approaches are often used to assess parental sensitivity, which many researchers view as the crucial determinant of the degree of dyadic meshing achieved. (At least in the first few months of life, infants lack the capacity to monitor their partners and modulate their own social behavior accordingly; the burden for doing so thus falls more heavily upon the adult interactants.) In addition to the structure or meshing of interaction, researchers have also focused on the "content" of interaction, with special interest in determining how and with whom infants tend to interact. The focus of the first section is on three simple questions: what to observe, how to record it, and how to interpret the data obtained.

---

[1] Space limitations prevent us from discussing the techniques available for assessing individual differences among infants. Both objective measures and parental report procedures have been used. Interested readers are referred to Rothbart and Derryberry's (1981) recent review of evidence concerning the concept of temperament.

The reasons for studying early social interaction are many and diverse. Some researchers aim simply to provide descriptive information, whereas others attempt to test predictions. The ethological attachment theorists (Ainsworth, Blehar, Waters, & Wall, 1978; Lamb, 1981a, 1981b), for example, believe that when the early interactions are smoothly meshed, infants develop expectations about these interactions and about the ways in which their caretakers will behave. These expectations about the behavior of specific people are then generalized to the other people with whom the infants later come into contact, and it is thus especially important to be able to assess these expectations. The "Strange Situation" procedure developed by Mary Ainsworth appears to do just that; this procedure and its correlates are thus described in the second substantive section.

Throughout these first two sections, the focus is upon the interactions between young children and their parents. By contrast, the third and fourth sections focus on interactions between children and people who are not family members. Section 3 deals with infants' reactions to strangers—a topic that has long been of interest to researchers because of the common presumption that all children pass through a period in which they respond negatively to strangers. This presumption has recently been questioned, which has led, in turn, to a refinement of measures and methods in this area. In the fourth section, positive rather than negative responses are central as the focus shifts to the nature and development of interactions and relationships among young children. The way children behave in interactions with peers both reflects the social style and competencies they have developed (e.g., in interaction with their parents) and has formative developmental significance of its own. Both topics are relevant to the contents of the fourth section. This is also the section in which, for the first time, many of the examples have to do with preschoolers rather than infants and toddlers.

STUDIES OF PARENT–CHILD INTERACTION

Developmental psychologists have long been interested in the nature and formative significance of parent–child relationships, although the questions of greatest interest have changed in the last few decades. Earlier work focused largely on the effects on children's personality development of parents' childrearing attitudes and practices (Baumrind, 1971; Hoffman & Saltzstein, 1967; Sears, Maccoby, & Levin, 1957). As noted earlier, most of the data were obtained in parental interviews that proved to have dubious validity and reliability. Furthermore, researchers tended to assume that the direction of influence usually ran from parents to infants, an assumption that was criticized most pointedly by Bell (1968, 1971). This critique led to a focus of attention upon the ways in which infants and young children elicit and maintain interactions with their caretakers. This in turn accentuated the trend toward reliance on observations rather than interviews, and encouraged a concern with preverbal infants and their parents, rather than with the more complex interactions between preschoolers and parents. When interviews are used today, they are typically used to supplement the information obtained by direct observation. As Parke (1978) noted recently, interviews provide the only way in which we can determine how parents perceive their children and their own behavior. Interviews may thus help us to understand *why* parents behave as they do. They remain, however, poor ways of determining how parents and children *actually* behave.

The focus of observational studies has changed in recent years. It is common today for researchers to aim for (*a*) detailed descriptions of the course of interaction, and (*b*) understanding of the contextual and developmental factors that account for changes in the interactive patterns. These aims result from theoretical interest in the formative significance of the quality of interactive meshing between infants and adults. Another impetus has come from technological advances that provide reasonably inexpensive tools for data collection, reduction, and analysis. Unfortunately, the availability of devices such as event recorders, computer analysis programs, and special videotape recorders has encouraged many researchers to gather more data than they can deal with—often without clearly articulated research questions in mind. The complexity of these devices and systems is such that questions must be clearly articulated in advance so that the problem (rather than the technology) determines what types of data will be gathered. It is regrettably common, however, for researchers to undertake "fishing expeditions"—unfocused attempts to "let the data determine the questions." These studies often result in masses of uninterpretable data or else publication of selected and unreplicable findings. In this section, we discuss the various techniques and approaches to the study of parent–child interaction. Our discussion is organized around three simple but crucial questions: (*a*) What behaviors are to be observed? (*b*) how should the observations be recorded?, and (*c*) how should the data be analyzed? Readers who wish to go beyond our brief discussion are referred to several recent anthologies (Cairns, 1979; Lamb, Suomi, & Stephenson, 1979; Sackett, 1978b; Schaffer, 1977).

What Should Be Observed?

Exactly how one describes an interaction depends on the issues of interest to the researcher. The refinement and sensitivity of the behavioral catalog will differ depending on whether one wishes to explore individual differences in interactive quality (e.g., Ainsworth & Bell, 1969; Ainsworth, Bell, & Stayton, 1971, 1974; Brazelton, Koslowski, & Main, 1974; Brazelton, Tronick, Adamson, Als, & Wise, 1975; Vietze, Abernathy, Ashe, & Faulstich, 1978) or broader normative trends (e.g., Kaye, 1977a, 1977b; Lamb, 1977a, 1977b; Stern, 1974; Stern, Beebe, Jaffe, & Bennett, 1977); changes in interactive quality occurring within the duration of a single observation (e.g., Freedle & Lewis, 1977; Jaffe, Stern, & Peery, 1973; Lewis & Lee-Painter, 1974) or over several months of development (e.g., Lamb, 1977a, 1977b, 1978a); the effects of the immediate physical and social context (e.g., Lamb, 1979) or the effects of enduring social relationship upon dyadic interactions (e.g., Parke, Power, & Gottman, 1979); the temporal sequence and interrelationships among behaviors (e.g., Bakeman, 1978, Bakeman & Brown, 1977) or the frequency of characteristic modes of interaction (e.g., Kaye, 1977a, 1977b; Lamb, 1977a, 1978a, 1978b; Stern, 1974).

The first decision has to do with the refinement of behavioral description. In the last few years, researchers have been able to achieve "micro"-level descriptions, in which the behaviors and expressions of interactants are described in great detail—usually with the aid of films or videotapes that allow sequences to be reviewed repeatedly and in slow motion. In Brazelton's research, for example, the quality of facial expression, vocalization, eye direction and focus, head position, and body posture of both parent and infant are recorded for each individual second during a 3-minute dyadic play interaction (Als, Tronick, & Brazelton, 1979). Such microanalytic descriptions have made it possible to determine that there are varying amounts of synchrony or reciprocal turn-taking (i.e., a sort of behavioral dialogue) occurring in these face-to-face interactions. Some mothers and infants in Brazelton's sample, for example, took turns looking and vocalizing at one another and exchanged smiles. Other mother–infant dyads were more dysjunctive and less reciprocal in their interactive exchanges (see Figure 3.1).

Much of this interactive patterning might have gone unrecorded if grosser measures or observational codes had been employed. Another advantage of choosing to provide a micro-level description is that it is possible to combine micro-descriptive units into macrounits, whereas it is impossible to break macrounits down into finer units. For example, Bakeman and Brown (1977) used 100 rather detailed codes in their initial observational records, and then selected 36 that appeared to be communicative (e.g., "mother kisses baby," "baby looks at mother") and created 10 "activity variables" (e.g., "mother stimulates baby to feed") for further analysis. At the most global level, they used the observational detail to determine, for each time unit, whether or not either mother or baby was behaving at all!

FIGURE 3.1. The mutual sharing of socioemotional signals between a mother and baby has recently been of interest to students of early social development. (Photo by R. Thompson)

As an alternative to this conceptually based creation of macrocodes, it is possible to use statistical techniques like factor analysis to combine variables into clusters (e.g., Clarke-Stewart, 1973; Cohen & Beckwith, 1979).

As one might expect, there are also drawbacks attendant upon the microanalytic approach. First, microanalytic descriptions usually demand a record that can be reviewed many times, and the presence of cameras may have an obtrusive effect on mother–infant interaction. Second, the setting is often highly structured in order to ensure that both interactants are in clear view, and this too may distort natural patterns of interaction. Third, the more detailed and complex the coding system, the more time has to be devoted to analyzing the record of each subject. As a result, microanalytic studies are seldom more than demonstration projects involving very small sample sizes. Generalizability and replicability often remain in question. Finally, it is quite easy to "lose the forest for the trees," unless the researcher frequently steps back from the detailed description and appraises the interaction from a *macro*analytic perspective.

Selecting a level of analysis typically demands a detailed understanding of the subjects and settings under examination. This understanding should then be employed to select units of analysis that approximate the unit of meaning employed by the communicating interactants. When studying social interaction and communication, the researcher should not use a coding system that parcels behavior more discretely than the interactants themselves do, and should not treat as similar behaviors those that the interactants do not deem functionally equivalent. Available technical sophistication makes it easy to make these mistakes.

One alternative to detailed and comprehensive microanalysis is to record a small subset of behaviors which one has reason to believe are indices of some underlying construct or reality. Thus, for example, Lamb (e.g., 1977a, 1977b) found that the frequency with which babies approached, stayed near, cried to, or asked to be held by certain people indicated to whom the infants were attached, and which attachment figures were preferred. The choice of these measures was theoretically determined, and the empirical findings confirmed that the measures were appropriately chosen. Stern (1974, 1977) studied behavioral dialogues by focusing only on mutual gaze patterns, and Kaye (1977a) studied communication during feeding by recording only maternal jiggling and infant sucking. The usefulness of this strategy of course depends on the ability to choose the appropriate measures: It is much more conservative to hedge one's bets and record as much as possible!

Another approach involves analyzing interactive activity at the level of the *dyad* rather than the individual. In his studies of mother–infant gazing patterns, Stern (1974) considers four dyadic states: neither mother nor infant looking at the other; only the infant looking; only the mother looking; mutual gaze. Vietze (Strain & Vietze, 1975; Vietze *et al.*, 1978) has used a similar strategy in studies of vocal interaction. After extensive analysis, Brazelton and his colleagues identified the clusters of maternal and infant behaviors that together constituted five dyadic states—initiation, greeting, mutual orientation, play dialogue, and disengagement (Als *et al.*, 1979). The advantage of the dyadic approach is that one can examine and compare mother–infant pairs as interactive systems, to which both partners contribute (see Figure 3.2).

Another strategy involves *categorizing* behaviors that are functionally similar. Such a "macro-level" strategy was employed in the Stanford Longitudinal Study. Maccoby (1979) grouped the behaviors of 18-month-olds and their mothers into just four categories: child positive, child negative, mother positive, and mother negative. Likewise, in multivariate analyses Lamb (1977a, 1977b) considered smiling, vocalizing, laughing, and proffering as "affiliative behaviors," and others have created descriptive categories like "distal social bids." Functional similarity can also be determined by the timing and sequence of activities, rather than the content

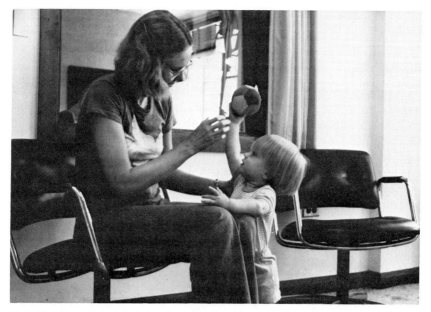

FIGURE 3.2. Dyadic social exchange between a mother and infant often centers on the sharing of toy play and other pleasant experiences. (Photo by R. Thompson)

of the behaviors, as Stern *et al.* (1977) showed in their analyses of dyadic interaction.

Another macro-level technique involves the use of *rating scales,* which require that the observer both observe and make evaluative judgments of the individual's or the partners' behavior (e.g., Ainsworth & Bell, 1969; Ainsworth *et al.,* 1971, 1974, 1978; Brody & Axelrad, 1978; Matas, Arend, & Sroufe, 1978). Obviously, the usefulness of these scales depends on the care with which they are employed by the observer; their advantages are (*a*) the fact that they synthesize a considerable amount of information into one score, while (*b*) capitalizing on the ability of humans to perform complex integrations and judgments.

In sum, the strategy chosen to describe an interaction sequence depends on the specific research question and the types of data needed to address that problem. Microanalytic strategies permit detailed, quantitative analyses of interactive synchrony and reciprocal behavior between social partners, while also permitting multiple "slices" through the data at different levels of descriptive detail. Because the techniques are labor-intensive, however, most studies involve very small samples, making generalization from their findings rather questionable. Furthermore, the procedures are somewhat intrusive, which also leads to doubt about validity. Broader ("macro") assessments allow researchers to assess relationships among variables, but do not permit detailed descriptive analyses.

How Are Observations to Be Recorded?

Whatever level of description they choose, researchers have to decide how to deal with temporal relations. Some behaviors (e.g., smiles) are most easily counted regardless of duration, whereas the duration of others (e.g., touching, sucking) constitutes essential descriptive information. In addition, it is usually important to know when behaviors occur in relation to one another, so it is common to record the time at which the behaviors of interest occur (e.g., whether they are recorded as incidence or duration measures). This usually implies that a film or audiotaped record is necessary, so that the time of each data entry can be noted.

From such a record, it is possible to determine how often certain behaviors occurred and how much time was filled by others. To obtain more detail, one can break the observational period into many brief time units, and then determine which behaviors occurred in each unit. Stern (1974; Jaffe et al., 1973), for example, scored maternal and infant gazes during intervals of .6 seconds, whereas Brazelton scored infant and maternal behavior every second (Als et al., 1979). If the investigator wishes to perform a sequential analysis (i.e., an analysis designed to determine whether certain behaviors consistently precede or succeed one another), it is important that the time units be smaller than the duration of the behaviors being recorded.

If sequential analyses are to be attempted, it is usual for researchers to use electronic recording devices to encode the occurrence of behaviors keyed in by the user (for examples, see the 1978 issue of *Behavior Research Methods & Instrumentation*). Written notes do not permit the onset and offset of activities to be recorded with sufficient accuracy (Lewis & Freedle, 1973; Lewis & Lee-Painter, 1974), whereas portable keyboards producing a computer-readable output allow observers to record when criterial behaviors occur in the most simple and accurate way. These devices automatically record when each key is depressed; computerization permits automated data reduction (Stephenson, 1979).

Nevertheless, it is important to remember that the reliability of any data acquisition device is never greater than the reliability of its human user. Regardless of the technological sophistication, therefore, it is often necessary to review the interaction several times, and this means that film records must be available. Film or videotaped records can be reviewd multiple times and slowed for more detailed study, but the film record itself is only the beginning of the complete analytic process. It is not uncommon for researchers to collect more extensive videotape records than they can hope to analyze. Furthermore, as we noted earlier, the process of filming may affect the behavior under study, especially when the interactions have to take place in contrived situations, because these permit easier filming. The representativeness of the behavior filmed then becomes questionable.

In all, each mode of data collection has attendant costs which must be weighed against the advantages. The relative costs and benefits will vary depending on the specific research question. No single method is suitable for every project, and every method has its applications and limitations.

Analytic Strategies

The data collection procedure employed is often dictated by the types of analyses the investigators hope to conduct. Observational data can be used simply to provide detailed descriptions, especially when the researchers wish to illustrate individual differences in dyadic functioning (e.g., Brazelton *et al.*, 1974). For example, one could compare a mother–infant dyad in which the mother sensitively adjusts her behavior in response to the baby's needs with a dyad in which the mother paces her behavior less effectively with respect to her baby's changing states. Alternately, by summing the frequencies of certain criterial behaviors in relation to interactions involving different people or occurring in different contexts, it is possible to demonstrate how relationships differ, or how interactions are context-dependent (Lamb, 1977a, 1977b, 1979). Thus, for example, one could show that infants direct more social bids to one person than to another, or that infants show more distress in an unfamiliar laboratory than in the home setting.

When they wish to understand the dynamics of interaction, however, investigators typically employ one of a variety of *sequential analysis* procedures (Bakeman, 1978; Gottman & Bakeman, 1979; Sackett, 1978a, 1979). In general, these procedures involve determining the conditional probability that a certain behavior (X) will occur given the prior occurrence of another behavior (Y). X and Y can be behaviors of a single subject, they may be performed by different individuals, or they may represent different dyadic states. If they wish to determine how likely certain behaviors or states are to co-occur, for example, researchers compute contingent probabilities at zero lag (i.e., they examine how likely the behaviors are to occur simultaneously). State transitional probabilities with lag = 1 (i.e., behavior Y occurs in the unit immediately preceding X) quantify the likelihood that certain behaviors precede or succeed one another within one time unit. Analyses with lag = 1 are especially useful when the range of behaviors recorded is small, or when dyadic states are involved (Bakeman & Brown, 1977; Jaffe *et al.*, 1973; Stern, 1974; Strain & Vietze, 1975).

Lagged sequential probability analyses operate by the same general principle, except that they quantify the probability that X occurs 2, 3, or more (lag = 2, 3, or n) time units or 2, 3 or more events after the occurrence of Y. When the number of lags or the number of behaviors involved is large, however, the number of calculations becomes prohibitive. Fortunately, Sackett (1979) has developed a probabilistic strategy for detecting stable sequential chains that makes analysis much easier, although it requires that the investigators have some prior knowledge of the phenomena being studied.

Sequential analyses are useful because they allow researchers to detect co-occurrences, sequences, and contingencies in the course of dyadic interactions, and most of the data collection procedures described above can generate data suitable for sequential analysis. Looking just at gaze exchange between mother and infant, for example, one can examine how often gazing is reciprocated or not, and the ways in which mutual gazing is contingent upon the prior gazing of one social partner. However reliably a sequence occurs, however, cause–effect relationships may not be involved, since a third factor may account for the sequential occurrence of both X and Y. Furthermore, lagged sequential analyses capitalize on the likelihood that some probabilities will be statistically significant, especially when many are being computed. This makes it important to guard against reporting sequences that are the result of chance relations. One possibility is to search for *consistency* of findings across related response modalities, or in repeated analyses of the data at different levels of description.

Summary

Interest in describing the dynamics of social interaction and the availability of sophisticated technological aids have combined to make the study of parent–child (particularly parent-*infant*) interaction popular. These data processing devices do not, however, relieve investigators of all taxing responsibilities. Researchers still must choose the level of detail at which the interactions will be described. Their decisions will depend on the specific research question under review, and so it is crucial that researchers have clear questions in mind before they begin to gather data. Having decided on the amount of detail to be sought, investigators must then decide how the data will be recorded and whether it will be necessary to make a film record, which can be reviewed repeatedly or slowly to ensure reliable and detailed data. Most often, researchers will try to encode the temporal relationships among the interactants' behaviors, so that some type of sequential analysis will be possible. Such analyses make it possible to determine quantitatively how well meshed the interactants' behaviors are, but the meaningfulness of any findings depends on the appropriateness of the original decisions about which behaviors to record. We are still only learning how to describe and study social interaction.

THE STRANGE SITUATION PROCEDURE AND ITS CORRELATES

As we noted earlier, many attempts to study social interaction are motivated by a desire to understand formatively significant relationships. Proponents of the ethological attachment theory, for example, argue that the degree of behavioral meshing between parent and infant determines how secure a relationship will be formed. When the interaction is well meshed, infants learn that the interaction is predictable, and that they can count on adults to respond promptly and appropriately to the infants' signals and needs. Such infants will develop secure, trusting attachment relationships. By contrast, when the interaction is not well meshed—that is, when adults respond inconsistently and inappropriately to the infants' signals and needs—insecure, mistrustful relationships result. In this section, we describe a procedure developed for assessing the security or insecurity of infant–parent attachments. We also discuss research confirming the relationship between prior parental behavior and the infants' behavior in the Strange Situation, as well as studies showing how the security of the parent–infant relationship affects the infant's later behavior with others.

The Strange Situation was first described by Ainsworth and Wittig in 1969. It is a laboratory procedure in which 1–2-year-old infants can be observed interacting with attachment figures. The focus is on the way in which the infants use the adults as sources of security in a mildly stressful situation. The setting is a comfortable laboratory playroom with many attractive toys. The parent is instructed to respond naturally to the infant's social bids, but not to initiate interaction with the baby. As Table 3.1 shows, stress is introduced by placing the child in a strange room, having an unfamiliar person enter on two occasions, and also by having the parent leave the child briefly. When stressed, it is usual for infants of this age to seek comfort or reassurance in proximity to or contact with the adult. Having obtained this reassurance, they then resume exploration of the novel toys.

According to attachment theorists, *securely attached* infants behave in precisely this fashion (Ainsworth *et al.,* 1978). They may retreat to the parent at first, or when the stranger enters, but they otherwise gain security enough—from the parent's mere presence—that they are able to explore. They are distressed by the separations (they often cry) and greet their

TABLE 3.1
Procedure for the Strange Situation

Episode	Persons present	Entrances and exits
1	Parent, baby	
		Stranger enters
2	Parent, baby, stranger	
		Parent leaves
3	Baby, stranger	
		Parent returns; stranger leaves
4	Parent, baby	
		Parent leaves
5	Baby	
		Stranger returns
6	Baby, stranger	
		Parent returns; stranger leaves
7	Parent, baby	

Note: All episodes are of 3 minutes' duration, although episodes 3, 5, and 6 are often abbreviated when infants are very distressed. The duration of episode 4 is extended when necessary.

parents enthusiastically when they return, either with distal social bids or, more commonly, by approaching and seeking contact. *Insecure* infants, however, respond in one of two ways. Some *avoid* the parent, so that they respond to the parent's return by cutting off or avoiding interaction, rather than by seeking it. Others are angry and *ambivalent,* mingling bids to interact with or be close to the adult with outbursts of angry rejecting behavior (see Figure 3.3).

Several initial studies indicated that these patterns of behavior were remarkably stable—when an infant was seen twice in the situation with the same attachment figure, it was very likely to behave in the same way both times (Connell, 1976; Waters, 1978). Over 80% of the infants seen twice with their mothers displayed the same pattern of behavior at 12 and 18 months. However, if the baby was seen with another attachment figure, the way he or she behaved often differed (Lamb, 1978c; Lamb, Hwang, Frodi, & Frodi, in preparation; Main & Weston, 1981; Owen, Chase-Lansdale, & Lamb, in preparation), suggesting that the way the infant behaved reflected a characteristic of a specific relationship more than a characteristic of the infant him- or herself.

Such a degree of stability is seldom obtained in psychological research. Indeed, Waters reported that when one analyzes data from the Strange Situation differently, less stability is obtained (Waters, 1978; Ainsworth *et al.,* 1978). More specifically, there is no significant stability, either between episodes of the same session or between different observations in the situa-

FIGURE 3.3. This infant tries to follow and searches for the parent who has just left him. An infant's reactions to brief separations from the parent in the Strange Situation—and their subsequent reunion—can provide important information concerning the security of the attachment relationship. (Photo by R. Thompson)

tion, when one tabulates the frequency or duration of *specific behaviors* like smiling, crying, vocalizing, and the like. There is greater stability over time, however, on several *rating scales* in which the observer synthesized information about the infant's behavior during a 3-minute episode (such as scales of proximity and contact seeking, avoidance, and resistance). The greatest stability is obtained when the behavior observed throughout the session is synthesized into a *single* categorical rating concerning the security of parent–infant attachment. This means that when appraising the general quality of the parent–infant relationship, it is more useful to employ a synthetic "macro" approach than the kind of microanalytic strategy earlier described. Complete instructions regarding the coding and classificatory procedures have been published recently (Ainsworth *et al.,* 1978). Ainsworth's procedures are not difficult to apply, but a great deal of practice is necessary before they can be employed reliably and sensitively.

More recent studies yield a very different picture concerning the stability of attachment classification over time. Waters (1978) deliberately selected a sample of mothers and infants from highly stable families in order to maximize attachment stability. Thompson, Lamb, and Estes (in press), with an unselected middle-class sample; and Vaughn, Egeland, Sroufe, and

Waters (1979), with a disadvantaged sample, reported stability over 6–7 months of only 50–60%. In both cases, instability was related to changing life circumstances (most notably, mother returning to work) and major socioemotional stresses on the family. Presumably, these changes or stresses are associated with changes in the quality of mother–infant interaction, which in turn lead to a renegotiation of the relationship and of each partner's expectations regarding the other.

The way infants behave in the Strange Situation appears to be determined by the way they have been treated in the preceding months of their lives (Ainsworth *et al.*, 1974, 1978). When adults respond promptly and appropriately, infants develop trust in the adults, and trust that the adults can be counted on to be accessible when they are needed. Such trust is a characteristic of secure relationships. When the adults respond less predictably and they find contact with their infants aversive, the babies develop a pattern of avoidance. Ambivalent patterns develop in infants whose parents have behaved inconsistently, and who also find interaction distasteful. According to Lamb (1981a, 1981b), infants' behavior in the Strange Situation reflects their expectations about the likely behavior and accessibility of the adults. Many researchers (e.g., Lamb, Sroufe) are now studying relationships between descriptions of early parent–child interaction (see preceding section) and the child's later behavior in the Strange Situation. Of course, the parent's behavior may change over time in response to changing family circumstances, leading to changes in the security of infant–parent attachment (Thompson *et al.,* in press; Vaughn *et al.,* 1979).

Behavior in the Strange Situation is also of interest to researchers because of its demonstrated predictive value (Ainsworth *et al.,* 1978). The results of several studies indicate that infants generalize their way of behaving with specific attachment figures to encounters with unfamiliar people. Thus Main (1973) found that infants who avoided their mothers in the Strange Situation at 12 months also avoided an unfamiliar tester and a woman trying to engage them in play more than 8 months later. Securely attached infants were later more cooperative with the examiner and showed more "game-like spirit" in interaction with the playmate. Thompson and Lamb (in preparation) reported that securely attached infants were more sociable with unfamiliar adults than were insecurely attached infants. Waters, Wippman, and Sroufe (1979) showed that infants who were securely attached to their mothers at 12 months were rated more socially competent in preschool 2 years later. Easterbrooks and Lamb (1979) showed a relationship between quality of attachment and social competence with unfamiliar peers. Finally, Matas *et al.* (1978) reported that securely attached infants were more enthusiastic, persistent, and happy in problem-solving situations. Not only do secure infants develop trust in their attachment figures, they also appear to have confidence in their own efficacy (Lamb, 1981b).

Summary

The Strange Situation procedure is likely to be used extensively in years ahead, both as a means of assessing the outcomes of relationships studied in early observations and to predict later social behavior. A secure attachment relationship does not guarantee optimal later development, but it provides the child with a strong base—a head start over children whose earlier relationships have been unsatisfactory.

REACTIONS TO UNFAMILIAR PEOPLE

Developmental psychologists have studied infants' responses to unfamiliar adults for several decades, largely because the emergence of fearful responses to strangers has long been described as a developmental milestone. Spitz (1965), for example, viewed the emergence of "stranger anxiety" around 8 months as an indication of a major reorganization of psychological functioning. Much of the recent interest, however, has been spurred by a published critique of the literature which in turn stimulated a reappraisal of both methodology and theoretical assumptions (Rheingold & Eckerman, 1973).

In their review of the literature, Rheingold and Eckerman (1973) could find no convincing demonstration that infants were primarily fearful when approached by an unfamiliar adult. Rather, fear or anxiety was regularly accompanied by positive or affiliative responses to strangers; seldom did more than half the infants in a sample exhibit frank fear. Rheingold and Eckerman also contended that the popular means of appraising stranger fear were operationally vague and of questionable validity and reliability.

Research techniques have improved greatly since the publication of this critique, and researchers have contested Rheingold and Eckerman's conclusion that wariness of strangers rarely occurs. Three issues have dominated recent discussions of this phenomenon: the nature of the research paradigm, data collection and analysis, and general questions about research strategy.

Research Paradigms

As Rheingold and Eckerman (1973) noted, the most common procedure to assess infants' reactions to strangers involves observing the baby's response when a stranger approaches and then withdraws (see Campos,

Emde, Gaensbauer, & Henderson, 1975; Morgan & Ricciuti, 1969; Scarr & Salapatek, 1970; Schaffer, 1966; Schaffer & Emerson, 1964; Waters, Matas, & Sroufe, 1975, for examples). Typically, these standardized sequences consist of four episodes:

1. Entry—the stranger appears in the doorway, then smiles and talks to the infant
2. Approach—the stranger slowly walks toward the infant, still talking and smiling
3. Contact—the stranger touches the infant and offers to or actually does pick it up
4. Withdrawal—the stranger slowly moves away from the infant

Modifications are made depending on the goals of the specific study. Other studies have looked closely at infants' behavior in episode 2 of the Strange Situation, in which the stranger sits quietly for 1 minute, talks to the parent for the next minute, and then tries to engage the baby in toy play (e.g., Bretherton & Ainsworth, 1974).

The differences between these two procedures are sure to have an impact on the infants' responses. The approach–withdrawal sequence culminates in a highly intrusive encounter between stranger and infant—usually a pickup—which is much more stressful than an encounter mediated by distal bids or attractive toys (Skarin, 1977; Waters, Matas, & Sroufe, 1975) (see Figure 3.4). In the Strange Situation, the baby is mobile, and so has a variety of response options; in the approach–withdrawal situation, the baby is often in an infant seat—immobilized and unable to seek the proximity of a parent if he or she is present. Infants respond more positively to strangers when on their parent's lap than when in an infant seat (Sroufe, Waters, & Matas, 1974). Furthermore, the brevity of the approach–withdrawal sequence may tax the infant's ability to appraise and understand the situation. In general, researchers have confirmed that stranger anxiety is greatest when interaction with the stranger is proximal, intrusive, and sudden, rather than distal and well modulated (Sroufe, 1977; Sroufe *et al.,* 1974).

Characteristics of strangers other than their behavior are also important. Male strangers evoke more negative reactions than do female strangers (Lewis & Brooks, 1974; Skarin, 1977), although even female adults are more fear-provoking than children are (Brooks & Lewis, 1976; Greenberg, Hillman, & Grice, 1973; Lewis & Brooks, 1974). The size of the stranger relative to the infant's viewing perspective (i.e., does the stranger tower over the infant?) is also important (Weinraub & Putney, 1978).

The naturalness of the encounter likewise affects the infant's response.

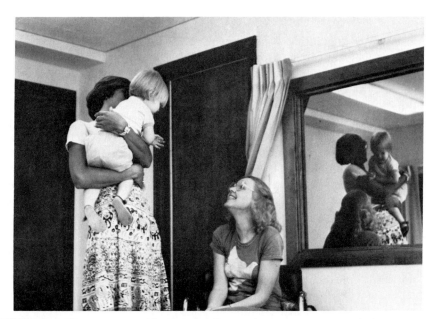

FIGURE 3.4. Close contact with an unfamiliar adult—such as being picked up and held—more regularly evokes negative reactions in infants than does social interaction across a distance. (Photo by R. Thompson)

Often the stranger's approach and withdrawal are so contrived and unnatural that the infant may react negatively to the unfamiliarity of the stranger's behavior, rather than to the stranger's unfamiliarity per se (Shaffran, 1974). Infants show less wariness in the familiar home environment than they do in unfamiliar laboratory settings (Skarin, 1977; Sroufe *et al.*, 1974), and they are less fearful when their mothers are close and accessible than when they are distant or absent (Campos, Emde, Gaensbauer, & Henderson, 1975; Morgan & Ricciuti, 1969; Skarin, 1977). Clearly, the social and nonsocial context affects the infant's appraisal of and response to the event.

In sum, the quality of the infant's response to a stranger depends on the setting, the way the stranger approaches, the accessibility of an attachment figure, and the behavior and individual characteristics of the stranger. The procedure employed in any study should be chosen in light of the specific goals, be they the elicitation of frank fear (Hiatt, Campos, & Emde, 1979) or the assessment of individual differences in sociability with strangers (Lamb, 1981c; Stevenson & Lamb, 1979; Thompson & Lamb, in preparation).

Data Collection and Analysis

Whether the infant's behavior is recorded live or from videotape records, most researchers compare the frequencies of occurrence of discrete behaviors that are believed to index fear or wariness (e.g., fussing, withdrawal, or avoidance) or affiliation (e.g., smiling, approaching) across the various episodes. Other researchers make global ratings—for example, of facial expression or motor activity.

Both approaches have their weaknesses. Frequency counts of discrete behaviors may overlook important information because behaviors are not viewed in the context of ongoing activity. A smile directed toward mother is not functionally equivalent to a smile directed toward the stranger, particularly if the latter is preceded by the cessation of toy play and is followed by gaze aversion. A more meaningful analytic unit would describe these three behaviors together as a "coy response." Viewing behaviors in clusters permits more refined and discriminating descriptions, although responses such as "active smile," "wary brow," "gaze aversion," and sobering" are not easily coded or described. These milder instances of wariness may also tell us more about the infant's appraisal of the stranger than the presence or absence of frank distress does.

When positive responses anchor one end of a rating scale and negative responses anchor the other, an implicit assumption is made that responses are *either* positive or negative. In fact, however, unfamiliar persons tend to elicit *both* positive responses (including curiosity) and negative reactions (Bretherton, 1978; Bretherton & Ainsworth, 1978). Sensitivity is lost when the cooccurrence of these responses is given the same score on a rating scale as a "neutral" response. By appraising both wariness and sociability separately, for example, Bretherton (1978) was able to show that over an 8-minute episode, 1-year-olds became increasingly sociable and decreasingly wary. When positive and negative responses are appraised separately, it is easier to compare the quality of responses to familiar and unfamiliar persons than when a single composite measure is used (Bretherton, 1978; Bretherton & Ainsworth, 1974) (see Figure 3.5).

Recently, several researchers have used convergent behavioral and psychophysiological measures in studies of reactions to strangers. Heart rate data have been used because heart rate is known to decelerate (the orienting response) when an organism is attending to a stimulus, whereas it accelerates (the defensive response) when the organism is avoiding a stimulus or processing aversive or fear-provoking stimuli (Campos, 1976). Thus we would expect heart rate to decelerate when babies are looking curiously at strangers, and to accelerate when wariness or fear is involved. Heart rate acceleration occurs in response to strangers in infants older than about 6 months (Campos, 1976; Lewis, 1974; Sroufe & Waters, 1977). Like

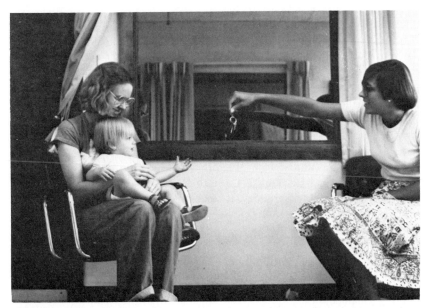

FIGURE 3.5. Infants frequently show both affiliative and wary tendencies in their responses to initial encounters with an unfamiliar adult. Here the infant smiles at the stranger and reaches for the keys she is offering, while pushing himself back on his mother's lap. (Photo by R. Thompson)

the behavioral data, therefore, cardiac data do not support Rheingold and Eckerman's (1973) conclusion that fearful reactions are rare.

One must be cautious when using heart rate data in this way, however. Movement affects heart rate, so it is important to restrict the subject's activity and to have behavioral records available to distinguish movement artifacts from indices of fear (Sroufe & Waters, 1977). As noted earlier, careful studies using cardiac activity measures confirm that wariness of strangers first occurs in the second half of the first year (Campos *et al.,* 1975; Skarin, 1977; Waters *et al.,* 1975). The degree of wariness reflected on cardiac and behavioral measures is generally congruent, and the pattern of contextual and developmental effects is similar for both types of measures. Nevertheless, cardiac data should always be supplemented by behavioral data so that accurate and appropriate inferences are drawn from the data.

Research Strategy

Since individual infants of any given age respond differently to strangers, longitudinal studies are more likely than cross-sectional studies to show how common a phase of negative responses to strangers is. Cross-sectional studies (like most of those reviewed by Rheingold and Eckerman, 1973) are likely to underestimate the incidence of wary reactions, because at any age some infants may have completed and others may not have begun the period of wariness. Longitudinal studies (e.g., Emde, Gaensbauer, & Harmon, 1976) show that most infants respond negatively to strangers during some part of the first year of life, although the onset, termination, and duration of this phase are highly variable. Moreover, longitudinal studies are also more likely to provide inportant information concerning individual differences in responsiveness to strangers. For instance, Thompson and Lamb (in preparation) found that ratings of stranger sociability at $12\frac{1}{2}$ and $19\frac{1}{2}$ months, correlated .40, indicating some stability in individual differences in reactions to strangers.

Summary

In all, a number of methodological factors have to be taken into account when studying infants' reactions to strangers. The fact is that infants' emotional responses are affected by a number of factors, among them the unfamiliarity of the stranger. Unfortunately, these factors are often confounded in research investigations, making it difficult to determine the relative importance of the stranger's unfamiliarity per se. Especially when the many responses are muted rather than exaggerated by these confounds, it is also essential to use measures that are sensitive enough to reflect the varied and subtle expressions of emotion that occur. It is usually preferable to use multiple convergent measures rather than single indices of "fear."

DEVELOPING RELATIONS WITH OTHER CHILDREN

Like the other topics discussed in this chapter, research on the relationships among children has blossomed in the last decade, largely because societal changes have produced a situation in which increasing numbers of children spend much of their time together. This increases the formative importance of peer relationships, and also increases the availability of peer groups for study.

Unlike research on reactions to strangers, the research on peer relations has not focused on negative responses. Instead, three other issues have been of primary interest to investigators. Most important has been the attempt to gather, by observation, descriptive accounts of the nature of the interaction between children of different ages. Related to this has been an attempt to determine how competently children interact—how well they mesh their behaviors with those of their partners. In this area, individual differences have been of greater import than in the descriptive investigations. Finally, studies have been designed to illustrate the processes whereby peers influence one another. Under the influence of the ethological perspective, which has become increasingly popular in developmental psychology, most studies have been conducted in minimally structured settings.

Descriptive Studies

Particularly when the subjects are infants, descriptive information about the nature of peer relationships has been the primary focus in research studies. In several of the studies conducted by Lewis and his colleagues (e.g., Lewis, Young, Brooks, & Michalson, 1975), for example, infants of around 1 year of age were brought together in a laboratory playroom. While the infants' mothers quietly looked on, concealed observers recorded the infants' behaviors, using measures based on those previously used in observational studies of parent–infant interaction (e.g., proximity, touch, look, vocalize). Eckerman, Whatley, and Kutz (1975), in a study of 12–18-month-old infants, and Lamb (1978a, 1978b), in two studies of sibling-infant interaction, later employed larger behavioral catalogs in essentially the same way. Unfortunately, although studies such as these give an indication of the amount and type of interaction taking place (e.g., there is much looking, but toys are infrequently offered), they do not reveal how well or poorly integrated the partners' behaviors are. With the exception of a few dyadic codes employed by Eckerman *et al.* and Lamb (e.g., play), social *interaction* is poorly described when discrete behavioral measures are used. Recognizing this, several researchers have taken an alternative route, focusing on the *structure* of the interaction sequences (i.e., the way in which the behaviors of the interactants are related to one another's behavior) rather than on the specific behavioral *content* (i.e., what behaviors each interactant emits).

There are several other problems with the techniques employed by Lewis, Eckerman, and Lamb. First, most specific behaviors occur fairly rarely, especially in brief laboratory sessions. Thus, quantitative comparisons across situations or ages may sometimes be insensitive to contextual or developmental differences because of a statistical "floor effect." Second, the more specific and refined the behavioral codes, the more likely they are to make some of the behavior unclassifiable and to break down complex social acts into component parts that fail to represent the complexity and nature of the acts (see first section of this chapter). Third, unfamiliar infants observed in an unfamiliar environment may behave abnormally, giving an inaccurate picture of their social abilities and propensities.

In their research, Mueller and Vandell (1979) and Becker (1977) have avoided these problems, and have pioneered alternative means of investigating early peer relationships. Mueller and his colleagues, for example, established play groups for young infants and then recorded the infants' behavior by way of concealed cameras (Mueller & Lucas, 1975). Subsequent analysis of the videotaped records revealed a series of stages in the types of peer interaction that occurred—stages that appeared to parallel the sensorimotor developmental stages described by Piaget (1952). Around 1 year of age, object-centered contacts predominated, and social exchanges or interactions were rare. In the second stage (beginning at around 15 months of age), infants actively sought and received "contingencies" from one another—that is, they responded to one another's actions, and they expected to receive such responses to their own actions. In the third stage (about 17 months), complementary interchanges began. It was now possible to predict not only *that* a partner would respond, but *how* he or she would respond. The children had developed rules about the content of social behavior that made social interaction more orderly and rule-governed than it was before. With age, the number of social behaviors in a sequence increased, as did their complexity.

To demonstrate these developmental trends, Mueller and his colleagues used a somewhat unusual scoring system. Instead of noting *which* social behavior was directed by one infant to another, they noted for many of their analyses *whether* a socially directed behavior (type unspecified) occurred, and *whether* a response was received. This procedure made it possible to assess the complexity of interactions by determining how many times the partners took turns. A somewhat similar procedure was employed by Jacqueline Becker (1977) in a study designed to determine whether the amount of experience with peers affected the amount and complexity of peer interaction. (It did.) In Becker's scoring system, the observers recorded each behavior as it occurred. Subsequently, the complexity of each socially directed behavioral "unit" was determined by counting the number of behaviors included in the unit. For example, if a baby just smiled at another, a complexity of 1 was scored. If the baby smiled, approached, and offered a toy, however, a complexity of 3 was scored. By combining Mueller's and Becker's measures, therefore, it would be possible to assess both the mean complexity of the socially directed units and the complexity of the sequence of social units comprising the interaction.

All of the methods described thus far have been used in attempts to identify and describe normative trends—both developmental differences and situational differences. Besides defining such normative trends, however, developmental psychologists typically want to explore individual differences among infants and children. Measures sensitive to normative trends may not be sensitive to stable and meaningful individual differences. In fact, we know from research on mother–infant interaction that behavioral frequency measures are usually *not* stable over time (Waters, 1978). There is some evidence, however, that these measures may be useful in research on peer interaction. In a longitudinal study of sibling–infant interaction, for example, Lamb (1978a) found great stability over a 6-month period in several frequency measures of sociability. In addition, Vandell (1979) has shown that there is individual stability over time in the complexity of the interactions infants engage in. These measures may thus be useful in investigations designed to explore the origins and consequences of individual differences in sociability with peers.

Social Competence

Researchers are probably most interested today in social competence with peers. Unfortunately, this term seems to have a variety of meanings. In many papers, social competence is confused with sociability, so that infants who direct more social behaviors to others are deemed more socially competent than others. We prefer to define social competence as an individual's ability to initiate social interactions, reciprocate others' initiatives, and maintain social interactions. Unfortunately, when one counts the number of interactions initiated, the proportion of initiatives that are successful in eliciting social responses, the amount of time spent in social interaction, or the mean length of each such bout, one finds that these measures do not tap a stable dimension of individual difference (Lamb, Easterbrooks, & Holden, 1980). These measures are neither stable over time nor significantly intercorrelated. Without further research, we will not know, of course, whether the measures are deficient (they fail to take into account the affective quality of social interaction, for example) or whether stable individual differences in social competence simply do not exist in young children.

Like Lamb *et al.* (1980), Gottman, Gonso, and Rasmussen (1975) have focused on social competence in preschool-aged children, but their approach has been different. After tabulating the frequency of a variety of discrete social behaviors, these investigators conducted factor analyses in order to determine what combinations of behaviors might constitute social competence and sociability. The stability of individual differences was not assessed, although, as would be predicted, the preschoolers who scored high on the competency factor were also more popular among their peers—that is, they were more commonly identified as friends or preferred playmates. Asher (1978) and his colleagues have conducted other studies demonstrating that friendship nominations are sensitive to individual differences in social competence. For example, Oden and Asher (1977) showed that children became more popular and more sociable after they were given training in how to interact with peers.

A very different way of investigating social competence has been employed by the Blocks (1980) and other researchers (e.g., Baumrind, 1977) at Berkeley. The technique employed by these researchers—Q-sort ratings—builds on the fact that trained observers gradually construct perceptions of children's behavior; they synthesize information that would be fragmented or unrecorded if only the frequency or complexity of social behaviors were recorded. Consequently, observers and teachers are asked to indicate how characteristic of specific children certain descriptions or adjectives are. By forcing their informants to classify only a certain proportion of the statements as "very descriptive," others as "somewhat descriptive," some as "not characteristic," and yet others as "extremely uncharacteristic," it appears possible to obtain quite sophisticated and reliable descriptions. As mentioned earlier, for example, Waters *et al.* (1979) recently showed that Q-sort descriptions of the social competence of preschoolers were systematically and predictably related to earlier measures of the security of mother–infant attachment. Although Q-sorts and other types of rating scales have not been used widely, they are likely to become more popular as researchers come to realize that human observers are better able to make sense of complex behavioral sequences than are complex statistical techniques.

Another group of researchers have chosen not to focus on constructs like social competence or sociability but to describe in detail the behavioral patterns that underlie such constructs. These descriptive efforts are similar in purpose to the ethologists' attempts to develop ethograms—detailed descriptions of interaction patterns. Thus, for example, Strayer and Strayer (e.g., 1976) have attempted to describe dominance and submissive behavior in different groups of young children. McGrew (1972) published a detailed description of behavior among nursery school children, including a particularly useful description of agonistic behavior. Blurton Jones (1972) has also provided valuable descriptions and an extensive behavioral catalog. By design, these human ethologists avoid the attribution of *meaning* or *purpose* to the behavior they observe. They believe that objective descriptions are far more useful, because they will ultimately allow us to define the meaning of behavior more accurately than if we rely upon our presumptions, intuitions, and biases. Now that several ethograms have been published, researchers are waiting for the ethologists to make good on this promise.

Peer Socialization

While researchers such as Becker and Mueller have characterized interactions by whether or not responses are received, much of the recent research on the process of peer socialization is focused on the communicative value of behavioral responses from peers. Several studies have thus explored the propensity of children to administer punishing and rewarding responses to one another, whereas others have sought to determine when such responses occur and how effective children's responses are in shaping the behavior of peers. Most studies of this type have focused on the responses children receive from peers when they engage in sex-typed behaviors in naturalistic settings (see Chapter 10). Several studies have demonstrated that when children engage in sex-appropriate activities, they are likely to elicit positive or rewarding responses from peers, whereas they elicit negative or punishing responses when they engage in sex-inappropriate activities (e.g., Fagot, 1977; Lamb & Roopnarine, 1979; Lamb et al., 1980). Such responses should shape the behavior of peers, making it more likely that they will behave in conventionally approved ways. Two studies have now demonstrated that reinforcing and punishing responses from peers are indeed effective: Punished activities terminate more rapidly, and reinforced activities terminate more slowly (Lamb & Roopnarine, 1979; Lamb et al., 1980). Furthermore, there is some evidence of a stable individual characteristic—susceptibility to peer influence. Specifically, Lamb et al. (1980) found that children who are most responsive to reinforcements from peers are also more responsive to punishments from peers. Studies of this sort illustrate one way of investigating the process of peer socialization and also point toward behavioral measures of individual differences whose origins and implications demand further investigation.

CONCLUSION

In this chapter we have tried to illustrate some of the diverse techniques used in the study of early social development. Recent methodological advances in this area have been considerable, and have permitted researchers to address and answer questions that were once untestable. Rather than attempting to be encyclopedic, however, we have sought to identify issues and research strategies that illustrate some of the considerations involved in research work in this area.

Across each of the domains we selected for discussion above, there run common themes that merit review. First, it is clear that well-defined research questions must define the arena and strategy for data collection and analysis—not the other way around. Technological sophistication is never a substitute for conceptual clarity. This means that critical constructs (such as "social competence with peers") must be clearly defined, theoretical assumptions must be rigorously tested (lest they be found erroneous), and cautious inferences must be drawn from the data. Above all, the "right" research strategy is the one that is best suited to studying the question(s) under consideration.

Second, understanding the subject of study is the essential prerequisite to research activity. This is especially true in the area of infancy, when the organism's behavioral repertoire—and the "meaning" of overt behavior—undergo striking change in a relatively short time span. In many ways, research on early social development is still in a stage of understanding the young infant: what it can do, and why.

Finally, it is clear that recent advances in research technology—videotape equipment, electronic recording devices, computer-based analytic packages, and the like—can be a real boon to research activity if used wisely. But they also have a number of disadvantages such as their intrusiveness, high cost, and labor-intensiveness, that also merit consideration. As always, the relative costs and benefits of these devices depend on what is being studied, and why.

Major contributions to this area in the future will depend on the ability of researchers to select theoretically important questions and to choose appropriate methodologies with which to study them. From the appearance of the field at present, we have every reason to be optimistic for the future.

REFERENCES

Ainsworth, M. D. S., & Bell, S. M. Some contemporary patterns of mother–infant interaction in the feeding situation. In A. Ambrose (Ed.), *Stimulation in early infancy*. London and New York: Academic Press, 1969.

Ainsworth, M. D. S., Bell, S. M., & Stayton, D. J. Individual differences in strange situation behavior of one-year-olds. In H. R. Schaffer (Ed.). *The origins of human social relations*. London and New York: Academic Press, 1971.

Ainsworth, M. D. S., Bell, S. M., & Stayton, D. J. Infant–mother attachment and social development: "Socialisation" as a product of reciprocal responsiveness to signals. In M. P. M. Richards (Ed.), *The integration of a child into a social world*. Cambridge, England: Cambridge University Press, 1974.

Ainsworth, M. D. S., Blehar, M. C., Waters, E., & Wall, S. *Patterns of attachment: A psychological study of the strange situation*. Hillsdale, N.J.: Lawrence Erlbaum Associates, 1978.

Ainsworth, M. D. S., & Wittig, B. A. Attachment and exploratory behavior of one-year-olds in a strange situation. In B. M. Foss (Ed.), *Determinants of infant behavior IV*. London: Methuen, 1969.

Als, H., Tronick, E., & Brazelton, T. B. Analysis of face-to-face interaction in infant–adult dyads. In M. E. Lamb, S. J. Suomi, & G. R. Stephenson (Eds.), *Social interaction analysis: Methodological issues.* Madison: University of Wisconsin Press, 1979.

Asher, S. Peer relationships. In M. E. Lamb (Ed.), *Social and personality development.* New York: Holt, Rinehart & Winston, 1978.

Bakeman, R. Untangling streams of behavior: Sequential analyses of observation data. In G. P. Sackett (Ed.), *Observing behavior* (Vol. 2). *Data collection and analysis methods.* Baltimore: University Park Press, 1978.

Bakeman, R., & Brown, J. V. Behavioral dialogues: An approach to the assessment of mother–infant interaction. *Child Development,* 1977, *48,* 195-203.

Baumrind, D. Current patterns of parental authority. *Developmental Psychology,* 1971, *4,* 1-103.

Baumrind, D. *Socialization determinants of personal agency.* Paper presented to the Society for Research in Child Development, New Orleans, March 1977.

Becker, J. A learning analysis of the development of peer oriented behavior in nine month old infants. *Developmental Psychology,* 1977, *13,* 481-491.

Bell, R. Q. A reinterpretation of the direction of effects in studies of socialization. *Psychological Review,* 1968, *75,* 81-95.

Bell, R. Q. Stimulus control of parent or caretaker behavior by offspring. *Developmental Psychology,* 1971, *4,* 63-72.

Block, J. H., & Block, J. The role of ego-control and ego-resiliency in the organization of behavior. In W. A. Collins (Ed.), *Minnesota symposia on child psychology* (Vol. 13). Hillsdale, N.J.: Lawrence Erlbaum Associates, 1980.

Blurton Jones, N. Categories of child–child interaction. In N. Blurton Jones (Ed.), *Ethological studies of child behaviour.* London: Cambridge University Press, 1972.

Brazelton, T. B., Koslowski, B., & Main, M. The origins of reciprocity: The early mother–infant interaction. In M. Lewis & L. A. Rosenblum (Eds.). *The effect of the infant on its caregiver.* New York: Wiley, 1974.

Brazelton, T. B., Tronick, E., Adamson, L., Als, H., & Wise, S. Early mother–infant reciprocity. In *Parent–infant interaction.* (Ciba Foundation Symposium 33.) Amsterdam: Elsevier, 1975.

Bretherton, I. Making friends with one-year-olds: An experimental study of infant–stranger interaction. *Merrill-Palmer Quarterly,* 1978, *24,* 29-51.

Bretherton, I., & Ainsworth, M. D. S. Responses of one-year-olds to a stranger in a strange situation. In M. Lewis & L. Rosenblum (Eds.), *The origins of fear.* New York: Wiley, 1974.

Brody, S., & Axelrad, S. *Mothers, fathers and children.* New York: International Universities Press, 1978.

Brooks, J., & Lewis, M. Infants' responses to strangers: Midget, adult and child. *Child Development,* 1976, *47,* 323-332.

Cairns, R. B. (Ed.). *Social interaction: Methods, analysis and illustration.* Hillsdale, N.J.: Lawrence Erlbaum Associates, 1979.

Campos, J. J. Heart rate: A sensitive tool for the study of emotional development in the infant. In L. Lipsitt (Ed.), *Developmental psychobiology: The significance of infancy.* Hillsdale, N.J.: Lawrence Erlbaum Associates, 1976.

Campos, J. J., Emde, R. N., Gaensbauer, T., & Henderson, C. Cardiac and behavioral interrelationships in the reactions of infants to strangers. *Developmental Psychology,* 1975, *11,* 589-601.

Clarke-Stewart, K. A. Interactions between mothers and their young children: Characteristics and consequences. *Monographs of the Society for Research in Child Development,* 1973, *38,* (Serial No. 153).

Cohen, S. E., & Beckwith, L. Preterm infant interaction with the caregiver in the first year of life and competence at age two. *Child Development, 1979, 50,* 767–776.

Connell, D. B. *Individual differences in attachment: An investigation into stability, implications, and relationships to structure of early language development.* Unpublished doctoral dissertation, Syracuse University, 1976.

Easterbrooks, M. A., & Lamb, M. E. The relationship between quality of infant–mother attachment and infant competence in initial encounters with peers. *Child Development, 1979, 50,* 380–387.

Eckerman, C. O., Whatley, J. L., & Kutz, S. L. Growth of social play with peers during the second year of life. *Developmental Psychology, 1975, 11,* 42–49.

Emde, R. N., Gaensbauer, T. J., & Harmon, R. J. *Emotional expression in infancy: A biobehavioral study.* New York: International Universities Press, 1976.

Fagot, B. I. Consequences of moderate cross-gender behavior in preschool children. *Child Development, 1977, 48,* 902–907.

Freedle, R., & Lewis, M. Prelinguistic conversations. In M. Lewis & L. Rosenblum (Eds.), *Interaction, communication, and the development of language.* New York: Wiley, 1977.

Gottman, J. M., & Bakeman, R. The sequential analysis of observational data. In M. E. Lamb, S. J. Suomi, & G. R. Stephenson (Eds.), *Social interaction analysis: Methodological issues.* Madison: University of Wisconsin Press, 1979.

Gottman, J., Gonso, J., & Rasmussen, B. Social interaction, social competence, and friendship in children. *Child Development, 1975, 46,* 709–718.

Greenberg, D. J., Hillman, D., & Grice, D. Infant and stranger variables related to stranger anxiety in the first year of life. *Developmental Psychology, 1973, 9,* 207–212.

Hiatt, S. W., Campos, J. J., & Emde, R. N. Facial patterning and infant emotional expression: Happiness, surprise, and fear. *Child Development, 1979, 50,* 1020–1035.

Hoffman, M. L., & Saltzstein, H. D. Parent discipline and the child's moral development. *Journal of Personality and Social Psychology, 1967, 5,* 45–57.

Jaffe, J., Stern, D. N., & Peery, J. C. "Conversational" coupling of gaze behavior in prelinguistic human development. *Journal of Psycholinguistic Research, 1973, 2,* 321–329.

Kaye, K. Thickening thin data: The maternal role in developing communication and language. In M. Bullowa (Ed.), *Before speech.* Cambridge, England: Cambridge University Press, 1977. (a)

Kaye, K. Toward the origin of dialogue. In H. R. Schaffer (Ed.), *Studies in mother–infant interaction.* London: Academic Press, 1977. (b)

Lamb, M. E. The development of mother–infant and father–infant attachments in the second year of life. *Developmental Psychology, 1977, 13,* 637–648. (a)

Lamb, M. E. Father–infant and mother–infant interaction in the first year of life. *Child Development, 1977, 48,* 167–181. (b)

Lamb, M. E. The development of sibling relationships in infancy: A short-term longitudinal study. *Child Development, 1978, 49,* 1189–1196. (a)

Lamb, M. E. Interactions between 18-month-olds and their preschool-aged siblings. *Child Development, 1978, 49,* 51–59. (b)

Lamb, M. E. Qualitative aspects of mother- and father–infant attachments. *Infant Behavior and Development, 1978, 1,* 265–275. (c)

Lamb, M. E. The effects of the social context on dyadic social interaction. In M. E. Lamb, S. J. Suomi, & G. R. Stephenson (Eds.), *Social interaction analysis: Methodological issues.* Madison: University of Wisconsin Press, 1979.

Lamb, M. E. The development of social expectations in the first year of life. In M. E. Lamb & L. R. Sherrod (Eds.), *Infant social cognition: Theoretical and empirical considerations.* Hillsdale, N.J.: Lawrence Erlbaum Associates, 1981. (a)

Lamb, M. E. Developing trust and perceived effectance in infancy. In L. P. Lipsitt (Ed.), *Advances in infancy research* (Vol. 1). Norwood, N.J.: Ablex, 1981. (b)

Lamb, M. E. The origins of individual differences in infant sociability and their implications for cognitive development. In H. W. Reese & L. P. Lipsitt (Eds.), *Advances in child development and behavior* (Vol. 16). New York: Academic Press, 1981. (c)

Lamb, M. E., Easterbrooks, M. A., & Holden, G. W. Reinforcement and punishment among preschoolers: Characteristics, effects and correlates. *Child Development,* 1980, *51,* 1230–1236.

Lamb, M. E., Hwang, C. P., Frodi, A. M., & Frodi, M. *Security of mother- and father-infant attachment and stranger sociability in traditional and nontraditional Swedish families.* Manuscript in preparation.

Lamb, M. E., & Roopnarine, J. L. Peer influences on sex-role development in preschoolers. *Child Development,* 1979, *50,* 1219–1222.

Lamb, M. E., Suomi, S. J., & Stephenson, G. R. *Social interaction analysis: Methodological issues.* Madison: University of Wisconsin Press, 1979.

Lewis, M. The cardiac response during infancy. In R. F. Thompson & M. M. Patterson (Eds.), *Methods in physiological psychology* (Vol. 1-C). *Recording of bioelectric activity.* New York: Academic Press, 1974.

Lewis, M., & Brooks, J. Self, other and fear: Infants' reactions to people. In M. Lewis & L. Rosenblum (Eds.), *The origins of fear.* New York: Wiley, 1974.

Lewis, M., & Freedle, R. Mother–infant dyad: The cradle of meaning. In P. Pliner, L. Krames, & T. Alloway (Eds.), *Communication and affect: Language and thought.* New York: Academic Press, 1973.

Lewis, M., & Lee-Painter, S. An interactional approach to the mother–infant dyad. In M. Lewis & L. Rosenblum (Eds.), *The effect of the infant on its caregiver.* New York: Wiley, 1974.

Lewis, M., Young, G., Brooks, J., & Michalson, L. The beginning of friendship. In M. Lewis & L. Rosenblum (Eds.), *Friendship and peer relations.* New York: Wiley, 1975.

Maccoby, E. E. *Parent–child interaction.* Paper presented to the Biennial Meeting of the Society for Research in Child Development, San Francisco, March 1979.

McGrew, W. *An ethological study of children's behavior.* New York: Academic Press, 1972.

Main, M. *Exploration, play and level of cognitive functioning as related to child-mother attachment.* Unpublished doctoral dissertation, Johns Hopkins University, 1973.

Main, M. & Weston, D. Security of attachment to mother and father: Related to conflict behavior and the readiness to establish new relationships. *Child Development,* 1981, *52,* in press.

Matas, L., Arend, R., & Sroufe, L. A. Continuity of adaptation in the second year: The relationship between quality of attachment and later competence. *Child Development,* 1978, *49,* 547–556.

Morgan, G., & Ricciuti, H. Infants' responses to strangers during the first year. In B. M. Foss (Ed.), *Determinants of infant behaviour IV.* London: Methuen, 1969.

Mueller, E., & Lucas, T. A developmental analysis of peer interaction among toddlers. In M. Lewis & L. Rosenblum (Eds.), *Friendship and peer relations.* New York: Wiley, 1975.

Mueller, E., & Vandell, D. Infant–infant interaction. In J. D. Osofsky (Ed.), *Handbook of infant development.* New York: Wiley, 1979.

Oden, S., & Asher, S. R. Coaching children in social skills for friendship making. *Child Development,* 1977, *48,* 495–506.

Owen, M., Chase-Lansdale, P. L., & Lamb, M. E. *Mothers' and fathers' attitudes, maternal employment, and the security of infant-parent attachment.* Manuscript in preparation.

Parke, R. D. Parent–infant interaction: Progress, paradigms and problems. In G. P. Sackett

(Ed.), *Observing behavior* (Vol. 1). *Theory and applications in mental retardation*. Baltimore: University Park Press, 1978.

Parke, R. D., Power, T. G., & Gottman, J. M. Conceptualizing and quantifying influence patterns in the family triad. In M. E. Lamb, S. J. Suomi, & G. R. Stephenson (Eds.), *Social interaction analysis: Methodological issues*. Madison: University of Wisconsin Press, 1979.

Piaget, J. *The origins of intelligence in children* (2nd ed.). New York: International University Press, 1952. (Originally published, 1936.)

Rheingold, H., & Eckerman, C. Fear of the stranger: A critical examination. In H. W. Reese & L. P. Lipsitt (Eds.), *Advances in child development and behavior* (Vol. 8). New York: Academic Press, 1973.

Rothbart, M. K., & Derryberry, D. Development of individual differences in temperament. In M. E. Lamb & A. L. Brown (Eds.), *Advances in developmental psychology* (Vol. 1). Hillsdale, N.J.: Lawrence Erlbaum Associates, 1981.

Sackett, G. P. A taxonomy of observational techniques and a theory of measurement. In G. P. Sackett (Ed.), *Observing behavior*. (Vol. 2). *Data collection and analysis methods*. Baltimore: University Park Press, 1978. (a)

Sackett, G. P. (Ed.). *Observing behavior*. (Vol. 2). *Data collection and analysis methods*. Baltimore: University Park Press, 1978. (b)

Sackett, G. P. The lag sequential analysis of contingency and cyclicity in behavioral interaction research. In J. D. Osofsky (Ed.), *Handbook of infant development*. New York: Wiley, 1979.

Scarr, S., & Salapatek, P. Patterns of fear development during infancy. *Merrill-Palmer Quarterly*, 1970, *16*, 53–90.

Schaffer, H. R. The onset of fear of strangers and the incongruity hypothesis. *Journal of Child Psychology and Psychiatry*, 1966, *7*, 95–106.

Schaffer, H. R. (Ed.). *Studies in mother–infant interaction*. New York: Academic Press, 1977.

Schaffer, H. R., & Emerson, P. E. The development of social attachments in infancy. *Monographs of the Society for Research in Child Development*, 1964, *29* (Ser. No. 94).

Sears, R. R., Maccoby, E. E., & Levin, H. *Patterns of child rearing*. Stanford, Calif.: Stanford University Press, 1957.

Shaffran, R. Modes of approach and the infant's reactions to the stranger. In T. Gouin Decarie (Ed.), *The infant's reaction to strangers*. New York: International Universities Press, 1974.

Skarin, K. Cognitive and contextual determinants of stranger fear in six- and eleven-month-old infants. *Child Development*, 1977, *48*, 537–544.

Spitz, R. A. *The first year of life*. New York: International Universities Press, 1965.

Sroufe, L. A. Wariness of strangers and the study of infant development. *Child Development*, 1977, *48*, 731–746.

Sroufe, L. A., & Waters, E. Heart rate as a convergent measure in clinical and developmental research. *Merrill-Palmer Quarterly*, 1977, *23*, 3–27.

Sroufe, L. A., Waters, E., & Matas, L. Contextual determinants of infant affective response. In M. Lewis & L. Rosenblum (Eds.), *The origins of fear*. New York: Wiley, 1974.

Stephenson, G. R. Plexyn: A computer-compatible grammar for coding complex social interactions. In M. E. Lamb, S. J. Suomi, & G. R. Stephenson (Eds.), *Social interaction analysis: Methodological issues*. Madison: University of Wisconsin Press, 1979.

Stern, D. N. Mother and infant at play: The dyadic interaction involving facial, vocal and gaze behaviors. In M. Lewis & L. Rosenblum (Eds.), *The effect of the infant on its caregiver*. New York: Wiley, 1974.

Stern, D. N. *The first relationship*. Cambridge, Mass.: Harvard University Press, 1977.

Stern, D. N., Beebe, B., Jaffe, J., & Bennett, S. L. The infant's stimulus world during social interaction: A study of caregiver behaviours with particular reference to repetition and timing. In H. R. Schaffer (Ed.), *Studies in mother-infant interaction.* London: Academic Press, 1977.

Stevenson, M. B., & Lamb, M. E. Effects of infant sociability and the caretaking environment on infant cognitive performance. *Child Development,* 1979, *50,* 340–349.

Strain, B. A., & Vietze, P. M. *Early dialogues: The structure of reciprocal infant-mother vocalization.* Paper presented to the Society for Research in Child Development, Denver, April 1975.

Strayer, F. F., & Strayer, J. An ethological analysis of social agonism and dominance relations among preschool children. *Child Development,* 1976, *47,* 980–989.

Thompson, R. A., & Lamb, M. E. *Quality of attachment and stranger sociability in infancy.* Manuscript in preparation.

Thompson, R. A., Lamb, M. E., & Estes, D. Stability of infant-mother attachment and its relationship to changing life circumstances in an unselected middle-class sample. *Child Development,* 1982, *53,* in press.

Vandell, D. L. A microanalysis of toddlers' social interaction with mothers and fathers. *Journal of Genetic Psychology,* 1979, *134,* 299–312.

Vaughn, B., Egeland, B., Sroufe, L. A., & Waters, E. Individual differences in infant-mother attachment at twelve and eighteen months: Stability and change in families under stress. *Child Development,* 1979, *50,* 971–975.

Vietze, P. M., Abernathy, S. R., Ashe, M. L., & Faulstich, G. Contingent interaction between mothers and their developmentally delayed infants. In G. P. Sackett (Ed.), *Observing behavior* (Vol. 1). *Theory and applications in mental retardation.* Baltimore: University Park Press, 1978.

Waters, E. The reliability and stability of individual differences in infant-mother attachment. *Child Development,* 1978, *49,* 483–494.

Waters, E., Matas, L., & Sroufe, L. A. Infants' reactions to an approaching stranger: Description, validation and functional significance of wariness. *Child Development,* 1975, *46,* 348–356.

Waters, E., Wippman, J., & Sroufe, L. A. Attachment, positive affect, and competence in the peer group: Two studies in construct validation. *Child Development,* 1979, *50,* 821–829.

Weinraub, M., & Putney, E. The effects of height on infants' social responses to unfamiliar persons. *Child Development,* 1978, *49,* 598–603.

4 Perceptual Development[1]

DANIEL W. SMOTHERGILL

One reason psychology is in business is to provide people a better understanding of what they are. In his presidential address to the American Psychological Association, George Miller (1969) referred to this as the "giving away of psychology," and it is surely a major societal responsibility of psychologists. The importance of some of the things psychologists study is obvious in this respect. Aggression is one good example; children's learning disabilities another. But other aspects of psychology may not strike the lay person as quite so obviously important. In such cases, and I believe perception is one of them, part of the giving away of psychology involves educating people as to why it is important that scientific research be conducted at all.

Consider perception. Suppose you were asked why things in the world look as they do. If you were to close this book and look at the front cover why would you have the particular perceptual experience that you would? Many people would probably regard this as a silly question. Things look as they do because of the way they are; they have to look that way! There is a sense in which this answer may well be correct (Gibson, 1979), but the question itself is enormously complex and important rather than simplistic.

An experiment conducted by de Groot (1965) serves to illustrate this point. De Groot was interested in how chess masters differ from weaker players. In one experiment, subjects attempted to reconstruct a chess board after seeing it for only 5 seconds. When the pieces were arranged in a way that could actually occur during the course of a game, the masters placed many more pieces correctly than did the weaker players. Why? Are chess

[1] The comments of Nancy L. Smothergill and Audrey M. Fullerton on earlier drafts are gratefully acknowledged.

STRATEGIES AND TECHNIQUES
OF CHILD STUDY

masters just better at remembering locations of chess pieces? To find out, de Groot repeated the experiment but this time the pieces were arranged at random on the board. Now the masters performed no better than the weaker players. These findings, along with others by Chase and Simon (1973), indicate that the skill a chess master possesses does not lie in greater memory capacity but in a highly developed ability to perceive chess pieces according to the rules and strategies of chess.

So perception cannot simply be explained as things "having to look that way." Two people looking at a chess game see things differently depending on their skillfulness at chess. More generally, this example suggests that *what one perceives is to some degree a product of one's past experiences.* The countless hours chess masters devote to playing the game are surely a major factor in their sophisticated chess-perception abilities.

If perception is indeed influenced by experience, it becomes apparent why the study of perception in children is important. Compared with adults, children are relatively inexperienced perceivers over a wide domain of situations and information. To what degree do children perceive the world differently from adults? Alternatively, in what ways are perception in children and adults the same? In the sections that follow, these questions will be taken up within the context of several selected research areas. The particular research areas that were chosen are ones that illustrate variety in both research techniques and substantive questions. We shall see that the research methods used to study perceptual development do not have to be elaborate, expensive, or new. Truly creative research is usually the result of ingenious coupling of method and question. The only real requirement for good research is that the method fit the question at hand.

SPATIAL LAYOUT

Chess is played according to a set of rules for moving various pieces over what can be regarded as a spatial layout. The rules are quite arbitrary. A very different game can be imagined in which pawns would be moved as kings and vice versa. Although this new game would surely be different from chess as we know it, the possibility of such a game makes the point that there is no necessary and inherent reason why pawns must behave in this way, kings in that way, and so on.

The world around us also can be considered a spatial layout, but one in which the structure is far from arbitrary. James J. Gibson (1979) emphasized this point in describing what he called *ecological optics.* To understand a bit of what Gibson meant by this expression, look at the sketches presented in Figure 4.1.

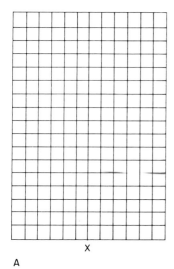

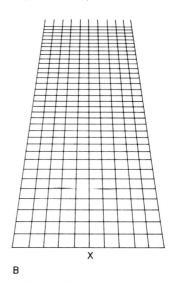

X   X

A   B

FIGURE 4.1. A. A simple spatial layout. B. A photograph of the layout.

The left side (A) of Figure 4.1 illustrates what might be regarded as an elongated chess board extending to the horizon. Imagine that an observer standing at the location marked X took a picture of this layout. The right side (B) of Figure 4.1 is intended to represent what that picture would look like. Notice how the sizes of the squares change from the bottom to the top of the picture: They become progressively smaller as the distance from location X increases. The optics of the situation are responsible for this. Objects farther away from a station point produce a smaller pattern of light rays than do objects close up.

Psychologists have long been attracted to the camera as an analogy for the eye, although some have felt that the analogy is misleading in crucial respects. The reason for presenting Figure 4.1 is not to take sides on the issue, but to illustrate the point that the light available to the eye is structured in certain ways. Specifically, there is a fixed structural relationship between projected element size and distance from the observer. A slightly more theoretical statement of this is to say that there is a *gradient of texture* such that items close to an observer project a relatively coarse texture upon the eye, whereas items farther away project a finer texture. Gibson emphasized the point that such structure is inherent in the optic array, and he theorized that perception is based on detecting the structure that is available in the optic array. In the present example, for instance, Gibson would claim that the perception of distance is based on the perceptual system detecting the regular changes in projected element size that accompany distance from the perceiver.

But a chessboard is an artificial spatial layout. Are there texture gradients in the real world (as the adjective in the expression *ecological optics* implies) that people might use in perceiving distance? The pictures reproduced in Figures 4.2 and 4.3 were taken by Phil Brodatz (1966) and are published in a remarkable book entitled *Textures*. Most of the pictures in Brodatz's book are close-ups of mundane objects and things in the environment. What makes them special is that they clearly show the intricate and unique texture that quite literally defines an entity as an oak tree, a brick, a pebble, etc. Actually, the pictures shown in Figures 4.2 and 4.3 are not close-ups of discrete things but long-range shots of two particular spatial layouts. Notice how in each instance there is both a specific texture that identifies the nature of the layout and a gradient of texture that provides distance information.

If, as Gibson claims, the environment has a structure that is there to be perceived, the study of perceptual development can begin by asking what kinds of environmental structure children perceive and when they are able to perceive it. We turn now to some research that has asked such questions regarding the perception of spatial layout.

FIGURE 4.2. Water (D38). (From *Textures: A Photographic Album for Artists and Designers*, Dover Publications, Inc., New York, N.Y., reproduced with permission of P. Brodatz, copyright © 1966 by P. Brodatz.)

FIGURE 4.3. Beach pebbles (D54). (From *Textures: A Photographic Album for Artists and Designers*, Dover Publications, Inc., New York, N.Y., reproduced with permission of P. Brodatz, copyright © 1966 by P. Brodatz.)

Infancy

When infants look out over a spatial layout do they perceive distance? For a psychologist, the question requires a research technique that will allow reasonably straightforward inferences to be drawn from the infants' behavior. An early method that continues to be productive was devised at Cornell University for studying the perception of distance in the downward direction, or depth. The method makes use of what is known as the visual cliff. A diagram is presented in Figure 4.4.

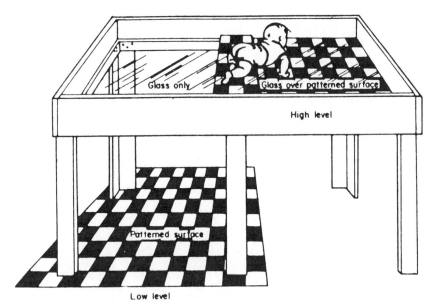

FIGURE 4.4. Diagram of a visual cliff. (From "A Comparative and Analytic Study of Visual Depth Perception," *Psychological Monographs*, by R. D. Walk and E. J. Gibson, 75, no. 15, whole no. 519. Copyright 1961 by the American Psychological Association, reprinted by permission.)

More chessboards? No, the squares you see in Figure 4.4 are checked material that is spread across both the "shallow" and "deep" sides of the visual cliff. The cliff is actually a large piece of strong glass with a board running down the middle dividing it into shallow and deep sides. On the shallow side the checked material is directly beneath the glass, whereas on the deep side the material rests on the floor several feet beneath the glass.

The test for depth perception is quite simple. The baby is placed on the center board and encouraged (usually by the mother) to crawl first to one side and then to the other. A baby unable to perceive depth would presumably be just as likely to crawl to one side as to the other. In contrast, a baby who could perceive depth might be expected to avoid crawling over the deep side and go only to the shallow side.

Walk and Gibson (1961) reported that almost all the babies who moved from the center board at all crossed to the shallow side but not the deep side. The youngest babies they tested were $6\frac{1}{2}$ months old. It would appear from these findings that depth perception is present at the time babies achieve independent locomotion.

A question left unanswered by Walk and Gibson's original findings was whether depth perception is present any earlier than $6\frac{1}{2}$ months. Notice how Walk and Gibson's method precludes answering this question: The method requries that the baby crawl, but crawling does not begin before 6 or 7 months at the earliest. Two solutions to the problem would seem possible. First, a totally different method might be used to assess depth perception. T. G. R. Bower (1965, 1974) took this tack. In a series of ingenious experiments using conditioning methods and visually guided reaching, Bower reported evidence of quite sophisticated spatial perception in young babies. Unfortunately, the reliability of these findings is uncertain at the moment because other investigators have been unable to replicate them (Dodwell, Muir, & Di Franco, 1976; Yonas, Bechtold, Gordon, Frankel, McRoberts, Norcia, & Sternfels, 1977). A second possible solution to the problem of studying depth perception in very young infants would be to retain the visual cliff as a research instrument but to use it in a way that does not require crawling. This is the approach that has been taken by Joseph Campos and his colleagues.

Campos's research group has measured heart rate when a baby is placed on the visual cliff. Heart rate is a physiological measure that has proved very useful in psychological research because certain changes in heart rate appear to be correlated with specific psychological states. At some risk of over simplification, it can be said that heart rate acceleration is a sign of fear, whereas heart rate deceleration occurs when one is attentive.

From this description, the application of the heart rate measure to the problem of early infantile depth perception would seem quite direct. If prelocomotive babies perceive depth, heart rate acceleration would be expected when the babies are placed on the deep side of the visual cliff. In the first experiment (Campos, Langer, & Krowitz, 1970) of this type, babies as young as $1\frac{1}{2}$ months were alternately placed on the deep and shallow sides of the cliff while their heart rate was monitored. The results were surprising. On the shallow side there was no change in heart rate from its normal (*baseline*) level. On the deep side there was a change in heart rate, but it was opposite to what was expected: Heart rate *deceleration* occurred rather than heart rate acceleration.

It is important to realize that regardless of the *direction* of change, the simple fact that a change in heart rate occurred on one side of the cliff but not the other means that the babies discriminated between the two sides. But why should heart rate deceleration, traditionally a sign of attention, occur on the deep side? One possibility is that for young babies the simple formulas of "acceleration = fear" and "deceleration = attention" do not hold. The babies may well have been afraid of the deep side, but fear in young babies may be indicated by deceleration of heart rate. The difficulty with this interpretation is that it was also found that behavioral measures of fear, such as crying, actually occurred *less* frequently on the deep side than on the shallow. This finding in conjunction with the heart rate findings suggests the possibility that young babies may respond to depth at an edge by attention rather than fear.

Suppose older babies were tested under similar conditions. Would they too show heart rate deceleration on the deep side or would they be afraid and show heart rate acceleration? Schwartz, Campos, and Baisel (1973) found that 5-month-olds predominantly showed deceleration on the deep side, whereas for 9-month-olds heart rate accelerated when the baby was placed on the deep side. Notice that these ages bracket the period during which crawling begins. Is the onset of crawling directly related to the apparent switch that occurs from depth being something that is interesting to something that is feared?

Some recent evidence points in this direction (Campos, Hiatt, Ramsay, Henderson, & Svejda, 1978). Two groups of babies just under 7 months old were tested on the visual cliff. The groups were virtually identical in age, but one group of babies had already begun crawling whereas the other group had not. Each baby was lowered toward both the deep and shallow sides twice while heart rate was monitored. The findings were clear. When lowered toward the shallow side neither group showed a change in heart rate. When lowered toward the deep side, however, the group that could locomote showed significant heart rate acceleration, but the group that could not locomote showed no change in heart rate. These findings strongly suggest that it is the onset of locomotion rather than age per se that is linked in an important way to the development of fear of depth. The more precise details of that linkage are unknown at this time and await further research.

Frame of Reference

Getting around the day-to-day spatial environment is so effortless that we are usually unaware of the complex skills by which it is accomplished. The actual complexity of what is involved is partially revealed on occasions when the system breaks down. Trying to get around in a strange city or (my personal favorite here) emerging from a subway station in an unfamiliar part of town, are examples of experiences in which our ordinarily smoothly functioning spatial abilities momentarily desert us and thereby reveal our dependence on them.

What are the psychological processes underlying the ability to navigate a spatial layout successfully? How can we describe the spatial world of a child who, presumably, does not have the same mastery of space as an adult? The research evidence on these questions is organized around some more or less specific concepts that have proved useful in thinking about the questions. One such concept is frame of reference.

Space is fundamentally a matter of location, of *where* things are. A bit of reflection shows that any attempt to specify where a thing is must locate it with respect to something else. For example, my coffee cup is located on my desk, to my right, several meters from the window. In each case a relation is specified between the cup and something else. Moreover, this example also illustrates an important distinction that can be made between two kinds of frames of reference: subjective or *egocentric* (Piaget, 1952) frames of reference in which locations are specified with respect to the self, and objective or *allocentric* frames of reference in which locations are specified with respect to external referents. This distinction has proved useful in guiding research on spatial development.

Linda Acredolo (1978) has studied the frames of reference used by infants. Her research strategy is quite simple. A baby is placed in a movable chair located in a small, artificial room. Initially, the back of the chair is against one wall so that the baby can look out at the room. There was little to see in the room used in Acredolo's major study. The walls behind and opposite the baby were blank as were the two side walls, except that each of the latter contained a window. A round table in the center of the room completed the sparse furnishings.

The babies first were trained to anticipate the experimenter's appearance at one of the side windows. On each trial, a buzzer sounded and about 3 seconds later the experimenter's face appeared at one of the windows, the same window on all trials. The experimenter remained visible and entertained the child for about 10 seconds. These trials continued until, on four of five consecutive trials, the baby anticipated the experimenter's appearance by turning to the window after the buzzer sounded but before the experimenter appeared.

Given that the babies learned where to look to see the experimenter, what frame of reference had they used? To find out, Acredolo moved the baby so that she was facing the table from the opposite side of the room. Several test trials were then conducted, on each of which the buzzer sounded but the experimenter did not appear at either window. The question of interest was the window at which the baby would look when the buzzer sounded. If the baby had coded the experimenter's location within an *objective* frame of reference it would be expected that the baby would continue to look at the same window as before. Since the baby was now on the opposite side of the room this would require turning the head in the *opposite* direction from before. (If this reasoning is not clear to you, imagine that you had learned that the experimenter appeared at the window to your left whenever the buzzer sounded. If you now moved across the room that same window would be to your right.)

According to a *subjective* frame of reference, locations are specified by the actions one performs with respect to them. Thus, if babies turned their heads to the left to see the experimenter during the first part of the experiment, they should also turn their heads to the left during the test phase even though they were now on the opposite side of the room.

Acredolo found that 6- and 11-month-olds typically turned in the same direction on test trials as they had during training, an indication of a subjective frame of reference. Sixteen-month-olds, in contrast, evidenced an objective frame of reference. They turned toward the window at which the experimenter had previously appeared.

These findings suggest a developmental trend in spatial reference frame from subjective to objective. Do they mean that, prior to 16 months, infants are unable to use an objective frame of reference? Some other findings suggest not. For example, Acredolo found that, when the window at which the experimenter appeared was made distinctive by surrounding it with a large yellow star, objective responding was facilitated for 11-month-olds but not for 6-month-olds. Do 6-month-olds ever use an objective frame of reference? Acredolo and Evans (1979) attempted to answer this question by making the side at which the experimenter appeared even more salient. Instead of just a star around the window, they surrounded it with a panel of flashing lights. In addition, the wall on which this window was located was striped rather than blank. Under these conditions, virtually none of the 6-month-olds consistently turned in the same direction as they had during training; that is, none gave evidence of using a consistent subjective frame of reference. However, only a third of the babies consistently responded on the basis of objective frame of reference. The other two-thirds were classified as mixed responders: They looked at both windows either within one trial or across several test trials.

These findings suggest that salient *landmarks* can serve to modify the spatial behavior of young infants, although the fact that most 6-month-olds do not show consistent use of an objective frame of reference, even when the correct side is made highly salient, suggests that subjective frames of reference exert a strong influence at that age. It would be interesting to know something about frames of reference prior to 6 months, but Acredolo has found it extremely difficult to train very young babies on the initial part of her procedure. A different procedure seems required. Recall that Campos altered the standard testing procedure on the visual cliff in order to adapt it to prelocomotive babies. Whether Acredolo's procedure can be modified in some way or whether an entirely new procedure will be needed to test frames of reference in babies less than 6 months old is unknown now. The pace of research progress in this area, however, would suggest that an answer will soon be forthcoming.

Landmarks

A landmark is a salient feature of the environment: a hill dominating an otherwise flat terrain, a bridge linking two parts of town, a cathedral, and so forth. Adults asked to describe what first comes to mind about a particular city will frequently describe distinctive landmarks (Lynch, 1960). Acredolo's findings about the effects of making one side of a room highly distinctive suggest that landmarks may be an important factor in the development of objective frames of reference.

Landmarks provide a potentially effective means for learning a spatial layout, but there are situations in which dependence on them can be a hindrance rather than a help. A study by Smothergill, Hughes, Timmons, and Hutko (1975) illustrates this point. Children between 4 and 10 years of age were shown a large Y-shaped figure that was drawn on tagboard and mounted on an easel. The two arms of the Y were covered with black felt. On each trial the experimenter placed a circular piece of yellow felt on the end of one of the arms. The child was asked to notice and remember the arm on which the yellow circle was located. An identical piece of yellow felt was then handed to the child with the instruction to put it on the same arm of a second Y which was located either alongside the model (Alongside condition) or on the opposite side of the same easel on which the model was located (Behind condition).

The youngest children, 4- and 5-year-olds, responded in a surprising way. When the Y to which they responded was located alongside the model they performed quite well as long as the Y was upright (the same orientation as the model); if the Y was inverted the number of correct responses was below chance level. Moreover, the pattern of results was exactly opposite to this when the Y was located behind the model: In that case, the youngest group performed quite well when the Y was inverted but below chance when it was upright.

How can these findings be interpreted? A quite likely possibility is that the children were coding the location of the yellow spot on the model with respect to landmarks in the surrounding environment. For example, imagine that the yellow spot was on the arm of the model that was closest to the door. If one location of the spot was coded as "arm nearer the door," the Alongside condition would be responded to "correctly" when the Y was upright but "incorrectly" when it was inverted. Conversely, in the Behind condition, responses would be "incorrect" when the Y was upright but "correct" when inverted. The terms *correct* and *incorrect* have been put in quotes because the results of the study illustrate that the correctness of any spatial judgment is a matter of how space is coded. The 4- and

5-year-olds in this study appear to have coded location in terms of proximity to a salient landmark. As experimenters, Smothergill *et al.* had implicitly coded space on the basis of a Euclidean spatial system and deemed responses as correct or not insofar as they conformed to correctness as defined within that system. A Euclidean definition of space is one that most adults in our culture regard as natural. Piaget (1952), however, has long pointed out that this is just one of many ways of organizing space and that the different organizations of space that are possible are each based on a particular geometry. Moreover, according to Piaget, there is a regular sequence of changes with development in the type of spatial organization a person regards as natural. Whereas for adults Euclidean space is natural, children are said to organize space at first on the basis of topology and later on the basis of projective geometry.

Let us return now to the findings of the Smothergill study and consider them from the perspective of Piaget's theory. The theory makes the proximity-based responding of the 4- and 5-year-olds understandable since proximity is a major characteristic of topological space, the type of spatial organization Piaget would impute to children of this age. An additional piece of evidence supporting the Piagetian analysis comes from the fact that the experimenter told the subject whether he or she was right or wrong on each trial. If a child had originally been unsure of how to respond, this feedback might be expected to have improved the child's performance as the task proceeded. Alternatively, if the child was incapable of dealing with the task at all, the feedback would have been useless, and responding would be expected to have been random throughout. Neither of these outcomes occurred. Instead, the 4- and 5-year-olds persevered throughout the experiment in responding in a coherent manner that was unperturbed by the experimenter's remarks that they were often wrong. This behavior is a sign that the children were attacking the problem from a different perspective from that of the experimenter—a perspective reflecting topological coding of space.

Cognitive Maps

A person very familiar with a particular spatial layout has an understanding of the layout that goes beyond his or her actual experience. For example, in going to work each day I typically bicycle down Circle Road, turn left at Stratford Road, right at Comstock, and then onto campus. I know other ways of getting to campus, some of which I have taken at one time or other, but there are many others I never have taken. The fact that I know possible routes that I have never actually taken indicates that my understanding of the spatial layout between home and campus is organized in some coherent way; that is, it is not simply a collection of the discrete paths I have actually traveled. Such a coherent organization of space is referred to as a "cognitive map," and some interesting research has recently been done on children's cognitive maps.

In one study (Pick, 1972), young children were asked questions about the layout of their own homes. Specifically, preschool children took a tour of their own homes during which they were asked which rooms were behind certain outside windows, interior walls, floors, and so on. Surprisingly, many children found questions about rooms adjacent to their own quite difficult in spite of the extensive experience it can be assumed they had had in getting around their own homes.

Pick's study represents an extremely simple but effective research strategy. The ecological validity of such research is extremely high because it deals with an aspect of the child's normal environment. Any single research strategy is limited, however. For example, the data from the Pick study give a fairly gross, qualitative indication of what children's cognitive maps may be like, but they do not specify the details in any precise way.

A method more suitable for studying the details of cognitive maps (but one that does so at a sacrifice in ecological validity) was employed by Kosslyn, Pick, and Fariello (1974). A sketch of the spatial layout specially constructed for this study is presented in Figure 4.5.

The horizontal and vertical lines you see in the figure represent barriers.

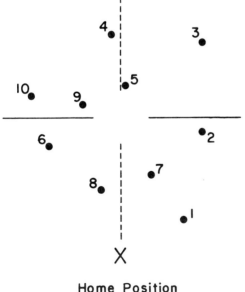

FIGURE 4.5. Experimental spatial layout used by Kosslyn, Pick, and Fariello (Copyright © 1974 by the Society for Research in Child Development, Inc.).

The horizontal barriers were opaque blankets hung from ceiling to floor, whereas the vertical barriers were low wooden fences that could easily be seen over. The numbers 1–10 designate specific locations at each of which there was a drawing of a small toy.

Subjects first were trained to go from the home position (X) to each position on the floor. The subject was given a toy on each trial and asked to find the drawing that went with it. Thus, if the subject was handed a plastic boat and the drawing of the boat was at location 4, the subject would walk around the layout until finding the drawing at that location. Preschoolers and adults were trained in this way until they could go quickly and without error from the home position to each of the 10 locations. The question Kosslyn and co-workers asked was whether in the course of this learning the subject also acquired an overall map of the layout. That is, did subjects learn something about the spatial relations *among* the 10 locations as well as the location of each drawing with respect to the home position?

To find out, the subjects' knowledge of the distances between all pairs of locations was assessed. With their backs to the layout, subjects were handed one of the toys (the "standard") and asked to select from the remaining nine the one that was closest to it in the layout. That done, subjects were asked to choose from the remaining eight toys the one that was the next closest to the standard, and so on. When all nine such judgments had been completed, the subjects were given another toy as the standard, and the procedure was repeated. This questioning continued until all 10 toys had served as the standard.

These judgments were then subjected to a statistical technique called *multidimensional scaling*. This technique uses distance judgments to generate a two-dimensional representation of the latent cognitive map underlying the judgments. These statistically derived maps can then be compared with a map of the actual spatial layouts to determine the degree of fit between the two.

The major finding was that both age groups acquired cognitive maps. There were some age differences. The adults' maps were somewhat more accurate; barriers seemed to have more of an effect on preschoolers than on adults. Overall, however, the similarity between the adults and preschoolers was striking. Another interesting aspect of these findings is the apparent spontaneity with which a cognitive map seems to be formed. Recall that the subjects received no explicit training regarding spatial relations *among* the locations. Quite likely, some pairs of locations were never walked between and, certainly, no subject systematically went from one location to another in an exhaustive manner during training. Yet a surprisingly accurate cognitive map of the layout was acquired, even by preschoolers. This result suggests that the acquisition of a cognitive map may be a fundamental and unintentional component of spatial learning. At the present time there is very little known about just how such maps are acquired in the process of learning particular routes.

Something of a paradox is revealed in comparing the findings of Kosslyn *et al.* with those of Pick (1972). According to the former, preschoolers easily acquire a sophisticated map of a novel spatial layout without deliberately trying to do so. But according to the latter, many preschoolers do not know which rooms are adjacent to which others in the very familiar spatial layout of their own homes. The key to the paradox may lie in the nature of the response required in each study. Specifically, the Kosslyn procedure required judgments of distance only. When scaled appropriately, those judgments revealed considerable organization: a cognitive map. This finding does not necessarily mean, however, that the subject was *aware* of the cognitive map. The procedure used in the Pick study, in contrast, would seem to require a more direct awareness of spatial layout because the subject was explicitly asked to identify which rooms were located behind certain walls.

The difference suggested here seems analagous to the insight from psycholinguistics that, whereas our normal speech is governed by grammatical rules of truly incredible complexity, we are not normally aware of those rules. Perhaps, if preschool children were asked to make judgments of the distances between rooms in their homes, multidimensional scaling would reveal the existence of a cognitive map even though those same children would be expected to do poorly on Pick's task. Rather than being incompatible, such findings would suggest that spatial development may be characterized by an increasing awareness of the rules and structures that guide behavior at earlier stages of development (cf. Rozin, 1975).

PERCEPTUAL LEARNING

Children learn to perceive more than the spatial layout of the surround. They come to perceive the people, cars, toys, trees, books, plays, social interactions, language, etc. that occur within the surround as well. What is the process by which perceptual learning occurs? Many theories of perceptual learning have been offered over the years. In this section we shall briefly discuss one of them, the differentiation theory proposed by Eleanor Gibson (1969). Gibson's theory has been chosen for discussion not because it is "The Correct View" (although your author admits a bias in favor of it), but because it has become the single most influential theory in the contemporary study of perceptual development. It also underlies several research studies that will be described later on in this section.

Gibson's theory addresses two questions. First, *what* happens when perceptual learning occurs? Second, *how* does perceptual learning occur?

In answer to the first question, Gibson claims that perceptual learning involves bringing perception into greater accord with the variables of stimulation the environment provides. The environment is held to be rich in information, and perceptual learning involves extraction of that information. Prior to perceptual learning the information one extracts about a particular thing may be global and imprecise. After perceptual learning the finely differentiated information specifying that particular thing is perceived. An example is provided by an experiment on wine tasting (Walk, 1966). College students were asked to take two sips of wine on each of several trials. Sometimes both sips were of the same wine and sometimes they were of different wines. The subject was simply asked to say on each trial whether the wines were the same or different. Walk found that his subjects could not do this very well. They particularly found it difficult to judge correctly when the two wines were actually the same. In the terminology of Gibson's theory, these subjects would be said to be unable to detect the invariant information that specified each wine.

How does perceptual learning occur? Gibson claims that simple practice in discriminating is usually sufficient. Walk (1966) modified his wine tasting experiment to test this hypothesis. One group was simply given practice discriminating wines by making same–different judgments. A second group received just as much practice and, in addition, was told after each judgment whether that judgment was correct or not. A third group was treated identically to the second group but also was given the name for each wine when their judgments were correct.

All three groups received the same number of training trials and then a test. The results were that all three groups improved compared to their performance before training, but there were no differences among the groups. Apparently, as Gibson's theory had predicted, simple discrimination practice is all that is needed to learn to perceive wines.

Perceptual learning is thought to occur in many different domains as children develop. One laboratory task in which the role of perceptual learning has been extensively studied is the discrimination–shift task. A diagram of the task is presented in Figure 4.6.

The subject first learns to solve the two problems depicted in the left half of Figure 4.6. The subject learns that in one problem the large black cube is correct and the small white cube is incorrect and in the other problem that the large white cube is incorrect and the small black cube is correct. When the child has mastered both problems the experimenter, without mention, introduces one of two changes. For one type of change, a *reversal shift,* the same dimension remains relevant as before, but the opposite value on that dimension is now correct. In the example in Figure 4.6, the brightness dimension was relevant in the original learning and *black* was the correct value. In the reversal shift shown in Figure 4.6 the correct choice is now

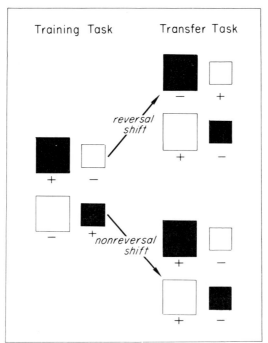

FIGURE 4.6. A discrimination—shift problem. (From "Vertical and Horizontal Processes in Problem Solving," *Psychological Review,* by T. S. Kendler and H. H. Kendler, *69,* 1–16. Copyright 1962 by the American Psychological Association, reprinted by permission.)

white: The brightness dimension has remained relevant but the correct value has changed. The second type of change that can be introduced is known as a *nonreversal* shift. Here the original dimension is no longer relevant. Size (in Figure 4.6) rather than brightness becomes relevant after a nonreversal shift and the correct value is big.

It has generally been found that children younger than 5 years find the nonreversal shift easier to learn than the reversal shift, whereas just the opposite is the case for children 7 years and older. It seems that the younger children do not solve the original problems dimensionally (i.e., brightness is relevant; black is correct), but, instead, simply learn which object to respond to in each problem. That strategy would result in faster learning of a nonreversal shift because the originally correct object remains the same in one of the two problems for that type of shift, whereas in a reversal shift neither of the originally correct objects remains so after the shift.

Louise Tighe (1965) suggested that this developmental change is the result of perceptual learning. She had 5- and 6-year-olds make same–different judgments to stimuli varying in height and brightness. The children were allowed to view a *standard* stimulus of a given height and brightness at the beginning of each perceptual training trial. The standard was then removed and a series of *comparison* stimuli was presented. Some comparisons differed from the standard in height, some in brightness, some in both height and brightness, and some were exactly the same as the standard. The subject's task was simply to say whether each comparison was the same as or different from the standard. No feedback was given for either correct or incorrect judgments.

Tighe's hypothesis that perceptual training would result in increased sensitivity to the dimensions of the stimuli was supported by results from a discrimination–shift task. The children who had received perceptual training solved the reversal shift more quickly than the nonreversal shift, whereas a group of untrained control subjects solved both shifts at the same rate.

Tighe's study has now been replicated several times and results have consistently supported those of the original study. In addition, there is now evidence that the specific mechanism by which perceptual training is effective in such tasks involves an improvement in stimulus ordering or *seriation*. Timmons and Smothergill (1975) found evidence for this in kindergartners. These researchers identified a group of children who were unable to arrange a collection of wooden dowels varying in height (or brightness) into a row so that each successive dowel was taller (or brighter) than the one immediately preceding it. Some of these children were then administered Tighe's perceptual training procedure, but others were not. When both groups were then tested again for seriation, it was found that the trained group performed better than the untrained group. This suggests that sensitivity to dimensional information is intimately connected with the ability to order along the dimension.

These findings also raise an interesting question about the relation between perception and cognition. Piaget and others have suggested that seriation is basic to children's understanding of number. Since seriation is improved by perceptual training, does this mean that a certain amount of perceptual learning is a prerequisite for cognitive development? If so, precisely how do perceptual development and cognitive development differ? Little is now known about such questions. The interface of perception and cognition promises to be a productive area of future research.

Social Perception

Following the ins and outs of discrimination–shift research can be tedious business for even the most analytic mind. Perhaps, then, you will be heartened to learn that perceptual learning has been studied in other areas as well. In this section we shall consider some very recent research on racial perception and how it is linked to perceptual learning.

Interesting work in this area has been done by Phyllis Katz and her colleagues. In a series of experiments, they have devised methods for studying race perception and have also studied the effects of perceptual learning on race perception. Katz initially devised a measure of racial stereotyping called the Projective Prejudice Test (PPT). It consists of a series of slides in each of which several children wearing large name tags are shown in an ambiguous situation. The experimenter provides a theme for each slide (e.g., "there was a fight" or "someone just won a trophy"), and the subject is asked who was the initiator or recipient of the action. Because subjects have no objective basis on which to make such a decision, their choice is taken as an index of the degree to which they categorize in terms of racial stereotypes. For example, a white girl who invariably chooses a black child as the initiator of aggression and a white child as the honor recipient would receive a higher racial stereotyping score than another white girl who distributed her choices of doing good and bad more evenly between the races.

In one study (Katz, Sohn, & Zalk, 1975), about 100 New York City elementary school children were administered the PPT. Several weeks later each child was asked to rate the degree to which two briefly presented pictures of faces were similar. The child did this by setting a lever at a position along a track on which one end was designated "no difference" and the other was designated "as different as they can be." These faces varied systematically in a number of ways. Some had curly hair and others straight hair; some were smiling and others were frowning; some were black and others white. What Katz and her colleagues were interested in was the relation (if any) between performance on the PPT and judgments of facial similarity.

They found that racial stereotyping on the PPT was related to judged dissimilarity of faces differing in color. Specifically, the more stereotyped children's PPT responses were, the greater the difference they assigned to faces different in color. This finding held for both black and white children of both sexes and at all grade levels (second, fourth, and sixth) studied.

In a second experiment, Katz (1973) studied the effects of perceptual learning on PPT scores and racially based judgments of facial similarity. Second- and sixth-grade students from an integrated New York City school were first given the PPT. About a month later, each child was assigned at random to one of three training conditions. All conditions consisted of 40 trials on which the child was presented one or two pictures of opposite-race faces (e.g., a black child saw a white face). There were four faces in each condition. In the Distinctive Label condition the child learned a particular name for each face. For example, one face was designated Marge, another Robin, and so forth. In the Perceptual Differentiation condition the child was shown a pair of faces for 1 second on each trial and then judged whether they were the same or different. Finally, in a Control condition children simply looked at the individual photos for 40 trials. Each child performed the lever-moving task described previously to pairs of faces, the same faces he or she had been presented during training, immediately afterwards. Several days later the PPT was readministered.

Before describing the findings, a word is in order regarding the Distinctive Label condition. The major opposition to Gibson's differentiation theory of perceptual learning has been the *acquired distinctiveness of cues*. This view arose within the learning theory tradition (cf. White, 1970), and asserts that physically similar stimuli can come to be perceived as different by a conditioning-like process involving the association of distinctive responses to each stimulus. Differentiation theory, in contrast, holds that perceptual learning occurs by comparing stimuli for similarities and differences rather than by conditioning. The dispute between proponents of an acquired distinctiveness position and those favoring differentiation theory has flared up and quieted several times over the past quarter of a century. Katz's question, in part, was which view would be better supported in terms of bringing about changes on the dependent variables of the study.

The findings generally did not favor one theory or the other: Both training conditions were effective in comparison to the Control condition. Both training groups now scored lower (i.e., gave less stereotyped responses) on the PPT than the control group, and both training groups judged the opposite-race faces as being more different from each other than did the control group.

Notice the convergence of these findings with those of Katz's previous study. Here perceptual learning increased the distinctiveness of opposite-race faces and also resulted in more egalitarian PPT scores. In the previous study, more egalitarian PPT scores were associated with judgments that were based on color. Taken together the findings provide evidence that racial stereotyping is linked to a perceptual disposition to maximize between-race differences and minimize within-race differences (at least for members of other races). But can a brief session of perceptual learning really decrease stereotyping and increase sensitivity to differences among members of other races?

Evidence that at least part of these findings are replicable was recently provided by Katz and Zalk (1978) in a study of white children. They compared the effects of four treatments on both PPT scores and a more behavioral measure of racial prejudice (distancing self from a member of another race). In general, perceptual learning by means of same–different judgments proved the most effective treatment. It reduced PPT scores for a period of at least 4–6 months in second-graders and also improved their scores on the behavioral distance measure for the same duration. Effects for fifth-graders were similar on tests given 2 weeks after training but were attenuated at the 4–6-month testing. Ideally, this very promising line of research will spur other investigators to attempt to replicate the basic phenomena and extend the inquiry in new directions.

ATTENTION

In concluding her comprehensive *Principles of Perceptual Learning and Development,* Eleanor Gibson (1969) described three developmental trends that emerged from the research literature she had reviewed. She termed one of these trends the *optimization of attention.* Although it has long been recognized that attention and perception are related intimately, only recently has the nature of that relationship become the subject of research. A very influential paper on the topic was published in 1973 by David LaBerge.

LaBerge suggested that perception can occur in two ways. The first, which characterizes highly practiced perception, is automatic in the sense that it occurs effortlessly. If someone held before you a card displaying the letter A and asked what you saw, your response would very likely be quick and accurate. Introspectively, you might report that the letter simply "appeared" to you and might even question how someone could possibly *not* see the A under the same conditions. That question, of course, overlooks the fact that you have literally had years and years of practice perceiving letters of the alphabet; the fact that highly practiced perception seems to occur automatically is no reason to assume the same is true for all perception (recall the case of the nonexpert chess player presented earlier).

The second way in which perception can occur according to LaBerge is by bringing attention to bear. Attention, so conceived, is assumed to be limited, and it would be inefficient to use attention for each and every aspect of what we perceive. Instead, attention is normally reserved for those perceptual acts that are relatively unpracticed. As a perceptual act becomes more practiced it requires progressively less attention; it occurs more automatically.

The argument so far is intuitive and can be summarized as saying that familiar things are perceived more or less automatically whereas unfamiliar things require attention. What is the experimental evidence in support of this automaticity theory, as it is termed? LaBerge designed a reaction–time experiment in which subjects were presented both familiar (e.g., b, p, d, q,) and unfamilar (e.g., レ , ⨼ , ⌐ , ⌐) letters. The purpose of this experiment was to demonstrate that whereas familiar letters are perceived automatically, the perception of unfamiliar letters requires attention.

Each trial began with the onset of a single familiar letter. After 1 second it was removed. A second later something else appeared and, depending on what it was, the subject was to do one of two things. If the original letter reappeared the subject was to push a button as quickly as possible; if any other single letter appeared the subject was to do nothing. On the majority of trials the original letter did reappear. This was intended to induce the subject to set his or her attention for the original letter.

On a small proportion of trials a pair of letters was presented after the original familiar letter. The subject was instructed to press the button as quickly as possible if the pair was identical (e.g., bb or ⌐⌐) but to do nothing if the pair consisted of different letters (e.g., bd or ⌐⌐).

LaBerge was interested primarily in reaction times to the identical pairs. He reasoned that the subject's attention was set for the original letter to reappear. Thus, when an identical letter pair (familiar or unfamiliar) appeared attention would not be set for it. If, as automaticity theory claims, attention is needed to perceive the unfamiliar but not the familiar, it should take longer to respond to the unfamiliar pair because attention would have to be switched to it for perception to occur, whereas the familiar pair could be perceived without attention.

The subjects were tested for 6 days and received many trials each day. On the first day, reaction time to unfamiliar letter pairs was slower than to familiar letter pairs, as theory predicted. Over successive days this difference narrowed until by the sixth day it had disappeared. The reason, LaBerge suggests, was that the repeated exposure of the unfamiliar letters had made them familiar, and they thus came to be perceived automatically.

These findings are consistent with automaticity theory but a critic might remain unconvinced. The theory claims that an additional something—attention—is needed to perceive the unfamiliar. Yet, a critic might say, all the experiment really demonstrates is that unfamiliar letter pairs require more time to respond to. Why need it be concluded that the extra time reflects the use of attention? Perhaps unfamiliar things just take longer to perceive.

To answer this objection LaBerge carried out a second experiment that was a slight variation on the first. In this experiment, the subject never saw pairs of letters. Each trial began with the onset of a single letter, either familiar or unfamiliar. After a second the letter disappeared and 1 second later a letter of the same type (familiar or unfamiliar) appeared. Most of the time the second letter was the same as the original; the subject was to push the button quickly on such trials. Sometimes the second letter was different from the original and on these trials the subject was to do nothing.

Following the reasoning of the first experiment, LaBerge expected that the subject's attention would be set for the original letter to reappear. Consider now what the theory would predict with respect to perception of the second letter when it was the same as the first. In the familiar condition, the theory would predict that response should be fast because familiar things are said to be perceived automatically. More interestingly, the theory predicts that perception should be fast in the unfamiliar condition as well, because attention, the ingredient needed for perceiving the unfamiliar, is already set for the original letter, so there is no need to switch attention from something else to the original letter when it appears. The prediction from the theory, then, was that response speed to the familiar and unfamiliar letters should be equally fast. The results were exactly that.

In sum, these experiments are important for automaticity theory because they go beyond the commonsense idea that we ordinarily perceive the familiar faster than the unfamiliar. They demonstrate that under some conditions—when attention is set appropriately—familiarity does not influence the speed of response. This finding bolsters the idea from automaticity theory that the reason the unfamiliar ordinarily takes longer to perceive is that a specific psychological process—attention—must be brought to bear.

Impact on Reading Research

Automaticity theory has had its greatest influence within child psychology in the area of reading. Reading is a learned skill that has as its overall goal the extraction of meaning from print (Gibson & Levin, 1975). This overall skill subsumes a number of subskills that are thought to correspond to various *units of analysis*. At a primitive level, for example, a reader must be able to perceive letters and identify the individual letters comprising a word. A somewhat higher unit of analysis than the single letter might be groups of letters that make up regular spelling patterns (e.g., sp). Beyond that are syllables, words, phrases, clauses, sentences, paragraphs, and so on. The actual units of analysis that are used in an act of reading are not well understood at this time. That reading can be viewed in terms of a hierarchy of such units is a working hypothesis that underlies a good deal of the research that is currently being done.

Automaticity theory has provided a conceptualization of the changes that occur as one learns to read. If, for example, letters are considered to be a relatively low level unit of analysis, the theory would hold that the child first learns to perceive letters with the aid of attention. With practice, letters would come to be perceived progressively more automatically, thereby freeing attention for a higher unit of analysis such as spelling patterns. Gradually, as perceptual learning of this higher unit improves, it too will be perceived automatically and thereby make attention available for the next higher unit of analysis, etc. In sum, the overall goal in learning to read, according to automaticity theory, is for the perception of lower-level units of analysis to become sufficiently automatic so that attention can be given to higher levels of comprehension.

Samuels (1978) draws an important prescription for reading teachers from automaticity theory. He advises the teacher to be aware of the difference between accurate reading and automatic reading. Children might read a passage with great accuracy but comprehend little because they are attending to individual words rather than to the meaning conveyed by groups of words, clauses, sentences, paragraphs, etc. Accurate reading, according to Samuels, should not be taken as the criterion for success at reading. The criterion should be automatic reading, which is achieved only by practice, practice, and more practice after the child has learned to read accurately.

To understand the research on reading automaticity, it is necessary to understand that automaticity can sometimes have a negative effect. Specifically, once it is presented to the eyes (for example), an automatically perceived stimulus *will* be perceived regardless of whether it is advantageous to do so. Special tasks can be contrived to demonstrate this. Consider, for instance, that your task is to name very quickly the color of the ink in which a word that is about to be presented to you is printed. Normally, this is an easy task. But suppose the word is a color name that differs from the color of the ink. The word might be *RED;* the ink color *blue*. Presumably, you read automatically. It follows that you would perceive the name of the word as well as the color of the ink. A conflict between the two would result, and your reaction time would be slowed. Demonstrated many years ago (Stroop, 1935), this is known as the Stroop effect.

The basic idea underlying the Stroop effect has been used to study the development of reading automaticity. Typically, subjects are told that they will see a series of pictures of common objects and that they are to name each object quickly when it is presented. Embedded within most of the pictured objects is a printed word that sometimes corresponds to the object and sometimes does not. An example of stimuli used in such research is presented in Figure 4.7.

What should happen on such a task? Automaticity theory would predict a difference in the performance of children who read automatically (skilled readers) and those who read accurately but not automatically (less skilled readers). Skilled readers should take longer to name pictures when the embedded word conflicts with the object than when it is consistent with the

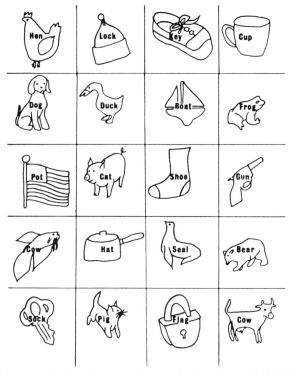

FIGURE 4.7. Stimuli used in interference task research. (From Rosinski, Golinkoff, & Kukish. Copyright © 1975 by the Society for Research in Child Development, Inc.)

object or when there is no word present. Less skilled readers, in contrast, should be relatively unaffected by the nature of the word (correspondence or noncorrespondence with the pictured object) or even its presence because they read by means of attention and their attention is directed to the object rather than the word.

A fair number of studies have now been conducted and indicate that skilled readers' picture naming is indeed slowed when word and object do not correspond. As this phenomenon has been studied in greater detail some very encouraging findings for automaticity theory have emerged. For example, Guttentag and Haith (1978) found that a noncorresponding word slows reaction time more if it belongs to the same conceptual category as the object (e.g., *BED* embedded in a picture of a chair) than if word and object belong to different categories (e.g., *BED* embedded in a picture of a banana). Also, word–picture noncorrespondence results in slower responding compared to a picture without a word (Ehri, 1976). These findings are quite sensible within an automaticity theory framework.

In contrast, the findings for less skilled readers have not been as supportive for the theory. Golinkoff and Rosinski (1976) found that poor readers were as slowed as good readers in a noncorrespondence condition. Assuming that the poor readers were at an "accuracy" stage and good readers at an "automaticity" stage, this result is difficult to understand from the perspective of automaticity theory. Moreover, very similar findings have been reported by others (Guttentag & Haith, 1978; Pace & Golinkoff, 1976). In the Guttentag and Haith study it was even found that the first-graders with less than a year of reading instruction (prime candidates for being at the accuracy stage) were slowed in a noncorrespondence condition.

It should be pointed out that there is some evidence from several of these studies that children who make frequent errors in reading respond about as quickly in noncorrespondence as in correspondence conditions. The theoretical meaning of this finding is unclear, however, because automaticity theory predicts this result for those who do read accurately (i.e., those who do not make errors), whereas the finding seems to occur for those who do not read accurately.

The difficulties that have been encountered in providing evidence for a stage of accurate-but-not-automatic reading pose a serious problem for automaticity theory. At least two types of explanations for why the problem has occurred can be entertained. One is that the theory itself may simply be wrong. There is no guarantee that any idea, even (or especially) an attractive one that captures the imagination of a field, will be substantiated by careful experimentation. Rather than being a cause of disappointment, it is perhaps to the credit of the theory that its hypotheses are so unambiguous that they can be proved wrong. Although it is too early to be sure, it is quite possible that in reality reading acquisition does not proceed by a stage of accuracy followed by a stage of automaticity.

A second possibility is that the interference tasks used in this research have not been entirely appropriate for testing the theory. The rationale underlying the use of interference tasks is that the subject will attend to the pictured object and not the word. If the subject does perceive the word, it is assumed to occur by automatic perception rather than by attention-based perception. Consider the possibility, however, that the word is so salient in these tasks that a reader (at either the stage of accuracy or automaticity) attends to it to some degree in spite of the experimenter's instruction to name only the pictured object. If this were the case, the conflict that would occur in the noncorrespondence condition would be between an attended-to word and an attended-to picture rather than, as a valid test of automaticity theory requires, between an automatically perceived word and an attended-to picture. Whatever the plausibility of this conjecture, it does serve to make clear that interference tasks do not provide for fine experimental control of attention, and it is therefore difficult to draw conclusions about whether the word stimuli used in such tasks are perceived automatically or by means of attention. This suggests that a different method might prove more fruitful for studying the general proposition that the process by which words are perceived changes in important ways as reading skill develops. A method discussed in the next section has yielded some encouraging preliminary findings in this respect.

Familiarization

Imagine that you are seated before a screen and a red circle appears for about 30 seconds, disappears for 10 seconds, reappears for 30 seconds, etc. The sequence continues until the red circle has been presented 30 times or so. The experimenter then introduces two response keys and instructs you to press one of them as quickly as you can whenever the red circle appears and the other as quickly as you can whenever a blue circle appears. Gordon Cantor (1969) and his colleagues found in a series of studies such as this that children respond more *slowly* to the familiarized stimulus. The finding has recently been replicated in adults (Kraut & Smothergill, 1978) as well.

Why does this occur? Kraut (1976) hypothesized that familiarization brings about changes in two components of attention. The notion of components of attention was originally introduced by Posner and Boies (1971) in describing the processes of *alertness, encoding* (set), and *capacity* (consciousness). Kraut's idea was that the familiarization procedure results in a decrease in alertness to a familiarized stimulus, but facilitation of its encoding. The observed effect of slower responses to a familiarized stimulus than to a novel stimulus would thus be the result of decreased alertness outweighing facilitated encoding.

Kraut tested this two-factor theory in a series of three experiments with 6- and 7-year-olds. Each experiment began with familiarization of a colored circle. In the first experiment, the familiarized stimulus was then pitted against a novel colored circle in a choice–reaction time task. As expected, the familiarized stimulus was responded to more slowly. The second experiment sought to demonstrate that alertness decrement occurs as a consequence of familiarization. A choice–reaction time task was used in which the subject responded to two geometric shapes. Six hundred milliseconds prior to onset of the target stimulus a warning signal occurred. On half the trials the warning signal was the familiarized stimulus, and on half the trials it was a novel colored circle. A warning signal normally speeds up reaction time responses; according to Posner and Boies's model it does so by raising alertness. Kraut predicted that responses would be slower on trials for which the familiarized stimulus was the warning signal because it would raise alertness less than a novel stimulus. Results confirmed this prediction.

Kraut's third experiment sought to demonstrate that familiarization also facilitates stimulus encoding. The demonstration required a procedure for getting around the alertness decrement effect of familiarization. As in the first experiment, the subject performed a choice–reaction time task in which the targets were the familiarized stimulus and a novel stimulus. Prior to target onset a warning signal occurred. The warning signal was the same geometric shape on all trials. Its purpose was to raise alertness to a constant level on each trial and thereby offset any differences in alertness associated with the target stimuli. As expected, the familiarized stimulus was responded to more quickly than the novel stimulus under these conditions—a reversal of what had been found in the first experiment.

These findings suggested that familiarization might be useful as a general tool for investigating patterns of alertness and encoding. For instance, a question that could be asked is whether the altertness decrement effect of familiarization is stronger than the encoding facilitation effect for all types of stimuli. An experiment conducted with college students sought to answer this question by contrasting colors and printed words (Kraut, Smothergill, & Farkas, in press). Subjects were familiarized to either a color or a printed word and then performed a choice–reaction time task in which the targets were the familiarized stimulus and a novel stimulus of the same type. The results indicated a clear difference for colors and words. For color, the familiarized stimulus evoked a slower response than the novel stimulus—a replication of previous findings. For printed words, just the opposite occurred: The familiarized stimulus evoked a faster response than the novel stimulus.

Does the finding for printed words mean, as two-factor theory would suggest, that encoding facilitation was a stronger effect than alertness decrement? If so, it should be possible to demonstrate that a decrement in alertness occurs to a familiarized printed word. This was demonstrated in a follow-up study by Kraut *et al.* (in press). College students were familiarized to a printed word prior to performing a choice–reaction time task on which the target stimuli were a pair of geometric shapes. Just before target onset one of two warning signals occurred. On half the trials the warning signal was the familiarized word and on half the trials it was a novel word. The pairings of warning signals and target stimuli were random across trials. If familiarization decreases the alerting capacity of a word, responses would be expected to be slower on trials for which the familiarized word was the warning signal. Results confirmed the expectation.

In sum, familiarization has been found to affect both the alertness and encoding components of attention for both colors and printed words.

Alertness is decreased and encoding is facilitated for both kinds of stimuli, but for colors alertness decrement is the stronger of the two effects, whereas for words encoding facilitation is the stronger effect.

These findings have recently been used as a basis for studying reading acquisition in children (Kraut, Smothergill, & Chedester, 1979). In one study, fifth-graders and first-graders were familiarized to a printed word prior to performing a choice–reaction time task in which the familiarized word and a novel word were the target stimuli. Testing was done in the spring, so the first-graders had had about 1 year of reading instruction. Findings were quite different for the two grade levels. The fifth-graders performed as adults: They responded faster to the familiarized word than the novel word. The first-graders, in contrast, responded *slower* to the familiar word than to the novel word. This latter finding has now been confirmed in a replication study (Kraut & Smothergill, 1979).

Comparing findings across these word familiarization studies indicates that fifth-graders and adults perform in one way and first-graders in another. The former, relatively skilled readers, show an encoding facilitation effect for familiarized words that is stronger than an alertness decrement effect also present. For relatively inexperienced first-grade readers, in contrast, familiarization of words appears to produce stronger alertness decrement than encoding facilitation.

Recall now the hypothesis from automaticity theory that there exists an accuracy stage in reading acquisition that precedes an automaticity stage. Recall, too, that attempts to provide evidence that these stages are indeed separate have not been notably successful. Although speculative, it is tempting to suggest that the relative strengths of alertness and encoding effects of familiarization may be a way of differentiating between the accurate and automatic modes of perceiving. The dominance of alertness over encoding for inexperienced readers may signal a stage of accuracy; the opposite pattern of findings for more experienced readers may be evidence for the automatic stage. Whatever the fate of this particular speculation, the familiarization research does indicate a clear difference in how words are responded to by skilled and less skilled readers. Automaticity theory has spurred the search for such differences, and it can be anticipated that others will be found as research continues.

CONCLUDING NOTE

Research findings often have a curious way of confirming an investigator's theoretical ideas. This impression seems all the more apparent when one reads the journals in which original research is published. Article after article seems to suggest that more often than not the investigator's theoretical hunches turned out to be supported by the experimental findings.

Intuitively, we know that this cannot always, or even frequently, be true, and at least two factors can be identified as responsible for this appearance of prescient knowledge. One is that the form in which journal articles are published is misleading. A reading of journal articles suggests that research is a cut-and-dried sequence of a theoretical idea leading to an experiment, the results of which confirm the theory. In fact, the process is usually much more intuitive, groping, and full of false starts. It is very often not until after a good deal of preliminary work has been done that a researcher clarifies the theoretical idea within which the research project makes sense. This then gives rise to one or two formal experiments whose outcome is well anticipated on the basis of the preliminary work.

A second reason is that powerful selective forces are at work in determining the research that gets published. As a rule, research results must be positive before a journal editor will consider publishing a study. The reason for this is that negative results are for the most part uninterpretable without follow-up research that positively identifies why the negative outcome occurred in the first place.

These two factors are responsible for much of the illusion that results invariably confirm researchers' theories. There is another more important and substantive aspect to this issue, however. Stated simply, it is this: How do we know whether the theoretical interpretation offered for a finding is correct? For example, we have seen that Kraut (1976) interpreted the slowed response that occurs to a familiarized color to be the net result of a combination of alertness decrement and encoding facilitation. How are we to know if Kraut is right? How can the *validity* of an interpretation of a result be established?

A very powerful principle that can be used to answer such questions was outlined for students of perception more than 25 years ago. Called *converging operations,* it is described as "Any set of two or more experimental operations which allow the selection or elimination of alternative hypotheses or concepts which could explain an experimental result [Garner, Hake, & Eriksen, 1956, p. 151]."

The essential concern underlying the need for converging operations, according to Garner *et al.,* is that any interpretation of a single result is simply a restatement, in theoretical terms, of the method by which the result was produced in the first place. To avoid such circularity, to determine whether an interpretation has real merit, at least one additional experiment needs to be conducted. The second experiment should use a different method from the first, and results from both experiments should converge upon the same common interpretation. Ideally, interpretations should be backed by findings from several converging operations, but a minimum of two is required to free any interpretation from the specificity inherent in the relation between the result and the method that produced it.

The notion of converging operations is a simple but powerful reminder of the continual interplay that must exist between theory and method. The challenge in producing a coherent theory of perceptual development lies as much in formulating good ideas as it does in creating methods for testing ideas.

REFERENCES

Acredolo, L. P. Development of spatial orientation in infancy. *Developmental Psychology,* 1978, *14,* 224-234.

Acredolo, L. P., & Evans, D. *Some determinants of the infant's choice of spatial reference system.* Paper presented at the meeting of the Society for Research in Child Development, San Francisco, March 1979.

Bower, T. G. R. Stimulus variables determining space perception in infants. *Science,* 1965, *149,* 88-89.

Bower, T. G. R. *Development in infancy.* San Francisco: W. H. Freeman, 1974.

Brodatz, P. *Textures.* New York: Dover, 1966.

Campos, J. J., Hiatt, S., Ramsay, D., Henderson, C., & Svejda, M. The emergence of fear on the visual cliff. In M. Lewis & L. A. Rosenblum (Eds.), *The development of affect* (Vol. 1). New York: Plenum, 1978.

Campos, J. J., Langer, A., & Krowitz, A. Cardiac responses on the visual cliff in prelocomotor human infants. *Science,* 1970, *170,* 196-197.

Cantor, G. N. Effects of stimulus familiarization on child behavior. In J. P. Hill (Ed.), *Minnesota symposia on child psychology* (Vol. 3). Minneapolis: University of Minnesota Press, 1969.

Chase, W. G., & Simon, H. A. Perception in chess. *Cognitive Psychology,* 1973, *4,* 55-81.

de Groot, A. D. *Thought and choice in chess.* The Hague: Mouton, 1965.

Dodwell, P. C., Muir, D., & Di Franco, D. Responses of infants to visually presented objects. *Science,* 1976, *194,* 209-211.

Ehri, L. C. Do words really interfere in naming pictures? *Child Development,* 1976, *47,* 502-505.

Garner, W., Hake, H. W., & Eriksen, C. W. Operationism and the concept of perception. *Psychological Review,* 1956, *63,* 149-159.

Gibson, E. J. *Principles of perceptual learning and development.* New York: Appleton-Century-Crofts, 1969.

Gibson, E. J., & Levin, H. *The psychology of reading.* Cambridge, Mass.: MIT Press, 1975.

Gibson, J. J. *The ecological approach to visual perception.* Boston: Houghton Mifflin Company, 1979.

Golinkoff, R. M., & Rosinski, R. R. Decoding, semantic processing, and reading comprehension skill. *Child Development,* 1976, *47,* 252-258.

Guttentag, R. E., & Haith, M. M. Automatic processing as a function of age and reading ability. *Child Development,* 1978, *49,* 707-716.

Katz, P. Stimulus predifferentiation and modification of children's racial attitudes. *Child Development,* 1973, *44,* 232-237.

Katz, P. A., Sohn, M., & Zalk, S. R. Perceptual concomitants of racial attitudes in urban grade-school children. *Developmental Psychology*, 1975, *11*, 135–144.

Katz, P. A., & Zalk, S. R. Modification of children's racial attitudes. *Developmental Psychology*, 1978, *14*, 447–461.

Kendler, T. S., & Kendler, H. H. Vertical and horizontal processes in problem solving. *Psychological Review*, 1962, *69*, 1–16.

Kosslyn, S. M., Pick, H. L., Jr., & Fariello, G. R. Cognitive maps in children and men. *Child Development*, 1974, *45*, 707–716.

Kraut, A. G. Effects of familiarization on alertness and encoding in children. *Developmental Psychology*, 1976, *12*, 491–496.

Kraut, A. G., & Smothergill, D. W. A two-factor theory of stimulus repetition effects. *Journal of Experimental Psychology: Human Perception and Performance*, 1978, *4*, 191–197.

Kraut, A. G., & Smothergill, D. W. *Replication of effect of familiarizing words in first grade children.* Unpublished manuscript, 1979. (Available from first author, Department of Psychology, Virginia Polytechnic Institute and State University, Blacksburg, Va. 24061.)

Kraut, A. G., Smothergill, D. W., & Chedester, A. E. *Familiarization and the development of attention: Verbal vs. non-verbal materials.* Paper presented at the meeting of the Society for Research in Child Development, San Francisco, March 1979.

Kraut, A. G., Smothergill, D. W., & Farkas, M. S. Stimulus repetition effects on attention to words and colors. *Journal of Experimental Psychology: Human Perception and Performance*, in press.

LaBerge, D. Attention and the measurement of perceptual learning. *Memory and Cognition*, 1973, *1*, 268–276.

Lynch, K. *The image of the city.* Cambridge, Mass.: MIT Press, 1960.

Miller, G. A. Psychology as a means of promoting human welfare. *American Psychologist*, 1969, *24*, 1063–1075.

Pace, A. J., & Golinkoff, A. M. Relationship between word difficulty and access of single-word meaning by skilled and less skilled readers. *Journal of Educational Psychology*, 1976, *68*, 760–767.

Piaget, J. *The origins of intelligence in children* (trans. M. Cook). New York: International University Press, 1952. (Originally published as *La naissance de l'intelligence chez l'enfant.* Neuchâtel: Delachaux & Niestlé, 1936.)

Pick, H. L., Jr. *Mapping children—Mapping space.* Paper presented at the meeting of the American Psychological Association, Honolulu, September 1972.

Posner, M., & Boies, S. Components of attention. *Psychological Review*, 1971, *78*, 391–408.

Rosinski, R. R., Golinkoff, R. M., & Kukish, K. S. Automatic semantic processing in a picture-word interference task. *Child Development*, 1975, *46*, 247–253.

Rozin, P. The evolution of intelligence and access to the cognitive unconscious. In J. Sprague & A. N. Epstein (Eds.). *Progress in psychobiology and physiological psychology* (Vol. 6). New York: Academic Press, 1975.

Samuels, S. J. Application of basic research in reading. In H. L. Pick, Jr., H. W. Leibowitz, J. E. Singer, A. Steinschneider, & H. W. Stevenson (Eds.), *Psychology.* New York: Plenum, 1978.

Schwartz, A. N., Campos, J. J., & Baisel, E. J. The visual cliff: Cardiac and behavioral responses on the deep and shallow sides at five and nine months of age. *Journal of Experimental Child Psychology*, 1973, *15*, 86–99.

Smothergill, D. W., Hughes, F., Timmons, S., & Hutko, P. Spatial visualizing in children. *Developmental Psychology*, 1975, *11*, 4–13.

Stroop, J. R. Studies of interference in serial verbal reactions. *Journal of Experimental Psychology*, 1935, *18*, 643–662.

Tighe, L. S. Effect of perceptual pretraining on reversal and nonreversal shift. *Journal of Experimental Psychology,* 1965, *70,* 379–385.

Timmons, S. A., & Smothergill, D. W. Perceptual training of height and brightness seriation in kindergarten children. *Child Development,* 1975, *46,* 1030–1034.

Walk, R. D. Perceptual learning and the discrimination of wines. *Psychonomic Science,* 1966 *5,* 57–58.

Walk, R. D., & Gibson, E. J. A comparative and analytical study of visual depth perception. *Psychological Monographs,* 1961, *75,* No. 15.

White, S. The learning theory approach. In P. H. Mussen (Ed.), *Carmichael's manual of child psychology* (3rd ed., Vol. 1). New York: Wiley, 1970.

Yonas, A., Bechtold, A. G., Frankel, D., Gordon, F. R., McRoberts, G., Norcia, A., & Sternfels, S. Development of sensitivity to information for impending collision. *Perception & Psychophysics,* 1977, *21,* 97–104.

5 Language Development

JILL G. deVILLIERS AND PETER A. deVILLIERS

INTRODUCTION

A few years ago the Harvard University student newspaper ran a series of cartoons poking gentle fun at some of the courses in the catalog. Among the courses so honored (alongside "Introduction to Attic Prose" and "The Romantic Hero") was the "Child Language" course that one of us taught. The cartoon pictured a rather mindless looking baby saying "ba-ba" into a microphone held by two serious, scholarly adults. There is a sense in which the cartoon was unnervingly close to the truth. If we concentrate just on the methods used to study children's language there are times when the notion of so many earnest adults paying rapt attention to every word spoken by a toddler seems foolish indeed. Consequently, although this chapter is about methods and techniques, and we are going to get to the complexities of collecting a sample of child speech soon enough, we are not going to begin with methods at all but rather with questions, issues that dominate the study of language acquisition. This will serve to motivate later discussions of methods, and also reflects our conviction that most techniques are created to investigate particular theoretical questions. Both the strengths and weaknesses of available methods are defined in large part by the extent to which they enable the investigator to illuminate these issues.

How does the child's knowledge of a particular grammatical construction, word meaning, or aspect of discourse change with age? In its simplest form this is the most atheoretical question motivating research on child language, and it has been the basis for a great many studies. Typically the investigator searches for general patterns in children's mastery of some aspect of language, although research of this type is not simply a matter of

STRATEGIES AND TECHNIQUES
OF CHILD STUDY

cataloging successive approximations to adult usage. In many cases, children go through a period of apparent regression after initial mastery, and the investigator goes beyond the superficial description to an account of the child's underlying knowledge of the rules and how this changes over time. For instance, the well-known mistakes on irregular past tense forms (e.g., *comed* and *falled* for *came* and *fell*) result from the child's overgeneralization of the regular past tense form to cases where English has exceptions. Similar observations have been reported for phonological (Ingram, 1976a) and lexical development (Bowerman, 1974). Systematic errors or patterns in the mastery of some feature of language can therefore provide evidence of the changing rule system of the child, and much research is concerned with identifying or describing those patterns and examining how general they are across children.

What is the relationship between theoretical analyses of adult language and the child's acquisition of those forms? A particular linguistic analysis suggests that construction X is grammatically less complex than construction Y. Are they acquired in that order? Many linguists hold that the grammars they write correspond to the adult's tacit knowledge of the language (*competence*) and are not a model of the processes underlying the production or comprehension of speech (*performance*). Nevertheless, developmental psycholinguists have suggested that if the linguistic theory captures a person's implicit knowledge of the language it may also predict the course of acquisition of that knowledge (Brown & Hernstein, 1975; Erreich, Valian, & Winzemer, 1980). Good examples of predictions of this sort are provided by Brown and Hanlon's (1970) study on tag questions, E. Clark's (1972, 1973a) investigations of lexical development as they relate to semantic feature analyses of word meaning (e.g., Bierwisch, 1970), and several papers in the volume by Goodluck and Solan (1978). Although alternative accounts have been offered for some of these patterns of acquisition, and theories of adult grammar and semantics frequently change (e.g., Chomsky, 1980; Halle, Bresnan, & Miller, 1978; Lyons, 1977), linguistic theory continues to be a rich source of hypotheses about language acquisition.

What is the relationship between cognitive development and language acquisition? Over the past 10 years this has been a major issue in the study of child language as researchers have sought a broader explanatory framework than that provided by purely linguistic analyses. Hypotheses about the relationship between cognitive and linguistic development vary in strength. The strongest hypothesis holds that specific cognitive attainments are sufficient for the acquisition of various language milestones—that language skills result from the child's intellectual developments. Few theorists explicitly espouse such a strong position, although hints of it may be found in some Piagetian writings (Piaget, 1955, 1962; Sinclair, 1971). A weaker version proposes that certain cognitive skills are necessary though not sufficient for the acquistion of a variety of language skills (Cromer, 1974, 1976; Miller, Chapman, & Bedrosian, 1977). In both cases the hypothesis is that cognitive development constrains the rate and pattern of language acquisition, in that particular linguistic abilities presuppose certain cognitive attainments (Sinclair, 1971; Bloom, 1973; Bowerman, 1978a).

The cognitive ability most frequently proposed as a prerequisite for the onset of meaningful speech is the capacity for mental representation of objects or events (Piaget, 1962). Research on this question has focused on the earliest stages of language acquisition, correlating the emergence of words or some other measure of linguistic development (e.g., periods of rapid vocabulary growth, or mean length of utterance) with performance on tasks designed to test the child's capacity for mental representation (such as object permanence, imitation, and symbolic play) (see Bates, Benigni, Bretherton, Camaioni, & Volterra, 1977, 1979; Bloom, 1973; Corrigan, 1978; Huttenlocher, 1974; Ingram, 1978; Miller *et al.,* 1977; Ramsay, 1977). Frequently the children have been classified according to Piaget's six stages of sensorimotor development based on their performance on these tasks. Significant positive correlations between performances on the cognitive and language tasks have been interpreted as indicating either that the particular cognitive skill is a prerequisite for the language skill or that both tasks reflect a common underlying cognitive capacity.

Unfortunately the correlational research has produced divergent results, and it has become clear that the cognitive hypothesis is not so simple as it sounds. Corrigan (1979) points out that a great deal of the confusion stems from different operational definitions of representation and object permanence. Many reasearchers have assumed that all measures of mental representation should be equivalent since they all tap into the same underlying cognitive structure. Yet there is no substantial synchrony in children's mastery of the tasks Piaget used to define his stages of sensorimotor development, and decalage appears to be the rule rather than the exception in early cognitive development (Feldman & Toulmin, 1975; Fischer, in press; Flavell, 1971; Uzgiris, 1976). Hence children can be at different levels in different skills, and changes in materials or methods of task administration within a skill influence a child's performance; so a child may fail on a supposedly prerequisite cognitive task for all the wrong reasons while succeeding on the linguistic task. Of course, the same problems of construct definition and the task-specific nature of children's performance can be raised about the language measures as well. Thus close synchrony between cognitive and linguistic development may only be found when essentially the same skills are required and the task demands are similar in the two domains. Studies must specify exactly which cognitive behaviors and which language behaviors were measured, and how they were assessed.

Precisely the same problems of task demands and construct definition arise in investigating cognitive and linguistic skills in the later preschool period; for instance, whether the acquisition of deictic expressions like pronouns, determiners, and demonstratives presuppose that the child has the capacity to take the other's point of view, hence not be egocentric (deVilliers & deVilliers, 1974; Maratsos, 1979; Webb & Abrahamson, 1976).

Another approach to the relationship between cognition and language acquisition involves cross-linguistic research. The acquisition of particular meanings (for example, the hypothetical, or deictic expressions) is studied across several languages that vary in the way in which those meanings are expressed. The logic of the research is quite simple: If a meaning is mastered in children's speech or comprehension at about the same age despite marked differences in the complexity of its expression across languages, then the acquisition of that linguistic form appears to depend primarily on cognitive rather than linguistic sophistication (Cromer, 1974). Cross-linguistic research can also reveal structural and functional aspects of languages that make them easy or hard to learn, thereby suggesting information processing biases that the child might bring to the task of language learning (Slobin, 1973, in press).

How can the child's general level of language development be captured by a reliable measure so that it can be used as an evaluative tool for clinical purposes, or to correlate with other linguistic or nonlinguistic abilities? A continuing concern of educators, clinicians, and researchers is to assess a child's level of language development much as one might arrive at an index of physical growth or visual acuity. Unfortunately language is a more complex achievement, and the measurement technique depends very heavily on the goal of the assessment. For instance, a common question—Is this particular child developing language normally for his age?—requires a whole range of different assessments: perception of speech sounds, articulation, vocabulary, sentence structure, and conversational ability. Furthermore, it presupposes that we know the normal range of these achievements at different ages and the extent of individual variation within normal children. There are tests available for the assessment of phonetic perception (e.g., Eisenson, 1972), articulation (see survey of these by Winitz, 1969), and vocabulary (e.g., the Peabody Picture Vocabulary Test, Dunn, 1965). However, the assessment of syntactic development is more difficult and controversial.

The length of the child's spontaneous utterances is a popular measure of syntactic development, either in words per sentence (Shriner, 1969) or morphemes per utterance (MLU; Brown, 1973). There are several well-known problems with length measures, however. First, two sentences can be the same length but different in complexity even to the untrained ear. Children below age 3 or so with the same MLU do not vary too widely in the range of structures they produce (Brown, 1973), so the measure can be defended for them, but not for atypical populations or older normal children. Second, there are unsolved problems in the definition of a "morpheme" in English and other languages. For example, should *falled* count as two morphemes although *fell* is only one? Should a child with only the negative auxiliary *can't* in his speech be credited with knowing the morpheme *n't?* A third problem is the way the length of a child's utterances can be influenced by contextual variables, socioeconomic background (Minifie, Darley & Sherman, 1963), or simply by what the child talks about (Brown, 1973). In short, while MLU is a useful and easily applied index of syntactic development in the earliest stages of speech, it has limited utility for older or very heterogeneous groups of children, unless it is supplemented with some other complexity index (e.g., Shriner, 1967). At present there is a clear need for a reliable and easily scored gauge of syntactic development between the ages of 3 and 6 years.

For clinical populations a profile of the child's abilities in syntax is more useful than a scale, and this is the approach adopted by Crystal, Fletcher, and Garman (1976), who measure such things as phrase and clause complexity and the means the child has available for combining these. This profile is then used to guide the nature and sequence of a language intervention program.

What experiences might be necessary for children to learn various aspects of language, and how might we enhance acquisition? What role might factors like parental expansions of utterances, modeling, imitation, or reinforcement play, and how might they interact with or be constrained by maturational factors? Questions of the influence of environmental factors on language acquisition have long been of interest to psychologists and linguists, both in order to extend learning theories from other domains of psychology to language and to devise training procedures for language-delayed children. But they acquired even greater interest following the claims of Chomsky (1965) and McNeill (1966) that available learning theories were inadequate to account for the hypotheses the child brings to the task of language acquisition, and that the quality of the input and feedback the child receives is of little importance in the process. Studies addressing these issues constitute a major area of current research, and they are discussed in depth later in this chapter.

METHODS

Spontaneous Speech

Data Collection. As the dominant questions in the field have shifted, details of the methodology have changed, but the classical technique for the study of child language continues to be the collection of samples of spontaneous speech. The history of the field of child phonology provides an illustration: The earliest period around the turn of the century was characterized by diary studies of individual children (e.g., Humphreys, 1880; Lindner, 1898); the middle period from 1930 into the 1960s was marked by large-scale cross-sectional studies aimed at establishing age norms for the correct pronunciation of particular speech sounds (Olmsted, 1971; Templin, 1957); and the most recent period has seen a return to detailed study of only a few children, either to test linguistic theories such as generative phonology (Chomsky & Halle, 1968; Schane, 1973) or to perform sophisticated spectrographic analyses of the speech (e.g., Macken & Barton, 1980).

The older diary studies, particularly of word pronunciation and use, provided a wealth of data for subsequent theorists (e.g., Ingram, 1976a), although they have some intrinsic limitations. The major problem is the tendency of the reporter to be selective in what is recorded. In the case of phonology, the investigator would simply note down a phonetic transcription of the words he heard while listening to the child. This was sometimes a "normalization" of the variations or only the most frequent pronunciation of the words. But variability in pronunciation is common in early speech, and it is now of greater interest to researchers (e.g., Ferguson, 1978). Furthermore, the contextual notes were frequently inadequate to tell if the word was an imitation of a preceding adult utterance, and since imitated utterances may be more advanced than spontaneous productions (Ingram, 1976b) it becomes important to record the preceding adult speech as well.

In the case of word meaning, a diary study can be invaluable in tracing the way a child's use of a term changes over time. Again it is essential to record the context of use in detail, not only the referential aspects of the situation, but also what actions the participants were engaged in. For instance, some children may use a word in a restricted *functional* context compared to adults; Svachkin (1973) mentioned a child who used the word *kat* only when she had thrown her toy kitty out of her crib, not in any other circumstances. Frequently young children extend a word to objects or events that adults would not use it for, and these overextensions play a pivotal role in current theories of lexical development (Barrett, 1978;

Braunwald, 1978; Clark, 1973a, 1978a; Nelson, Rescorla, Gruendel, & Benedict, 1978). While careful contextual notes can reveal these divergent uses and suggest their function, diary studies have the inherent problem that overextensions are recorded but underextensions are missed. When a child fails to name an object in a natural setting, the adult cannot tell whether he or she does not know the word or simply chooses not to name the object (Anglin, 1977). Underextension errors are more likely to be revealed in elicited naming or comprehension tasks.

For the study of syntax, diary studies are less useful than a representative sample of the child's speech at different ages, although longitudinal records of a particular construction, such as the negative, can be informative (e.g. deVilliers and deVilliers, 1979a). It is usual practice now for diary studies to be supplemented by high quality reel-to-reel tape recordings taken at regular intervals, either to provide a check on the reliability of transcriptions of the child's speech (Ingram, 1976b) or to provide additional information about such things as frequency or variability of usage and the nature of the verbal interaction between the parent and child.

There is some variation in the definition of a representative sample of the child's spontaneous speech, again reflecting the goals of the enterprise. The most usual practice is to record an hour or two of spontaneous speech in conversation with a familiar adult such as the mother and in familiar surroundings. The activities during the recording should be sufficiently varied to elicit a range of conversational topics and functions from the participants: not, for instance, just labeling the pictures in a book. It is imperative to have detailed contextual notes to supplement the recording: information about what the child is doing, what he is looking at, and who is being addressed. As young children's speech is usually in response to someone else's utterances, both sides of the conversation should be recorded. If the focus of interest is phonology, the researcher should make a careful phonetic transcription while he can see the child's mouth, as the tape recording, no matter how high the quality, can be ambiguous on its own (Ingram, 1976b). The transcript taken at the time of the interaction should later be checked against the tape by at least one independent transcriber. The International Phonetic Alphabet (IPA) is frequently used in the transcription of child speech, but for detailed analysis it has been modified by an additional system of diacritic symbols to capture information such as an exaggerated friction or tongue protrusion that may be present in children's pronunciation (Bush, Edwards, Luckau, Stoel, Macken, & Petersen, 1973). Unfortunately, as the detail becomes finer, the less agreement there is among transcribers (Johnson & Bush, 1971), so the IPA is still the system most widely adopted.

For the study of grammatical development, a general guideline is that

150–200 utterances is a minimal sample from which to draw inferences, If the researcher is studying development over time, a typical sample is a 1–2-hour recording once every 2 weeks, but during periods of rapid change the frequency of sampling may have to be increased.

With the increased current interest in the development of communicative competence and conversational skills, the techniques of recording discourse have expanded to include the use of videotape. Because of the much greater investment of time and equipment, the sampling is usually smaller. Sometimes particular scenarios are chosen for study, such as looking at a book (Ninio & Bruner, 1978) or feeding rituals (Bruner, 1975). Alternatively, only those portions of the videotape containing an aspect of interest, say *requests* (Haselkorn, 1979), are selected for detailed study.

Analysis. Having collected transcripts of spontaneous speech, the researcher must address the difficult questions of analysis. Finding the most illuminating level of description is the ever-present problem in all aspects of child language, since there are multiple possible descriptions of child phonology, word use, grammatical structure, and function. To a large extent choice is governed by the questions the researcher is trying to answer and his or her theoretical stance, although we suggest that it is frequently illuminating to employ several different levels of analysis in the same study. Parallel concerns are found in each of the domains of language, but we shall consider each in turn to allow discussion of issues specific to each area.

Phonology. There are four general approaches to the analysis of children's phonology: *phones, phonemes, distinctive features,* and *phonological rules.* In the first approach, the focus is on individual speech sounds and how accurately they are produced. For instance, Olmsted (1971) measured the frequency and likelihood of error of individual phones in samples of speech from 100 children aged 1:3–4:6 years. His interest was in whether their relative difficulty could be predicted from their frequency or confusability for adults, as well as in the variations in pronunciation within each child's speech. Recent research has extended this type of phonetic analysis to preverbal vocalizations, in an attempt to study the influence of various language environments on this stage of development (Nakazima, 1962), and to explore the continuity of preverbal patterns of pronunciation and later speech (Oller, Wieman, Doyle, & Ross, 1976).

The second approach concerns the child's mastery of those contrasting sounds in his native language (i.e., phonemes) that signal differences in meaning. Jakobson (1968) argued that phonological development consists of a progressive opposition between classes of speech sounds, a process that is systematic and universal. It has proved difficult to test the specific predictions made by the theory about the order of acquisition of phoneme contrasts, since much of the data required for a phonemic analysis is absent from early child speech. Many phonemes in the adult language are identified by noting minimal pairs of words such as *bit* and *pit* whose single sound difference indicates a contrast in meaning. Child speech supplies few such pairs, although Braine (1971) gives an illustration of the subtle cues that could be used by the researcher. Young children often produce a [d] for an initial /d/, /t/, /δ/, and /θ/, saying *dat* for *that,* for example. At the same time an initial /g/ or /k/ might sometimes be produced as [g] and sometimes as [d]; hence the child says either *gat* or *dat* for *cat.* Braine argues that even though the child uses *dat* for both *cat* and *that,* the fact that *cat* is only sometimes *dat* while *that* is always *dat* suggests that he knows the words begin with different speech sounds. This is an interesting example of how a phonemic analysis of child speech might proceed. Nevertheless, variability in pronunciation is so pervasive in child phonology that it seems a fragile cue on which to base the analysis. Ferguson (1978) argues that in the earliest stages of speech the units of sound opposition may not be phonemes but whole syllables or even words, and a phonemic analysis is inappropriate for that stage. Finally, there is the danger that a child may in fact be making a phonemic contrast that adults cannot hear, because it does not cross the adult phoneme boundary. Macken and Barton (1980) found that at an intermediate stage in the mastery of stop consonants, some children produced a consistent contrast between initial voiced and unvoiced stop consonants that the adult researchers could only distinguish by spectographic analysis of voice onset time. It remains to be seen how widespread this phenomenon is across children and across different phonemes before its impact on phonemic analyses of child speech can be assessed, but it could greatly complicate such an analysis.

Jakobson and Halle (1956) analyzed phonemes into clusters of *distinctive features,* a supposedly universal set of articulatory and acoustic aspects of speech sounds such as [± voice], [± continuant], and so forth. Each phoneme could be characterized by a distinct set of such features. Menyuk (1968) analyzed the consonants produced by English- and Japanese-speaking children in terms of their accuracy in producing the appropriate distinctive features. Errors often consisted of a failure to observe a single distinctive feature, so the child might produce *dis* for *this,* or *gup* for *cup.* The order in which children came to control the production of distinctive features was the same for English and Japanese speakers.

The distinctive feature approach has the advantage that it looks at the nature of errors of pronunciation and the reasons they may occur. In the fourth approach to child phonology, errors are also a major source of information about the child's developing system of rules. The focus is much less on individual speech sounds but rather on a system of pronunciation incorporating many words, so a fairly large sample of different words is required for this analysis. Linguists then try to capture the broad regularities in the child's pronunciation, by proposing a set of phonological rules or simplifying processes that govern the child's production of speech sounds in combination with others. For illustration, take a child who says *pop* for *top* and *tat* for *pat*. A phonetic analysis could only describe this as a rather odd substitution of [p] for [t] in one word, and [t] for [p] in another. But suppose the child also says *gog* for *dog* and *kick* for *thick*. The most economical description is that the child assimilates the place of articulation of the initial consonant to that of the final consonant, keeping the voicing and other features the same. This process is a common one in child speech, and a number of such rules or simplifying processes have been proposed as universals (Ingram, 1976a, 1976b). Typically the linguist describes these regularities by writing phonological rules that relate the child's form of the word to the adult form, although there is some controversy as to whether a child at this stage can in fact be presumed to hear the adult form correctly (Edwards, 1974; Ingram, 1974; Smith, 1973). A detailed phonological rule system for one child at different stages of development is provided by Smith (1973), and this area is a fertile one in current research with both normal and abnormal populations (Ingram, 1976b).

Word Meaning. Linguists have tried to draw parallels between word meaning and phonology in analyzing the meaning of a term into a set of distinctive semantic features, such as [± animate] or [± male], that distinguish it from other related terms (Bierwisch, 1970; Katz & Fodor, 1963). The approach works rather well for restricted semantic domains such as kinship terms—*father, brother, son,* and *nephew* would be [+ male], whereas *mother, sister, daughter,* and *niece* would be [− male]— though it runs into complications for so-called "natural kind" terms like *tiger* or *gold* (see Putnam, 1975). Eve Clark (1973a) suggested that semantic development should be viewed as the acquisition and differentiation of semantic feature entries for words. This semantic feature hypothesis explained the overextensions of early words by suggesting that the child had only partial lexical entries for those words. Subsequent research has questioned the adequacy of the semantic feature hypothesis alone in accounting for the general pattern of lexical development and criticized its freedom in inventing semantic features. Increased stress is being placed on conceptual development and strategies that the child may adopt to interpret words (Clark & Clark, 1977; E. Clark, 1979), and on specific knowledge the child may have picked up about the use of particular words in limited contexts (Carey, 1978). Nevertheless, semantic feature theories have stimulated a great deal of research on the acquisition of words in particular semantic domains (e.g., spatial adjectives, Clark, 1972;

kinship terms, Haviland & Clark, 1974; verbs of possession, Gentner, 1975; spatial prepositions, Clark, 1977). A few of these studies looked at word use in spontaneous speech (e.g., Brown, 1973; Nelson, 1976), but most of them used elicited production and comprehension tasks, so we will consider them in more detail in other sections of the chapter.

In the same way that the child acquires a phonological system relating many words, there is evidence that a semantic system is being acquired. Bowerman (1978b) has shown from longitudinal study of her two daughters how errors of word choice can give evidence of the growth of a sense of semantic relatedness among words. For instance, the child might say *give* or *let* in a context requiring *put* or *make,* even though she had used these words appropriately before. These errors seemed to reflect the organization of the child's lexicon into a coherent network of related terms. Spontaneous errors in word use may therefore reveal a change in the child's knowledge that is not readily apparent in other language tasks.

Syntax. The first major approach to children's syntax consisted of attempts to write grammars that would capture the child's knowledge at particular points in time (e.g., Brown, Cazden, & Bellugi, 1969; Brown & Bellugi, 1964; Miller & Ervin, 1964). Primarily these were phrase structure grammars that borrowed categories such as *subject* or *noun phrase* from adult syntax to describe the child's first sentences. In contrast, Braine (1963a) argued that his three subjects were developing their own pivot grammar with a limited set of rules and categories, which was not simply a reduced adult grammar. These arguments paved the way for the preoccupation in current research with the *psychological reality* of the rules proposed for child speech.

Instead of adopting adult linguistic categories and searching for their embryonic forms, researchers are now more likely to arrive at a description of early grammar that tries to capture the child's limited knowledge at that time. For instance, in the early stages, children talk about a restricted range of events and relationships that may best be analyzed as a set of formulae for expressing semantic relations (Brown, 1973). A fairly small set of such formulae accounts for early sentences in a variety of languages:

agent + action	Teddy fall
action + object	kick ball
agent + object	me lunch
action + locative	fly roof
entity + locative	birdie tree
possessor + possessed	Daddy chair
attribute + entity	red truck
demonstrative + entity	here Mommy

The semantic relations approach emphasizes the continuity of prelinguistic and linguistic development, and universal aspects of early sentences (deVilliers & deVilliers, 1978), but it has raised many methodological problems.

Since the researcher must arrive at an interpretation of the meaning the child intends to express, the question arises as to whether an adult-centered view is being imposed on the child when the sentences are analyzed. As adults we make distinctions, both conceptually and linguistically, between *locations, possessions,* and *attributions,* for example, but how do we know the child does? We can be sure only if the child marks the distinction by some formal means, such as word order in English or inflections in other languages, and several writers have suggested that the "rich interpretation" of the child's utterances should be constrained by evidence of consistent formal encoding of the various relations (e.g., Schaerlaekens, 1973, Schlesinger, 1979).

Unfortunately this criterion may be too strong, for it is often the case that some utterances that have the same surface form are produced in quite different contexts and clearly have different meanings. The classic example is Bloom's (1970) subject who said *Mommy sock,* once when her mother was putting on the child's sock, and once when she found her mother's stocking. The interpretation must clearly be *agent–action* on the one occasion, and *possessor–possessed* on the second, despite the identical form of the sentences. Second, adult English is not completely consistent in its use of word order: The possessive can be produced in two different forms, *Mommy's sock* and *the sock belonging to Mommy,* and the child might recognize that variability is allowed and express the relation without fixed word order.

Further problems arise in justifying the linguistic categories chosen for description. In theory, any given utterance can be given a multitude of descriptions: Should it be *Daddy + kick, agent + action, human + motion, animate + cause to move,* or *subject + predicate?* There is some variation in the categories chosen by researchers and in the frequency of those categories in children's speech (Bowerman, 1978a). It is sometimes difficult to determine whether this reflects real differences in individual children's formulas or different criteria adopted by the investigators. The best solution at present is for researchers to be as explicit as possible about their procedures for arriving at a level of description.

Beyond the first sentences, research has usually focused on a much narrower area of syntax than entire grammars. For instance, Brown's (1973) study of inflectional development, Bellugi's (1967) thesis on negation, and Limber's (1973) discussion of relative clauses all investigated how children's rules for particular constructions change over time. Nevertheless, there has been little coordinated research on how children's grammars are best represented at the later stages, in part because linguistic theory never stays still long enough for developmental researchers to catch up with current accounts of adult grammar. It is also the case that researchers of child language are in a more difficult position with respect to data. They have access only to "performance" data with little or no supplemental information from the speaker's intuitions, and the system they study is evolving rapidly rather than remaining stationary. The focus on particular constructions rather than entire grammatical systems is therefore understandable. Unfortunately, however, when the rules in question are studied in isolation from the child's grammar as a whole, many of the criteria used in adult linguistics to justify a particular formal description over other alternatives—criteria such as overall parsimony, completeness, and so forth —are less applicable. Consequently it would be informative for future studies to examine the acquisition in the same children of a range of construction types that might be related in the adult grammar (see Brown & Hanlon, 1970, for this kind of study).

Pragmatics. The issues of analysis that arise within pragmatics are highly similar to those within syntax: How can the child's intention be determined, and what categories are available for description? The debate concerns what the child is using the proposition *for* in discourse: Is it a *request,* a *label,* a *demand?* To distinguish these *speech acts* (Searle, 1969) is usually not difficult for the listener, but researchers need to know what cues the listener is using, and whether the child controls those cues.

Once again, some researchers have searched for evidence that the child uses linguistic markers to distinguish speech acts, the most obvious being intonation. Unfortunately, the evidence that young children consistently use intonation to signal different functions is equivocal at best (Bloom, 1973; Crystal, 1979; Dore, 1975; Halliday, 1975: Menyuk & Bernholtz, 1969). Consequently, nonlinguistic cues like persistence toward an apparent goal, or gestures reliably associated with speech must frequently be used to infer the child's intentions (Bates, 1976; Carter, 1979).

The familiar problem of how finely to slice the categories of description recurs in the area of pragmatics (deVilliers & deVilliers, 1978). At one extreme, each utterance performs a different act; at the other extreme, all utterances invoke a response from a listener. The problem comes in arriving at a finite list of functions with just the right degree of specificity. Rather than applying functional categories devised for adult speech, Halliday (1975) derived a list of functions from his own child's use of language. The list has two major divisions: *pragmatic* functions, including instrumental, regulatory, and interactional functions, and *mathetic* or learning functions incorporating personal, heuristic, imaginative, and informative uses. Definitions of these are given in Table 5.1.

Halliday's son differentiated between the two broad classes of function by a rising versus a falling intonation contour, and there was a developmental order in the emergence of the functions. Pragmatic and personal functions were the first to be used, even before conventional speech appeared, whereas the last function to emerge was the informative, that considered by Halliday to be intrinsic to language and to require some understanding of the notion of dialogue. Although Halliday's system can be criticized on the grounds that few criteria are provided for reliably classifying individual utterances, the general distinction it makes between pragmatic and ideational (mathetic) aspects of language has proved useful in illuminating individual differences in early language acquisition (Nelson, 1978). Furthermore, the system stresses the continuity between preverbal and verbal communication in the child, a position supported by several other researchers (e.g., Bates *et al.,* 1977, 1979; Bruner, 1975). Wells (1973) and Dore, Gearhart, & Newman (1978; see also Dore, 1979) have published much more extensive schemes of pragmatic classification, which may be necessary for the analysis of older preschool children's conversations, and there is no doubt that the functional analysis of children's early language will continue to be a fertile area of research. However, specification of criteria for the selection of categories and for the classification of individual utterances is essential if such analyses are to be reliably performed and if findings are to be comparable across studies.

An alternative approach in studying the acquisition of functional aspects

TABLE 5.1
Definition of Halliday's (1975) Pragmatic Functions for
Early Child Speech

Instrumental:	The "I want" function—the child uses speech to express demands and desires.
Regulatory:	"Do as I tell you." The child attempts to regulate the actions of others.
Interactional:	"You and me." Speech is used for social or affective communication.
Personal:	The child draws attention to himself and his actions—"here I come."
Heuristic:	"Tell me why." The child requests an explanation for a statement or event.
Imaginative:	The "let's pretend" function.
Informative:	Language is used to impart information. "I've got something to tell you."

of language is to focus on a particular type of speech act and examine its development over time. For instance, philosophers have worked out the conditions of knowledge and other circumstances between speaker and listener that make a particular speech act, say a *promise* (Searle, 1975), appropriate. The child language researcher can then examine the child's conversation in either natural or contrived circumstances to see if he or she respects these conditions of use. Antinucci and Voltcrra (1973) analyzed children's denials from this perspective, and Garvey (1975) took a similar approach to contingent queries and requests.

Elicited Production

It is often desirable to arrange a situation that would elicit a particular verbal response from a child, because the natural frequency of certain phonemes or grammatical constructions may be so low that normal sampling of spontaneous speech would either miss them or provide too few examples for meaningful analysis.

Elicited naming of pictures is a technique widely used to examine the child's pronunciation of a range of speech sounds, but there are some limitations to such tasks. Usually only a couple of words are elicited for each speech sound, but there are a great many influences on the child's pronunciation of a sound: the number of syllables, the stress pattern, opportunities for assimilation to other sounds, and so forth. Ideally the test words should vary along all these dimensions. In addition, the pronunciation of a word in isolation can be different from its pronunciation in a sentence context. So although elicited production tasks are easy to administer, they should be regarded as supplemental information to a spontaneous speech sample if a comprehensive description of the child's phonological system is to be achieved.

In studying word meaning, elicited production tasks have also proven useful. The child could be asked to name objects or their properties (Anglin, 1977; Bartlett, 1977), to describe objects that vary along spatial dimensions such as height or width (Wales & Campbell, 1970), or to use deictic expressions to direct a listener to the location of an object (deVilliers & deVilliers, 1974). Several factors may influence the likelihood that a child will come up with the appropriate words in these tasks. These include the view of the object and how typical it is of its class (a German shepherd is more likely than a chihuahua to be called a *dog;* Anglin, 1977), and the number of dimensions along which the items to be described may vary. A child may know that particular items such as swimming pools can be *deep* and *shallow,* but not that holes or boxes can be described by those adjectives (Carey, 1978). To assess the child's grasp of the general meaning of a word, a variety of eliciting stimuli should therefore be presented.

The earliest elicitation task for investigating children's productive use of morphological endings was Berko's (1958) "wug" test. The child might be shown a picture of a funny little creature and told: "Here is a wug. He is wearing a hat. Whose hat is it? It is the ——." If the child provides the appropriate inflected form of nonsense syllables in a number of such contexts, he or she provides evidence of mastery of the morphological rules in English for such inflections as the possessive, the plural, the past tense, and the third person singular. The use of nonsense syllables assures that the child could not just be providing the inflected word from rote memory, and the phonological form of the nonsense syllables can be varied to determine the extent to which the child controls the various forms of any particular inflectional rule. The "wug" test and similar versions with real words in place of nonsense syllables (MacWhinney, 1978) have been used extensively with both normal (see Derwing & Baker, 1979, for a review) and retarded children (Denver & Gardner, 1970).

Puppet games can also be used to elicit grammatical constructions from young children. Typically the roles of the puppets are first modeled by the experimenter, and then the child is asked to work the puppet. Kuczaj (1978) used this technique to elicit past tenses; for example, the experimenter's puppet would say, "I will throw the ball," and the child's puppet had to say, "I already ____ the ball." By devising suitable roles for the puppets it is possible to elicit negative sentences, questions, and tag questions (Brown and Herrnstein, 1975; deVilliers & deVilliers, 1979b). The advantages of this method lie in the control that can be exercised over the lexical items produced as well as the increased frequency of rare constructions. Preschoolers usually enter into the spirit of the game and enjoy working the puppets, so a substantial number of utterances can be collected.

Carefully designed pictures have also been employed in the elicitation of certain sentence types. For example, Tager-Flusberg, deVilliers, and Hakuta (in press) obtained many conjoined sentences from 3- to 5-year-olds by presenting pictures depicting multiple agents, actions, or objects, and asking the children to describe them for an adult who could not see them. Usually the pictures are presented in conjunction with modeling or some other cue about the kind of response that is expected (Whiteburst, Ironsmith, & Goldfein, 1974). Without such direction, a child can "misread" the picture, say something tangential, or fail to pay attention to the details that the experimenter has carefully depicted. The child may also fail to produce the desired construction because he or she assumes that the experimenter already knows what is in the picture. We have found it helpful to show children slides of the pictures in a small viewer, pointing out that we cannot see what is in the picture so they must describe it fully.

Procedures that elicit speech acts of various kinds would be enormously helpful for studies of the emergence of different functions in children's speech. Snyder (1978) and Dale (1980) attempted to elicit declaratives and imperatives from 1–2-year-olds. For example, to elicit an imperative, the child would be given part of a desirable toy, say a xylophone, and the experimenter would then hold up another essential part, such as the mallet. To elicit naming, a novel object would be introduced into a repetitive situation; for instance, after the child had been given a series of identical blocks to put into a bucket he or she would be offered a baby's bottle. In Dale's study, the tasks designed to produce imperatives were generally more successful in revealing developmental trends than the declarative tasks, but both functions could be reliably scored. A set of structured tasks of this kind would enable researchers to refine their criteria for scoring speech acts, and also make possible the testing of quite heterogeneous populations in similar controlled situations. However, this work has only begun, and it remains to be seen how wide a range of functions can be reliably elicited.

Imitation

Elicited imitation as a technique for child language research has its proponents and its critics. The procedure could be used to increase the frequency of rare responses from the child, particularly in the areas of phonology and syntax. The debate arises over whether the responses elicited are a true reflection of the child's spontaneous speech. Templin (1957) found no apparent differences in her subjects' pronunciation between imitation and naming tasks, but she only tested a few examples of each sound. Subsequent work (Ingram, 1976b) has sometimes found imitated words to be in advance of the child's spontaneous pronunciation.

In the area of syntax, Slobin and Welsh (1973) claimed that children filter the sentences to be imitated through their own grammar; hence elicited imitation could be very useful in mapping out the limits of the child's knowledge. However, Bloom and Lahey (1978) argue that short-term memory is the major variable at work, and some children can mimic complex sentences that are not in their productive capacity, whereas others will not perform to their usual standards. If imitation tasks are regarded as memory tasks, then the experimenter must control for these variables known to influence short-term memory. As Tager-Flusberg et al. (in press) point out, redundancy and sentence length covary with many interesting linguistic phenomena, so the results of imitation tasks are not readily interpretable in terms of the *linguistic* complexity of the sentences.

Finally, Bloom (1974) demonstrated that the lack of nonlinguistic context in imitation tasks is a problem; children's grammatical knowledge can be underestimated when they are speaking with no contextual support. In a demonstration of this Bloom gave a child sentences to imitate that he had produced earlier in his spontaneous speech in context, and in the imitation task he could not produce them accurately. To some extent this problem can be alleviated by providing pictures along with the sentences, and introducing a short delay before the child has to repeat them. Picture-cued delayed imitation may have advantages over the standard techniques of elicited production in the control that can be exercised over what the child produces (e.g., Gaer, 1969).

Perception

The area of infant speech perception is a very active, relatively new field of research made possible by the development of novel methodological paradigms. There are three general procedures in use at this time. Two involve measurement of habituation/dishabituation, and the third is an instrumental conditioning paradigm.

The two habituation procedures have the following aspect in common: A syllable of natural or synthesized speech is presented to the infant over and over until the child satiates or habituates to the sound. The experimental group is then presented with a new syllable differing in some minimal way from the old one, say in the voice-onset-time of its initial consonant. The control group receives no change in the stimulus. If the experimental group shows recovery or dishabituation of behavior related to the speech sound, while the controls do not, perception of the difference in speech sounds is inferred.

In the high-amplitude sucking paradigm (HAS), the infant sucks at a pressure-sensitive nipple in order to hear the syllable, and an increase in the rate of sucking when the syllable is changed is used as the index of discrimination (Eimas, Siqueland, Jusczyk, & Vigorito, 1971). In the alternative procedure the infant's deceleration of heart rate (HR), a component of the orienting response, is the variable of interest (Morse, 1978). The HAS procedure has been used successfully with infants only 48 hours old (Butterfield & Cairns, 1974), but it is most appropriate for infants aged 1–4 months. After 6 months of age, infants show less interest in nonnutritive sucking. The HR procedure has a wide age range of application, although it requires a modification in the rate of syllable presentation when used with very young infants (Morse, 1978).

The infant's state of arousal is a critical factor for both types of test (Williams & Golenski, 1979), and a rather high percentge of subjects have to be excluded from the studies because they fall asleep or cry. Another disadvantage is that data on individual children are scanty, and intergroup comparisons must be made to reveal the presence of discrimination. Finally, a failure to observe dishabituation is difficult to interpret, since it can occur for many reasons other than a failure to hear the difference in sound.

The third paradigm has the advantage that a much larger amount of individual data can be collected, even across several sessions (Eilers, Wilson, & Moore, 1979; Eilers, Gavin, & Wilson, 1979). The infant sits on his or her mother's lap or in a baby chair and listens to a speech syllable. An obvious change in the speech sound is a signal for the child to turn the head to one side, where the activation of an attractive toy reinforces the behavior. Once this response is established, the researcher can introduce more subtle changes in the stimulus syllable, interspersed with trials in which there is no change. This visually reinforced infant speech discrimination procedure (VRISD) promises to increase the information available about speech sound perception in infants aged 4–12 months, although care must be taken to ensure double-blind testing, in which neither the mother nor the experimenter knows which kind of trial is being presented to the infant (Aslin & Pisoni, 1980).

Comprehension

The infant speech perception procedures tell us only that young children can perceive a difference in sound, not that they can respond to that difference in some linguistically relevant manner. For instance, the child still has to learn which of these sound differences carries differences in meaning in his or her native language. Research conducted with 1–3-year-old children suggests that this development may be quite extended in time. (Edwards, 1974; Garnica, 1973; Svachkin, 1973). A typical procedure from the studies employs an object identification task, in which a pair of distinctive objects are given nonsense syllable names that differ by a single phonological feature, say *pok* versus *bok*. The child can be asked to do things with the objects such as "Put the hat on *pok*" or "Give *bok* a ride on the truck." Ten to twelve different tests are usually given for a particular distinctive feature contrast such as voiced–unvoiced, so that an individual child's ability to associate a speech sound contrast with a difference in reference can be assessed.

Object identification tasks are also used extensively in the assessment of semantic development. The child is asked to pick out one of a set of pictures or objects in an array to assess his comprehension of a noun or adjective, or the task can be transformed into a hide-and-seek game in which the location of a candy or small toy is indicated in terms of the meaning contrasts being investigated (e.g., "The M&M is over *here*" versus "The M&M is over *there*"; Clark & Sengul, 1978; deVilliers & deVilliers, 1974; Wales,

1979). Alternatively, the child can be asked to perform some action on the array, such as "Put the block *in/on/under* the box" (Clark 1973b; Wilcox & Palermo, 1974) or "Make it so there is *more/less* water in this glass" (Carey & Potter, 1977; Palermo, 1974).

In testing comprehension of syntactic structures, the two major methods are *picture-cued comprehension* and *act-out comprehension*. The former involves asking the child to pick out the picture in an array which corresponds to the sentence spoken by the experimenter (or presented on a tape recording). There are two considerations that influence the usefulness of this task. First, young children are not very good at scanning and extracting information from an array of pictures (Kennedy, 1970), so the number of pictures in the array has to be quite small, say four or fewer. Unfortunately the alternatives depicted are then restricted, and they might not include the particular interpretation the child gives to the sentence. If the alternatives are too implausible, the child could also guess at the correct interpretation without really understanding the grammatical construction.

Act-out comprehension avoids these problems, as the child is free to act out practically anything with dolls or toy animals. Typically, the researcher provides the child with the appropriately limited set of toys and ascertains beforehand that the child knows their names, because the focus of interest is on whether the child can figure out the syntactic relationship between the objects in a sentence such as "The cat that kicked the dog licked the mouse" (deVilliers, Tager-Flusberg, Hakuta, & Cohen, 1979). The drawbacks of the task include the distractible quality of manipulable toys for small children, and the limited set of verbs that can be used in the task. Generally the sentences have to contain action verbs, and unambiguous ones at that, since verbs like *belong to* or *imagine* or *like* cannot readily be acted out; yet this may give a biased picture of how productive the syntactic rule is across a variety of verb types (see Maratsos, Kuczaj, Fox, & Chalkley, 1979). Nonetheless, act-out comprehension is an enjoyable procedure for small children and it has provided valuable information about how they process rather complex sentences.

Results from comprehension tests of semantic and syntactic development are rendered awkward to interpret because children adopt response strategies that mask their understanding of the linguistic stimuli. Discussion of this issue is pervasive in the literature (see Richards, 1979; Wannemacher & Ryan, 1978), but we will select a couple of examples to highlight the problem, one from semantic and one from syntactic development. Clark (1973a) predicted that in the acquisition of word meaning, children would only gradually acquire all of the semantic features necessary for understanding the full meaning of the terms; that is, their lexical entries would be incomplete. The particular prediction that concerns us here involved polar opposites: Clark argued that the last feature learned for opposite relational terms would be their appropriate polarity, so the child should go through a stage in which he or she confused *big* and *little, tall* and *short,* and so on. Furthermore, Clark predicted that children would understand the positive or unmarked term of a pair first: so *big* before *little,* and *more* before *less.* If this was so, children at this stage would be expected to regard *little* as a synonym for *big, short* as a synonym for *tall,* and *less* as a synonym for *more.* In fact when 3-year-olds are given a glass of water and a jug and told "make it so the glass has less to drink in it," they often pour more in instead (Palermo, 1973, 1974). However, this may be an artifact of the testing situation and nonlinguistic response biases the child brings to it, rather than reflecting the child's knowledge of the meaning of *less.* Carey and Potter (1977) essentially repeated Palermo's experiments, but on some trials they substituted a nonsense syllable for *less,* hence: "make it so that the glass has *tiv* to drink in it." The order of *tiv, more,* and *less* trials were random across subjects. Almost all of the children who added water upon hearing *less* also added water for *tiv.* Since it is hardly possible that the children had any lexical entry for *tiv,* their apparent confusion with *more* and *less* in this task probably stems from an existing tendency to pour water into rather than out of glasses. The tendency may even be a more general one that involves adding rather than subtracting when manipulating quantities (Carey & Potter, 1977; Wilcox & Palermo, 1977). The choice of stimulus objects and what the child is asked to do with them thus influences the results of comprehension tests of this sort, and it is essential that the experimenter take into account the a priori probabilities of the response options (Richards, 1979; Wilcox & Palermo, 1974).

Other research has demonstrated that the number of dimensions along which the test stimuli vary (Brewer & Stone, 1975), and the number of response options available to the child (Wannemacher & Ryan, 1978) can determine the pattern of results. It is an unfortunate truth that different tasks can elicit different response strategies from children, so they frequently give inconsistent responses across a range of tasks testing the same semantic contrast (Carey, 1978; Wannemacher & Ryan, 1978). The research into semantic development has to take into account the contribution of nonlinguistic strategies as well as the generalizability of the child's knowledge of a word to other materials and tasks.

In fact, though, the interpretation of these comprehension results depends quite heavily on the investigator's view of semantics. Some researchers regard response biases and task differences as confounding factors in the study of "dictionary" knowledge the child possesses: knowledge of synonymy, ambiguity, antonymy, and hierarchical relationships between words, regarded by some linguists as being the proper domain of semantic theory (Katz, 1972; Lyons, 1977). Others (e.g., Whitehurst, 1979) define meaning more functionally, in terms of the way words are used and responded to. For them, any strategies adopted by the child to understand words and how they are being used by the speaker constitute an essential part of semantic development. Perhaps the most appropriate position holds that semantic development is a combination of learning both abstract lexical information and strategies for communicating and understanding (e.g., E. Clark, 1978a, 1979).

Analogous considerations arise for comprehension tests of syntax. For instance, on hearing a passive sentence a young child might respond on the basis of the likely relationship between the two nouns rather than on their structural relationship. Irreversible passives such as "The banana was eaten by the monkey" will be readily understood (Bever, 1970; Chapman, 1978; Strohner & Nelson, 1976), as will semantically biased ones, such as "The girl was scratched by the cat." However, if the sentence portrays a relatively unlikely event, such as "The car was bumped by the man," the child will act out its reverse.

In contrast to this "probable-event strategy," other children might respond on the basis of the more usual active sentence word order, that the first noun mentioned is the agent of the action. Then reversible passives will be systematically misinterpreted.

Strategies are identified when a consistent pattern of errors emerges, but it is important that individual data be analyzed, not group data, which can obscure the range of strategies used by the children (Bridges, 1980). Once again, it becomes difficult to assess the importance of comprehension strategies vis-à-vis grammatical development: Should they be regarded as confounding factors in performance that obscure the real knowledge children have at this stage, or as an important stage in the mastery of complex sentence structures? It is possible that strategies should be divided into two types: *nonlinguistic response strategies* that have nothing to do with the sentences but arise from the testing situation, and *comprehension strategies* that are much more dependent on the sentences' structure and content (Chapman, 1978). Further work is needed to clarify whether the responses children give on these tasks relate in any way to other measures of their grammatical knowledge (e.g., deVilliers and deVilliers, 1974).

Metalinguistic Awareness

A number of tasks have been developed to get at children's awareness of words, both as arbitrary symbols that need not bear any inherent relation to the objects or events for which they stand, and as the components of sentences. For instance, several studies have asked children quite directly for their definition of what a word is (Papandropolou & Sinclair, 1974; Piaget, 1928; Vygotsky, 1962), following this up with further questions to explore the limits of the child's awareness: "Is *big* a word?" "Is *the* a word?", and so on. Berthoud-Papandropolou (1978) used several additional tasks with the same group of children, including asking the child to provide words having different properties that could be true of either the word or its referent—a *short* word or a *hard* word, for example. The youngest children, preschoolers, tended to confuse words and their referents, so gave as a long word an example like *train.* Some 6-year-olds demonstrated an interesting vacillation between properties of the object and the word, one of them giving *newspaper* as a long word "because there is a lot of written stuff." In another task, the children were asked to count the number of words in sentences produced by the experimenter, and then to specify what they were.

There are also a wide variety of tasks to tap children's awareness of the component sounds in words. For example, Bruce (1964) asked children questions such as: "Take the word *pink.* Now take off the *p* sound. What word is left over?" Zhurova (1973) set up a game in which the child had to say the first sound in a toy animal's name in order for the animal to be allowed past a toy sentry on a bridge. Liberman (1973) required his subjects to tap on a table to indicate the number of speech sounds in a word. Surprisingly few preschoolers can perform these tasks, despite years of sound play (Weir, 1962). Read (1978) and Lundberg (1978) stress the relationship between the awareness of speech sound segments and readiness to read.

A somewhat different task designed to explore 5-year-olds' judgments of the similarity between speech sounds was developed by Read (1978). He introduced a puppet called Ed and told the children that Ed liked to find words that sounded like his name; words like *fled, bed,* and *head.* Then the children were given a number of choices, such as "Would Ed like food or fed?" Finally, this was extended to vowels that were not the same as the one in the puppet's name, as in "Would Ed like *aired* or *aid?*" The technique can easily be extended to other classes of speech sounds besides vowels, and it seems to be a valuable one for exploring preschoolers' awareness of phoneme similarities.

Other work has concentrated more on the child's awareness of word meaning; for instance, the hierarchical relationships among words like *living thing, plant, flower, rose,* and so on (Anglin, 1978). Werner and Kaplan (1952) asked children to formulate a definition of a new word after it had been introduced to them in a set of sentences, to see what information could be gleaned from verbal context alone. Their task used rather abstract words and demanded an explicit definition, but with suitable modifications the task could be used with preschoolers to examine their awareness of the meaning relations between the words in a sentence.

Children's intuitions of grammar take on additional interest because of the role ascribed to adult's intuitions in modern generative grammars. The first successful attempt to elicit 2-year-olds' judgments of well-formedness was by Glietman, Glietman, and Shipley (1972). The experimenter said simple imperative sentences that were either correct or reversed, and the mother at first modeled the role of judge, saying "good" or "silly" to each sentence, repeating the good ones and correcting the silly ones. DeVilliers and deVilliers (1972, 1974) used puppets to play the roles of speaker and judge, and asked the child to take over the "teacher" puppet after a few sentences had been modeled. Although the primary motivation for studies of this kind was to decide among competing grammars of spontaneous speech, children's ability to make judgments of grammar seems to lag behind their performance in speaking and understanding (deVilliers & deVilliers, 1974). However, elicted judgments have provided useful information about more advanced rule systems, such as the acceptability of overgeneralized past tense endings (Kuczaj, 1978).

One problem that remains unsolved is how to communicate to the child the basis for making such judgments. Gleitman and co-workers used the words *good* and *silly,* but these may cue the child to the meaning rather than the structure of the sentence; deVilliers and deVilliers selected *right* and *wrong,* but these words carry moral connotations. Perhaps the most important data from which to infer the basis for the child's judgments come from the corrections they make of the incorrect sentences. But Scholl and Ryan (1975) point out that this introduces an element of differential punishment for judging a sentence to be wrong. In their own experiment, Scholl and Ryan asked children to point either to a photograph of a woman or to one of a 3-year-old girl, depending on whom they thought "the talk belonged to." The stimulus sentences were either syntactically primitive or correct, and the 5–7-year-old subjects tended to ascribe the more primitive ones to the 3-year-old girl. Unfortunately this task requires the child to have some intuitions not only of acceptability, but also of the way adults and children differ in their speech. It therefore does not seem possible to use it with young children.

The syntactic judgments of still older children have not been fully explored, although the suggestion has been made that they are capable of giving reasoned arguments about grammar (Gleitman *et al.,* 1972). Studies of middle childhood might answer some of the difficult questions about the transition to adult-like grammar, as well as providing interesting information about the development of metalinguistic skills in their own right (e.g., Moore, 1975).

Finally, Clark (1978b) has suggested the use of children's corrections of speech errors, either spontaneous corrections of their own or elicited corrections of errors produced by the experimenter, as a source of evidence for their awareness of speech sounds, syntax, and word meanings. This is potentially a rich source of information, but it remains to be established whether these are frequent enough in the spontaneous speech of the child or can be elicited reliably enough to enable meaningful analysis.

Studies of the Context and Processes of Acquisition

Over the past 10 years there has been increased interest in environmental variables that may contribute to language development, particularly the language input to the child and the context of social interaction in which he or she learns to speak. Originally the mother's speech was transcribed primarily because it made the child's utterances easier to understand, but now the dialogue between adult and child is considered of paramount significance. The kinds of analysis take several forms.

The Linguistic Input. Most of the earliest studies looked at mother's speech to children in the same way as children's spontaneous speech had been analyzed. They measured such things as mean utterance length, syntactic complexity, and well-formedness, and the frequency of repetitions, expansions, imperatives, and questions in transcripts of mothers speaking to other adults or to their children. When compared to speech between adults, mother-to-child speech was demonstrated to be much simpler, more grammatical and repetitious, and confined to topics in the here and now—an input apparently more tailored to the child's language learning task than had been believed (Broen, 1972; Brown, & Bellugi, 1964; Brown, et al., 1969; Phillips, 1973; Snow, 1972; see Snow, 1977, for a review). Several researchers then correlated these general features of the mother's speech with the child's age or various measures of his or her language production or comprehension in an attempt to discover what factors determine parent's modification of their speech and how such modifications might affect the child's rate and pattern of language acquisition (Cross, 1978; Newport, 1976; Newport, Gleitman, & Gleitman, 1977; Phillips, 1973). However, the interpretation of correlations between relatively gross measures of language production is problematic (Brown, 1977; deVilliers & deVilliers, 1979b; Newport et al., 1977), and recent studies have turned to more specific measures of the form and function of the speech of parent and child. Some investigators have concentrated on the frequency of particular constructions in the speech of parents to their children at different ages (e.g., indirect questions: Bellinger, 1979), others on the way parental usage of forms changes over time relative to the child's use of the same forms (e.g., semantic relations: van der Geest, 1977; coordinated sentences: deVilliers, Tager-Flusberg, & Hakuta, 1977; wh- questions: Savic, 1975). For example, van der Geest (1977) reported that mothers began using particular semantic relations frequently in speaking to their children only after the children first referred to that relationship in their own speech. The frequency of usage in parental speech peaked just before the child began using that relationship with any substantial frequency. DeVilliers and deVilliers (1979a) analyzed both the form and function of negative sentences in longitudinal spontaneous speech samples from three children and their parents. Differences between the parents in use of initial-*no* or *don't*-imperative forms that served the function of rejection of an ongoing or pending course of action were later mirrored in differences between the children, suggesting a strong influence of parental speech on the pattern of acquisition of negative forms and functions by their children. Shatz (1979), however, found that parents employed a wide range of form–function mappings in questions to their children, although she did not study the children's use of these forms. To summarize, a great deal has been learned about the nature and determinants of the language input to children at different points in development (see Snow, 1977, 1979, for reviews) but the role of this input in enhancing or promoting language growth has not been clearly demonstrated. Some evidence suggests that the extent to which parental utterances are semantically related to preceding child utterances is predictive of rapid early development (Cross, 1978). Studies of hearing children with deaf parents indicate that some minimal exposure to verbal interactions with speakers and perhaps some degree of simplification of the speech the child hears are necessary for normal acquisition (Bard & Sachs, 1977). But there have been too few fine-grained analyses relating parental usage of forms for various communicative functions to their children's mastery of those functions, and too few cross-linguistic and cross-cultural studies (but see Blount, 1977; Harkness, 1977; Snow, Arlman–Rupp, Hassing, Jobse, Joosten, & Vorster, 1976). Furthermore, most studies of the linguistic input to the child, especially after age 2 have concentrated on syntactic and semantic aspects of parental speech rather than pragmatic or conversational aspects (but see below; Berko, Gleason, & Weintraub, 1978; Shugar, 1978).

Early Verbal and Social Interaction. Microscopic analysis of videotaped interactions between mother and child in different settings has demonstrated the support the adult provides for the child's earliest attempts at communication. Bruner and his co-workers (Bruner, 1977, 1978; Ninio & Bruner, 1978), for instance, have documented the kinds of interactions in which the parent elicits a verbal response from the child, expands on it, and provides feedback, thus creating a richly structured dialogue around the minimal repetoire of the 1–2-year-old child (see also Messer, 1978, 1980). While the examples given by Bruner are rich and convincing, it is another matter to demonstrate that these patterns are necessary for language acquisition to occur, given the wide cultural variation in childrearing even in the United States, and here too there is a great need for cross-cultural work (see Schieffelin, in press). Some features of maternal behavior, such as the increased use of gesture in accompaniment to speech to infants and toddlers, have been held to provide assistance to the language-learning child, but largely on intuitive grounds. Shatz (in press) examined the relation of maternal gestures to various aspects of language and found it to be rather complex, so that the child could not easily use gesture as a clue to, say, the sentence mood or underlying semantic relations. At the pragmatic level of analysis, although there was not a great deal of consistency across the mothers Shatz studied, there were some regular relations between the patterns of gesturing and the focus of conversation—in particular, whether the utterance was related to action or reference. However, the children did not respond significantly better to utterances accompanied by gesture than to other utterances serving the same communicative function. It should be noted that the children in Shatz's study were rather older (19–34 months) than those observed by Bruner, and there may be age differences in the importance of gestures. Nevertheless, Shatz's research illustrates how intuitions about the utility of some frequent adult behavior for language acquisition may not be borne out by more fine-grained analyses of how the nonlinguistic and linguistic systems interrelate in conversations and how the child responds to them.

Processes. Several analyses of spontaneous speech between mother and child have tried to isolate occasions for learning that fit principles or processes from established learning theories. For example, researchers have looked at children's spontaneous imitations of the speech addressed to them, examining how frequently such imitations take place, what was imitated, and whether the child's imitations were in advance of his or her own spontaneous speech, to see if imitation might facilitate the child's acquisition of those forms (e.g., Bloom, Hood, & Lightbown, 1974; Ervin-Tripp, 1964; Folger & Chapman, 1978; Leonard, Schwartz, Folger, Newhoff, & Wilcox, 1979; Ramer, 1976). A primary methodological issue in these studies is the definition of what is to constitute an imitative utterance. The criteria used by most researchers have been particularly conservative, confining analysis to utterances that immediately follow the adult utterance without any intervening speech on the part of the child, that are structurally (in the case of syntactic imitation) or phonologically (in the case of lexical imitation) recognizable as a copy of the preceding adult utterance, and do not have any material (lexical or syntactic) added that was not in the adult sentence. But these criteria may be too restrictive to capture the full influence of the form of a parental utterance on the subsequent speech of the child. Whitehurst and Vasta (1975) have argued for a much broader definition of imitation, suggesting that cases in which the child uses the passive construction to describe events after hearing it modeled by an adult should also be considered cases of imitation. In this sense a child who asks a lot of questions because his parents do would also be considered to be imitating their speech even though the child's questions might not be about the same things or have exactly the same grammatical form as the parents' questions. The danger is that too broad a definition of imitation may come to include almost any case in which the child seems to have learned something from the adult utterance so that "imitated" becomes almost synonymous with "learned." Our everyday concept of imitation does seem to include more than just immediate copying of an utterance, but it also requires a certain degree of restriction to the form or content of the utterance on which it is based. The crucial methodological point is that studies should clearly define the criteria employed for identifying cases of imitation and confine interpretation of their results to that sense of imitation.

Other attempts to determine influences on the child's progress in language have involved tracing the adult responses contingent upon certain child utterances. For instance, Brown and Hanlon (1970) divided their subjects' utterances into grammatical and ungrammatical, and looked to see whether they were differentiated by the adults' responses. Did the mother correct ungrammatical forms, or only approve grammatical utterances? Was the mother more likely to understand grammatical utterances? Analyses that look at a particular construction type in this way can also be done. In principle such analyses are simple; in practice they are much more difficult. Identifying nonsequiturs, for example, presumes that the researcher knows what the child intends by an utterance even when the parent apparently does not, and this may be an infrequent state of affairs.

Some researchers have tried to identify interactions in which the adult seems to teach the child a construction or form by explicit modeling or repetition and expansion (e.g., Moerk, 1980). But it has proven difficult to establish from the analysis of spontaneous speech that these interactions really do facilitate acquisition. For every case in which the child seems to pick up the correct use of a phrase or expression from the immediate parental input, there are as many in which the frequency of parental modeling of a form or their responses to the child's use of that form seem to have no effect on the child's speech (Pinker, in press). A good illustration of the difficulty in establishing the effectiveness of what appears on intuitive ground to be an important learning opportunity for the child is the case of parents' expansions of their children's telegraphic utterances. Brown and Bellugi (1964) first drew researchers' attention to the prevalance of this response in mothers' speech. For example, a child who says "Truck fall" might hear the response "Oh dear, the truck fell over." These expansions supply missing grammatical features while keeping the content constant, and, since they follow closely after the child's own attempt to comment on the situation, they would seem to provide an ideal learning experience. Brown *et al.* (1969) noted that expansions were frequent in the responses of the mothers of two of the three children they studied—some 30% of the children's utterances were expanded by the mothers. Those children also showed the most rapid language development. Expansions were much less frequent in the speech of the third mother, and her child was the slowest in acquiring language. But Brown *et al.* point out that besides the problems of generalizing from three children, this relationship could have been confounded by many factors. The third mother also talked less in general in the recorded play sessions, and it was not clear to what extent expansions by the other two mothers represented attempts to clarify the children's utterances for the observers rather than being natural aspects of their verbal interaction with their children. Subsequent studies of mothers' speech to their children have reported widely varying frequencies of expansion, and few have found any substantial correlations between frequency of expansions in mothers' speech and rate of language development in the child (e.g., Newport, 1976). It is not even clear that a consistent correlation should be expected, since it is plausible that the relationship between the frequency of expansions and the child's language development would be a curvilinear one, first increasing in frequency as the child is able to make telegraphic comments about a situation and then decreasing in frequency as the child produces more complete utterances.

Training Studies. The problems with identifying and establishing the effectiveness of particular learning processes in spontaneous interactions between parent and child make it preferable to undertake experimental studies that directly manipulate a particular kind of input or feedback to the child. One of the earliest of these studies was by Cazden (1965), who attempted to modify the rate of language acquisition in a group of preschool children by providing immediate expansion by an adult of all of their utterances during a 40-minute period each day. One control group (the modeling group) received an equal amount of speech in response to their utterances but not in the form of direct syntactic expansions; a second control group received no special attention but did play with the adult researchers and the same materials. There were four children in each group, and the groups were matched on a variety of measures such as initial language level, age, and talkativeness. The children received this treatment every school day for a period of 3 months, but postintervention measures of language development were generally not significantly different across the three groups. The trend in overall growth was modeling best, then expansion, and then the no-treatment group.

Several reasons could be given for the failure of expansions to enhance acquisition in this study. First, the richness and variety of linguistic responses to children's utterances may be a more important determinant of rate of acquisition, and Cazden's modeling group received a syntactically more varied and semantically richer input from the adult researcher than the expansion group. Second, one function of adult expansion is to confirm for the child the relationship between his or her utterance and the context. But expansion of every utterance by the adult may have led to the loss of their effectiveness, and the children may have stopped listening to the adult after a while.

Nelson, Carskaddon, and Bonvillian (1973) supported this interpretation of Cazden's results. In their study the adults not only expanded the children's incomplete utterances, but also recast complete utterances into different syntactic forms while retaining the same semantic content. So, for example, a child saying "I see a doggie" might hear in response, "Oh, you see a dog, do you?" or "What is the doggie doing?" The adult thus provides the child with alternative, varied, syntactic means of encoding the situation rather than just completing the encoding the child had attempted. The recast sentence group later performed better on a sentence imitation task and produced more complex predicate forms than a control group that heard new sentences modeled by the adult but did not have their own sentences recast.

Several studies have demonstrated the efficacy of modeling or modeling plus imitation as a means of modifying the child's use of sentence forms (see Whitehurst & Vasta, 1975; Brown, 1979, for reviews). For example, Whitehurst *et al.* (1974) modeled passive sentences for young children who did not use them productively, and the children were subsequently able to produce novel passive forms in response to pictured events. The children exposed to modeled passive sentences also comprehended them better in a later act-out test than children who had only been exposed to active sentences. In this study the modeled sentences described pictured actions. A subsequent experiment by Brown (1976) demonstrated that the greatest improvement in comprehension of passive forms is achieved if the modeled passive sentences are embedded in an acted-out story in which they make pragmatic sense. These and other experiments show that intensive exposure to a construction in an experimental situation facilitates productive use and improves comprehension of that construction in similar situations. But the limits of these training procedures with respect to generalization to new situations, different lexical items, and different semantic relations are still being mapped out (see J. G. deVilliers, 1980).

There are three general designs for training studies of this sort. The simplest is to take a single pretested group of children, give them some intensive exposure or treatment, and then look for improvement on posttest language measures. The assumption is that time alone, multiple testing, or simply increased attention from the adult, will not effect a change by itself. To control for these factors, a stronger design uses two (or more) groups matched on age and pretest language measures, only one of which is given the training procedure being investigated. Interpretation of any subsequent differences between the groups in language production or comprehension depends crucially on the initial matching of the groups on tests of general intelligence and linguistic ability, frequently an issue if there are only a few children in each group, and on the number of variables that distinguish the treatment given the experimental group(s) from that given the control group(s). For example, general factors like the sheer amount of attention or language input from the adult need to be controlled for if the effects of a specific type of intervention are to be determined. One control for this is to look for selective facilitation of the language development of the experimental group relative to the control group (e.g., significant differences in specific syntactic aspects, but no difference in general measures of language development like mean length of utterance (Nelson *et al.,* 1973); or better comprehension of passive sentences but not of active forms (Whitehurst *et al.,* 1974)).

A still more sophisticated control is to use a multiple baseline design. In this procedure two groups might be matched on their initial level of mastery of a range of syntactic structures. One group would then be exposed to some form of training on one type of syntactic feature, the other group to the same type of training on a different syntactic feature. In the language posttest the investigator would look for differential improvement between the groups on the two aspects of syntax in order to determine the efficacy of the intervention. Nelson (1977) used this design to demonstrate the effectiveness of contingent recasting–expansion of children's utterances. Children who on a pretest showed no productive use of either complex questions or verb forms like the future tense or multiple-verb sentences were divided into two groups. For one group the experimenter recast many of their utterances in the form of complex questions like tags and negative questions; for the other the recastings took the form of complex verbs. At the end of the treatment period, the first group showed usage of complex questions in their spontaneous speech but still very few complex verb forms; the second group used significantly more complex verbs but almost no complex questions. The groups showed the same amount of gain in general measures like MLU and mean number of elements per noun phrase.

While such studies may establish the effectiveness of particular training procedures in enhancing acquisition, sometimes with important implications for therapy programs with language-delayed children, it is an extra step to establish that these processes actually play any substantial role in the natural language acquisition of the normal child. They therefore need to be supplemented with analyses of the range of situations in which children learn language. Thus, for example, recastings contingent on children's utterances are infrequent in the speech of some mothers to their children. So, although this form of language input may be effective in facilitating syntactic development when it is highlighted in training procedures, it does not appear to be essential for normal language acquisition.

A different kind of training study is concerned not so much with the effects of certain variables on the rate or pattern of language acquisition, but with how children generalize or spontaneously use a new word or grammatical form when it has been introduced to them in a natural interaction setting. Carey (1978) introduced a new color term to nursery school children and then followed their use and generalization of the term to new exemplars as well as their subsequent comprehension of the word when it was used by adults. The method comes close to the study of spontaneous word use in diaries, except that the researcher has control over the conditions of first exposure to the form and can follow it more carefully. One can also study precisely how much information is conveyed by limited exposure to new terms in varying circumstances, but research along these lines is only just beginning (see Mervis, 1976, for a study of the effects of exemplar prototypicality on the learning of a new lexical item). Leonard *et al.* (1979) used this new-word training technique to investigate the conditions under which young children imitate lexical items and whether such imitations facilitate later spontaneous use by the child.

Artificial Grammars. Training artificial languages is yet another technique for investigating the nature of language acquisition. The aim of this approach is generally to design the language to have some particular property and then to see how hard or easy it is for children to learn it. The particular study might focus on the nature of the language's rule system and the way it is learned and generalized (e.g., J. G. deVilliers, 1980), or look at the success of different training procedures (e.g., appropriate referential context versus no referential context: Moeser & Bregman, 1972). Good reviews and critiques of miniature artificial-language research are provided in Moeser (1977) and Schlesinger (1977). Although little research of this type has been done with children since Braine's (1963b) work demonstrating the learnability of pivot grammars by 4-year-olds, it is likely that current interest in the process of rule learning and generalization will lead to renewed use of the method. The possible problems with such research are easy to state: (*a*) If the new rule or rules resemble the rules already in their language, children may simply respond by analogy to what they already know; (*b*) If the new rule is particularly alien to their own grammar, the children may fail to see it as a linguistic task and treat it as a problem-solving game, not using their usual language acquisition strategies. Clearly there is no way to decide these issues in advance of collecting sufficient empirical data with these procedures and seeing how the results might or might not illuminate key issues in natural language acquisition.

CONCLUSIONS

In the preceding discussions there are a number of recurring issues that deserve mention in a concluding summary. Perhaps the single most important issue concerns the competence–performance distinction, namely the problem of drawing conclusions about the child's knowledge from his or her performance on some task. The problem has taken several manifestations in present research, among them the following:

1. How is it possible to decide, from among competing descriptions of the child's categories or rules, which level is psychologically real for the child? The question has received most attention in discussions of early semantic relations in child speech, but precisely parallel concerns arise in deciding among pragmatic or functional descriptions, and in settling on the right level of analysis in phonology. While this is a troublesome question for adult linguistics, it is even more so for child language where the range of tasks is severely restricted.
2. What is the relation between response strategies and true linguistic knowledge? This problem was especially evident in research on word meaning development, but also arose in research on the comprehension of complex sentences. It becomes necessary to decide whether a dividing line between performance strategies and abstract knowledge can really be defended and, if so, where it should be drawn.

3. The differential demands of particular experimental tasks can cause wide variability in performance: Which should be taken as the true index of the child knowledge? At one extreme, it may be possible to strip a task to the minimum and thereby demonstrate that a child can attend to some linguistic dimension at a very early age. However, the validity of the task as part of the language can then be called into question, especially if the child does not show the ability in natural circumstances. Perhaps the best solution to this recurring problem is for researchers to utilize diverse methodology in attacking any problem area, and to allow the task results to complement one another. By comparing results across tasks it is then possible to highlight constraints or strategies made available by any single task. The hope is that the child's knowledge can be pieced together like a jigsaw puzzle from this evidence.

A second major issue that arises again and again is that of individual differences in normal development. Until recently the concern has been with universals of language acquisition, and typically a very small, homogeneous population of children has been studied in depth. It is now becoming imperative that we know the range of variation among normally developing children, not only to broaden our perspective on the process of acquisition and the variety of routes to adult competence, but also for clinical comparison and assessment.

While not strictly methodological issues, these problems are basic to the interpretation of the data that are obtained via the wide range of methods we have described. Advances in our understanding of language acquisition depend on their resolution as well as on the refinement of techniques and strategies of study.

REFERENCES

Anglin, J. M. *Word, object and conceptual development.* New York: Norton, 1977.

Anglin, J. M. From reference to meaning. *Child Development,* 1978, *69,* 969–976.

Antinucci, F., & Volterra, V. Lo sviluppo della negazione nel linguaggio infantile: Uno studio pragmatico. In *Studi per un modello del linguaggio: Quaderni della ricerca scientifica,* Rome, 1973.

Aslin, R. N., & Pisoni, D. B. Effects of early linguistic experience on speech discrimination by infants: A critique of Eilers, Gavin, and Wilson (1979). *Child Development,* 1980, *51,* 107–112.

Bard, B., & Sachs, J. *Language acquisition patterns in two normal children of deaf parents.* Paper presented to the second annual Boston University Conference on Language Acquisition, October 1977.

Barrett, M. D. Lexical development and overextension in child language. *Journal of Child Language,* 1978, *5,* 205–219.

Bartlett, E. *Acquisition of the meaning of color terms.* Paper presented to the Biennial Conference of the Society for Research in Child Development, New Orleans, 1977.

Bates, E. *Language and context.* New York: Academic Press, 1976.

Bates, E., Benigni, L., Bretherton, I., Camaioni, L., & Volterra, V. From gesture to first word: On cognitive and social prerequisites. In M. Lewis & L. Rosenblum (Eds.), *Interaction, conversation, and the development of language.* New York: Wiley, 1977.

Bates, E., Benigni, L., Bretherton, I., Camaioni, L., & Volterra, V. *The emergence of symbols: Communication and cognition in infancy.* New York: Academic Press, 1979.

Bellinger, D. Changes in the explicitness of mothers' directives as children age. *Journal of Child Language,* 1979, *6,* 443–458.

Bellugi, U. *The acquisition of negation.* Unpublished doctoral dissertation, Harvard University, 1967.

Berko, J. The child's learning of English morphology. *Word,* 1958, *14,* 150–177.

Berko Gleason, J., & Weintraub, S. Infant language and the acquisition of communicative competence. In K. E. Nelson (Ed.), *Children's language* (Vol. 1). New York: Gardner Press, 1978.

Berthoud-Papandropolou, I. An experimental study of children's ideas about language. In A. Sinclair, R. J. Jarvella, & W. J. M. Levelt (Eds.), *The child's conception of language.* New York: Springer-Verlag, 1978.

Bever, T. G. The cognitive basis for linguistic structure. In J. R. Hayes (Ed.), *Cognition and the development of language.* New York: Wiley, 1970.

Bierwisch, M. Semantics. In J. Lyons (Ed.), *New horizons in linguistics.* Baltimore: Penguin Books, 1970.

Bloom, L. M. *Language development: Form and function in emerging grammars.* Cambridge, Mass.: MIT Press, 1970.

Bloom, L. *One word at a time: The use of single word utterances before syntax.* The Hague: Mouton, 1973.

Bloom, L. Talking, understanding and thinking. In R. L. Schiefelbusch & L. L. Lloyd (Eds.), *Language perspectives: Acquisition, retardation and intervention.* Baltimore: University Park Press, 1974.

Bloom, L., Hood, L., & Lightbown, P. Imitation in language development: If, when and why. *Cognitive Psychology,* 1974, *6,* 380–420.

Bloom, L., & Lahey, M. *Language development.* New York: Wiley, 1978.

Blount, B. G. Ethnography and caretaker–child interaction. In C. E. Snow & C. A. Ferguson (Eds.), *Talking to children.* Cambridge, England: Cambridge University Press, 1977.

Bowerman, M. F. Learning the structure of causative verbs: A study in the relationship of cognitive, semantic and syntactic development. *Papers and Reports on Child Language Development* (Stanford University), 1974, *8,* 142–148.

Bowerman, M. F. Words and sentences: Uniformity, individual variation, and shifts over time in patterns of acquisition. In F. D. Minifie & L. L. Lloyd (Eds.), *Communicative and cognitive abilities—Early behavioral assessment.* Baltimore: University Park Press, 1978. (a)

Bowerman, M. F. Systematizing semantic knowledge: Changes over time in the child's organization of word meaning. *Child Development,* 1978, *49,* 977–987. (b)

Braine, M. D. S. The ontogeny of English phrase structure: The first phase. *Language,* 1963, *39,* 1–13. (a)

Braine, M. D. S. On learning the grammatical order of words. *Psychological Review,* 1963, *70,* 323–348. (b)

Braine, M. D. S. The acquisition of language in infant and child. In C. Reed (Ed.), *The learning of language.* New York: Appleton-Century-Crofts, 1971.

Braunwald, S. R. Context, word and meaning: Toward a communicational analysis of lexical acquisition. In A. Lock (Ed.), *Action, gesture and symbol: The emergence of language.* New York: Academic Press, 1978.

Brewer, W. F., & Stone, J. B. Acquisition of spatial antonym pairs. *Journal of Experimental Child Psychology,* 1975, *19,* 299–307.

Bridges, A. SVO comprehension strategies reconsidered: The evidence of individual patterns of response. *Journal of Child Language,* 1980, *7,* 89–104.

Broen, P. A. The verbal environment of the language-learning child. *Monographs of American Speech and Hearing Association,* December 1972, No. 17.

Brown, I. Role of referent concreteness in the acquisition of passive sentence comprehension through abstract modeling. *Journal of Experimental Child Psychology,* 1976, *22,* 185–199.

Brown, I. Language acquisition: Linguistic structure and rule-governed behavior. In G. J. Whitehurst & B. J. Zimmerman (Eds.), *The functions of language and cognition.* New York: Academic Press, 1979.

Brown, R. *A first language: The early stages.* Cambridge, Mass.: Harvard University Press, 1973.

Brown, R. Introduction to C. E. Snow & C. A. Ferguson (Eds.), *Talking to children.* Cambridge, England: Cambridge University Press, 1977.

Brown, R., & Bellugi, U. Three processes in the child's acquisition of syntax. *Harvard Educational Review,* 1964, *34,* 133–151.

Brown, R., Cazden, C., & Bellugi, U. The child's grammar from I to III. In J. P. Hill (Ed.), *Minnesota Symposium on Child Psychology* (Vol. 2). Minneapolis: University of Minnesota Press, 1969.

Brown, R., & Hanlon, C. Derivational complexity and order of acquisition in child speech. In J. R. Hayes (Ed.), *Cognition and the development of language.* New York: Wiley, 1970.

Brown, R., & Herrnstein, R. J. *Psychology.* Boston: Little Brown, 1975.

Bruce, L. J. The analysis of word sounds by young children. *British Journal of Educational Psychology,* 1964, *34,* 158–170.

Bruner, J. S. The ontogenesis of speech acts. *Journal of Child Language.* 1975, *2,* 1–19.

Bruner, J. S. Early social interaction and language acquisition. In H. R. Schaffer (Ed.), *Studies in mother–infant interaction.* London: Academic Press, 1977.

Bruner, J. S. Berlyne memorial lecture: Acquiring the uses of language. *Canadian Journal of Psychology,* 1978, *32,* 204–218.

Bush, C. N., Edwards, M. L., Luckau, J. M., Stoel, C. M., Macken, M. A., & Petersen, J. D. *On specifying a system for transcribing consonants in child language: A working paper with samples from American English and Mexican Spanish.* Stanford, Calif.: Stanford Univeristy Department of Linguistics, 1973.

Butterfield, E. C., & Cairns, G. Discussion summary—Infant reception research. In R. Schiefelbusch & L. L. Lloyd (Eds.), *Language perspectives—acquisition, retardation, and intervention.* Baltimore: University Park Press, 1974.

Carey, S. The child as word learner. In M. Halle, J. Bresnan, & G. A. Miller (Eds.), *Linguistic theory and psychological reality.* Cambridge, Mass.: MIT Press, 1978.

Carey, S., & Potter, M. Less may never mean more. In P. Smith & R. Campbell (Eds.), *Proceedings of the Stirling conference on the psychology of language.* New York: Plenum, 1977.

Carter, A. L. Prespeech meaning relations: An outline of one infant's sensorimotor morpheme development. In P. Fletcher & M. Garman (Eds.), *Language acquisition.* Cambridge, England: Cambridge University Press, 1979.

Cazden, C. *Environmental assistance to the child's acquisition of grammar.* Unpublished doctoral dissertation, Harvard University, 1965

Chapman, R. S. Comprehension strategies in children. In J. Kavanagh & W. Strange (Eds.),

Speech and language in the laboratory, school, and clinic. Cambridge, Mass.: MIT Press, 1978.

Chomsky, N. *Aspects of a theory of syntax.* Cambridge, Mass.: MIT Press, 1965.

Chomsky, N. *Rules and representations.* New York: Columbia University Press, 1980.

Chomsky, N., & Halle, M. *The sound pattern of English.* New York: Harper & Row, 1968.

Clark, E. On the child's acquisition of antonyms in two semantic fields. *Journal of Verbal Learning and Verbal Behavior,* 1972, *11,* 750–758.

Clark, E. What's in a word? On the child's acquisition of semantics in his first language. In T. E. Moore (Ed.), *Cognitive development and the acquisition of language.* New York: Academic Press, 1973. (a)

Clark, E. Non-linguistic strategies and the acquisition of word meaning. *Cognition,* 1973, *2,* 161–182. (b)

Clark, E. Strategies and the mapping problem in first language acquisition. In J. Macnamara (Ed.), *Language learning and thought.* New York: Academic Press, 1977.

Clark, E. Strategies for communicating. *Child Development,* 1978, *49,* 953–959. (a)

Clark, E. Awareness of language: Some evidence from what children say and do. In A. Sinclair, R. Jarvella, & W. J. M. Levelt (Eds.), *The child's conception of language.* New York: Springer-Verlag, 1978. (b)

Clark, E. Building a vocabulary: Words for objects, actions and relations. In P. Fletcher & M. Garman (Eds.), *Language acquisition.* Cambridge, England: Cambridge University Press, 1979.

Clark, E., & Sengul, C. J. Strategies in the acquisition of deixis. *Journal of Child Language,* 1978, *5,* 457–475.

Clark, H., and Clark, E. *Psychology and language.* New York: Harcourt Brace Jovanovich, 1977.

Corrigan, R. Language development as related to stage 6 object permanence development. *Journal of Child Language,* 1978, *5,* 173–189.

Corrigan, R. Cognitive correlates of language: Differential criteria yield differential results. *Child Development,* 1979, *50,* 617–631.

Cromer, R. The development of language and cognition: The cognition hypothesis. In B. Foss (Ed.), *New perspectives in child development.* Harmondsworth, England: Penguin Books, 1974.

Cross, T. Motherese: Its association with rate of syntactic acquisition in young children. In N. Waterson and C. E. Snow (Eds.), *The development of communication.* New York: Wiley, 1978.

Crystal, D. Prosodic development. In P. Fletcher & M. Garman (Eds.), *Language acquisition.* Cambridge, England: Cambridge University Press, 1979.

Crystal, D., Fletcher, P., & Garman, M. *The grammatical analysis of language disability.* New York: Elsevier, 1976.

Dale, P. S. Is early pragmatic development measurable? *Journal of Child Language,* 1980, *7,* 1–12.

Derwing, B., & Baker, W. J. Recent research on the acquisition of English morphology. In P. Fletcher & M. Garman (Eds.), *Language acquisition.* Cambridge, England: Cambridge University Press, 1979.

Dever, R. B., & Gardner, W. I. Performance of normal and retarded boys on Berko's test of morphology. *Language and Speech,* 1970, *13,* 162–181.

deVilliers, J. G. The process of rule learning in child speech: A new look. In K. E. Nelson (Ed.), *Children's language,* Vol. II. New York: Gardner Press, 1980.

deVilliers, J. G., & deVilliers, P. A. Competence and performance in child language: Are children really competent to judge? *Journal of Child Language,* 1974, *1,* 11–22.

deVilliers, J. G., & deVilliers, P. A. Semantics and syntax in the first two years: The output of form and function and the form and function of the input. In F. Minifie and L. L. Lloyd (Eds.), *Communicative and cognitive abilities: Early behavioral assessment.* Baltimore: University Park Press, 1978.

deVilliers, J. G., Tager-Flusberg, H. B., & Hakuta, K. Deciding among theories of the development of coordination in child speech. *Papers and Reports on Child Language Development* (Stanford University), 1977, *13,* 118-125.

deVilliers, J. G., Tager-Flusberg, H. B., Hakuta, K., & Cohen, M. Children's comprehension of relative clauses. *Journal of Psycholinguistic Research,* 1979, *8,* 499-518.

deVilliers, P. A., & deVilliers, J. G. Early judgments of semantic and syntactic acceptability by children. *Journal of Psycholinguistic Research,* 1972, *1,* 299-310.

deVilliers, P. A., & deVilliers, J. G. On this, that and the other: Nonegocentrism in very young children. *Journal of Experimental Child Psychology,* 1974, *18,* 438-447.

deVilliers, P. A., & deVilliers, J. G. Form and function in the development of sentence negation. *Papers and Reports on Child Language* (Stanford University), 1979, *17,* 56-64. (a)

deVilliers, P. A., & deVilliers, J. G. *Early language.* In J. Bruner, M. Cole, & B. Lloyd (Eds.), *The developing child* series. Cambridge, Mass.: Harvard University Press, 1979. (b)

Donaldson, M., & Balfour, G. Less is more: A study of language comprehension in children. *British Journal of Psychology,* 1968, *59,* 461-471.

Dore, J. Holophrases, speech acts and language universals. *Journal of Child Language,* 1975, *2,* 21-40.

Dore, J. Conversation and preschool language development. In P. Fletcher & M. Garman (Eds.), *Language acquisition.* Cambridge, England: Cambridge University Press, 1979.

Dore, J., Gearhart, M., & Newman, D. The structure of nursery-school conversation. In K. E. Nelson (Ed.), *Children's language,* Vol. I. New York: Gardner Press, 1978.

Dunn, L. M. *Peabody picture vocabulary test.* Circle Pines, Minnesota: American Guidance Service, 1965.

Edwards, M. L. Perception and production in child phonology: The testing of four hypotheses. *Journal of Child Language,* 1974, *1,* 205-219.

Eilers, R. E., Gavin, W., Wilson, W. R. Linguistic experience and phonemic perception in infancy: A cross linguistic study. *Child Development,* 1979, *50,* 14-18.

Eilers, R. E., Wilson, W. R., & Moore, J. M. Speech discrimination in the language-innocent and the language-wise: A study in the perception of voice onset time. *Journal of Child Language,* 1979, *6,* 1-18.

Eimas, P., Siqueland, E., Juszyck, P., & Vigorito, J. Speech perception in infants. *Science,* 1971, *171,* 303-306.

Eisenson, J. *Aphasia in children.* New York: Harper and Row, 1972.

Erreich, A., Valian, V. V., & Winzemer, J. Aspects of a theory of language acquisition, *Journal of Child Language,* 1980, *7,* 157-179.

Ervin-Tripp, S. Imitation and structural charge in children's language. In E. H. Lenneberg (Ed.), *New directions in the study of language.* Cambridge, Mass.: MIT Press, 1964.

Feldman, C. F., & Toulmin, S. Logic and the theory of mind. In T. Cole & W. Arnold (Eds.), *Nebraska symposium on motivation,* Vol. 23. Lincoln: University of Nebraska Press, 1975.

Ferguson, C. A. Learning to pronounce: The earliest stages of phonological development in the child. In F. D. Minifie & L. L. Lloyd (Eds.), *Communicative and cognitive abilities—Early behavioral assessment.* Baltimore: University Park Press, 1978.

Fischer, K. W. A theory of cognitive development: Control and construction of a hierarchy of skills. *Psychological Review,* in press.

Flavell, J. H. Stage-related properties of cognitive development. *Cognitive Psychology,* 1971, *2,* 421-453.

Folger, J. P., & Chapman, R. S. A pragmatic analysis of spontaneous imitations. *Journal of Child Language,* 1978, *5,* 25-38.

Gaer, E. Children's understanding and production of sentences. *Journal of Verbal Learning and Verbal Behavior,* 1969, *8,* 289-294.

Garnica, O. The development of phonemic speech perception. In T. E. Moore (Ed.), *Cognitive development and the acquisition of language.* New York: Academic Press, 1973.

Garvey, C. Requests and responses in children's speech. *Journal of Child Language,* 1975, *2,* 41-63.

Gentner, D. Evidence for the psychological reality of semantic components: The verbs of possession. In D. A. Norman, D. E. Rumelhart, & the LNR Research Group (Eds.), *Explorations in cognition.* San Francisco: Freeman, 1975.

Gleitman, L. R., Gleitman, H., & Shipley, E. The emergence of the child as grammarian. *Cognition,* 1972, *1,* 137-164.

Goodluck, H., & Solan, L. (Eds.), *Papers in the structure and development of child language.* University of Massachusetts Occasional Papers in Linguistics, Vol. 4, 1978.

Halle, M., Bresnan, J., & Miller, G. A. *Linguistic theory and psychological reality.* Cambridge, Mass.: MIT Press, 1978.

Halliday, M. K. Learning how to mean. In E. H. Lenneberg & E. Lenneberg (Eds.), *Foundations of language development: A Multidisciplinary approach,* Vol. 1. New York: Academic Press, 1975.

Harkness, S. Aspects of social environment and first language acquisition in rural Africa. In C. E. Snow & C. A. Ferguson (Eds.), *Talking to children.* Cambridge, England: Cambridge University Press, 1977.

Haselkorn, S. L. Success or failure: Does it affect young children's request strategies? *Papers and Reports on Child Language Development* (Stanford University), 1979, *17,* 73-80.

Humphreys, M. W. A contribution to infantile linguistics. *Transactions of the American Philological Association,* 1880, *11,* 5-17.

Huttenlocher, J. The origins of language comprehension. In R. L. Solso (Ed.), *Theories in cognitive psychology.* Hillsdale, N. J.: Lawrence Erlbaum Associates, 1974.

Ingram, D. Phonological rules in young children. *Journal of Child Language,* 1974, *1,* 49-64.

Ingram, D. Current issues in child phonology. In D. M. Morehead & A. E. Morehead (Eds.), *Normal and deficient language.* Baltimore: University Park Press, 1976. (a)

Ingram, D. *Phonological disability in children.* New York: Elsevier, 1976. (b)

Ingram, D. Sensorimotor intelligence and language development. In A. Lock (Ed.), *Action, gesture and symbol: The emergence of language.* New York: Academic Press, 1978.

Jakobson, R. *Child language, aphasia, and phonological universals.* The Hague: Mouton, 1968.

Jakobson, R., & Halle, M. *Fundamentals of language.* The Hague: Mouton, 1956.

Johnson, C. E., & Bush, C. A note on transcribing the speech of young children. *Papers and Reports on Child Language Development* (Stanford University), 1971, *3,* 95-100.

Katz, J. J. *Semantic theory,* New York: Harper and Row, 1972.

Katz, J. J., & Fodor, J. A. The structure of a semantic theory. *Language,* 1963, *39,* 170-210.

Kuczaj, S. A. II. Children's judgments of grammatical and ungrammatical irregular past-tense verbs. *Child Development,* 1978, *49,* 319-326.

Leonard, L., Schwartz, R., Folger, J., Newhoff, M., & Wilcox, M. Children's imitations of lexical items. *Child Development,* 1979, *50,* 19-27.

Liberman, I. Y. Segmentation of the spoken word and reading acquisition. *Bulletin of the Orton Society,* 1973, *23,* 65-77.

Limber, J. The genesis of complex sentences. In T. E. Moore (Ed.), *Cognitive development and the acquisition of language.* New York: Academic Press, 1973.

Lindner, G. *Aus dem naturgarten der Kindersprache.* Leipzig: Th. Ljieben's Verlag, 1898.

Lundberg, I. Aspects of linguistic awareness related to reading. In A. Sinclair, R. J. Jarvella, & W. J. M. Levelt (Eds.), *The child's conception of language.* New York: Springer-Verlag, 1978.

Lyons, J. *Semantics* (Vol. 1). London: Cambridge University Press, 1977.

Macken, M. A., & Barton, D. The acquisition of the voicing contrast in English: A study of voice onset time in word-initial stop consonants. *Journal of Child Language,* 1980, *1,* 41–74.

MacWhinney, B. The acquisition of morphophonology. *Monographs of the Society for Research in Child Development,* 1978, *43,* 1–22.

Maratsos, M. P. Learning how and when to use pronouns and determiners. In P. Fletcher & M. Garman (Eds.), *Language acquisition.* Cambridge, England: Cambridge University Press, 1979.

Maratsos, M. P., Kuczaj, S. II, Fox, D., & Chalkley, M. A. Some empirical studies in the acquisition of transformational relations: Passives, negatives and the past tense. In W. A. Collins (Ed.), *The Minnesota symposia on child psychology,* Vol. 12. *Children's language and communication.* Hillsdale, N. J.: Lawrence Erlbaum Associates, 1979.

Menyuk, P. The role of distinctive features in children's acquisition of phonology. *Journal of Speech and Hearing Research,* 1968, *11,* 138–146.

Menyuk, P., & Bernholtz, M. Prosodic features and children's language production. *Quarterly Progress Report of the Research Laboratory of Electronics,* 1969, *93,* 216–219.

Mervis, C. *Acquisition of object categories.* Unpublished doctoral dissertation, Cornell University, 1976.

Messer, D. J. The integration of mothers' referential speech with joint play. *Child Development,* 1978, *49,* 781–787.

Messer, D. J. The episodic structure of maternal speech to young children. *Journal of Child Language,* 1980, *7,* 29–40.

Miller, J. F., Chapman, R. S., & Bedrosian, J. L. *Defining developmentally disabled subjects for research: The relationship between etiology, cognitive development and communicative performance.* Paper presented to the Second Annual Boston University Conference on Language Acquisition, October 1977.

Miller, W., & Ervin, S. The development of grammar in child language. In U. Bellugi & R. Brown (Eds.), *The acquisition of language. Monographs of the Society for Research in Child Development,* 1964, *29.*

Minifie, F., Darley, F., & Sherman, D. Temporal reliability of seven language measures. *Journal of Speech and Hearing Research,* 1963, *6,* 139–148.

Moerk, E. L. Relationships between parental input frequencies and children's language acquisition: A reanalysis of Brown's data. *Journal of Child Language,* 1980, *7,* 105–118.

Moeser, S. S. Semantics and miniature artificial languages. In J. Macnamara (Ed.) *Language learning and thought.* New York: Academic Press, 1977.

Moeser, S. D., & Bregman, A. S. The role of reference in the acquisition of a miniature artificial language. *Journal of Verbal Learning and Verbal Behavior,* 1972, *11,* 759–769.

Moore, T. E. Linguistic intuitions of twelve-year-olds. *Language and Speech,* 1975, *18,* 213–216.

Morse, P. A. Infant speech perception: Origins, processes, and *alpha centauri.* In F. Minifie & L. L. Lloyd (Eds.), *Communicative and cognitive abilities—Early behavioral assessment.* Baltimore: University Park Press, 1978.

Nakazima, S. A comparative study of the speech developments of Japanese and American English in childhood. *Studies in Phonology,* 1962, *2,* 27–39.

Nelson, K. Some attributes of adjectives used by young children. *Cognition,* 1976, *4,* 13–30.

Nelson, K. Early speech in its communicative context. In F. Minifie & L. L. Lloyd (Eds.),

Communicative and cognitive abilities: Early behavioral assessment. Baltimore: University Park Press, 1978.

Nelson, K. Rescorla, L., Gruendel, J., & Benedict, H. Early lexicons: What do they mean? *Child Development,* 1978, *49,* 960–968.

Nelson, K. E. Facilitating syntax acquisition. *Developmental Psychology,* 1977, *13,* 101–107.

Nelson, K. E., Carskaddon, G., & Bonvillian, J. D. Syntax acquistion: Impact of experimental variation in adult verbal interaction with the child. *Child Development,* 1973, *44,* 497–504.

Newport, E. Motherese: The speech of mothers to young children. In N. Castellan, D. Pisoni, & G. Potts (Eds.), *Cognitive theory,* Vol. II. Hillsdale, N. J.: Lawrence Erlbaum Associates, 1976.

Newport, E., Gleitman, L., & Gleitman, H. Mother, I'd rather do it myself: Some effects and non-effects of maternal speech style. In C. E. Snow & C. A. Ferguson (Eds.), *Talking to children.* Cambridge, England: Cambridge University Press, 1977.

Ninio, A., & Bruner, J. S. The achievement and antecedents of labelling. *Journal of Child Language,* 1978, *5,* 1–16.

Oller, D. K., Wieman, L. A., Doyle, W. J., & Ross, C. Infant babbling and speech. *Journal of Child Language,* 1976, *3,* 1–12.

Olmsted, D. *Out of the mouths of babes.* The Hague: Mouton, 1971.

Palermo, D. More about less: A study of language comprehension. *Journal of Verbal Learning and Verbal Behavior,* 1973, *12,* 211–221.

Palermo, D. Still more about the comprehension of "less." *Developmental Psychology,* 1974, *10,* 827–829.

Papandropoulou, I., & Sinclair, H. What is a word? Experimental study of children's ideas on grammar. *Human Development,* 1974, *17,* 241–258.

Phillips, J. Syntax and vocabulary of mothers' speech to young children: Age and sex comparisons. *Child Development,* 1973, *44,* 182–185.

Piaget, J. *Judgement and reasoning in the child.* London: Routledge & Kegan Paul, 1928.

Piaget, J. *The language and thought of the child.* Cleveland: Meridian Books, World Publishing, 1955.

Piaget, J. *Play, dreams and imitation.* New York: Norton, 1962.

Pinker, S. On the acquistion of grammatical morphenes. *Journal of Child Language,* in press.

Putnam, H. The meaning of 'meaning.' In K. Gunderson (Ed.), *Language, mind, and knowledge.* Minneapolis: University of Minnesota Press, 1975.

Ramer, A. L. H. Syntactic styles in emerging language. *Journal of Child Language,* 1976, *3,* 49–62.

Ramsay, D. *Object word spurt, handedness and object permanence in the infant.* Unpublished doctoral dissertation, University of Denver, 1977.

Read, C. Children's awareness of language, with emphasis on sound systems. In A. Sinclair, R. J. Jarvella, & W. J. M. Levelt (Eds.), *The child's conception of language.* New York: Springer-Verlag, 1978.

Richards, M. M. Sorting out what's in a word from what's not: Evaluating Clark's semantic features acquisition theory. *Journal of Experimental Child Psychology,* 1979, *27,* 1–47.

Savic, S. Asects of adult–child communication: The problem of question–acquisition. *Journal of Child Language,* 1975, *2,* 251–260.

Schaerlaekens, A. M. *The two-word stage in child language development: A study based on evidence provided by Dutch-speaking triplets.* The Hague: Mouton, 1973.

Schane, S. *Generative phonology.* Englewood Cliffs, N.J.: Prentice-Hall, 1973.

Schiefflin, B. Cultural variations in a dialog. In R. Schiefelbusch (Ed.), *Communicative competence: Acquisition and intervention.* Baltimore: University Park Press, in press.

Schlesinger, I. M. Relational concepts underlying language. In R. L. Schiefelbusch & L. L. Lloyd (Eds.), *Language perspectives: Acquisition, retardation and intervention.* Baltimore: University Park Press, 1974.

Schlesinger, I. M. Miniature artificial languages as research tools. In J. Macnamara (Ed.), *Language learning and thought.* New York: Academic Press, 1977.

Scholl, D. M., & Ryan, E. B. Child judgments of sentences varying in grammatical complexity. *Journal of Experimental Child Psychology,* 1975, *20,* 274–285.

Searle, J. *Speech acts.* Cambridge, England: Cambridge University Press, 1969.

Searle, J. R. Indirect speech acts. In P. Cole & J. L. Morgan (Eds.), *Syntax and semantics,* Vol. 3. *Speech Acts.* New York: Seminar Press, 1975.

Shatz, M. How to do things by asking: Form–function pairings in mother's questions and their relation to children's responses. *Child Development,* 1979, *50,* 1093–1099.

Shatz, M. On mechanisms of language acquisition: Can features of the communicative environment account for development? In L. Gleitman & E. Warner (Eds.), *Language acquisition: The state of the art.* New York: Cambridge University Press, in press.

Shriner, T. H. A comparison of selected measures with psychological scale values of language development. *Journal of Speech and Hearing Disorders,* 1967, *10,* 828–835.

Shriner, T. H. A review of mean length of response as a measure of expressive language development in children. *Journal of Speech and Hearing Disorders,* 1969, *34,* 61–68.

Shugar, G. W. Text analysis as an approach to the study of early linguistic operations. In N. Waterson & C. E. Snow (Eds.), *The development of communication.* Chichester, England: Wiley, 1978.

Sinclair, H. Sensorimotor action patterns as a condition for the acquisition of syntax. In R. Huxley & E. Ingram, *Language acquisition: Models and methods.* New York: Academic Press, 1971.

Slobin, D. I. Cognitive prerequisites for the development of grammar. In C. A. Ferguson & D. I. Slobin (Eds.), *Studies of child language development.* New York: Holt, Rinehart & Winston, 1973.

Slobin, D. I. Universal and particular in the acquisition of language. In L. R. Gleitman & E. Warner (Eds.), *Language acquisition: State of the art.* Cambridge, England: Cambridge University Press, in press.

Slobin, D. I., & Welsh, C. A. Elicited imitation as a research tool in developmental psycholinguistics. In C. A. Ferguson & D. I. Slobin (Eds.), *Studies of child language development.* New York: Holt, Rinehart & Winston, 1973.

Smith, N. *The acquisition of phonology: A case study.* Cambridge, England: Cambridge University Press, 1973.

Snow, C. E. Mothers' speech to children learning language. *Child Development,* 1972, *43,* 549–565.

Snow, C. E. Mother's speech research: From input to interaction. In C. E. Snow & C. A. Ferguson (Eds.), *Talking to children.* Cambridge, England: Cambridge University Press, 1977.

Snow, C. Conversations with children. In P. Fletcher & M. Garman (Eds.), *Language acquisition.* Cambridge, England: Cambridge University Press, 1979.

Snow, C., Arlman-Rupp, A., Hassing, Y., Jobse, J., Joosten, J., & Vorster, J. Mother's speech in three social classes. *Journal of Psycholinguistic Research,* 1976, *5,* 1–20.

Snyder, L. S. Communicative and cognitive abilities and disabilities in the sensori-motor period. *Merrill-Palmer Quarterly,* 1978, *24,* 161–180.

Strohner, H., & Nelson, K. E. The young child's development of sentence comprehension: The influence of event probability, non-verbal context, syntactic form and strategies. *Child Development,* 1976, *45,* 567–576.

Svachkin, N. K. The development of phonemic speech perception in early childhood. In C. A. Ferguson & D. I. Slobin (Eds.), *Studies of child language development.* New York: Holt, Rinehart & Winston, 1973.

Tager-Flusberg, H., deVilliers, J. G., & Hakuta, K. The development of sentence coordination. In S. Kuczaj (Ed.), *Language development: Syntax and semantics.* Hillsdale, N. J.: Lawrence Erlbaum Associates, in press.

Templin, M. *Certain language skills in children: Their development and interrelationships.* Institute of Child Welfare Monograph, *26,* Minneapolis: The University of Minnesota Press, 1957.

Uzgiris, I. Organization of sensorimotor intelligence. In M. Lewis (Ed.), *Origins of intelligence.* New York: Plenum, 1976.

van der Geest, T. Some interactional aspects of language acquisition. In C. E. Snow & C. A. Ferguson (Eds.), *Talking to children.* Cambridge, England: Cambridge University Press, 1977.

Vygotsky, L. S. *Thought and language.* Cambridge, Mass.: MIT Press, 1962.

Wales, R. Deixis. In P. Fletcher & M. Garman (Eds.), *Language acquisition.* Cambridge, England: Cambridge University Press, 1979.

Wales, R., & Campbell, R. N. The development of comparison and the comparison of development. In *Proceedings of psycholinguistics conference at Bressarone.* Amsterdam: North Holland, 1970.

Wannemacher, J. T., & Ryan, M. L. "Less" is not "more": A study of children's comprehension of "less" in various task contexts. *Child Development,* 1978, *49,* 660–668.

Webb, P. A., & Abrahanson, A. Stages of egocentrism in children's use of 'this' and 'that': A different point of view. *Journal of Child Language,* 1976, *3,* 349–367.

Weir, R. *Language in the crib.* The Hague: Mouton, 1962.

Wells, G. *Coding manual for the descriptions of child speech.* University of Bristol School of Education, 1973.

Werner, H., & Kaplan, E. The acquisition of word meaning: A developmental study. *Monographs of the Society for Research in Child Development,* 1952, *15.*

Whitehurst, G. J. Meaning and semantics. In G. J. Whitehurst & B. J. Zimmerman (Eds.), *The functions of language and cognition.* New York: Academic Press, 1979.

Whitehurst, G., Ironsmith, E. M., & Goldfein, M. Selective imitation of the passive construction through modeling. *Journal of Experimental Child Psychology,* 1974, *17,* 288–302.

Whitehurst, G., & Vasta, R. Is language acquired through imitation? *Journal of Psycholinguistic Research,* 1975, *4,* 37–58.

Wilcox, S., & Palermo, D. "In," "on" and "under" revisited. *Cognition,* 1974, *3,* 245–254.

Wilcox, S., & Palermo, D. S. *If less means more do does dax.* Paper presented at the 49th annual meeting of the Midwestern Psychological Association, Chicago 1977.

Williams, L., & Golenski, J. Infant behavioral state and speech sound discrimination. *Child Development,* 1979, *50,* 1243–1246.

Winitz, H. *Articulatory acquisition and behavior.* New York: Appleton-Century-Crofts, 1969.

Zhurova, L. Y. The development of analysis of words into their sounds by preschool children. In C. A. Ferguson & D. I. Slobin (Eds.), *Studies of child language development.* New York: Holt, Rinehart & Winston, 1973.

6 Cognitive Development: A Piagetian Perspective

SCOTT A. MILLER

For close to 60 years some of the most interesting and ingenious research in cognitive development came from the Swiss psychologist Jean Piaget. For at least the last 15 years much of the work by other students of children's thinking has been in some way inspired by Piaget. It is to the broad topic of Piagetian research, both in its original form and in more recent follow-ups, that the present chapter is devoted.

Piaget's work has been influential in two ways. First, his studies have provided the experimental tasks that have most intrigued later reseachers of cognitive development. The oft-studied conservation problem is the best-known example, having served as the focus of literally hundreds of studies. Conservation is by no means the only example, however. Rather, it often seems that whatever the topic—infant intelligence, classification, role taking, adolescent thinking—Piaget was there first with procedures that have set a mold for virtually all later studies.

In addition to providing experimental tasks, Piaget's studies have also furnished the theoretical issues that have most engaged developmental researchers. Does the child's thinking proceed through qualitatively distinct stages, or is development a more quantitative and continuous-looking process? Is there a consistent patterning to development, with certain abilities emerging concurrently and others in predictable sequence, or is development more variable? How does the child move from one level of understanding to the next? None of these questions is unique to Piaget; all of them, however, have thus far found their fullest expression in the context of Piagetian theory and research.

Although Piaget's studies have been seminal, they have not gone unquestioned. Indeed, much later research in cognitive development has been motivated by perceived deficiencies in the original Piagetian research.

161

STRATEGIES AND TECHNIQUES
OF CHILD STUDY

Some researchers have questioned whether Piaget's experimental tasks really measure what Piaget thinks they measure. Others have concentrated on the theoretical issues sketched above, such as the validity of the notion of stages. Our discussion, therefore, will hardly consist of an unbroken string of praise for Piaget. Instead, much of the chapter will be devoted to studies whose goal has been to correct, extend, or revise the original Piagetian work.

Certain limitations in the coverage should be noted. Although work by many researchers in addition to Piaget will be considered, the focus will remain on tasks and issues that are either identical or close in form to those developed by Piaget. Thus many interesting approaches to the study of children's thinking will be omitted. A major such approach, the information-processing viewpoint, is discussed in Chapter 7.

A second limitation is chronological. This chapter will discuss research procedures that are appropriate for verbal, postinfancy subjects. Some methodological aspects of infant research are discussed in Chapter 2.

PIAGET'S APPROACH

Piaget has published some 25 books that report research concerned with cognitive development beyond infancy. Most of these books contain dozens of original tasks and variations thereof. Clearly, an exhaustive summary of this work would require several additional books. The goal of this section is more modest: to identify some of the most important general themes that characterize the Piagetian approach, and to preview the issues that will concern us when we turn to follow-up work and evaluation. The section is divided into two parts: an initial orientation to the Piagetian view of intelligence, followed by a sampling of important and frequently studied Piagetian tasks.

The Piagetian View of Intelligence

As they develop, children come to know thousands of things that they initially did not know. Prolific though Piaget has been, even he has studied only a small proportion of these cognitive attainments. How do Piaget and his many able co-workers (most notably Barbel Inhelder) decide which of the innumerable cognitive acquisitions of childhood are worthy of study? What are the criteria that define a "Piagetian task," the leitmotivs that run through the Piagetian research program?

In this section we will suggest five criteria that, taken together, capture much of what is meant by the "Piagetian view of intelligence." In the next section we will flesh out this rather abstract characterization with a consideration of specific tasks.

The first and most important characteristic of the Piagetian approach is a focus on basic, epistemologically central kinds of knowledge. No researcher, of course, deliberately sets out to study trivial kinds of knowledge. Piaget, however, has been far more successful than anyone else at identifying concepts that really do appear fundamental to the child's understanding of the world. Doubtless part of the basis for this success lies in Piaget's early training in philosophy and his life-long desire to use psychological research to address basic philosophical questions about knowledge (Piaget, 1952a). Again and again in Piaget's books the focus of the research returns to classic issues of epistemology—to the child's understanding of space, time, and causality, of classes and relations, of invariance and change. Questions can be raised about the validity of the experimental procedures used or about the general theoretical surrounding in which the research is embedded. No one, however, has ever doubted that the kind of knowledge studied by Piaget is knowledge that is worth knowing about.

A second characteristic follows from this first. Because of his focus on epistemologically basic kinds of knowledge, Piaget has never been very much concerned with individual differences among children. His interest, rather, has been in the commonalities of development—in concepts that are mastered by all children as they develop, precisely because such concepts are necessary for any child's understanding of the world. Whether the concepts that Piaget studies really do have the universality that he claims is an interesting empirical question beyond the scope of this chapter (see Dasen, 1976, for a recent discussion). The point for now is simply that one of the many ways in which Piaget departs from many American psychologists is in his concern with commonalities rather than individual differences.

The statement that Piaget neglects individual differences requires qualification. There is one very important individual difference that runs through all of Piaget's work, and that is the difference between developmentally less mature and developmentally more mature children. All of the abilities studied by Piaget show a progression from incomplete mastery in early childhood to an eventually full or at least more nearly complete mastery by late childhood or adolescence. Indeed, there would be little point in studying these abilities if no such progression occurred; it is only when we know, for example, that conservation is *not* always understood that conservation becomes an interesting concept to study. As Flavell (1963) long ago noted, one of the great contributions of Piaget's work has been the demonstration that there is much seemingly very basic knowledge that is not always present but rather must somehow be mastered in the course of development.

Our next characteristic again follows naturally. Many of the cognitive changes of childhood are essentially quantitative changes, a matter of acquiring more facts, getting faster or more efficient at solving problems, etc. Piaget's interest has always been much more in qualitative changes—in the *how* of children's thinking, and not just in how much the child knows or how quickly the child can do things. Thus (to take the conservation problem as our example again), when the child moves from not understanding to understanding conservation, the change is not merely a matter of learning a new fact or eliminating a bothersome error. Rather, the change (or at least this is Piaget's claim) is the result of a qualitative reorganization of the underlying cognitive system. Again, we can defer consideration of the validity of the Piagetian claim; the point for now is simply that the *intent* of the research has always been to identify qualitative changes with development.

A qualitative change such as the nonconservation-to-conservation shift does not occur in isolation. A fourth characteristic of the Piagetian approach is its emphasis on the interrelation of different cognitive abilities. There is probably no instance in Piaget's writings of a cognitive task being studied solely for its own sake; rather, the continual attempt is to specify the relations that hold across a range of seemingly diverse tasks. In its most general form this emphasis on the interrelation of cognitive skills is linked to Piaget's belief in broad stages of development, such as the concrete operational stage of middle childhood. At a more molecular level the emphasis leads to a number of specific claims about sequences and concurrences in development, claims that will concern us when we turn later to the issue of patterning in development.

There is still one important component of the Piagetian view of intelligence that remains to be noted. According to Piaget, intelligence is a system of action, and intellectual adaptation always involves some form of action upon the world. During infancy the actions are literal and overt; during the age period that concerns us they are generally internal and covert. The system of actions, or "operations," that develops during middle and late childhood supposedly underlies solutions to all of the various tasks that we will be considering. This, too, is a claim to which we will return in our discussion of issues.

Let us briefly summarize the various criteria for a "Piagetian task" that we have discussed. Such a task (at least according to Piaget) taps very basic knowledge about the world, is eventually mastered by all children everywhere, reveals a qualitative change in mental functioning in the movement from nonmastery to mastery, is mastered in conjunction with other related tasks, and requires some sort of mental action for its solution.

As noted, such an abstract listing of characteristics can take us only so far in understanding the Piagetian approach. Let us turn now to some specific tasks.

A Sampling of Tasks

The tasks to be discussed are all important ones within Piaget's system, and all have led to interesting follow-up work. This section will introduce the tasks in their typical Piagetian form; each will be returned to subsequently in the discussion of issues and follow-up research.

We can begin with a task that we have already made reference to, the conservation problem. *Conservation* refers to the knowledge that some quantitative property of an object or collection of objects is not changed by a change in perceptual appearance. There are many possible quantitative properties, and hence many possible forms of conservation. If Piaget has not studied all of these possible forms, he has certainly come close. Number, amount, mass, weight, volume, length, distance, area, speed, time—these are among the forms of conservation that have received close attention from Piaget.

Despite the diversity in content examined, all conservation tasks share certain features. Some of the most commonly studied forms are illustrated in Table 6.1. As can be seen, the starting point for any conservation problem is the establishment of initial equality between the two stimuli.[1] Typically, the experimenter presents the stimuli in a way that makes the equality as obvious as possible—for example, the two rows of chips in exact one-to-one correspondence, the two columns of water exactly the same height. The child is asked explicitly about the equality, usually in the same words that will be used for the later conservation question, and the task proceeds only when the child has agreed that the stimuli are equal. If the child does not agree to the equality, then the experimenter must adjust the stimuli or reword the question until agreement is reached.

---

[1] Actually, not all conservation tasks involve two stimuli. In both Piaget's original work and more recent studies, there have been occasional examinations of one-stimulus, or "identity," conservation. In the case of number, for example, we might start with a single row of chips which is then spread. The conservation question might be something like the following: "Is the number of chips the same now as when we started, or is it more or less?" Some studies indicate that such identity conservation may be mastered earlier in development than the more often studied "equivalence," or two-stimulus, conservation. This is still a matter of dispute, however (see Brainerd & Hooper, 1975; Miller, 1978).

TABLE 6.1
Conservation Tasks in Different Content Domains

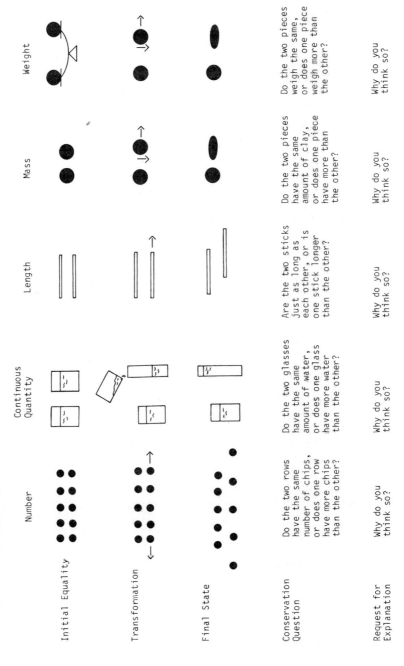

The perceptual transformation follows. It is important to stress that the transformation does not involve any deception or withholding of information; rather, the chips are spread, the water poured, and so on in full view of the child. There are many possible ways to transform stimuli in any content domain, and thus the methods shown in Table 6.1 should be taken simply as examples. The important point is that the transformation produce an end state in which the stimuli no longer *look* the same. By definition, conservation involves the recognition of invariance in the face of change, and a task is simply not a conservation task unless it poses some perceptual obstacle to the correct answer.

The final phase is the questioning of the child with regard to the equality or inequality of the stimuli. Again, there are many different approaches that can be used, and the particular wordings given in Table 6.1 are simply examples. It is possible, however, to state certain guidelines that should be followed in most cases. It is good practice to specify the quantitative dimension that is being asked about—thus "same *number*," and not simply "same." It is clearly desirable to use wording that is comprehensible to the child; thus "just as long" is probably preferable to "same length" (verbal pretests are sometimes used to assure that the wording is comprehensible). It is also good practice to present both the correct and the incorrect alternatives in the question, that is, to ask the child not only about "same" but about "same" versus "more." Presenting both alternatives precludes simple "yes saying" on the part of the occasional child who will acquiesce in whatever the adult says. Finally, it is usually sensible to balance the order of the "same" or "more" alternatives across trials or across children. Some children have a tendency to respond with the last-named alternative, and failure to balance can consequently produce misleading results.

As Table 6.1 indicates, the basic judgmental question is often supplemented by a request for an explanation. Explanations are usually of greatest concern following correct judgments, the interest being in whether the child can provide an adequate rationale for his or her answer. (Obviously, however, it would be poor procedure to probe *only* correct judgments.) Examples of adequate rationales are "You didn't add any or take any away," "You just spread them out," and "You could pour it back and it would be the same." An inadequate rationale, in contrast, would be "They look like it," or "I figured it out." Again, various ways of wording the question are possible. Whatever the initial wording, further probes may be necessary to elicit some coherent answer.

It should be stressed again that the intent of Table 6.1 is to present a general framework for assessing conservation, not to mandate *the* technique that must be followed. Variations in approach are not only possible but quite desirable if the child's understanding is to be fully examined. In addition to the types of variation already mentioned, two further possibilities can be noted. One is variation in the nature of the stimulus. Number, for example, has been examined with stimuli as diverse as paper clips, M&Ms, and the child's own fingers. Weight has been studied with clay balls, wire coils, and the child's own body. The second possible variation concerns the context in which the problem is presented. Especially with young children, it may sometimes be helpful to embed the problem in the context of a simple story or game. A continuous quantity task, for example, might be presented in terms of the need to divide a pitcher of juice equally. Such simple stories are common in Piaget's own studies of conservation. (It is possible to devise more radical departures from the typical conservation format than those described here; these methods, however, we will reserve for our later section on Assessment.)

What we have discussed thus far is a general, "standard" framework within which conservation assessment usually proceeds. Readers who have dipped into Piaget's original studies of conservation will recognize that Piaget himself has not always adhered to this "standard" approach; furthermore, there are some specific Piagetian emphases that are not captured in our general description. Let us turn, therefore, to some points specific to the original work. We can begin with two examples of Piagetian protocols, both drawn from *The Child's Conception of Number* (Piaget & Szeminska, 1952). The first example deals with conservation of continuous quantity; the second, with conservation of number. In both cases the numbers in parentheses give the child's age in years and months. In the first example the different letters are used to designate glasses of different diameter.

Blas (4:0): *Have you got a friend?—Yes, Odette.—Well look, we're giving you, Clairette, a glass of orangeade* (A_1, ¾ full), *and we're giving Odette a glass of lemonade* (A_2, also ¾ full). *Has one of you more to drink than the other?—The same.*—This is what Clairette does: She pours her drink into two other glasses (B_1 and B_2, which are thus half filled). *Has Clairette the same amount as Odette?—Odette has more.—Why?—Because we've put less in* (She pointed to the levels in B_1 and B_2, without taking into account the fact that there were two glasses).—(Odette's drink was then poured into B_3 and B_4.) *It's the same.—And now* (pouring Clairette's drink from $B_1 + B_2$ into L, a long thin tube, which is then almost full)?—*I've got more.—Why?—We've poured it into that glass* (pointing to the level in L), *and here* (B_3 and B_4) *we haven't.—But were they the same before?—Yes.—And now?—I've got more.* Clairette's orangeade was then poured back from L into B_1 and B_2: *Look, Clairette has poured hers like Odette. So, is all the lemonade* ($B_3 + B_4$) *and all the orangeade* ($B_1 + B_2$ *the same?—It's the same* (with conviction).—Now Clairette does this (pouring B_1 into C_1 which is then full, while B_2 remains half full). *Have you both the same amount to drink?—I've got more.—But where does the extra come from?—From in there* (B_1).—*What must we do so that Odette has the same?—We must take that little glass* (pouring part of B_3 into C_2).—*And is it the same now, or has one of you got more?—Odette has more.—Why?—Because we've poured it into that little glass* (C_2).—*But is there the same amount to drink, or has one got more than the other?—Odette has more to drink.—Why?—Because she has three glasses* (B_3 almost empty, B_4 and C_2, while Clairette has C_1 full and B_2) [this quotation and subsequent quotations from Piaget & Szeminska, 1972, are reprinted with permission of Humanities Press, Inc., New Jersey].

Boq (4:7): *Put as many sweets here as there are there. Those* (6) *are for Roger. You are to take as many as he has.*—(He made a compact row of about ten, which was shorter than the model.)—*Are they the same?—Not yet* (adding some).—*And now?—Yes.—Why?—Because they're like that* (indicating the length).—(The 6 in the model were then spread out.) *Who has more?—Roger.—Why?—Because they go right up to there.—What can we do to make them the same?—Put some more* (adding 1).—(The 6 were then closed up and his were spread out.)—*Now I've got more* [p. 75].

Perhaps the most immediately obvious characteristic of Piaget's studies is that they lack the systematic, standardized approach that was advocated above and that is so familiar in American research. Instead, the Genevans favor a style of testing that has been dubbed the *clinical method.* The essence of the clinical method is flexibility—the possibility for the experimenter to adjust to the child and to tailor subsequent questions and manipulations to what the child has just said or done. Thus, a particular task may be presented in a variety of ways across children, and no two children may receive exactly the same questions, stimuli, or sequence of events.

The clinical method has some obvious drawbacks. Most generally, the variability in the method, coupled with Piaget's idiosyncratic style of reporting, makes it impossible to determine exactly what procedures were administered to exactly how many children with exactly what results—precisely the information that readers of American journal articles tend to regard as essential. As Flavell (1963) has noted, the result is that the reader must take a lot on faith. Furthermore, the information that *is* provided, in the form of protocols such as those quoted above, is not always reassuring with regard to the validity of the method. It is not hard for any critical analyst of the Piagetian protocols to find instances of what appear to be unclear or leading wording, inappropriate reinforcement, unnecessary and possibly biasing variation across tasks or subjects, etc.

At the same time, it would take a supercritical analyst not to be convinced that there is *some* validity to Piaget's conclusions. When used by a skilled researcher—and there is no doubt that Piaget and his many highly trained testers are skilled—the clinical method can be a discovery procedure par excellence. The flexibility of the method allows the researcher to probe the phenomena of a new content domain in a way that would be impossible in a series of preset, rigidly standardized studies. It also permits the probing of an individual child's understanding in a way that would be impossible if all children had to be tested in exactly the same manner. A Piaget without the clinical method would doubtless be more readily assimilable for modern readers; it is doubtful, however, that there would be nearly as many interesting discoveries to assimilate.

Two further points about Piaget's methodology can be made. First, the procedures tend to be highly verbal. In Piaget's earliest studies (e.g., Piaget, 1926) the procedures were often totally verbal; a verbal question would be posed about a phenomenon such as the movement of the clouds or the origin of the sun, and the child would give a verbal response to the question. In the later work, which includes the conservation studies, the questioning is usually in reference to some concrete set of stimuli, and the child is sometimes allowed to respond through some nonverbal manipulation of the stimuli. Such a nonverbal response can be seen in our second protocol, in which the child's initial task is to set down candies to match those in another child's collection. Even here, however, the task is conveyed through verbal instructions, and the child can respond appropriately only if he or she can understand the instructions. Furthermore, as both of the quoted protocols reveal, the child is still often required to respond in words. This dependence of Piagetian assessment upon language will be a central issue in our later Assessment section.

The second point concerns the drawing of inferences. Like any researcher, Piaget attempts to go beyond a description of the child's behavior to draw inferences about the bases for the behavior. A primary question in cognitive assessment concerns the extent to which the child's behavior reflects a genuine understanding of the concept being studied. Does the child "really have" conservation, for example? Piaget's inferences in this respect tend to be conservative; that is, he is unwilling to credit a child with genuine understanding until the child's behavior makes it absolutely clear that such understanding is present. This conservativeness is reflected in the insistence on a wide range of procedures and questions to probe the genuineness of apparent understanding. It is also reflected in the requirement that the child provide not only a correct answer but also a logically adequate explanation for the answer. And it is reflected in the occasional use of a verbal counter-suggestion technique, in which the experimenter probes the child's confidence in his correct answer by posing an alternative possibility (e.g., "But another little boy told me that this one had more"). Piaget's concern, in short, seems to be with false positives, or overestimations of the child's ability. As we will see shortly, this concern contrasts with a general concern in more recent research with false negatives, or underestimations of the child's ability.

Many of the points that have been made with respect to conservation assessment are general ones that hold for other Piagetian tasks as well. Our discussion of the remaining tasks can therefore be briefer. We will begin with some work on classification. As might be expected from our earlier discussion, Piaget's methods for studying classification are many and varied. A general goal has been to move beyond simply categorizing how children sort objects (a focus in many research programs) to probe the child's understanding of the nature of classes. A particular interest has been the child's mastery of the principle of class inclusion. *Class inclusion* refers to the knowledge that a subclass is included in but does not exhaust its superordinate class—that dogs, for example, belong to but do not exhaust the class of animals. Behaviorally, class inclusion is typically assessed by asking the child to compare the sizes of a superordinate class and the largest subclass contained within it. At issue is whether the child realizes that the subclass must be smaller than the superordinate. The following example illustrates a class inclusion problem with flowers as the superordinate class. It also illustrates another surprising Piagetian discovery: children do not at first realize that a subclass cannot exceed its superordinate. Class inclusion, like conservation, must be developed.

> Ar. (5:0): *Look, are there a lot of flowers or a few in this field* (a drawing representing 20 poppies and 3 bluebells)?—*A lot.—What color are they?—**They're red and blue.**—The red ones are poppies and the blue ones are bluebells.—Yes.—I want to make a very big bunch. Must I pick the flowers or the poppies?—**The poppies.**—Show me the poppies.* (She pointed correctly.) *—Show me the flowers.*—(She made a circular movement to indicate the whole of the drawing.)—*Then will the bunch be bigger if I pick the flowers or the poppies?—**If you pick the poppies.**—If I pick the poppies, what will be left?—**The bluebells.**—And if I pick the bluebells, what will be left?—**The poppies.**—And if I pick the flowers, what will be left?*—(Reflection.) *Nothing at all.—Then which will be bigger, the bunch of flowers or the bunch of poppies?—**I've told you already.**—Think* (repeating the question).—***The bunch of poppies will be bigger.**—And what about the bunch of flowers?—**It won't be the same.**—Will it be bigger or smaller?—**Smaller.**—Why?—**Because you've made a big bunch of poppies*** [Piaget & Szeminska, 1952, p. 167].

Apart from the "clinical method" style of questioning, the above excerpt illustrates a fairly typical procedure for assessing class inclusion. Generally, the child is presented with a single superordinate class (such as flowers) which is divided into two subclasses, one of which is larger than the other. Let us refer to the superordinate class as A, the larger subclass as B, and the smaller subclass as B′. As in the conservation task, there is no deception involved; the child is already familiar with A's, B's, and B′'s, and may even explicitly agree that all of the objects are A but only some of them are B. Nevertheless, when asked to compare A and B, the child becomes confused and makes a B–B′ comparison instead. Apparently, once the child has focused on an object as a member of a particular subclass, he or she is unable to think about it simultaneously as belonging to the super-ordinate class; the only comparison left, therefore, is with the other subclass.

As with conservation, class inclusion tasks can be presented in a variety of ways. We will simply list a few of these variations, all of which may affect the child's ability to respond correctly.

One obvious variation is in the materials involved. Inhelder and Piaget (1964) noted, and subsequent research has confirmed, that class inclusion may be easier with some materials than with others. (One example reported by Inhelder and Piaget was that flowers were easier than animals.) Another possible variation is in the ratio that holds between the subclasses. Although something like the 85–15% ratio in our quoted example is common, it is possible to use any ratio down to 50–50—or, for that matter, to use three or four subclasses rather than two. It is also possible to present a series of nested classes, in which a particular class may be both subclass and superordinate. Inhelder and Piaget, for example, questioned children about a stimulus array that included ducks, birds other than ducks, and animals other than birds. The questioning need not follow the A-versus-B format described thus far. In one of Inhelder and Piaget's studies the child's understanding of class inclusion was probed through questions about "all" and "some." For example, in a collection of two red squares, two blue squares, and five blue circles, are all the squares red? Are all the circles blue? This example leads to another variation: In some cases the class relation reflects a natural semantic hierarchy (e.g., more ducks or more birds?), whereas in some cases it does not (e.g., more blue shapes or more circles?). In the second case, but not the first, one must be given information about the particular stimulus set in order to respond. Finally, class inclusion tasks vary in the manner in which the information about classes is presented. In some cases the actual objects are shown, in some cases (as in our example) a picture is used, and in some cases the presentation is completely verbal.

We turn next to some work on the child's understanding of relations. In general, Piaget believes that a dual focus on classes and relations can capture much of what is essential to intelligence; indeed, his model of middle childhood thought is partitioned into structures concerned with classes and structures concerned with relations (see Flavell, 1963, for the most helpful summary). The aspect of relational knowledge on which we will concentrate is transitivity. *Transitivity* refers to reasoning of the following sort: If $A = B$ and $B = C$, then $A = C$. Or, if $A > B$ and $B > C$, then $A > C$. It refers, in short, to the ability to combine information from two comparisons to deduce the logically necessary outcome of a third comparison. Like conservation and class inclusion, it is another very basic-seeming concept that is not always understood by children.

Potentially, transitivity can be examined in any quantitative domain. In fact, research on transitivity, both by Piaget and by others, has concentrated largely on two domains: length and weight. Length is usually studied with sticks of different lengths; weight, with clay balls of different weights. In both cases, the starting point is the comparison of A with B and B with C. With sticks the comparison is usually in the form of juxtaposition and visual examination; with clay balls a two-pan balance scale is typically used. The child is usually required to verbalize the results of the two comparisons; the child may also be required to recall them immediately before making the A–C judgment. The essential point in presenting the A–C test is that the correct answer not be perceptually apparent. With weight this requirement can be met by using balls of identical size. With length the usual procedure is to use sticks that are quite close in length (e.g., 20″ and $20\frac{1}{4}$″) and to ask the A–C question with the sticks either widely separated or out of sight. In some studies the sticks have been placed in Müller-Lyer arrows to create an illusion that is opposed to the correct answer.

The transitivity procedure just described can be said to involve a "passive inference," in the sense that the information necessary for the inference is carefully fed into the child (Bryant, 1974). Piaget's original studies (Piaget, Inhelder, & Szeminska, 1960) also included a test for a more "active" or "spontaneous" inference. In this task the child's job was to build a tower of bricks on one table so that it was the same height as an already constructed tower on a second table. Since the tables were of different heights and separated by a screen, simple visual comparison of the tops of the towers was not sufficient. There were, however, various rods and strips of paper nearby that could be used as measuring instruments. In its simplest form, the problem could be solved by finding a rod (B) that was the same height as the constructed tower (A) and then using the rod to build the new tower (C); thus A = C because A = B and B = C. Note, however, that in this case the child must realize the possibility of measurement and carry out the relevant operations unassisted. Not surprisingly, such active inference tasks turn out to be more difficult than the more often studied passive inferences.

All of the tasks described thus far are used by Piaget to diagnose the movement from preoperational (early childhood) to concrete operational (middle childhood) thought. Such thought is concrete in the sense that it remains closely tied to immediate, tangible reality, and may at first be limited in its generality by this dependence on concrete features of the world. Thus, as we saw, a budding conservation concept cannot at first be applied to all relevant stimuli and situations, and a burgeoning knowledge of class inclusion is not at first completely generalizable. According to Piaget, by some time around adolescence most children overcome such limitations and enter a final stage of development, the formal operational stage. The essence of *formal operational reasoning* is the capacity for hypothetico-deductive thought—the ability to move beyond immediate reality to generate *all* the possibilities for a situation and then systematically determine which of the various possibilities in fact hold true. Such thought, according to Piaget, reflects a reversal in the relation between reality and possibility. For the concrete operational child the starting point is always immediate reality, from which very limited extensions can be made into the world of the possible. For the formal operational child the starting point is the whole world of possibility, from which the child can work back, via various logical operations, to what happens to be true in the situation under study.

Inhelder and Piaget's (1958) procedures for studying formal operations consist mainly of various problems in scientific reasoning. We will describe one of these, the pendulum task. The apparatus for the pendulum task is a simple pendulum consisting of a bar, hanging string, and weight attached to the string. The subject's task is to determine which of the possible causal variables (length of string, amount of weight, height of drop, force of push) determine the frequency of oscillation of the pendulum. It turns out that only the length of the string matters. The real interest, however, is not in the correct answer but in the procedures by which the child attempts to arrive at the answer. Can the child isolate all of the potentially relevant factors, systematically test all of the possibilities, and draw logical conclusions from the results of these tests? As the following protocols suggest, the younger child is unlikely to be able to sustain such a hypothetico-deductive chain; the older child is much more likely to succeed.

PER (10:7) is a remarkable case of a failure to separate variables: He varies simultaneously the weight and the impetus; then the weight, the impetus, and the length; then the impetus, the weight, and the elevation, etc., and first concludes: *It's by changing the weight and the push, certainly not the string.— How do you know that the string has nothing to do with it—Because it's the same string.*—He has not varied its length in the last several trials; previously he had varied it simultaneously with the impetus, thus complicating the account of the experiment.—*But does the rate of speed change?—That depends, sometimes it's the same. . . . Yes, not much. . . . It also depends on the height that you put it at* [the string]. *When you let go low down, there isn't much speed.* He then draws the conclusion that all four factors operate: *It's in changing the weight, the push, etc. With the short string, it goes faster,* but also *by changing the weight, by giving a stronger push,* and *for height, you can put it higher or lower.—How can you prove that?—You have to try to give it a push, to lower or raise the string, to change the height and the weight* [he wants to vary all factors simultaneously] [Inhelder & Piaget, 1958, p. 71; this quotation and subsequent quotations from Inhelder & Piaget, 1958, are reprinted with permission of Basic Books, Inc.]. EME (15:1), after having selected 100 grams with a long string and a medium length string, then 20 grams with a long and a short string, and finally 200 grams with a long and a short, concludes: *It's the length of the string that makes it go faster or slower; the weight doesn't play any role.* She discounts likewise the height of the drop and the force of her push [Inhelder & Piaget, 1958, p. 75].

Subsequent research on formal operations has stuck fairly closely to the original Inhelder and Piaget approach, generally using either the original tasks or slight variations of them. Recently, however, there have been some interesting attempts to break away from the physics–chemistry problems that have dominated formal operational studies to search for comparable reasoning in other content domains. We will consider some of this work in our section on Assessment.

The final task that we will describe is directed to a very important ability within Piaget's system; it has also spawned more follow-up work than any other Piagetian task with the possible exception of conservation. The development in question is *role taking:* the ability to put oneself in the point of view of someone whose perspective is different from one's own. Role taking has a converse in *egocentrism:* the failure to break away from one's own perspective to adjust to the perspectives of others. Piaget's first book (Piaget, 1926) set forth the thesis that egocentrism is prevalent in young children and only gradually diminishes across childhood. Much research since then, by both Piaget and others, has been directed to this thesis.

There are many contexts in which role taking can occur and many kinds of role taking that can be examined. We will limit our discussion to two of the most often studied forms. One is generally labeled "visual [or spatial] perspective taking"—the ability to figure out how someone else's visual experience differs from one's own. In Piaget's original research (Piaget & Inhelder, 1956), the primary measure of visual perspective taking was the three-mountains task pictured in Figure 6.1. The child was seated on one side of the display and given the job of figuring out how the display would look to a doll placed at various other points around the landscape. Note that a correct response requires at least two components: an initial realization that the doll does not see the same view as oneself, and some subsequent ability to calculate what the doll in fact does see. Research since Piaget's has followed the same basic format: presentation of a display whose appearance varies with perspective, coupled with a requirement that the child judge how the display would look from at least one perspective other than his or her own. Variations in procedure have been of two main sorts. One is in the complexity of the display, with a trend in recent research toward simpler displays than the Piagetian mountains. The other

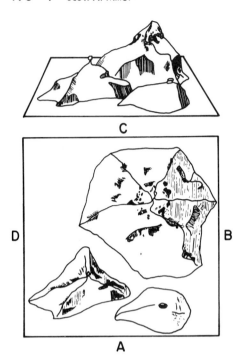

FIGURE 6.1. Three-mountains task for assessing visual perspective taking. (From *The Child's Conception of Space,* by J. Piaget and B. Inhelder, 1956. Reprinted by permission of Routledge & Kegan Paul Ltd./W. W. Norton.)

is in the mode of response required of the child. Thus the child may convey his or her understanding of different perspectives by selecting a picture that matches the view seen by another, by moving the other to a location presented in a picture, by rearranging the stimuli to show how the display would look from another perspective, or by rotating the display to obtain the perspective viewed by the other. The first three of these techniques, it can be noted, were used in the original Piaget and Inhelder study.

A second much-studied context for role taking is communication. In talking to others there is an obvious need to adjust one's message to the needs of the listener—to take into account what the other person knows, sees, feels, etc. That young children's speech does not always show such adjustments is evident to anyone who has ever conversed with a young child; it has also been amply demonstrated by research. Two main techniques of study have been used, both in Piaget's original work and in more recent follow-ups. One is to record and analyze children's spontaneously occurring speech—for example, in a nursery school or playground setting. The other is to pose an experimental task in which the child attempts to communicate information to a listener who initially, for any of several possible reasons (difference in immediate perceptual input, lack of relevant past experience, lower developmental level), does not share his or her knowledge.

In the following example the child's task is to describe one stimulus out of an array so that a listener with an identical array can pick the same stimulus (Glucksberg, Krauss, & Higgins, 1975, p. 321). Note that the two children are separated by a screen and hence cannot see each other or each other's arrays.

Speaker: *It's a bird.*
Listener: *Is this it?*
Speaker: *No.*

As noted, role taking has become a very popular research topic in recent years. Since we will have space in later sections only to touch on this recent work, one general point will be made here. Virtually any role-taking study taps more than simply the avoidance of literal egocentrism—that is, the realization that the other's perspective is *somehow* different from one's own. Often the additional response requirements may be quite demanding. In a communication task, for example, successful performance may depend not only on role taking but also on perceptual analysis of the stimuli and adequate vocabulary to convey their attributes. In a visual perspective-taking task, correct solution may require not just a realization of different perspectives but also a complex process of spatial calculation. Much recent role-taking research has had the goal either of simplifying the role-taking task or of breaking it clearly into component skills. Such research has led to at least two general conclusions: Young children are not as strongly or exclusively egocentric as Piaget claimed, and role taking is not a single ability but a multifaceted process that undergoes many changes as children develop (for elaboration of these points, see recent reviews by Gelman, 1978, and Shatz, 1977).

ISSUES AND METHODS OF STUDY

With this sampling of tasks as background, we are ready to turn to some central issues. Of the many issues that might be discussed, we will concentrate on three. They can be summarized as follows: What exactly does the child know? How does this knowledge relate to other developing abilities? How does new knowledge enter the cognitive system? To anticipate our subsequent terminology, these are the issues of Assessment of Knowledge, Patterning of Knowledge, and Origins of Knowledge.

Although we will discuss the three issues separately, it should be clear that they are not really independent questions. Rather, answers to any one of the questions are influenced by how one thinks about and studies the other two. To some extent, however, it is both possible and useful to consider them separately.

Assessment of Knowledge

The assessment question is a basic one: What exactly is it that our tasks are measuring? For any concept of interest, what are the possible ways to probe a child's understanding, and what conclusions can be drawn from these different methods? This issue was necessarily considered to some extent in our discussion of the basic Piagetian approach; in this section we will examine it both more fully and more critically.

A reasonable first question is why we should be concerned about precise assessment of cognitive skills. What does it matter, for example, if some understanding of conservation turns out to be elicitable at age 5 rather than $5\frac{1}{2}$ or 6? By now, certainly, everyone knows that age norms are unimportant to Piaget's theory. There are several answers to this "merely age norms" criticism. One is that description is a valid part of any science, and it is clearly best to make our descriptions (of conservation or anything else) as accurate and specific as possible. Beyond this descriptive goal, the question of assessment is relevant to a number of more functional issues in developmental psychology. Indeed, assessment is critical for all of the issues that we will be examining subsequently. It is impossible, for example, to evaluate claims about patterning in development without precise methods for assessing the various abilities in question. Similarly, studies that attempt to trace the origins of knowledge require assessment at various points in the movement from not understanding to understanding. Finally, the issue of assessment is also of obvious educational relevance, since our conceptions of educational "readiness" necessarily depend on the abilities that our current assessment techniques can reveal.

Piaget's Approach. We will begin our discussion of each issue with a review of Piaget's approach to the problem. We can then move on to alternative methods. In the case of assessment, we have already described the basic Piagetian techniques for assessing concepts like conservation and class inclusion. We have also indicated some general characteristics of the approach that cut across specific content areas. These include (a) an emphasis on a variety of tasks and variations of those tasks in the study of any cognitive domain (b) a "clinical" method of questioning that allows a flexible probing of the child's understanding (c) an attempt when possible to relate the questioning to concrete, manipulable materials (d) a dependence, nevertheless, on language both in the questions directed to the child and the child's responses and (*e*) a general conservativeness in drawing positive inferences about the child's ability.

Criticisms and consequent revisions of Piaget's assessment procedures have been of two main sorts. One sort can be summarized under the general heading of "cleaning up"—that is, attempts to alter certain idiosyncratic and bothersome aspects of Piaget's techniques to bring the approach more into line with standard (and familiar) experimental methodology. Included in this category are studies that attempt to standardize procedures that are left variable in Piaget, correct potentially unclear or biasing aspects of wording or stimulus presentation, apply standard statistical procedures to the data, etc. Revisions of this sort are virtually automatic in Piaget-inspired research these days, and will not be focused on as such.

The second kind of revision is more drastic. The motivation for studies in this category is a belief that Piaget's procedures may result in a fundamental miscalculation of the child's ability. The attempt, therefore, is to devise a major change in the methods of assessment and thereby arrive at a truer picture of the child's competence. Almost always, the specific concern has been that Piagetian techniques may underestimate children's ability, and the changes therefore have been in the direction of simplification. Although a variety of aspects of Piagetian assessment have been deemed worthy of change, the heavy verbal loading of the tasks has undoubtedly been the most frequent impetus for change.

If space permitted, it would be desirable to discuss follow-up research in this second category for each of the five tasks that were described in the previous section. Because space does not permit, the attempt instead will be to identify a few general approaches that are applicable across a variety of Piagetian concepts. We can still draw upon our five prototypical tasks for specific examples.

Nonverbal Choice Procedures. Probably the most common criticism of Piagetian assessment is that the child's understanding of concepts like conservation and class inclusion is filtered through words like "same" "more," "less," and "number." Perhaps the child who fails the conservation task really understands the concept but is simply confused about what the experimenter means by these words. An obvious way to test this possibility would be to assess conservation without using the usual words. Suppose, for example, that we allow children simply to pick the row of candies that they would like to eat or the glass of juice that they would like to drink. Could we then use such choices to draw inferences about their ability to conserve number or quantity?

An example of such a nonverbal choice technique is shown in Figure 6.2. The candies were first presented in one-to-one correspondence, thus mak-

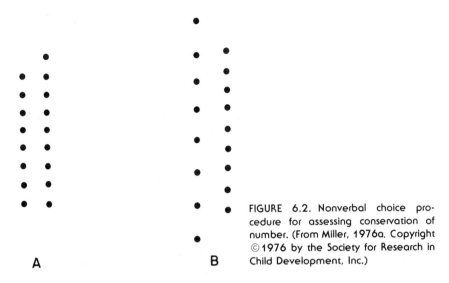

FIGURE 6.2. Nonverbal choice procedure for assessing conservation of number. (From Miller, 1976a. Copyright © 1976 by the Society for Research in Child Development, Inc.)

A   B

ing the greater number in the row of nine readily apparent. The children were asked which row they would pick if they could have one row to take home to eat, and almost all children indicated the row of nine. A conservation transformation was then performed, after which the children were in fact allowed to select a row to keep. The inference drawn was that selection of the row of nine indicated conservation; selection of the row of eight, nonconservation.

The kind of nonverbal choice procedure just described is not limited to conservation. Siegel, McCabe, Brand, and Matthews (1978) applied a similar technique to the assessment of class inclusion. The subjects in their study were shown a collection of candies (class A in our earlier terminology), some of which were smarties (subclass B), and some of which were jelly beans (subclass B′); they were then allowed to decide whether to eat all the candies or all the smarties. The procedure is also not limited to edible stimuli such as candies. King (1971) devised a game in which the child had to select either the longer or shorter of two sticks to successfully complete a bridge. Since the sticks were embedded in Müller-Lyer arrows prior to the choice, selection of the appropriate length stick could be taken as evidence of the ability to conserve length in the face of a perceptual change. Finally, the nonverbal choice procedure is not limited to situations in which there is some natural, preexisting basis for making a choice between the stimuli (as there is when choosing a collection of candy to eat). In what was probably the first of the "nonverbal" Piagetian studies, Braine (1959) used instrumental conditioning to train children to select the longer of two sticks. Once this response had been established, the problem was embedded in a transitivity paradigm of the $A>B$, $B>C$, $A?C$ sort. Consistent selections of stick A rather than stick C were taken as evidence of transitivity.

While the nonverbal choice procedure has its virtues, it also has its limitations. Although other applications might be imagined, the procedure is most obviously suited to tasks that involve a choice between different quantities; thus many interesting concepts fall outside its scope. Whenever candies or other consumable stimuli are used, there are possible problems of satiation or politeness; not all children will consistently attempt to pick the greater amount. When assessing conservation, it is necessary to depart from the typical conservation-of-equality framework and use unequal quantities in the two collections; otherwise there would be no logical basis for making a choice. The use of unequal quantities means that the non-conservation illusion is less than in the conservation-of-equality paradigm, raising the possibility that the child may be able to arrive at the correct answer through direct perception rather than logical reasoning. An obvious example of this problem from one of the earliest pick-the-candies studies is illustrated in Figure 6.3. Despite some initial excitement about apparent

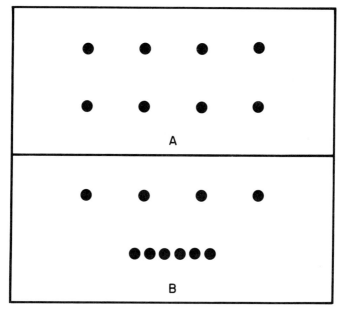

FIGURE 6.3. Nonverbal choice procedure with an obvious quantitative difference between the two collections. (From "Cognitive Capacity of Very Young Children" by J. Mehler and T. G. Bever, *Science, 158,* 141–142. Copyright 1967 by the American Association for the Advancement of Science.)

conservation in 2-year-olds, it now seems clear that selection of the row of six in this situation cannot be taken as evidence of conservation. Most generally, nonverbal choice techniques, in their attempt to avoid false negatives, turn out to be susceptible to various sorts of false positives, and the exact yield from such studies to date is therefore problematic. A very general conclusion from such research is that the verbal demands of the typical Piagetian task do result in some underestimation of young children's ability; the degree of underestimation, however, is probably not great (see Miller, 1976b, and Siegel, 1978, for fuller discussions).

Surprise Procedures. The possible utility of surprise as a diagnostic tool was first clearly advocated by Charlesworth (1964, 1969). The rationale is straightforward. The understanding of a concept (such as conservation) creates an expectancy that that concept will be confirmed whenever relevant evidence occurs. If evidence appears and the concept is *not* confirmed, this violation of expectancy will produce surprise. The surprise then serves as evidence that the concept was in fact understood. If, for example, the child is surprised at an apparent occurrence of nonconservation, the surprise tells us that the child expected conservation to hold true. The further argument, of course, is that such surprise may reveal an understanding of the concept at a time when the child is unable to pass the usual verbal test.

We will consider two examples of surprise studies, one directed to conservation and one to role taking. Gelman (1972) devised a game in which young children ($2\frac{1}{2}$ to 6) learned, through a series of choice trials, that a plate with three toy mice affixed to it was a "winner" and a plate with two toy mice was a "loser." Once the child had learned to pick the winner consistently, there was a single test trial on which a surreptitious change was produced in the winning plate. Two kinds of change were examined: subtraction of a mouse, or spreading or bunching of the row of mice. Among the responses measured was the child's surprise when the plate was uncovered and the change revealed. Gelman reported that fully 85% of the children showed surprise when confronted with a change in number; in contrast, only 27% were surprised by the spreading or bunching. Various other responses to the change were also recorded, such as search for a missing mouse, and they yielded the same conclusion: The children treated subtraction as an operation that was relevant to number and displacement as an operation that was irrelevant. Yet the age group tested was one which typically fails the standard conservation-of-number test.

Shantz and Watson (1970, 1971) developed a visual perspective-taking task in which the change in perspective was dependent on the child's own movement rather than the presence of another person. In their procedure the child first viewed the stimulus display through a window and then walked 180° around the display to look through a second window. In some cases the display was surreptitiously rotated while the child walked; thus the second view proved, quite illogically, to be identical to the first. About a third to a half of the 3–6-year-old subjects expressed surprise when shown the trick perspective. This proportion included a number of children who had failed a verbal test in which they attempted to predict the new perspective before moving. Thus the surprise measurement proved a useful supplement to the standard verbal assessment.

The diagnostic utility of surprise is clear in research programs such as Gelman's and Shantz and Watson's. Attempted applications of surprise techniques have not always proved so informative, however. Two main problems can be identified. First, investigators have sometimes failed to draw a clear link between their trick manipulation and the concept being violated. In some conservation-of-quantity studies, for example, the quantity of water has magically increased by six or seven times upon pouring. Surprise at such a change has been taken as evidence of conservation. The problem with such a procedure is that the change in quantity is so extreme that even many nonconservers may find it surprising. If a study is to provide evidence of conservation, it must utilize a change that *only* a conserver could possibly find surprising.

The second problem is one of measurement. Surprise can be a useful diagnostic tool only if we have ways to record its occurrence or nonoccurrence accurately. Most studies to date have inferred surprise from facial expressions and verbalizations; a few have attempted to utilize physiological responses as well. Various problems are evident. It is rare to find a really adequate description of the criteria used to infer surprise. Studies recording facial expressions have often failed to blind their raters with respect to the child's experimental condition or developmental level. In most studies the ratings have been made on the spot rather than from replayable videotapes. A few reports do not even include reliabilities for the ratings. In general, it seems fair to say that the degree of reported surprise varies inversely with the care with which surprise has been measured. Clearly, some improvement in methodology is necessary if surprise is to become a generally useful diagnostic construct.

Procedures to Enhance the Naturalness of the Task. The rather inelegant heading for this section encompasses a variety of specific procedural alterations. They do have a common goal, however, which is to move Piagetian assessment away from the rather artificial confines of the typical laboratory setting toward more natural, familiar, and ecologically valid situations for cognitive performance. The usual assumption has been that the increase in naturalness and familiarity will result in a more positive picture of the child's abilities. Whether or not this assumption is borne out, any increase in naturalness and hence external validity is clearly to the good.

Again, we will consider examples with respect to two abilities. A number of recent conservation studies have had as their starting point a belief that the usual method of assessing conservation is in some respects a rather strange and confusing situation for a young child. Consider the typical conservation-of-number task. The experimenter begins by carefully laying out two rows of objects in one-to-one correspondence, after which the child is explicitly asked whether the numbers are the same or different. Once the child has agreed to the equality, the experimenter deliberately spreads or bunches one of the collections, and the question about equality is repeated. Such a procedure embodies a specific focus on number and the operations that may affect number that is clearly not present in the child's usual dealings with objects. The only apparent reason for the spreading or bunching is the possibility that this action may affect number. The only apparent reason for repeating the question about equality so soon after the child has said "same" is the possibility that the answer has changed in the interim. In short, the typical procedure may bias the child toward a kind of error that he would be less likely to make in more natural settings.

Several recent studies have attempted in various ways to reduce the artificiality of the standard task. Rose and Blank (1974) devised a conservation-of-number test in which the initial question about equality was omitted and only the final posttransformation question was asked. Performance was much better in this new one-question version than on the standard test, leading Rose and Blank to conclude that the usual procedure of asking the same question twice makes some children think that they should change their answer. Since the initial answer was "same," the result would be an inflated level of apparent nonconservation. (It should be noted that replications of this claim have been inconsistent, with Silverman (1979) finding support and Miller (1977) finding no support.) McGarrigle and Donaldson (1974) invented a task in which the perceptual displacement of the stimuli was produced in an apparently accidental manner, occurring through the machinations of a naughty Teddy Bear. Their 4–6-year-old subjects were much less likely to believe that the number had changed when Teddy spread the stimuli than when the identical change was produced by the deliberate action of the experimenter. Finally, Light, Buckingham, and Robbins (1979) examined the effects of transformations that were not accidental but *incidental*—that is, changes produced deliberately but in a casual manner in the context of some other activity. Again, the modified form of transformation led to much better performance than did standard, very explicit changes.

Although the specific procedures vary, the studies just reviewed seem to carry a common message. The standard conservation task includes a number of features that are not found in the child's usual dealings with objects, features that may bias the child toward a nonconservation answer. When these features are removed, the probability of nonconservation decreases.

The second content area that we will consider is formal–operational reasoning. As noted earlier, Inhelder and Piaget's (1958) techniques for assessing formal operations consist of explicit problems in scientific reasoning drawn largely from the domain of the physical sciences. Noting this limitation in content and situation, several recent investigators have attempted to increase the naturalness and familiarity of the assessment. Kuhn and Brannock (1977) argued that the kind of situation studied by Inhelder and Piaget, in which the subject must actively generate and manipulate variables, is a less common real-life occurrence than is a situation in which the subject can simply observe naturally occurring variations and draw inferences from them. They therefore devised a "natural experiment," in which subjects received information about how certain variables related to plant growth and then made predictions about future outcomes. Sinnott (1975) concentrated on the familiarity of the content, reasoning that subjects might demonstrate higher levels of performance if tested with more familiar content than pendulums or chemical solutions. In her study, therefore, the problems posed had to do with such topics as cooking, furniture arrangement, and tire rotation. Finally, Capon and Kuhn (1979) sought to move the assessment out of the laboratory and into a more natural environment. In their study the capacity for proportional reasoning was tested via purchase decisions made by shoppers in a supermarket.

It should be noted that the procedural variations just described have not always led to better performance than the traditional methods. More generally, it should be clear that moving an assessment closer to real life does not mean that children will necessarily perform better. Recall the earlier distinction between "active" and "passive" transitive inferences. The former are doubtless more typical of whatever the real-life situations may be in which transitivity occurs, yet for a period in development children find the latter kind of task much easier. The general point is that there is a distinction between optimal performance and typical performance. Clearly, we need assessment techniques for both sorts of issues.

Conclusions. The studies reviewed in this section, as well as much other recent work that we have not had space to include, lead to four general conclusions.

1. The general validity of the assessment techniques devised by Piaget

has been amply confirmed by follow-up research. Despite a number of specific points of dispute, it seems clear that the overall Piagetian view of development has a good deal of truth to it.

2. When Piaget's techniques have led to miscalculations of the child's ability, the miscalculation has almost always been one of under-estimation. The procedural simplifications introduced in more recent work have often revealed that the young child's competence is greater than previously suspected. It has become clear that it can be dangerous ever to assert flatly that the child "does not have" a certain ability.

3. Assertions that the child "has" a certain ability may be equally problematic, however. The research reviewed here has not necessarily demonstrated that a full-fledged mastery of concepts like conservation is present substantially earlier than claimed by Piaget. A clearer message is that the development of any concept is not simply an abrupt "doesn't have" to "has" transition, but rather involves various precursors, component skills, different levels or substeps in the movement toward full mastery, etc. What the methodological innovations of recent years have done is to make possible the charting of various levels or forms of understanding not revealed in the original Piagetian work.

4. It is important in cognitive assessment to devise situations that will elicit the child's optimal level of performance. It is also important to devise situations that will elicit performance typical of that in the child's natural environment. The two are not necessarily the same thing, and studies to date, despite a few recent efforts, have been more successful at the former than at the latter.

Patterning of Knowledge

The issue of patterning is the issue of organization: How are cognitive abilities related? Two main kinds of relation are claimed in Piaget's theory and have been the focus of follow-up research. One is the possibility that two abilities emerge in an invariant *sequence*. Not all sequences are of interest, of course; no one conducts research to verify or to explain the fact that children crawl before they learn calculus. The sequences that elicit study are those that may reveal theoretically interesting relations between the abilities in question. Is ability A perhaps a necessary building block in the development of ability B? Is A perhaps a related but simpler skill, requiring some but not all of the cognitive equipment necessary for B? Such hypotheses can be entertained only if children do in fact master A before B.

The second possibility is that two (or more) abilities emerge in *concurrence*. As with sequences, the goal of research on concurrences is to move beyond simply eliciting correct answers to reveal something about the underlying basis for correct response. In this case the possibility of interest is that the different abilities may have a common underlying basis—may, in Piagetian terms, be reflections of the same underlying cognitive structures. If so, then the abilities should emerge at least roughly in synchrony.

We can again begin with a summary of Piaget's approach to the issue, after which we can move on to follow-up work.

Piaget's Approach. With the exception of the work on infant intelligence, the great majority of Piaget's studies are cross-sectional rather than longitudinal—that is, they examine different children at different ages, rather than tracing the development of the same child over time. The lack of longitudinal study makes it impossible to demonstrate directly that every child attains ability A before ability B, since a given child is studied just once and within-child change is never assessed. Nevertheless, the lack of longitudinal study is not in itself fatal to the goal of identifying sequences and concurrences. As shown in Table 6.2, it is possible to find strong evidence for sequences or concurrences in cross-sectional data from different age groups—or, for that matter, in data from one age group of varying developmental level. What is critical is the pattern of successes and failures on the tasks being compared. If an A-before-B sequence exists, then three of the four logically possible outcomes can in fact occur; the only one that is impossible is success on B in conjunction with failure on A. If an A–B concurrence exists, then two of the four possible outcomes can occur; ruled out, however, are both A without B and B without A.

What is needed, then, is within-subject analysis—that is, testing of the same subject on each of the tasks that we wish to compare. It is precisely this kind of analysis that is lacking in Piaget's writings. Although it does seem clear that Piaget occasionally tests the same child across a number of tasks, his analyses rarely provide systematic information about within-subject performance.[2] Instead, the usual approach is to infer sequences or

TABLE 6.2
Patterns of Success and Failure and Their Relation to Sequences and Concurrences

Hypothesized relationship	Congruent patterns	Incongruent patterns
A–B Sequence	A+ B+ , A+ B− , A− B−	A− B+
A–B Concurrence	A+ B+ , A− B−	A+ B− , A− B+

Note: + denotes success, − denotes failure.

[2] Some of the more recent research from Piaget's Genevan co-workers does occasionally provide within-subject analyses. See Inhelder (1971).

188 : Scott A. Miller

concurrences from the mean age at which the tasks are passed. Thus, if task A is passed at an earlier average age than task B, an invariant sequence may be claimed; if A and B are passed at about the same age, a concurrence may be claimed. It should be noted that such age norms are not Piaget's only basis for claims about sequences and concurrences; of perhaps equal importance is a theoretical analysis that says that the abilities in question *should* emerge in the order predicted. In any case, the empirical grounding for the claims is often not very compelling.

The mere adoption of a within-subject approach is not sufficient to ensure clear conclusions about sequences and concurrences. Also important is the variable of task sensitivity, or what Flavell (1971) has called the "hit rate" of the tests. As Flavell notes, any cognitive task involves more than simply the logical principle to which it is directed (e.g., the transitivity principle in the case of a transitivity task). Rather, any task includes specific stimuli that may be more or less interesting, particular wording that may be more or less comprehensible, demands on memory that may be more or less heavy, etc. All of these additional, extralogical factors may affect performance; indeed, a main point of our preceding section was that such task variations often *do* affect performance. The challenge in comparing different abilities then becomes to ensure that these additional task demands are as comparable as possible across the different tests. It is only if the task sensitivity of the different tests is equated that valid conclusions about relative difficulty can be drawn.

Let us try an example to make this point clearer. Suppose that we select a test for ability A that is maximally sensitive (i.e., likely to elicit successful performance if the child has any understanding of A at all). Suppose that our test for ability B is considerably less sensitive and, in fact, full of obstacles to correct response. We may well find that success comes earlier on A than on B, perhaps even in what appears to be an invariant sequence. Yet the ontogenetic reality may be that B is actually mastered concurrently with or perhaps even earlier in development than A.

It seems fair to say that Piaget's studies often fail to equate task sensitivity when drawing conclusions about relative difficulty. It should be noted, however, that Piaget has not been unaware of the possible effects of task variations on intertask comparisons; indeed, as the following passage shows, he has cited such effects as an excuse for the absence of systematic cross-task comparisons in his research.[3]

---

[3] In the following passage the term *ordination* refers to operations concerned with the ordinal properties of number, for example, arranging or counting objects in a certain order. The term *cardination* refers to operations concerned with the cardinal properties of number, for example, realizing that two sets of 10 objects contain the same number.

Clearly then, the same processes and the same levels are to be found in the development of both ordination and cardination. But obviously any attempt to express the situation in statistical form and to apply correlation formulae to these tests would involve us in questions for which we must confess we have little interest. Is, for instance, this or that problem of ordination of which we have made use, of exactly the same difficulty as this or that other problem, either of ordination or cardination, independently of ordination and cardination in general? It is obvious that in each test a considerable number of heterogeneous factors intervene, e.g., the words used, the length of the instructions given, their more or less concrete character, the relationship between the instructions and the individual experience of the child, the number of elements involved, the intervention of numbers the child knows, etc., etc. We noticed wide differences in the results of the various tests of cardinal correspondence, showing that we never succeed in measuring understanding of this correspondence in its pure state and that the understanding is always with respect to a given problem and given material. The calculation of the correlation between the levels of cardination and ordination, without the accompaniment of an extremely thorough qualitative analysis, could therefore give only misleading results, unless our experiments were transformed into "tests" in which statistical precision could no doubt easily be obtained, but at the cost of no longer knowing exactly what was being measured [Piaget & Szeminska, 1952, p. 149].

Pairwise Comparisons. The simplest approach to the issue of patterning is the kind of pairwise comparison that was outlined in Table 6.1. Let us consider two examples. McManis (1969) sought to determine the relative difficulty of conservation and transitivity. All subjects received tests, balanced for order, for four concepts: conservation of length, transitivity of length, conservation of weight, and transitivity of weight. Although the task variables were at least roughly equated (e.g., similar stimuli, similar wording), an examination of the procedures suggests that the tests for transitivity were probably somewhat more rigorous than those for conservation. In any case, McManis found that the majority of children performed comparably on conservation and transitivity, either passing both or failing both. When a discrepancy did occur, however, conservation turned out to be much easier: There were 35 instances of success on conservation coupled with failure on transitivity, compared to only five instances of the reverse pattern.

Brainerd (1973) also examined the relative difficulty of conservation and transitivity for both length and weight. His procedures differed from those of McManis in several ways. Perhaps the most important differences were that his transitivity tasks did not include a countervailing perceptual illusion (e.g., placement of the sticks in Müller-Lyer arrows), and the analyses were based on correct answers only, without the requirement of an adequate explanation. Brainerd's results proved quite different from those of

McManis: The majority of pairwise comparisons (across several samples and studies) indicated that transitivity was easier than conservation. In Brainerd's Study II, for example, there were 51 instances of transitivity without conservation, and only six instances of the reverse.

Most of the general points that can be made about these studies apply also to the other research to be considered in this section and consequently will be reserved for later. Three quick points can be made here, however. First, not all studies are as inconsistent in their outcomes as the McManis and Brainerd research; there are *some* well-established patterns in cognitive development. Second, inconsistency in outcome, while perhaps not rampant, is also not atypical; many other examples of discrepancies between studies could easily be cited. Finally, while the inconsistencies in outcome almost certainly relate to variations in procedure, the issue of which investigator has done the best job of equating task sensitivity—and therefore whose results come closest to reflecting developmental reality—remains in most cases quite debatable.

Scaling Approaches. The studies just considered compared performance on only two tasks at a time. Suppose that we are interested in looking simultaneously at the relative difficulty of a much larger number of tasks. Calculations of all possible pairwise comparisons would be both unwieldy (e.g., 45 comparisons in the case of 10 tasks) and difficult to interpret. There is an alternative, however, in the form of *scalogram analysis*. The logic of the scalogram approach is the same as that of the paired-comparisons approach, extended, however, to apply to multiple rather than single comparisons. Suppose that our hypothesis is that a set of six abilities develops in the order A-B-C-D-E-F. There are a number of possible patterns of performance that are compatible with such a sequence, including success on all tasks, failure on all tasks, success on A only, success on A and B only, etc. There are also a (larger) number of possible patterns that are incompatible with such a sequence—specifically, any in which a supposedly later ability (e.g., B) is mastered before a supposedly earlier ability (e.g., A). What the scalogram analysis does is determine whether the obtained patterns of performance are or are not compatible with a model of sequential emergence.

Let us try an example. Kofsky (1966) sought to verify a hypothesized sequence in the development of classification abilities derived from the work of Inhelder and Piaget (1964). She devised tests for 11 different classification skills, varying in expected difficulty from simple resemblance sorting to the class inclusion concept described earlier. As far as possible, common stimuli, labels, and methods of presentation were used across the 11 tests. The individual patterns of response were analyzed in various ways, all of which yielded the same conclusion: The 11 abilities showed some but far-from-perfect scalability. Thus, had the scalability been perfect, there would have been only 12 patterns of response (failure on all tasks, success on the easiest only, success on the two easiest only, etc.). There were in fact 63 patterns, and only 27% of the subjects showed a perfectly scalable pattern. Two further measures of scalability were calculated: Loevinger's test of interitem homogeneity (Loevinger, 1947) and Green's index of reproducibility (Green, 1956). The conclusion from both was that certain subsets of items appeared to show sequential emergence; overall, however, there were many deviations from both the theoretically expected and the empirically most common sequence.

The Kofsky study is a good framework for making several points about scaling approaches. First, as might be guessed from our rather cursory reference to the Loevinger and Green statistics, the determination of scalability involves a number of specific techniques and a number of complexities that we will not have the space to explore here. Useful sources with respect to the pros and cons of various scaling techniques, especially as applied to cognitive development, are books by Green, Ford, and Flamer (1971) and Wohlwill (1973). A second point concerns the distinction between theoretically predicted and empirically derived sequences. A scalogram analysis can be used to test for a theoretically predicted sequence, as in Kofsky's test of Piaget's model of classification. More generally, however, the scalogram can reveal whatever ordering is present in the obtained pattern of responses, whether that order was predicted or not. Finally, as in all methods for assessing patterns, the scalogram approach is only as good as the tests that go into it. If the tests are unreliable or of differential sensitivity, the scalogram can hardly be expected to yield an accurate picture of development.

Correlational Approaches. A third approach to the study of patterning involves the calculation of correlations among responses to the various tasks of interest. Adoption of a correlational approach is most likely when performance is scored along some ordered continuum of correctness or developmental level, rather than being limited to dichotomous, pass–fail categories. It is also most likely when the guiding hypothesis for the research is that of a common underlying basis for the different abilities being measured. The general expectation is then of a positive correlation among responses to the various tasks, that is, at least some degree of concurrence in their mastery.

We will consider role taking as our content area for the discussion of correlational approaches. We have already noted that role taking is not a single cognitive entity but a multifaceted process with numerous different applications. We already expect, therefore, to find less than perfect concurrence in the response to different role-taking tasks. Nevertheless, the question can be asked whether there is at least *some* concurrence—some indication of a common underlying basis, some justification for assigning the label "role taking" to all of the various measures. It is this question to which the correlational studies are directed.

One of the most ambitious attempts to evaluate the construct of role taking was reported by Rubin (1978). His study included tests for two different forms of role taking: cognitive role taking, or the ability to figure out what someone else knows; and affective role taking, or the ability to figure out what someone else feels. The battery for assessing cognitive role taking comprised four tasks (including the Glucksberg *et al.* communication task described earlier); that for affective role taking comprised two tasks. Also included were measures of verbal IQ, social status, and response time on a test of cognitive style. The tasks were administered to children at four different age levels, and all possible correlations of response to one task with responses to the other tasks were calculated.

In general, Rubin found little support for a general construct of role taking. The correlations among the various role-taking tasks were moderate at best, most falling in the .10 to .25 range. This pattern of low correlations held both within a particular form of role taking (e.g., cognitive) and across all role-taking measures combined. The finding of a weak relation among role-taking measures confirmed the results of most previous studies of the issue (e.g., Kurdek & Rodgon, 1975), although occasional reports of stronger correlations have appeared (e.g., Rubin, 1973).

The Rubin study can be used to illustrate several general points about correlational research. Suppose that the correlations among Rubin's role-taking measures had been substantially higher—would the results then have confirmed the notion of a general role-taking ability? The answer is that high correlations in themselves would not be sufficient, because there would be no way to be certain that role taking was the critical process responsible for the correlations. Perhaps, to take an obvious alternative, the correlations might be a simple reflection of the fact that high-competent children tend to do well whatever the task, and low-competent children tend to do poorly whatever the task. What we need, in short, is evidence not just for *convergent* validity— the fact that the role-taking measures correlate—but also for *discriminant* validity—the fact that other, theoretically unrelated measures do *not* correlate. This, in fact, was Rubin's purpose in including the measures of IQ, social status, and cognitive style. Had the role-taking correlations been higher, then the correlations with these other, supposedly unrelated measures would have become an important test of the role-taking hypothesis.

A second issue concerns the interpretation of correlations in multi-age samples. Suppose that Rubin had calculated correlations for his entire 5–10-year-old sample and had found substantial interrelations of performance across the different role-taking tasks. Clearly, such a finding could come about simply because older children tend to do better on all tasks than younger children, thus assuring some degree of correlation across any tasks that we might measure. There are two ways to control for this possibility, both of which were in fact used by Rubin. One is to calculate correlations within rather than across age. The other is to utilize a statistical procedure known as *partial correlation*. Partial correlation is a technique for statistically removing the contribution of one variable to a correlation and determining whether the resulting correlation remains significant. In this case what would be done is to calculate correlations across the entire sample but to partial out the effects of age in determining the final correlations. When Rubin utilized this procedure he found the same low concurrence among role-taking measures that had held within each age group separately.

There are two remaining points to be made about the correlational approach. The first is similar to a point made with regard to pairwise comparisons: the larger the number of tasks, the larger the number of possible correlations and the more difficult the job of making sense of the pattern of significant and nonsignificant results. Again, however, there is an alternative to the consideration of every separate test; in this case the alternative is a technique known as *factor analysis*. As with scalogram approaches, factor analysis involves a number of complexities that are beyond our scope here; the interested reader is referred to Comrey (1973) for a helpful introduction. Briefly, the goal of factor analysis is to abstract the structure in a set of responses by reducing an initially large matrix of correlations to a much smaller set of clusters or "factors," that is, sets of tasks that correlate among themselves and thus may have a common underlying basis. In role-taking research the goal would be to determine whether the various role-taking measures tend to cluster together on a single common factor. Rubin (1978) did not include such an analysis; Rubin (1973) did, however, and reported some clustering and thus some support for a general role-taking construct.

The second point concerns the scope of the correlational approach. The fact that we have limited our discussion to role taking does not mean that correlational analyses are unsuited for other issues within Piagetian theory. In fact, the correlational approach, including its factor-analytic extensions, has also been used to examine Piagetian claims about interrelations among both concrete operational (e.g., Toussaint, 1974) and formal operational (e.g., Bart, 1971) tasks.

Conclusions. Most of the general points to be made about research on patterning have already been touched on in the discussion of particular approaches and need be only briefly reiterated here.

1. Two things are necessary for the study of patterning: within-subject testing and equating of task sensitivity. The latter may often be hard to achieve. Our earlier discussion of this issue should not be taken as implying that we can never decide whether one study has been more successful in equating its tasks than another—there *are* criteria for judging the validity of a task and the comparability of different tasks. Nevertheless, the point remains that the determination of task sensitivity, and therefore the evaluation of intertask comparisons, is often very difficult.

2. Recent research on patterning has seen the increased utilization of sophisticated and powerful statistical techniques, including the scaling and factor analytic approaches briefly described here. The availability of this impressive statistical battery, however, should not make us lose track of the fact that the necessary starting point for any study is accurate assessment of the abilities in question.

3. Results from research on patterning have been mixed. There do seem to be some well-established sequences in development. Really clear demonstrations of concurrence are much less common.

4. In evaluating the results of studies of patterning it has sometimes been frustratingly difficult to be clear about exactly what Piaget's theory predicts. In the case of the conservation–transitivity comparison, for example, some researchers have assumed that Piaget's theory implies simultaneous emergence, whereas others have assumed that conservation should emerge before transitivity. More generally, there has been considerable disagreement about exactly how much concurrence is implied by Piaget's stage model, and therefore how troublesome for the theory is the pervasive finding of nonconcurrence (see Flavell, 1977, and Wohlwill, 1973, for further discussions).

Origins of Knowledge

The question of origins is the question of where knowledge comes from. How, for example, does the child move from not understanding to understanding conservation? This overall question can be divided into two (related) subquestions. One concerns the underlying cognitive basis for correct responses. When an understanding of conservation emerges, does this understanding reflect a set of mental actions or "operations," as is claimed in Piaget's theory? Or is there perhaps a different underlying basis, such as internal use of language or application of a new information-processing strategy? The issue, in short, is what is the nature of the knowledge that our assessment techniques reveal.

The second question concerns the experiences through which new knowledge is acquired. Does the child come to master concepts like conservation through direct experience with the world of physical objects? Is interaction with adults or peers important? Do biological–maturational factors contribute? And whatever the contributors may be, exactly how do they operate? If adults are important, for example, is it because they transmit information verbally to the child? Reinforce correct answers? Provide models of appropriate responding? Or what?

Two preliminary points should be made before proceeding to the discussion of relevant evidence. First, the mass of potentially relevant evidence is huge. Even more than for the preceding topics, therefore, our coverage will be selective, concentrating on a few illustrative approaches from which some general conclusions can be drawn.

The second point is that despite the mass of relevant evidence we really know very little about how new knowledge develops. The issue is obviously an especially difficult one to study, and there are limitations to any approach that might be tried. This is a theme that will be developed as we go.

Piaget's Approach. Piaget's theory has long set forth some definite claims about how cognitive change comes about. Very briefly, the essential claims include the following. The underlying basis for true knowledge always lies in a complex system of interrelated actions. During infancy the actions are external; later in development they are internal. The system of actions stems from the child's active constructive involvement with the world, as opposed to a passive taking in of information. This active involvement applies to both the physical world and the social world. In both cases, what children must do is "assimilate" experiences to their current cognitive structures, that is, fit new experiences into what they already understand. This need to build upon what one already knows sets definite constraints on how rapidly cognitive progress can occur.

Through what kinds of evidence has Piaget arrived at this conception of cognitive change? We have already noted that his work on postinfancy development is almost all cross-sectional; thus there clearly can be no long-term tracing of the growth of knowledge in a particular child. We can now add that the post infancy work is also almost all what we might call diagnostic—that is, it is oriented to assessing abilities that the child already possesses, rather than to studying the acquisition of new abilities. Thus the studies of conservation, for example, include many ingenious tests for assessing what children do or do not know about conservation, but no real test of how it is that the child moves from not knowing to knowing.

There is only one aspect of Piaget's research that escapes these limitations, and that is the work on infant intelligence (e.g., Piaget, 1952b). It is only for infancy that Piaget has attempted long-term longitudinal study; it is also only for infancy that his work includes extensive observations of children in the process of acquiring new knowledge. And indeed, it seems clear that many of Piaget's basic ideas about cognitive change derive from the study of infant intelligence. It is here, for example, that the assimilation-accommodation model was formulated, and here that the notion of intelligence as action was first clearly set forth. It seems likely that much of Piaget's thinking about the origins of knowledge in later development was shaped by the studies of infancy.

Apart from the infancy work, at least two other sources for Piaget's ideas about cognitive change can be identified. One is a logical analysis of the abilities in question. For each of the abilities we have discussed, Piaget's original writings include a detailed analysis of the presumed underlying logic. Class inclusion, for example, is analyzed in terms of the logical addition of classes, with the correct $A > B$ solution dependent upon the realization that B and B' add together to form A and that A minus B leaves a remainder of B' (again, the reader is referred to Flavell, 1963, for a fuller discussion). Piaget's argument seems to be that logical analyses of this sort can reveal the cognitive processes by which children arrive at their answers—if class inclusion is describable in this way, then children must solve it this way. Clearly, however, this argument is not necessarily valid. As long as other bases for correct response can be imagined—and other bases always *can* be imagined—the logical analysis is not sufficient. It may be a useful starting point, but further evidence is necessary.

Piaget also occasionally makes use of the explanations that children offer for their answers. If, for example, a child explains conservation of quantity in terms of the fact that the increase in the height of the water is compensated for by the decrease in width, this explanation may be taken as evidence that the child arrived at the correct answer through a logical multiplication of the two dimensions. Piaget sometimes puts special stress in this regard on the explanations offered by transitional subjects (i.e., children who show some but imperfect understanding), because they are the ones who presumably are in the process of mastering the concept. Even with transitional subjects, however, there is a basic limitation in the use of explanations, and that is that there is simply no guarantee that post hoc explanations reveal anything about the processes that went into solving the problem. Furthermore, Piaget's use of explanations tends to be selective; in fact, children offer many justifications that bear no obvious relation to Piaget's theory of underlying process.

Clearly, then, we need other sources of evidence. We turn now to what has been the most popular paradigm for attempting to explicate cognitive change: the training study.

Training Studies. The goal of training research is to determine whether children who do not understand a concept can be induced to understand it through the provision of selected experiences. The concept that has been studied most is conservation, and the specific goal has therefore been to see what kinds of experiences are effective in teaching nonconservers to conserve. The hope has been that successful training can tell us something about the underlying nature of the concept and the real-life routes to its development.

The training literature is now both very large and very diverse. It includes, it should be noted, some recent studies by Piaget's Genevan co-workers; see Inhelder, Sinclair, and Bovet (1974) for a summary. Rather than trying to pick a few representative studies, we will begin with a general summary of what training studies to date have found. We will then move on to some of the methodological issues that must be considered when evaluating training research. Further reviews and discussion can be found in Beilin (1978), Brainerd (1978), Kuhn (1974), and Modgil and Modgil (1976).

A first conclusion from training studies is that it is by no means easy to train concepts like conservation. There are a number of quite sensible-looking training procedures that have had little or no success. A second conclusion must be immediately added, however, and that is that it is by no means impossible to demonstrate successful training. There are now a large number of training studies that have produced what seem to be genuine advances in knowledge. A wide range of different procedures have proved effective. These include some that were explicitly derived from Piaget's theory—for example, training in the logical operations thought to underlie correct responses. They also include some that seem quite antithetical to Piaget—for example, instrumental conditioning or TV modeling. There may well be more commonality across the successful methods than is suggested by the diverse labels and interpretations given the studies by their authors; indeed, one major question in evaluating training research is whether the investigator's interpretation of what was important really captures the critical processes that led to success. Nevertheless, it is very doubtful that all successful training procedures can be reduced to any one common factor; the diversity is just too great.

Determining the basis for successful training is one important issue in the evaluation of training research. Another important issue is perhaps logically prior: Exactly how successful was the training? We noted earlier that Piaget tends to insist on rigorous criteria before crediting a child with genuine understanding of a concept. We can add now that this insistence becomes even more marked in the case of training studies. In the Piagetian view, genuine training implies not only the ability to give correct answers, but also the ability to provide a logical justification for the answers, generalize the correct response to related tasks, and maintain the correct answer over time and in the face of a challenge. The validity of some of these criteria can be questioned on both theoretical and empirical grounds (e.g., normal, nontrained development is at first far from perfectly generalizable). Nevertheless, the general point is certainly valid: What we are interested in is not simply whether children can parrot the correct answer to problems on which they have been directly trained (a fairly easy result to bring about) but whether they genuinely understand the concept. As would be expected, the apparent success of training tends to decrease as the rigor of the criteria increases. The conclusion in our preceding paragraph remains valid, however: Many studies have produced impressive gains in knowledge even when quite rigorous criteria are applied (e.g., Gelman, 1969).

A further issue concerns the distinction between experiences that are *sufficient* to bring about cognitive progress and experiences that are *necessary* to bring about cognitive progress. What training studies have identified is a large number of different kinds of experiences that appear sufficient, in a laboratory setting, to produce cognitive change. Clearly, however, the more kinds of experiences there are that are sufficient, the harder it becomes to argue that any one kind of experience is *necessary*. In a way, training studies are a victim of their own success. Fifteen years ago, when successful training was still a rare phenomenon, it was possible to maintain that a study had identified *the* basis for cognitive change. Such a position is hard to maintain today. Rather, to the extent that training studies have any relevance to normal development, the message may be that there can be multiple routes to the mastery of a concept like conservation. Some children may acquire conservation through one set of experiences, others through a somewhat different set of experiences, and still others through a still different set of experiences.

The final issue concerns the distinction between experiences that are sufficient to produce cognitive change and experiences that are typical in bringing about such change. All training studies involve a laboratory setting that is at least somewhat different from the real-life situations in which children make cognitive progress. In some cases the laboratory experience is radically different from any experience that children encounter in their natural environment. The question arises, therefore, of whether the training results can be generalized to the real-life situations in which we are interested. This question is of course not unique to training studies; rather the issue of the external validity of laboratory research is a very familiar and a very general issue in psychology. The familiarity of the issue, however, should not blunt its application to the training literature. Despite the large number of successful training studies, it is debatable whether any investigator has done a convincing job of relating his or her procedures to real-life, nontrained development.

Studies of Natural Variations in Experience. We have just seen that the artificiality of the typical training study may limit the conclusions that can be drawn. An obvious alternative is to seek out naturally occurring variations in experience. The goal is the same as that of training studies: to identify experiences that seem to be critical in the acquisition of knowledge. In this case, however, the experiences are naturally occurring rather than experimentally produced; thus we no longer need worry about the artificiality of the laboratory situation. At the same time, of course, we have bought this naturalness at the price of a severe decline in experimental control. This is a point that will be returned to shortly.

A number of different kinds of study fall under the heading of natural variations in experience. We will limit ourselves to one kind, with just brief mention of some other possibilities. The approach we will consider concerns the study of naturally occurring deprivations, that is, cases in which a particular kind of experience is unavailable to the child as he or she develops. The rationale for studies of this sort is the same as that for training research. Just as we can determine the importance of some factor by seeing what happens when we add it to the child's experience, so can we determine the importance of a factor by seeing what happens when it is subtracted from the child's experience.

Let us consider two examples. Piaget's stress on the child's active involvement with the world, including quite literal motoric involvement during infancy, would seem to imply that children deprived of such involvement would be severely handicapped in their intellectual development. Decarie (1969), Jordan (1972), and Kopp and Shaperman (1973) have all reported studies of individuals who, for various reasons, suffered severe limitations from birth in their ability to interact motorically with the world. Although some retardation in the speed of development was evident, the detrimental effects were not pronounced, and most of the subjects seemed to achieve a normal level of functioning. These data suggest that Piaget's theory of the origins of knowledge may overestimate the importance of literal, motoric action during the early years. In a more pro-Piaget vein, a number of studies have examined the cognitive development of deaf children, concentrating especially on the subset of deaf children who can be characterized as truly language-deficient. Although difficulties in development do sometimes occur, deaf children are not invariably retarded, and there are numerous instances of comparable performance by deaf and hearing children on Piagetian tasks (Furth, 1970). This finding has been seen as supportive of Piaget's theory, with its emphasis on general experience and its deemphasis of language, and as incompatible with opposing theories that place a heavy stress on language.

There are several problems that arise in interpreting such studies. It is often not clear exactly what the degree of deprivation has been. It may also not be clear just which aspects of the deprivation are important. Consider those cases in which deaf children perform more poorly than hearing children. Does this finding reflect the deaf child's language deprivation, his or her more general auditory deprivation, the restrictions in social interaction imposed by deafness, or what? In a well-designed experimental study the independent variable could be precisely defined and other variables ruled out. In research with naturally occurring variations, such control is impossible. A final problem concerns the generalization from the atypical case (such as a paralyzed or deaf child) to normal development. The most that studies of natural deprivation can demonstrate is that a particular kind of experience is not necessary for some aspect of development. They cannot demonstrate that such experiences do not typically contribute to development. It may well be, for example, that in the normal case motoric action during infancy plays a central role in the development of intelligence, just as Piaget claims. When such action is impossible, however, the child may be able to compensate via other kinds of experience and eventually reach the same level of development.

As noted, the studies of natural deprivation are just one example of research concerned with the effects of natural variations in experience. It is also possible to examine the effects of less extreme environmental variations. It can be asked, for example, whether natural, across-home variations in the physical or social environment early in life relate to the speed or quality of the child's intellectual development (e.g., Wachs, 1979). The same question can be asked cross-culturally: Are there differences between cultures that are associated with differences in the speed or the nature of cognitive development (e.g., Bruner, Olver, & Greenfield, 1966)? Studies of this sort escape some of the problems associated with a focus on atypical cases, such as deaf or paralyzed children. At the same time, such research remains naturalistic-correlational; as such, it is subject to the same problems of specifying variables and establishing cause-and-effect conclusions.

Longitudinal Studies. In this case we will begin with our illustrative study. Tomlinson-Keasy, Eisert, Kahle, Hardy-Brown, and Keasey (1979) tested a sample of grade-school children on five different occasions across a 3-year period. The tests consisted mainly of a variety of Piagetian tasks, including problems of class inclusion and conservation. The aspect of the study on which we will concentrate concerns the prediction of later development from earlier development. Suppose that we know which children have or have not mastered certain concepts by age 6; can we predict which of these children will have mastered a related set of concepts by age 8? To the extent that such prediction is possible, our data may tell us something about the building blocks of development—what it is that leads to what.

One segment of Tomlinson-Keasey et al.'s (1979) findings is illustrated in Figure 6.4. Shown here are the correlations between conservation of mass and class inclusion both within a particular time and across time. It can be seen that moderate correlations exist between the two abilities at any given time. From this finding alone it is impossible to know whether one ability contributes to the other or both reflect some other set of factors. What becomes critical in determining causality is the pattern of cross-time correlations presented on the two diagonals. Here it can be seen that conservation of mass at time 1 is moderately predictive of class inclusion at time 3; class inclusion at time 1, however, is not at all predictive of conser-

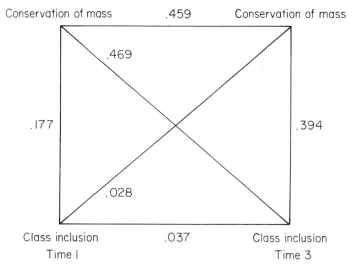

FIGURE 6.4. Cross-lagged panel correlations for conservation of mass and class inclusion across two times of measurement. (From Tomlinson-Keasey *et al.* Copyright © 1979 by the Society for Research in Child Development, Inc.)

vation of mass at time 3. This finding suggests that the direction of effect is from conservation to class inclusion rather than the reverse—that conservation (or, more probably, various component skills that underlie conservation) is a building block in the eventual mastery of class inclusion. Such "cross-lagged" correlations, in which patterns of correlation are tracked over time, have become a widely used tool for extracting causality from correlational data (see Kenny, 1975, for a much fuller discussion).

Research of the sort just described is directed to the issue that we have labeled the nature of knowledge—that is, what is the underlying cognitive basis for correct answers on tasks like class inclusion? The cross-lagged approach can also be used to examine the other issue that we have considered in this section, that of the experiential bases for cognitive change. What is needed are measurements at two different times of two things: aspects of the environment that may be important, and aspects of cognitive development that we wish to explain. If variations in the environment at time 1 prove predictive of variations in cognitive development at time 2, then we are in a position to argue (assuming that all assumptions of the cross-lagged approach have been met; again, see Kenny 1975) for a cause-and-effect conclusion. Although studies of this sort have not yet appeared, they seem a likely direction for future research.

Conclusions. Again, most of our general conclusions have been previewed in the discussion of particular approaches.

1. The question of cognitive change is an especially difficult one to study. Despite a large number of studies devoted to the issue, including many approaches not included here, our understanding of how knowledge develops remains very limited. This limitation, it should be noted, is not unique to Piagetian sorts of development; rather it applies to just about any interesting developmental change that we might consider. We know far more, for example, about the new linguistic rules that children master as they develop than we do about how it is that this mastery occurs (see Chapter 5). Similarly, information-processing psychologists have been far more successful at describing the different states that the cognitive system moves through than they have been at explaining the transition from one state to the next (see Chapter 7).

2. The general weakness of the experimental approach to the study of cognitive change is its artificiality and the consequent uncertainty about the generalizability of the results. The general weakness of the naturalistic approach is its lack of experimental control and the consequent uncertainty about cause-and-effect relations. To some ex-

tent, however, the weaknesses of one approach are compensated for by the strengths of the other. The obvious conclusion is that we need both, preferably used in close conjunction with each other. This prescription is, of course, just a specific instance of a very general point about the value of converging operations.

3. Probably Piaget's most fruitful work on the issue of cognitive change is to be found in the studies of infancy. The infancy studies are longitudinal in a very intensive, almost daily measurement sense; they also include a unique blend of detailed naturalistic observations supplemented by continual, small-scale experimentation. The application of such an approach to the study of older children would be enormously difficult, and might easily result in a mass of uninterpretable information. Nevertheless, this may well be a direction in which research should attempt to move. Whether any researcher ever attempts a total embodiment of the Piaget infancy approach, it seems clear that the field of cognitive development, dominated as it has been by cross-sectional studies in laboratory settings, would benefit from more longitudinal study, more naturalistic–observational study, and more combinations of the longitudinal and the naturalistic-observational approaches.

CONCLUSIONS

That the Piagetian approach to the study of intelligence has had a bountiful yield is indisputable. Piaget's studies, as well as the thousands of follow-up studies they inspired, have provided an enormous amount of useful information about how children think and about how thinking changes across childhood. Such studies have also helped to delineate central theoretical questions concerning both the nature of intelligence and the nature of development.

That the Piagetian approach has not answered all the questions it raised should be clear from the preceding pages. In some cases the ingenuity of Piaget's techniques and the insightfulness of the questions asked have not been matched in the actual execution of the research. The overly verbal procedures and the failure to report within-subject analyses are two obvious examples. Perhaps an even more important obstacle to complete resolution, however, has been the intrinsic difficulty of many of the issues addressed. Questions such as how cognitive abilities interrelate or how children acquire new knowledge are among the most difficult questions developmental psychologists can face. That generations of post-Piaget psychologists have also failed to solve these problems is ample testimony to their difficulty.

It is always somewhat hazardous to predict future directions for a research tradition. Three tentative predictions will be offered here, however. First, the history of Piaget-inspired research has been a history of the gradual importation of research tools from other traditions for use in attacking Piagetian problems. The greater standardization and statistical precision of the first follow-up studies are an early example. More recent examples can be seen in the increased use of techniques such as scalogram analysis, factor analysis, and cross-lagged correlations. This trend seems likely to continue.

Our second and third predictions are related. It seems quite possible that the number of directly "Piagetian" studies will decline in the coming years. Indeed, such a decline is already evident for certain topics. Studies of conservation, for example, are no longer so ubiquitous as they once were, and training studies do not enjoy the popularity they did 5 or 10 years ago. In part, such a decline may reflect the fact that some of the questions that motivated such studies are no longer questions; despite our many caveats, some problems *have* been solved. In part, however, a decline in traditional sorts of Piagetian research may reflect a general shift from an emphasis on replicating and testing Piagetian ideas to an emphasis on using such ideas and extending them to new content areas. Many examples can be cited. The currently popular topic of "social cognition," or the child's understanding of the social world, has been heavily influenced by Piaget. Studies of memory and of language development have a much more Piagetian look than was true 8 or 10 years ago. Our third prediction is for a continuation of this trend toward a "Piagetianizing" of other research areas.

Twenty years from now is a book of this sort likely to contain a separate chapter on Piagetian research? It is quite possible that it will not. What seems certain, however, is that many of the topics that are covered will bear the imprint of Piagetian thinking and Piagetian research.

REFERENCES

Bart, W. M. The factor structure of formal operations. *British Journal of Educational Psychology,* 1971, *11,* 70–77.

Beilin, H. Inducing conservation through training. In G. Steiner (Ed.), *Psychology of the 20th century* (Vol. 7). *Piaget and beyond.* Zurich: Kindler, 1978.

Braine, M. D. S. The ontogeny of certain logical operations: Piaget's formulation examined by nonverbal methods. *Psychological Monographs,* 1959, *73* (5, Whole No. 475).

Brainerd, C. J. Order of acquisition of transitivity, conservation, and class inclusion of length and weight. *Developmental Psychology,* 1973, *8,* 105–116.

Brainerd, C. J. Learning research and Piagetian theory. In L. S. Siegel & C. J. Brainerd (Eds.), *Alternatives to Piaget: Critical essays on the theory*. New York: Academic Press, 1978.

Brainerd, C. J., & Hooper, F. H. A methodological analysis of developmental studies of identity conservation and equivalence conservation. *Psychological Bulletin,* 1975, *82*, 725–737.

Bruner, J. S., Olver, R. R., & Greenfield, P. M. (Eds.). *Studies in cognitive growth*. New York: Wiley, 1966.

Bryant, P. E. *Perception and understanding in young children*. New York: Basic Books, 1974.

Capon, N., & Kuhn, D. Logical reasoning in the supermarket: Adult females' use of a proportional reasoning strategy in an everyday context. *Developmental Psychology,* 1979, *15*, 450–452.

Charlesworth, W. R. Development and assessment of cognitive structures. *Journal of Research in Science Teaching,* 1964, *2*, 214–219.

Charlesworth, W. R. The role of surprise in cognitive development. In D. Elkind & J. H. Flavell (Eds.), *Studies in cognitive development*. New York: Oxford University Press, 1969.

Comrey, A. L. *A first course in factor analysis*. New York: Academic Press, 1973.

Dasen, P. R. *Piagetian psychology: Cross-cultural contributions*. New York: Gardner Press, 1976.

Decarie, T. G. A study of the mental and emotional development of the thalidomide child. In B. M. Foss (Ed.), *Determinants of infant behaviour* (Vol. 4). London: Methuen, 1969.

Flavell, J. H. *The developmental psychology of Jean Piaget*. Princeton, N.J.: Van Nostrand, 1963.

Flavell, J. H. Stage-related properties of cognitive development. *Cognitive Psychology,* 1971, *2*, 421–453.

Flavell, J. H. *Cognitive development*. Englewood Cliffs, N.J.: Prentice-Hall, 1977.

Furth, H. G. A review and perspective on the thinking of deaf people. In J. Hellmuth (Ed.), *Cognitive studies* (Vol. 1). New York: Brunner/Mazel, 1970.

Gelman, R. Conservation acquisition: A problem of learning to attend to relevant attributes. *Journal of Experimental Child Psychology,* 1969, *7*, 167–187.

Gelman, R. Logical capacity of very young children: Number invariance rules. *Child Development,* 1972, *43*, 75–90.

Gelman, R. Cognitive development. In L. W. Porter & M. R. Rosenzweig (Eds.), *Annual review of psychology* (Vol. 29). Palo Alto, Calif.: Annual Reviews, 1978.

Glucksberg, S., Krauss, R. M., & Higgins, T. The development of communication skills in children. In F. Horowitz (Ed.), *Review of child development research* (Vol. 4). Chicago: University of Chicago Press, 1975.

Green, B. F. A method of scalogram analysis using summary statistics. *Psychometrika,* 1956, *21*, 79–88.

Green, D. R., Ford, M. P., & Flamer, G. B. (Eds.). *Measurement and Piaget*. New York: McGraw-Hill, 1971.

Inhelder, B. Developmental theory and diagnostic procedures. In D. R. Green, M. P. Ford, & G. B. Flamer (Eds.), *Measurement and Piaget*. New York: McGraw-Hill, 1971.

Inhelder, B., & Piaget, J. *The growth of logical thinking from childhood to adolescence*. New York: Basic Books, 1958.

Inhelder, B., & Piaget, J. *The early growth of logic in the child*. London: Routledge and Kegan Paul, 1964.

Inhelder, B., Sinclair, H., & Bovet, M. *Learning and the development of cognition*. Cambridge, Mass.: Harvard University Press, 1974.

Jordan, N. Is there an Achilles heel in Piaget's theorizing? *Human Development,* 1972, *15,* 379–382.

Kenny, D. A. Cross-lagged panel correlation: A test for spuriousness. *Psychological Bulletin,* 1975, *82,* 887–903.

King, W. L. A nonarbitrary behavioral criterion for conservation of illusion-distorted length in five-year-olds. *Journal of Experimental Child Psychology,* 1971, *11,* 171–181.

Kofsky, E. A scalogram study of classificatory development. *Child Development,* 1966, *37,* 191–204.

Kopp, C. B., & Shaperman, J. Cognitive development in the absence of object manipulation during infancy. *Developmental Psychology,* 1973, *9,* 430.

Kuhn, D. Inducing development experimentally: Comments on a research paradigm. *Developmental Psychology,* 1974, *10,* 590–600.

Kuhn, D., & Brannock, J. Development of the isolation of variables scheme in experimental and "natural experiment" contexts. *Developmental Psychology,* 1977, *13,* 9–14.

Kurdek, L. A., & Rodgon, M. M. Perceptual, cognitive, and affective perspective-taking in kindergarten through sixth-grade children. *Developmental Psychology,* 1975, *11,* 643–650.

Light, P. H., Buckingham, M., & Robbins, A. H. *Conservation: Accident and incident.* Paper presented at the meetings of the Developmental Section of the British Psychological Society, Southampton, September 1979.

Loevinger, J. A systematic approach to the construction and evaluation of tests of ability. *Psychological Monographs,* 1947, *61* (4, Whole No. 285).

McGarrigle, J., & Donaldson, M. Conservation accidents. *Cognition,* 1974, *3,* 341–350.

McManis, D. L. Conservation and transitivity of weight and length by normals and retardates. *Developmental Psychology,* 1969, *1,* 373–382.

Mehler, J., & Bever, T. G. Cognitive capacity of very young children. *Science,* 1967, *158,* 141–142.

Miller, S. A. Nonverbal assessment of conservation of number. *Child Development,* 1976, *47,* 722–728. (a)

Miller, S. A. Nonverbal assessment of Piagetian concepts. *Psychological Bulletin,* 1976, *83,* 405–430. (b)

Miller, S. A. A disconfirmation of the quantitative identity–quantitative equivalence sequence. *Journal of Experimental Child Psychology,* 1977, *24,* 180–189.

Miller, S. A. Identity conservation and equivalence conservation: A critique of Brainerd and Hooper's analysis. *Psychological Bulletin,* 1978, *85,* 58–69.

Modgil, S., & Modgil, C. *Piagetian research: Compilation and commentary* (Vol. 7). Windsor, England: NFER Publishing, 1976.

Piaget, J. *The language and thought of the child.* New York: Harcourt Brace, 1926.

Piaget, J. Autobiography. In C. Murchison & E. G. Boring (Eds.), *History of psychology in autobiography* (Vol. 4). Worcester, Mass.: Clark University Press, 1952. (a)

Piaget, J. *The origins of intelligence in children.* New York: International Universities Press, 1952. (b)

Piaget, J., & Inhelder, B. *The child's conception of space.* London: Routledge and Kegan Paul, 1956.

Piaget, J., Inhelder, B., & Szeminska, A. *The child's conception of geometry.* New York: Basic Books, 1960.

Piaget, J., & Szeminska, A. *The child's conception of number.* New York: Humanities, 1952.

Rose, S. A., & Blank, M. The potency of context in children's cognition: An illustration through conservation. *Child Development,* 1974, *45,* 499–502.

Rubin, K. H. Egocentrism in childhood: A unitary construct? *Child Development,* 1973, *44,* 102–110.

Rubin, K. H. Role taking in childhood: Some methodological considerations. *Child Development,* 1978, *49,* 428–433.

Shantz, C. U., & Watson, J. S. Assessment of spatial egocentrism through expectancy violation. *Psychonomic Science,* 1970, *18,* 93–94.

Shantz, C. U., & Watson, J. S. Spatial abilities and spatial egocentrism in the young child. *Child Development,* 1971, *42,* 171–181.

Shatz, M. The relationship between cognitive processes and the development of communication skills. In C. B. Keasey (Ed.), *1977 Nebraska Symposium on Motivation.* Lincoln: University of Nebraska Press, 1977.

Siegel, L. S. The relationship of language and thought in the preoperational child: A reconsideration of nonverbal alternatives to Piagetian tasks. In L. S. Siegel & C. J. Brainerd (Eds.), *Alternatives to Piaget: Critical essays on the theory.* New York: Academic Press, 1978.

Siegel, L. S., McCabe, A. E., Brand, J., & Matthews, J. Evidence for the understanding of class inclusion in preschool children: Linguistic factors and training effects. *Child Development,* 1978, *49,* 688–693.

Silverman, I. W. Context and number conservation. *Child Study Journal,* 1979, *9,* 205–212.

Sinnott, J. Everyday thinking and Piagetian operativity in adults. *Human Development,* 1975, *18,* 430–443.

Tomlinson-Keasey, C., Eisert, D. C., Kahle, L. R., Hardy-Brown, K., & Keasey, B. The structure of concrete operational thought. *Child Development,* 1979, *50,* 1153–1163.

Toussaint, N. A. An analysis of synchrony between concrete-operational tasks in terms of structural and performance demands. *Child Development,* 1974, *45,* 992–1001.

Wachs, T. D. S. Proximal experience and early cognitive–intellectual development: The physical environment. *Merrill-Palmer Quarterly,* 1979, *25,* 3–41.

Wohlwill, J. *The study of behavioral development.* New York: Academic Press, 1973.

7 Cognitive Development: An Information-Processing Perspective

ROBERT KAIL AND JEFFREY BISANZ

A 6-year-old child taking the Stanford-Binet Intelligence Scale is likely to be asked "In what way are an apple and a peach alike?" (Terman & Merrill, 1960, p. 86). Suppose a hypothetical 6-year-old responds by saying "They are both round," How should we interpret this child's response? What significance should we ascribe to it? Answers to these questions would vary, depending on the theoretical framework of the psychologist.

A psychometric psychologist, who specializes in measurement and testing of psychological characteristics, would probably note that the child's answer corresponds to one of those listed in the test manual as a correct response. Consequently, the child would receive credit for the response. The credit received on this problem, plus points received on other items in the scale, would be used to provide a numerical estimate of the child's "intelligence" relative to that of his or her peers.

A second psychologist, an adherent to the views of Jean Piaget, would argue that the psychometrist's emphasis on determining a quantitative expression of intelligence ignores important qualitative changes in thought that occur as children develop. The Piagetian psychologist would argue that a child in the concrete operational stage of intellectual development would probably answer the question by saying "fruit." This is because the concrete operational child recognizes that apples, oranges, plums, and the like can be combined to form the higher-order category of fruit, an accomplishment referred to as the "primary addition of classes" (Flavell, 1963, p. 173). The fact that our hypothetical 6-year-old answered with the shared *perceptual* characteristic of roundness suggests that this child may still be in the preoperational stage of intellectual development, for at this

209

STRATEGIES AND TECHNIQUES
OF CHILD STUDY

Copyright © 1982 by Academic Press, Inc.
All rights of reproduction in any form reserved.
ISBN 0-12-715080-3 0-12-715082-X (p)

stage children's reasoning tends to be based more on images and actions than on such abstract notions as "fruit."

Yet another psychologist, an information-processing psychologist, would share the Piagetian psychologist's claim that the psychometrist has ignored many interesting facets of the child's response. However, the information-processing psychologist's interpretation of the child's answer would differ from the Piagetian interpretation. Our third psychologist would begin by noting the similarity between human thought and the activities of a computer. That is, the information-processing psychologist argues that human thought is analogous to computer operations that perform specific actions on data. In the case of our hypothetical 6-year-old, the information-processing psychologist would point out that to determine the similarity of an apple and a peach, a child presumably must retrieve information from long-term memory about peaches and apples, just as a computer might search data banks for information. The child must then compare the information retrieved to determine in what way apples and peaches are similar (if at all). A variety of procedures are available for determining if two things are similar. The information-processing psychologist would be interested in determining the procedures and information our 6-year-old used to arrive at the shared feature of roundness.

Thus to the information-processing psychologist, as for the Piagetian, the child's response is merely the "tip of the iceberg," the overt product of many underlying mental processes. The Piagetian and information-processing psychologists differ, however, in their descriptions of those mental processes. For the Piagetian, mental processes resemble logical relations and operations; for the information-processing psychologist, they are akin to computer operations that interpret and manipulate data.

The Piagetian approach to research on cognitive development is presented in Chapter 6. The information-processing perspective is the focus of the present chapter. It is difficult to provide a complete characterization of the information-processing perspective, for it currently encompasses a diverse set of theories and research paradigms. To make the task manageable, we have tried to extract common themes and assumptions, and we have had to ignore many important ideas and research topics. The chapter is divided into four sections. In the first section, we analyze the notion of information processing as a framework for conceptualizing developmental change. In the second section, we consider some of the strategies of research associated with the information-processing approach. In the third section, we evaluate the usefulness of the approach for research on developmental phenomena. Finally we speculate on the future of this approach as a framework for developmental research.

THE INFORMATION-PROCESSING PERSPECTIVE
AND COGNITIVE DEVELOPMENT

Exploring the Computer Analogy

To understand the behavior of a cognitive system, whether computer or human, one must examine the processes that intervene between input and output. In a computer system these processes are specified in a "program" that provides instructions for what the computer is to do. Consider the program represented in Figure 7.1A that could determine the sum of two numbers. The program involves a number of specific steps. First, the program reads two numbers, say 4 and 3. Second, a counter is set to 0. Third, the counter is incremented X times, which would be 4 in our example. Next the counter is incremented Y times, 3 in our example. The resulting value of the counter, 7, provides the sum of X and Y.

Each of the steps in this program may be referred to as a *routine*. The organization of these routines in a program is referred to as the *executive routine* or *control structure*. Each routine, in turn, may be composed of "simpler" *subroutines* that, when organized appropriately, carry out the function of the routine. Thus the program is structured into hierarchical

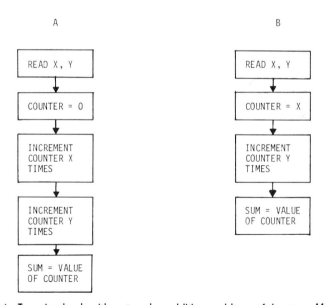

FIGURE 7.1. Two simple algorithms to solve addition problems of the type, $M + n = ?$.

"levels" of operation, with each superordinate routine composed of an organized set of subordinate routines.

Now consider the cognitive processes of a child who is determining the sum of two numbers. In effect, the information-processing perspective leads us to ask questions about human problem solvers that are analogous to those we would ask about the computer. We would attempt to discover the *processes* (routines) that are required to solve the problem and to identify the *strategy* or *plan* (executive routine) that integrates specific processes into a functional package yielding the desired results. We would also inquire about the kinds of information that are necessary to perform this task, how this knowledge is *represented* (formatted and interrelated) in memory, and how new information from the environment is incorporated into the system.

Using the computer metaphor, we can also make several hypotheses about *changes* in processing that might occur with development.

1. As children develop they may employ strategies or processes that either were simply not available earlier or were used inappropriately. For example, most 3- and 4-year-olds cannot answer questions like "5 + 3 = ?", whereas 7- and 8-year-olds do so readily. The nature of developmental change here is that older children have acquired a set of rules for addition (perhaps similar to those shown in Figure 7.1) that younger children simply do not have.

2. The efficiency and accuracy of a strategy or process may improve over development. For example, the addition algorithm depicted in Figure 7.1B is more efficient than the one depicted in Figure 7.1A: Instead of first setting the counter to 0, then incrementing X times, the algorithm in Figure 1B simply sets the counter to X, then increments it Y times, eliminating one step from the previous algorithm. Increased efficiency in processing with development might consist of using the more efficient second algorithm rather than the first algorithm.

3. The capacity for information that can be manipulated and/or stored in active memory may grow larger with age, thus permitting more complex processing. For example, suppose a child were taught to extend the algorithm represented in Figure 7.1B for use with multidigit numbers, such as 345 + 221 = ?. The child might attempt to apply the algorithm to the ones column, to hold the result in memory, to apply it again to the tens column, to hold this new result in memory, and so on. Processes would be similar to those in Figure 7.1B, but now the child must hold the result for each column in memory while simultaneously applying the algorithm to a new column. Older chil-

dren might solve such problems more effectively than younger children, because they are able to hold and manipulate more information at one time than younger children.

4. The speed of specific processes may increase with age in a way that enhances performance. Any of the processes in either of the two algorithms might be executed more rapidly as children grow older. The speed with which the counter is incremented, for example, might increase with development.

5. Certain kinds of factual knowledge may become available that influence how effectively the system processes information. We might expect that, for example, as children's knowledge of arithmetic becomes more elaborate, they would no longer use either of the two computational algorithms but instead would search long-term memory directly for the answer to an addition problem (but see Groen & Parkman, 1972).

These potential sources of development change certainly do not form an exhaustive list, and they are not mutually exclusive. However, they do illustrate the diversity of change that can be easily conceptualized from the perspective of information processing.

Comparison of the Information-Processing Perspective and Piaget's Approach

Characteristics of the information-processing perspective are sometimes described in textbooks (e.g., Lindsay & Norman, 1977) and in advanced theoretical papers, but questions related to development are often addressed superficially or ignored altogether. To illustrate some implications of this approach for understanding cognitive development, it is useful to compare Piaget's view, as described in Chapter 6 of this volume, with the perspective of information processing. Such a comparison could be misleading and confusing unless one recognizes the difference between (a) a general perspective or framework and (b) a particular theory formulated *within* that framework. *Information processing* refers to a framework for constructing and testing theories about human performance and development; it does not denote any single theory. In contrast, Piaget's theory is an instance of a theory based on the "organismic" framework (Reese & Overton, 1970). Comparing Piaget's theory with the information-processing framework is therefore analogous to comparing a single species of dog with the entire genus of cats: Observed similarities and differences are influenced by the fact that particular theories (the species level) tend to involve features that are not necessarily characteristic of the general framework (the genus level). Specific information-processing theories of cognitive development have emerged (e.g., Case, 1978a; Klahr & Wallace, 1976; Pascual-Leone, 1970), but no single theory has dominated the perspective. Consequently, it is more instructive to compare Piaget's theory with the general framework of information processing than with any particular theory within that framework.

View of Cognitive Development. Several aspects of Piaget's theory that are described in Chapter 6 serve as points of comparison for understanding how cognitive development is viewed in information-processing theories. Like Piaget, information-processing theorists assume that cognitive functioning is accomplished by means of an organized system of actions. Indeed, one of the major goals of any information-processing theory is to specify the precise nature and organization of the actions, or processes, that transform information obtained from the environment or from long-term memory. This assumption has very explicit methodological implications in information-processing theories. Not only is cognition active, but underlying cognitive processes take place over real time. Thus it is possible, in principle, to measure the duration of a particular process. Procedures for doing this constitute one of the major methodological contributions of the information-processing perspective and will be discussed later.

Another point of comparison concerns the concept of *stage*. Most traditional developmental theories, like Piaget's, describe developmental change as a succession or sequence of stages. In information-processing theories, cognitive activity at any point in time is described in terms of a *model*. The model includes the processes, strategies, and other information-processing characteristics that are believed to underlie performance. For example, the flow diagrams in Figure 7.1 represent models, if very simple ones, of how children might solve addition problems. Development can be described, in part, with a sequence of such models, each representing a different point in development.

Specifying a model is therefore comparable to describing a stage in traditional theories, but with three important exceptions. First, and most obviously, there is considerable difference in the language and theoretical concepts employed. For example, Piagetian theorists might emphasize concepts like "reversibility" and "reflective abstraction," whereas information-processing theorists are likely to employ ideas like "short-term memory," "activation," and "automaticity."

Second, there is a difference in the criteria for the adequacy of a model or stage description. In traditional theories, stages are supposed to be relatively *stable* and *pervasive:* They are stable to the extent that they characterize cognition over a lengthy period of time; they are pervasive in the sense that they describe cognition as it is manifested on a wide variety of tasks. For example, in Piaget's theory the claim is made that the "stage" of concrete operational thought spans several years and accurately represents a child's cognitive skills in a variety of contexts. The validity of a stage theory rests largely on evidence for its stability and pervasiveness.

The criteria of stability and pervasiveness can be accommodated easily in information-processing theories, and they would enhance the generality of any model. But they are not always necessary. Some aspects of performance may show stability and pervasiveness and others may not. For example, a child solving a set of difficult arithmetic problems may alter his or her strategy drastically several times. The model describing performance at the beginning of a set would be quite different from the models describing performance at the middle or end, but these models need not be considered trivial just because they change so rapidly. Similarly, some aspects of the child's performance may generalize to solution of science problems, and some may not. Information-processing models may be used to represent both general (i.e., stable and pervasive) *and* specific aspects of performance. Indeed, a major criticism of Piaget's theory, from the point of view of information processing, is that the influence of task-specific factors is often ignored (e.g., Case, 1978b; Pascual-Leone, 1970).

Another difference between traditional developmental theories, such as Piaget's, and theories based on the information-processing approach involves the distinction between *qualitative* and *quantitative change,* a topic that has a long and confusing history in developmental psychology (Flavell, 1971; Flavell & Wohlwill, 1969). Briefly, qualitative changes are considered to be changes in kind or form, whereas quantitative changes are changes in degree. Most traditional theories have made qualitative change the hallmark of development, whereas quantitative change is viewed as inherently less interesting. The reasons for this are often more related to metatheoretical assumptions about development than to compelling theoretical or empirical analyses. Information-processing theories are not necessarily limited by this restriction. The list of possible sources of developmental change cited earlier include instances that appear to be qualitative (such as acquiring a new strategy) and others that appear to be quantitative (such as improved efficiency of processes or greater memory capacity). Information-processing theories are open to the possibility that developmental change may have both qualitative and quantitative components.

Focus of Research. The Piagetian and information-processing approaches can also be contrasted in terms of those aspects of cognitive development that are of particular interest. Two contrasts are especially noteworthy.

First, characteristic of Piagetian research is a concern with epistemological issues. The child's knowledge of mathematics, logic, and the physical world provides the primary focus of Piagetian research. Many developmental psychologists with an information-processing orientation share Piaget's interest in these phenomena (e.g., Klahr & Wallace, 1976; Trabasso, 1977). However, information-processing psychologists are also interested in aspects of cognitive functioning that fall beyond the usual scope of Piagetian research. Children's understanding of words, their meanings and usage, would be one example of such an area. Another would be the question of how children perceive letters and words in the course of reading. Perhaps the best way to summarize this contrast is to say that information-processing psychologists tend to study a larger number of phenomena under the rubric of cognitive development than do Piagetians.

A second difference in research focus concerns individual differences. For Piagetian psychologists individual differences are of little interest, primarily because the concepts and processes central to Piaget's theory are presumed to be nearly universal aspects of development. Information-processing psychologists tend to take a more neutral position, believing that the universality of a developmental phenomenon is a matter subject to empirical inquiry rather than a theoretical given. A typical information-processing psychologist would probably propose that some aspects of cognitive development are very nearly universal, whereas others may differ from child to child.

Goal of Research. Having considered the concept of development and the focus of developmental research from an information-processing perspective, it is hardly surprising to conclude that specifying a child's "mental program" is the goal of most information-processing research. According to Klahr and Wallace (1976, p. 5):

> Faced with a segment of behavior of a child performing a task, we pose the question: "What would an information-processing system require in order to exhibit the same behavior as the child?" The answer takes the form of a set of rules for processing information: a computer program. The program constitutes a model of the child performing the task. It contains explicit statements about the capacity of the system, the complexity of the processes, and the representation of information—the data structure—with which the child must deal.

That is, information-processing psychologists attempt to provide flow diagrams (as in Figure 7.1) or computer programs that represent the sequence of cognitive processing that occurs in a child's mind as he or she attempts to solve a problem. By comparing the flow diagram (or program) for children of different ages, the information-processing psychologist hopes to determine changes in cognitive processing. Of course, these cognitive processes can never be seen directly, so they must be inferred from children's behavior.[1] Fortunately, information-processing psychologists have devised several powerful methods for generating and evaluating models of these unobservable processes, and it is to these methods that we now turn.

METHODS OF INFORMATION–PROCESSING RESEARCH

In this section we describe some of the general methods used to construct, test, and revise information-processing models of cognitive performance.

Task Analysis

The first step in constructing an information-processing model is *task analysis,* which refers to an investigator's hypothetical description of the psychological processes required for performance on a particular task (Resnick, 1976). A task analysis may be very simple, such as the primitive analyses of addition represented in Figure 7.1, or it may be very complex, such as the elaborate analyses done of performance on difficult problems taken from tests of intelligence (e.g., Hunt, 1974; Sternberg, 1977). The complexity of a task analysis will depend partly on the task and partly on the sophistication and elegance of the cognitive theory used in analyzing the task. In principle, task analysis in some form has long been used in many areas of psychological research. For example, Gagné (1968) proposed that the general task of acquiring complex skills or knowledge could be analyzed hierarchically into specific tasks that required simpler levels of learning. What distinguishes task analysis in information processing is the emphasis on identifying processes that take place over real time, as well as the use of theoretical constructs derived from the computer analogy.

In conducting a task analysis, an investigator often uses several sources

---

[1] For years introductory psychology textbooks have defined psychology as the science of behavior, where behavior refers to the observable responses of an organism. Modern cognitive psychology, in contrast, is essentially defined as the study of events that *cannot* be observed directly (Pachella, 1974).

of information. Existing theories are consulted, as are previous data from experiments conducted with tasks similar to the task of interest. Psychologists are also making increasing use of work in *artificial intelligence,* which refers to research on how to make computers solve complex problems in an "intelligent" manner. For example, programs have been written that enable computers to play chess or to solve physics problems. Such programs provide precise models of procedures that are *sufficient* to perform a task, although there is no guarantee that human problem solvers could or would use these same procedures. An information-processing theorist will use this information to outline an initial model that will yield specific predictions about behavior. The accuracy or validity of the model is not so critical: Indeed, it is assumed that the model will be wrong in interesting ways that will be revealed by empirical research. The goal of the initial task analysis is only to establish a starting point for research.

Given a model that leads to certain expectations about behavior, the next step is to test those predictions and to revise the model accordingly. Three methods appear to be particularly useful in the information-processing approach: rule assessment, measurement of response latencies, and computer simulation. We will describe each of these in some detail.

Rule Assessment

An information-processing model can be evaluated by comparing its predictions with children's behavior. To do this, an investigator creates problems for which various potential models yield different predictions. Children are tested on a number of these problems, and their responses are compared to those predicted by the different models. In effect, we are "assessing" the validity of the "rules" specified in the models, hence the name of this method. If a child's pattern of responses corresponds (at a statistically significant level) to the pattern predicted by a model, we would suspect that the child solves the problem using the processes described in that model.

An Example: Reasoning about Balance. Use of this research strategy can be illustrated by considering experimentation by Siegler (1976, 1978) on children's and adolescents' understanding of the concept of balance. In this work a child is shown a balance scale in which differing numbers of weights have been placed at various distances to the left and right of a fulcrum. The child's task is to determine which—if either—side of the balance scale will go down when the supporting blocks are removed.

Drawing upon previous work by Inhelder and Piaget (1958) and by Lee (1971), Siegler (1976) proposed that understanding of the concept of balance progresses through four ordered stages, which are depicted in Figure 7.2 in the form of flowcharts. A child using rule 1 believes that weight alone determines if the scale will balance. At the next stage—rule 2—a child again emphasizes weight, but considers distance (correctly) in the event that the weights to the left and right of the fulcrum are equal. Rule 3 represents yet another advance: A child at this level realizes that both weight and distance must be examined, but is stumped when one side has greater weight while the other has the greater distance. A child using rule 4 overcomes this limitation by multiplying the distance by the weight for each side and comparing the products: The side with the greater product will go down.

Each of these four rules makes specific predictions about the kinds of problems that will and will not be solved, as well as predictions about the kinds of errors that will be expected. Consequently, by judiciously selecting problems and examining an individual's performance on a large number of problems, Siegler (1976) was able to infer with considerable confidence which of rules 1–4 (if any) was being used by a child.

The way in which these inferences about rule usage were made is probably best demonstrated by considering the actual kinds of problems that were used in Siegler's (1976) research. Six classes, shown in Figure 7.3, were used. In balance problems, an equal number of weights appeared to the left and to the right of the fulcrum, at comparable distances; consequently, the scale would balance. On weight problems, the distance from the fulcrum was constant, but one side had more weight on it and therefore would go down. Distance problems were the complement to weight problems: The number of weights was constant on the two sides, but they were placed differently. The side with the greater distance would go down.

In the remaining classes of problems, the two sides differ in both weight and distance. In conflict–weight problems the side with the greater weight would go down, whereas in conflict–distance problems the side with the greater distance would go down. Finally, in conflict–balance problems, the greater distance on one side equals the greater weight on the other side, with the result that the scale balances.

Also shown in Figure 7.3 are the specific patterns of responses predicted by each of the rules for each of the types of problems. Consider, for example, rule 2, which says that a child uses weight principally, considering distance information only when the two sides have equal weights. On balance, weight and distance problems a child should be consistently correct: On balance problems the child using rule 2 should note the comparable number of weights and predict that the scale will balance; on weight problems the child will note that one side has greater weight and correctly predict that this side should go down; on distance problems a

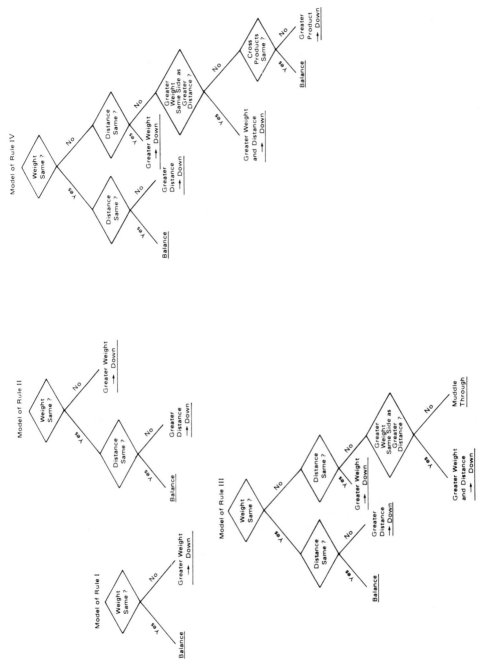

FIGURE 7.2. Four rules used to decide which of the two sides of a balance scale will go down (from Siegler, 1976).

Problem type	Rules			
	I	II	III	IV
Balance 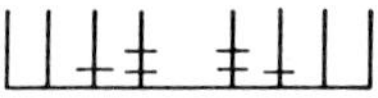	100	100	100	100
Weight 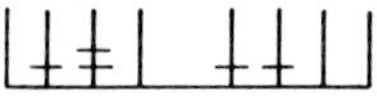	100	100	100	100
Distance 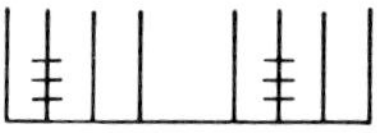	0 (Should say "balance")	100	100	100
Conflict-weight 	100	100	33 (Chance responding)	100
Conflict-distance 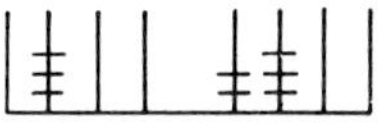	0 (Should say "right down")	0 (Should say "right down")	33 (Chance responding)	100
Conflict-balance 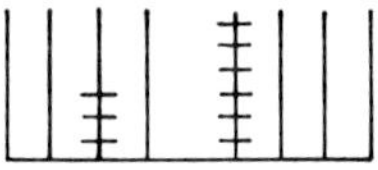	0 (Should say "right down")	0 (Should say "right down")	33 (Chance responding)	100

FIGURE 7.3. Six types of problems used by Siegler (1976) and the predictions made by each of four rules on the various problems.

child will note the equality of weight on the two sides, then proceed to examine the distances from the fulcrum and correctly judge that the side with the greater distance would go down.

It is in the various conflict problems that rule 2 begins to lead to erroneous judgments. On conflict–weight problems, the subject would notice the difference in weight and immediately judge that this side should go down. Again this is a correct answer, but it is a fortuitous one in that the child completely ignored the fact that the sides also differed with regard to the distance of the weights from the fulcrum. On conflict–distance problems the child will determine that the products differ in weight and immediately conclude that the side with the greater weight will go down. This, of course, is completely wrong. Thus we expect children using rule 2 always to err on conflict–distance problems, and to do so in a specific way: They should consistently pick the side with the greater number of weights, which in fact is the lighter rather than the heavier of the two sides. Finally, on conflict–equal problems, the rule 2 algorithm will again lead the subject to answer erroneously. As before, the child should consistently pick the side with the greater number of weights to go down.

In summary, a child using rule 2 should always respond accurately on balance, weight, distance, and conflict–weight problems. This same individual should always judge incorrectly on conflict–distance and conflict–balance problems. Furthermore, these errors should always consist of the child's judging that the side with the greater number of weights should go down. Similar distinctive patterns of responding (summarized in Figure 7.3) can be determined for each of the remaining rules by following the flowcharts in Figure 7.2 for the various classes of problems.

Siegler (1976) tested individuals ranging in age from 5 to 17 years on a total of 30 of these problems. Use of a rule was attributed to an individual if 26 of those responses conformed to the pattern predicted by that rule. Of the 120 individuals tested, 107 were readily classified as using one of the four rules. And, as would be expected, use of rules was age-related: 5- and 6-year-olds typically used rule 1, whereas 16- and 17-year-olds used either rule 3 or 4.

Methodological Issues. The methodological message is clear: When models are stated precisely, they can be evaluated with great power. That is, by providing a detailed, comprehensive account of the child's mental activity between the presentation of the balance and the child's response, Siegler (1976) was able to create different kinds of problems that would provide unambiguous data regarding the validity of his theory.

Perhaps the best way to see these assets more clearly is to examine how the results of this experiment could have been analyzed. A traditional approach would be to focus on the number of correct judgments and analyze these data with an analysis of variance. Such an analysis would have revealed significant age differences and significant differences among problems in difficulty. Of greater interest would be the finding of an interaction between age and type of problem. Subjects at all ages solved balance and weight problems easily. Performance on distance, conflict–distance, and conflict–balance problems improved with age. Finally, performance on conflict–weight problems actually declined with age.

What are the shortcomings of this form of analysis compared with the rule-assessment procedure used by Siegler (1976)? First and most important, we learn nothing about the processes used by children to solve the problems; we learn only that certain kinds of problems are more difficult than others for children of various ages. Second, we learn nothing about the behavior of individual children; the data from individuals are simply combined to form averages for the different age groups. In contrast to these shortcomings, the rule-assessment methodology (*a*) clearly specifies the rules used to solve problems, and (*b*) does so for individual children rather than looking only at group averages.

Two other virtues of these procedures should be mentioned. One concerns the characterization of the young child's (i.e., age 5 or 6 years and younger) cognitive skills. In most theories of development, these children are described in decidedly negative terms. As Gelman (1978) suggests, "When viewed through the eyes of many a cognitive developmentalist, the child of 5 years or younger is remarkably inept." For example, Piaget's description of children in the late preoperational period (i.e., approximately 4–7 years of age) is essentially a catalog of children's failures: They do not conserve, they do not take the perspective of other persons, they do not coordinate weight and distance information to determine if a scale will balance. The focus of the rule-assessment methodology is different. The goal is to characterize those cognitive skills that the child does possess—limited though they may be—rather than to try to define cognitive functioning at this stage of development in terms of processes that are absent.

The second virtue is related to the first. Most developmentalists would agree—at least in spirit—that models of development should "state both early and later forms of competence and provide an easy interpretation of each model as both a precursor and successor of other models in a developmental sequence" (Klahr & Siegler, 1978). Information-processing models like those shown in Figure 7.3 certainly meet this criterion. The models provide specific characterizations of (*a*) early, limited competence, (*b*) the ultimate level of proficiency, and (*c*) the steps involved in moving between these levels of skill.

The rule-assessment methodology does have several drawbacks that we need to consider. First, a relatively large number of problems must be administered to determine if a child's responses conform reliably to simple models. For some areas of research, the necessary number of trials simply cannot be administered feasibly. For example, when the "stimulus" is more complicated than a simple balance scale (e.g., presentation of a film or videotape, as in studies investigating children's role-taking ability), each trial may involve 15–20 minutes of testing, which severely limits the total number of trials per child. This, in turn, precludes reliable assessment of the extent to which a child's responses conform to those of an information-processing model. In addition, if complicated models are to be evaluated, the number of problems needed to distinguish the models may grow so large as to make it impractical to use these procedures without some modification.

Second, this method assumes that children respond consistently on all problems (i.e., that children follow the same rule in solving every problem).

If this assumption cannot be met, the rule assessment procedures will be of limited utility. For example, in experiments on learning, children may use several different rules in rapid succession as their learning progresses. Unless children adhere to one rule for many trials, typically there will be insufficient data to evaluate the relationship between children's responses and those predicted by a model.

Third, the rule-assessment method provides no information regarding the *order* in which cognitive processes are implemented. Consider, for example, rules 3 and 4 in Figure 7.3. The predictions of these models for the six types of problems would be exactly the same if children first examined the distance of the weights from the fulcrum, then considered the number of weights.

The fourth point is not really a limitation in the method so much as a clarification of it. In Siegler's (1976) work the vast majority of children conformed to one of the four rules. Does this mean that the rule actually described the child's cognitive processing? Strictly speaking, no. Conceivably the current model is not correct but merely happens to make the same predictions as some other as yet unthought of model that is the "true" description of a child's cognitive processing.

An information-processing psychologist's response to this dilemma would include several parts. First, the psychologist would note that information-processing research "rests on the proposition that there may be several ways to skin a cat, but probably not dozens of ways. Hence if *one* way (not admitting magical processes) is found, it may be similar to the way in which cats are actually skinned" (Simon, 1972, pp. 20–21). Second, by putting additional constraints on an information-processing model—notably that it be consistent with what is known about the physiology of the nervous system and cognitive processing in other tasks—we can increase the likelihood that the model corresponds to actual human cognitive processing (Simon, 1972). Third, given the absence of precise models of cognitive development, discovery of a model that consistently predicts a child's behavior represents a considerable advance, even if we cannot be sure that the model is merely mimicking the "true" model.

Response Time

A research strategy associated almost entirely with the information-processing approach is the measurement of response time to detect cognitive processes. Information-processing psychologists assume that any mental activity requires a finite amount of time to execute, an amount of time that is potentially measurable. By setting up experimental conditions appropriately, we can infer the kinds of processing that probably occur.

As before, the various methods based on the collection of response time data are best illustrated with an example.

An Example: Subtraction. Consider the equation $9 - 5 = ?$. Like most adults you probably thought "4" effortlessly. If asked to elaborate on how you determined that "4" was correct, you, like most adults, cannot; you simply say, "I just know it."

How might an individual arrive at an answer? Research by Woods, Resnick, and Groen (1975) suggests how individuals solve subtraction problems, and, more importantly, demonstrates how information-processing psychologists use response time to study cognitive processes. These investigators proposed four models of subtraction (for single-digit integers). A high-speed mental counter that can be incremented or decremented by one unit at a time is specified in each model.[2] Consider the general problem, $m - n = ?$, where m and n are both integers and $m > n$. One model assumes that the counter is first incremented m times, then is decremented n times. The answer is the final value listed on the counter. A second model uses a procedure in which the counter is set at m units (rather than incrementing from 0 m times, as in model 1, then is decremented by n units. Again, the answer is the final value listed on the counter. A third model holds that the counter is first set to n and is incremented until m is reached. The answer is the number of increments needed to reach m. A final model holds that individuals may use either model 2 or model 3, selecting for a particular problem the procedure that involves fewer operations.

How can we decide which of these hypothesized models, if any, actually describes the mental activities of a child or adult trying to answer $9 - 5 = ?$. By making a straightforward assumption, response latencies can be used to evaluate the different models. The assumption is simply this: Incrementing or decrementing the counter one unit always takes an individual the same amount of time.

Given this assumption, the models all predict that the time to subtract two single-digit integers should be described by a linear function of the type $RT = a + bx$. In this equation RT refers to total response time, and a is a constant referring to the amount of time needed to execute processes that are the same regardless of the actual number to be subtracted. Included here would be the time to read the problem initially and the time needed to emit a response. That is, we assume that the time needed to read or say a 4 or 6, for example, is approximately the same as the time needed to read or say a 7 or 8.

---

[2] These models seem bizarre when encountered initially, particularly the notion of a mental counter. In fact, the models are simply mental analogues of the various ways of subtracting on one's fingers.

Of greater theoretical interest is the other term in the linear equation, bx, for the models differ in their predictions regarding this term. The x in this term denotes the amount of time needed to change the counter by one unit; the b refers to the number of times that the counter must be changed to determine the answer. It is in predictions regarding b that the four models differ. That is, the models vary systematically in terms of the number of times that the counter must be changed to answer the same subtraction problem.

According to the first model, the counter is incremented m times, then decremented n times. Consequently, the total number of changes, b, is equal to $m + n$, and the model predicts that response time should be described by the function $RT = a + (m + n)x$. The second model assumes that a counter is set at m, then decremented n units. Consequently, $b = n$ for this model and the predicted function would be $RT = a + nx$. In the third model, the counter is set to n, then incremented to m, a total of $m - n$ changes in the counter; thus, $b = m - n$ and $RT = a + (m - n)x$. Finally, the fourth model holds that either model 2 or model 3 may be used, with the model requiring the fewer steps on a particular problem generally being chosen. In this case, the counter will be changed either n units (model 2) or $m - n$ units (model 3), whichever is smaller. Consequently, $b = min(n, m - n)$, where min refers to the minimal or smaller value, and $RT = a + (min(n, m - n))x$.

The data required to evaluate these models should be reasonably clear. Response latencies are needed from a set of problems in which m and n are varied systematically so that we can compute the various linear functions. Woods *et al.* (1975) tested second and fourth graders on 54 problems of the type $m - n$, reflecting all possible combinations of m and n, subject to the constraints that $m = 1$-9, $n = 0$-8, and $m > n$. Each child's latency data was compared to the predictions of the various models. Thus, for example, model 2 predicts that response latencies should be positively correlated with n. That is, solution time should increase linearly as n increases, regardless of the value of m. For a small number of second graders, latency data were most accurately characterized by this model. Correlations computed between n and solution time ranged from .59 to .71 for individuals; when solution time for each of the 54 problems was averaged across individuals, then correlated with n, $r - .84$.

The vast majority of children—30 of 40 second graders and all fourth graders—used rule 4 rather than rule 2. That is, their data were most accurately described by the function $RT = a + (min(n, m - n))x$. Correlations between $min(n, m - n)$ and solution time ranged from .45 to .67 for individual second graders and .33 to .60 for individual fourth graders. Correlations based on group data were .75 for second graders and .64 for fourth graders.

At this point we must digress momentarily, for by learning more about the information-processing interpretation of response time we will find that there are additional data of interest in the Woods *et al.* (1975) study. The use of response time data is not limited to identifying particular processes or the sequence in which such processes are executed. Recall that a fundamental assumption of the information-processing perspective is that any given process occurs over a finite and potentially measurable period of time. A number of methods have been developed to determine how *speed* of processing may vary among individuals. In experimental research with children, the suggestion has often been made that differences in the speed of simple, "basic" processes may account for changes in cognitive performance with age as well as for differences between normal children and mentally retarded or learning disabled children (Day, 1975; Kail & Siegel, 1977; Stanovich, 1978).

There are at least two general ways in which processing speed may underlie cognitive achievements. First, children who process information more quickly might acquire a greater amount of information in a given period of time (other factors being equal). For example, reading a book requires that meanings of words be processed hundreds of times per page; even small differences in the speed of this semantic processing could result in large differences in the amount of information that is obtained from reading for a fixed period of time (Hunt, 1976). Second, rapid processing may be a prerequisite for success on some cognitive tasks. It is well known that information held in active memory tends to be lost over time if it is not "refreshed" or rehearsed. Greater processing speed may generally make it possible to hold and manipulate more information simultaneously, which in turn might permit an individual to perform complex and "intelligent" cognitive functions more readily.

Returning now to the Woods *et al.* (1975) study, recall that the data for a substantial number of the second graders was best characterized by model 2, according to which $RT = a + nx$. Woods *et al.* found that response time for these children increased approximately .42 seconds for each increment of n. That is, problems like $9 - 2$, $8 - 2$, $7 - 2$ (i.e., where $n = 2$) were solved approximately .42 seconds more rapidly than problems like $9 - 3$, $8 - 3$, $7 - 3$ (i.e., $n = 3$) which, in turn, were solved approximately .42 seconds more rapidly than problems such as $9 - 4$, $8 - 4$, $7 - 4$ (i.e., $n = 4$). In other words, it apparently took second graders an average of approximately .4 seconds to change their counters one unit.

For the remaining children at grade 2 and all at grade 4, model 4 was the most appropriate. In this case response latencies were a linear function of the smaller of n or $m - n$. Woods *et al.* (1975) again found that response time of second graders increased approximately .42 seconds for each unit increment in $min (n, m - n)$. Thus, problems like $9 - 1$ (where $n = 1$) or $8 - 7$ (where $m - n = 1$) were answered about .42 seconds faster than problems like $4 - 2 (n = 2)$ and $5 - 3 (m - n = 2)$. For fourth graders the same linear increase was observed, but response latencies were only .25 seconds longer per unit increase in $min (n, m - n)$.

The Woods *et al.* (1975) study is a complicated one, but understanding its various details is a worthwhile enterprise, for the study provides a clear demonstration of the ways in which latency data can be used to reveal both qualitative and quantitative change. At the qualitative level, there is a shift from reliance on model 2 among the younger children to the more efficient model 4. At the quantitative level, we find that second graders who use model 4 execute the central process in the model (i.e., changing the counter) less rapidly than fourth graders using the model. Thus, development in the skill of subtracting single digit integers consists of (*a*) implementation of a more efficient algorithm, and (*b*) an increase in the speed with which that algorithm is executed.

Methodological Issues. One distinct asset of response time methods is that they can be used to understand cognitive performance at many "levels" of analysis. For example, such methods have been used to study the development of relatively lengthy reasoning processes in complex, problem-solving tasks (e.g., Sternberg & Rifkin, 1979), as well as the development of rapid comparison processes on much simpler tasks as in the work of Woods *et al.* (1975). Response time methods have proved to be powerful and effective tools in testing and revising hypothetical models. However, there are a number of methodological issues associated with the use of response times.

One issue concerns the reliability of latency data. Reaction time methods are most frequently used to detect processes or between-task differences that are very small. For example, the time to change the counter in the subtraction experiments described earlier is between $\frac{1}{4}$ and $\frac{1}{2}$ second. Often psychologists are interested in processes that occur during even briefer durations. Consequently, measurement techniques must be very sensitive and measurement error must be minimized.

A number of standard techniques are generally applied to accomplish these goals. First, reaction time experiments are designed so that each subject contributes data in each experimental condition of the task. This is known as a "within-subjects" or "repeated-measures" design, in which each child serves as his or her own control. Compared to methods in which different conditions involve different children ("between-subjects" designs), the within-subjects design permits more sensitive tests of differences among conditions. Second, a relatively large number of trials are given as preexperimental or "warm-up" trials. Latencies are often not even recorded on these trials. The rationale is that warm-up trials allow a child to become familiar with the task and to settle on a single processing strategy. As a result, latencies will be less variable than if a child constantly changes his or her approach as new facets of the task are experienced. Third, to gain reliable estimates of response time in each condition, a large number of test trials are administered; analyses are normally based on median or mean latencies for the conditions.

Each of these procedures to increase the accuracy of measurement has the side effect of increasing the amount of practice a child receives. This in turn can produce a number of interpretive complications that are often ignored. First, extended practice may significantly change cognitive processing. Second, a within-subjects design requires that a child experience different experimental conditions in a particular order. If this order is not counterbalanced or randomized across subjects, and if practice results in systematic changes over trials, than what appears to be a difference in processing may in fact be due simply to practice. Third, practice on a large number of trials may produce processing quite unlike that used outside an experimental setting, and hence the generality of any conclusions may be diminished considerably.

Another issue involves analysis of response time data. Response times can, under some conditions, be extremely variable both within and between subjects. Researchers sometimes use nonlinear transformations (e.g., logarithmic or reciprocal transformations) to reduce variability in their data and thereby make the data more suitable for statistical analysis. Pachella (1974) has argued that such a practice is unwarranted. Many measures used in psychology bear an arbitrary relationship to the construct they represent. For example, "trials to criterion" in a learning experiment does not necessarily relate to "learning" in a precisely linear fashion. However, a basic assumption of the information processing approach is that any given process requires a finite amount of *real time* for its function. Thus time has direct meaning and is not an arbitrary scale. The difference between 400 and 500 milliseconds is equivalent in a real and interpretive sense to the difference between 1400 and 1500 milliseconds. Nonlinear transformations distort this equivalence and should not be used in analyses of reaction time data unless justified by special considerations. (For a detailed discussion of this point, see Pachella, 1974.)

Little has been said to this point about error data. Response times on incorrect responses are typically discarded, since the underlying processes usually cannot be inferred. Problems of interpretation may arise, however, if error rates vary greatly across conditions and/or groups of children. For example, suppose mean latencies for conditions X and Y are both 900 milliseconds, but error rates are 5% and 20%, respectively. Total times are equivalent, but the discrepant error rates raise the possibility that children may have been more lax in their decisions for condition Y than for condition X. Perhaps children were sacrificing accuracy for speed in condition Y by processing in an incomplete or inaccurate manner that is not captured by the hypothesized model. If so, reaction times for conditions X and Y would not be directly comparable. Consequently, it is important to inspect the relationship between latencies and error rates to determine if any potentially confounding criterion differences exist. (For additional discussion of this problem, see Pachella, 1974, and Wickelgren, 1977.) In some cases it may be possible to circumvent potentially confounding problems like these by using canonical correlations (e.g., Sternberg, 1977) or by modeling correct and incorrect response latencies separately.

One additional problem that is common to response time methods is known as the "assumption of pure insertion," which refers to the belief that "it is possible to delete (or insert) completely mental events from an information-processing task without changing the nature of the other constituent mental operations [Pachella, 1974, p. 48]." For example, in the subtraction experiment described earlier it is assumed that a problem requiring two decrements of the counter is fundamentally comparable to one requiring three decrements; we presume that the additional, "inserted" decrementing operation required in the second problem does not alter previous processes (such as encoding and prior decrementing operations) or subsequent processes (such as reading the final result listed on the counter). This assumption of pure insertion makes it possible to analyze the data from the subtraction study in the way described earlier. If, however, performance on the two problems (or tasks) is not directly comparable in the ways specified by our models, then our analyses and interpretations will necessarily be wrong. Assumptions about the comparability of different tasks or problems can often be tested experimentally, and the results can provide insights into how to further revise and refine models of processing (see Pachella, 1974).

In addition to the issues already described, response time methods share a number of limitations with rule assessment methods. As already mentioned, a relatively large number of trials is usually required for accurate and reliable analyses. It is also important that subjects respond in a consistent and stable manner across trials. For example, if a child switches randomly between model 1 and model 4 in solving subtraction problems, the resulting latency measures may be impossible to interpret. Furthermore, reaction time methods and analyses tend to become somewhat unwieldly as stimulus complexity and the number of responses available to the subject increase. Finally, problems often exist in determining whether or not a given model provides a "sufficient" explanation for the data, and in deciding if one model is significantly superior to another model.

It is important to recognize that many of the issues raised in this section are specific instances of more general issues relevant to much psychological research. For example, the issues of assuming comparability among tasks and of detecting subtle inconsistencies in the way children respond are difficult and important for Piagetian psychologists as for information-processing psychologists. This rather lengthy collection of methodological issues should not detract from the fact that, *when used appropriately,* response time methods can be valuable tools for revealing cognitive processes.

Computer Simulation

The rule-assessment and response-latency methods share a common limitation: They become unwieldy when we attempt to apply them to models that have more than a handful of processes. For evaluating these more complicated models, *computer simulation,* often in conjunction with rule-assessment or response-latency methods, is emerging as a powerful technique. The thrust of this approach is to create a working computer program that will "behave" as a child of a particular age might behave. That is, if a child finds problem A more difficult than problem B, the program should too; if a child generally answers problem C more rapidly than problem D, the program should as well.

An Example: Seriation of Weight. One of the fundamental operations that differentiates the preoperational child from the concrete operational child in Piaget's system is that of *seriation.* Given a scale and several blocks identical in size but varying in weight, a child is asked to arrange them in order from heaviest to lightest. A child in the late preoperational stage, say a 5- or 6-year-old, typically will weigh pairs of blocks and order them correctly, but no effort is made to coordinate the weights of the various pairs. A child of this age might, for example, produce the ordering 6 2 4 1 5 3, where 6 refers to the heaviest block and 1 to the lightest. Each pair of blocks is ordered correctly ($6 > 2$, $4 > 1$, $5 > 3$), but the child has (apparently) made no effort to relate the various pairs. A child in the early concrete operational stage (7 or 8 years of age) will fare more successfully: Now the child produces ordered clusters consisting of three or four blocks, but the clusters remain uncoordinated (e.g., $6 > 4 > 1$, $5 > 3 > 2$). Not until 9 or 10 years of age do children successfully order the blocks, most commonly doing so with a strategy of finding the heaviest block from the set, placing it, determining the heaviest block from those remaining, placing it, and so on, until all blocks have been ordered (Baylor & Gascon, 1974; Baylor, Gascon, Lemoyne, & Pothier, 1973).

In a series of papers, Baylor and several colleagues (Baylor *et al.*, 1973; Baylor & Gascon, 1974; Baylor & Lemoyne, 1975) have provided a detailed information-processing analysis of the processes underlying solution of the seriation problem at each of the Piagetian stages. Here we will focus on their description of the preoperational stage, for the simplicity of the child's thinking at this level makes it an excellent vehicle for demonstrating the use of computer simulation.

As a starting point for their analysis, Baylor *et al.* (1973) present a detailed description of the efforts of one 6-year-old, Nathalie, to seriate seven blocks. Shown in Table 7.1 are the 10 steps involved in Nathalie's solution. The first column in Table 7.1 depicts the sequence of blocks in the original, unordered array; the second column indicated blocks currently in the balance; the third presents the outcome of a weighing; and the fourth column indicates the positions of the blocks in the ordered series that the child is constructing.

We see that Nathalie first placed blocks 5 and 2 in the balance and discovered that 5 was heavier (step 1). She took 5 out of the balance and began to construct her series (step 2), then placed block 2 next to 5 (step 3). Nathalie next selected blocks 1 and 7, determined that 7 was heavier (step 4), then placed it (step 5) and block 1 (step 6) at the end of the series. The

TABLE 7.1
Nathalie's Solution of the Weight Seriation Problem

	Unordered array	Balance	Weighing	Ordered array
Initial position	3 6 4 1 7 2 5			
Step 1	3 6 4 1 7	2 5	5 > 2	
Step 2	3 6 4 1 7	2		5
Step 3	3 6 4 1 7			5 2
Step 4	3 6 4	1 7	7 > 1	5 2
Step 5	3 6 4	1		5 2 7
Step 6	3 6 4			5 2 7 1
Step 7	3	6 4	6 > 4	5 2 7 1
Step 8	3	4		5 2 7 1 6
Step 9	3			5 2 7 1 6 4
Step 10				5 2 7 1 6 4 3

Note: These data are modified from Figure 1 of Baylor *et al.* (1973). (Copyright 1973 by the Canadian Psychological Association, reprinted by permission.)

TABLE 7.2
Production System for Nathalie

Rule	Conditions	Actions
P1	PO > 1 • PB = O	MOVE (block • block, PO (end position • next end position); PB)
P2	PB = 2	WEIGH (block • block) (= = > heavier block; lighter block); MOVE (heavier block, PB; PF (right end)); MOVE (lighter block, PB; PF (right end))
P3	PO = 1 • PB = 0	MOVE (block, PO; PF (right end))
P4	PO = 0	STOP

Note: From Baylor *et al.* (1973), Figure 2. PO refers to the original, unordered set of objects; PF refers to the final set of ordered objects; PB refers to the balance. (Copyright 1973 by the Canadian Psychological Association, reprinted by permission.)

process was repeated with blocks 6 and 4 (steps 7, 8, 9), leaving only block 3, which Nathalie placed at the end of the string without weighing it (step 10).

Baylor *et al.* (1973) created a computer program that would simulate Nathalie's behavior.[3] The essential unit of their program is called a *production*. Quite simply, a production consists of a condition or set of conditions and an associated action or set of actions to be taken whenever the condition(s) occurs. In a *production system* (i.e., a program comprised of a set of productions), productions are considered in sequence until the conditions of a particular production are met. The actions associated with this production are taken, then the productions are again considered in sequence, beginning with the first. This process occurs iteratively until the problem is solved. (For a more detailed description of production systems as they are used in computer simulation of cognitive phenomena, see Anderson, 1976; Klahr & Wallace, 1976; and, especially, Newell & Simon, 1972).

The best way to understand such a system is to examine some productions and watch them "in action." To explain Nathalie's behavior, Baylor *et al.* (1973) devised the four productions presented in Table 7.2. Each production consists of the condition(s) that must be met and the action(s) to be taken when those conditions are satisfied. The first production (*P1*), for example, has two conditions: (*a*) there must be more than one block in the

---

[3] The model presented here is one of the earliest formulations of the Baylor-Gascon work. In subsequent publications the model has been revised (Baylor & Gascon, 1974; Baylor & Lemoyne, 1975). We are presenting the initial model because its simplicity makes it useful pedagogically.

original unordered series ($PO > 1$), and (b) the balance must be empty ($PB = 0$). If *both* conditions exist then the actions to the right of the arrow are taken. Two blocks are moved from the unordered series (PO) to the balance scale (PB). Furthermore, the specific blocks to be chosen are the blocks at the end (i.e., the rightmost block) and the next-to-end positions. *P2* states that whenever two blocks are in the balance ($PB = 2$), several things should occur: (a) weigh them, (b) place the heavier block at the right end of the ordered series, then (c) place the lighter block at the right end of the series (i.e., to the right of the heavier block). *P3,* like *P1,* has two conditions that must be met. There must be only one block left ($PO = 1$) *and* the scale must be empty ($PO = 0$). When these conditions hold, the child moves the lone remaining block directly to the right end of the ordered series, without weighing it. Finally, *P4* indicates that when there are no blocks remaining in the unordered series ($PO = 0$) that processing can stop.

Table 7.3 depicts the actions of *P1–P4* when we ask the production system to seriate the seven blocks given to Nathalie. *P1–P4* are examined in sequence, beginning with *P1,* to determine if the conditions of any production are met. The search is brief, as *P1* is satisfied (there is more than one block in the unordered series and the scales are empty). Consequently, the action side of *P1* is implemented, with the end block and the next-to-end block being placed on the scales. Once the action of *P1* is executed, *P1–P4* again are scrutinized. This time both conditions of *P1* are *not* met, but the condition of *P2* that the balance be full ($PB = 2$) is. The actions associated

TABLE 7.3
Production System Solution of the Weight Seriation Problem

	Unordered array	Balance	Weighing	Ordered array
Initial position	3 6 4 1 7 2 5			
P1	3 6 4 1 7	2 5		
P2	3 6 4 1 7		5 > 2	
	3 6 4 1 7			5 2
P1	3 6 4	1 7		5 2
P2	3 6 4		7 > 1	5 2
	3 6 4			5 2 7 1
P1	3	6 4		5 2 7 1
P2	3		6 > 4	5 2 7 1
	3			5 2 7 1 6 4
P3				5 2 7 1 6 4 3
P4	STOP			5 2 7 1 6 4 3

Note: These data are modified from Figure 1 of Baylor *et al.* (1973). (Copyright 1973 by the Canadian Psychological Association, reprinted by permission.)

with *P2* are implemented: The blocks are weighed, revealing that block 5 is heavier than block 2, thus 5 is first placed at the end of the ordered array, followed by 2, to the right of 5.

At this point *P1–P4* are examined again, with the conditions of *P1* being satisfied. When the actions of *P1* are executed (blocks 1 and 7 are placed on the scale), the condition of *P2* will be satisfied and it will be executed (1 and 7 will be weighed and placed at the end of the ordered array). The *P1–P2* cycle will be repeated one more time, with blocks 6 and 4. At this point the program will again scan the productions, beginning with *P1*. For the first time the conditions of neither *P1* nor *P2* are satisfied. However, the two conditions of *P3*—that one block remain and that the balance be empty— are met and *P3* is executed. As a consequence, the final block, 3, is placed at the right end of the ordered series. Having implemented the actions of *P3,* each of the productions is again tested, with *P4* being the only one whose conditions are met, and the action taken is to terminate processing.

Methodological Issues. By comparing Tables 7.1 and 7.3 we can see that Baylor *et al.*'s (1973) production system simulates Nathalie's behavior perfectly. At each step the program's output mirrors Nathalie's actions with the blocks. Does this mean that the production system is an accurate description of Nathalie's cognitive activities as she solves the seriation task? Not necessarily. First, it should not be terribly surprising that the model simulates Nathalie's data, since these are the very data that were used to construct the model in the first place. We would want to evaluate the behavior of the production system in experimental situations other than those that led directly to its formulation. For example, according to the model, the number of ordered blocks should not affect the quality of performance: Nathalie should consistently construct an array consisting of $n/2$ ordered pairs, where n denotes the total number of weights.[4] We would want to compare Nathalie's behavior with that of the production system in this and several other novel conditions before placing much faith in the viability of the model.

If the model matched Nathalie's behavior in all such tests, would this prove that the production system was an accurate description of Nathalie's cognitive processing? No, but this is the same problem that we encountered earlier in describing rule-assessment and response-time methods. Current information-processing research places a great deal of emphasis on the *sufficiency criterion:* If a model is sufficient to account for a child's behavior, it will be accepted, even though it may only be mimicking the predictions of the "true model."

---

[4] When n is an odd number, $(n - 1)/2$ ordered pairs are expected.

Two additional issues can be mentioned briefly. First, to use computer simulation, an investigator must initially select a computer language to be used. Various languages have different strengths and weaknesses, and it is possible for psychologically irrelevant but language-related characteristics to have a subtle influence on the nature of one's psychological theories and models. For example, a language in which mathematical computations are cumbersome (e.g., LISP) may bias a theorist toward phenomena and/or models that involve minimal calculations. Similarly, a language with a built-in, limited-capacity "working memory" (e.g., PSG) may influence theory and research in the direction of hypotheses about "working memory." Investigators need to be aware of influences that derive from the nature of the computer language chosen.

Second, judicious decisions must be made about the "level" of analysis that is to be emphasized in simulating behavior. A "complete" simulation of any relatively complex behavior would be extraordinarily difficult. For example, a complete simulation of how an individual solves a geometry problem would require that we model everything from the perception of geometric patterns (an entire area of research itself!) to the student's concepts of geometry theorems (see Greeno, 1978). Certainly a distinct asset of the computer simulation approach is that it allows for integration of a very complex set of hypotheses about cognition (e.g., Anderson, 1976). However, it is normally necessary to restrict one's efforts to only part of the total picture and to make simplifying assumptions about the rest that do not appear to be grossly inaccurate. For example, Baylor et al. (1973) focused primarily on the processes of selecting and comparing blocks and chose to ignore details about how children perceived the blocks and balance scale visually.

In summary, it should be clear from this discussion that the most important asset of simulation work is the precision with which theories can be formulated. Given a set of interpretable instructions, the program will run and lead to a specific outcome. (Very subtle weaknesses in one's theory become starkly obvious when they cause a program to fail!) As a consequence, simulation models can be evaluated readily and improvements in the theory can be assessed easily. As Klahr and Wallace (1972) summarize the situation:

When information processing analysis is combined with computer simulation, the result is a theorizing medium which provides both ease of detection of mutual contradictions and ambiguity, and an explicit method for determining the exact behavioral consequences of theoretical statements. These are precisely the attributes which the major theories of cognitive development lack [p. 155].

SUMMARY AND EVALUATION

It may be useful to retrace our steps and recall some of the critical features of the information-processing framework before we evaluate the approach. Cognition is considered to be analogous to the activities of a computer: Cognitive processes occur over real time and can be organized into various superordinate strategies or procedures that operate on information from memory and from the environment. The organized set of processes and operating characteristics that is presumed to underlie cognitive performance is called a model. Such models are formulated initially by means of task analysis, then are evaluated and reformulated by some combination of rule assessment, response time, and computer simulation methods. Cognitive development is characterized in terms of a sequence of such information-processing models.

Our description of the information-processing framework is by no means exhaustive, but it does provide some of the core concepts that are commonly found in extant theories and research. It is now appropriate to step back, to view the framework from a distance, and to note some of its apparent strengths and weaknesses.

Assets

One clear advantage of the information-processing approach is its great breadth of application. Virtually any type of cognitive performance can, in principle, be modeled. Investigators may use the framework to model logical reasoning abilities, or they may use it to examine perceptual skills, mnemonic strategies, comprehension skills, or any other cognitive activity. The value of such a flexible framework is that it may ultimately make possible the integration of theories and research on diverse phenomena.

A second asset is that information-processing models can be specified with great precision, and hence they tend to be readily testable. The importance of this characteristic for research on cognitive development bears underscoring. For example, there is much research in developmental psychology derived from Piagetian theory. A consistent problem in this literature is that critical tests of the theory are nearly impossible due to the absence of precise descriptions of how a child's logical structures are translated into performance on any given task. The generality of available explanations makes Piagetian theory compatible with almost any experimental outcome.

There also is an enormous amount of research in developmental psychology that can be characterized as investigations of "developmental change in the effect of variable X on process Y." Sometimes research of this type is simply descriptive and there is no real interest in determining the processes underlying experimental outcomes. More often, however, hypotheses *are* stated regarding expected effects, but these hypotheses are derived from theories that are usually stated vaguely or perhaps not at all. In this case, when the expected results are not obtained, it is difficult to know whether (*a*) the theory was wrong, (*b*) the hypotheses did not follow from the theory, or (*c*) both. Information processing is, perhaps, the only available framework that provides the potential for the precision needed to construct and evaluate theories.

A third advantage of the information-processing perspective has to do with conclusions made about a child's cognitive ability. It seems to be characteristic of theories and clinicians that findings regarding a child's performance on a task are quickly translated into statements about that child's intellectual competence (Siegel, Kirasic, & Kail, 1978). Thus, for example, Piaget's finding that preschool children typically do not infer that A > C given A > B and B > C leads to a conclusion regarding the preschool child's inability to reason inferentially (Trabasso, 1977). The information-processing approach, with its emphasis on the manifold processes intervening between presentation of a problem to a child and the child's solution of that problem, underscores the hazardous nature of any quick and simple conclusions about a child's intellectual competence from that child's performance.

Fourth, information processing provides an excellent framework for considering psychological differences between individuals of the same age. Two of the studies cited earlier (Siegler, 1976; Woods *et al.,* 1975) demonstrate this feature. In Siegler's (1976) work, for example, children of the same age often varied considerably in the sophistication of their rules. Among the 9- and 10-year-olds, as one case in point, three children used rule 1, nine used rule 2, twelve used rule 3, and two used rule 4. Without the information processing analysis used to generate the rules, the result would simply have been that 9- and 10-year-olds differed considerably in the number of problems solved correctly, a finding that tells us little about factors underlying individual differences. With the rule analysis, individual variation was meaningful.

Liabilities

One potential drawback of the information-processing approach has to do with how it is applied. Because of the value placed on specificity, researchers have a tendency to focus on narrow domains of behavior. The result of this policy is that a number of highly precise "minitheories" are generated that account for a small and specifically defined set of behaviors, but little effort is made to integrate these theories. This seems to be a characteristic of researchers rather than anything attributable to the information-processing framework per se (Newell, 1973). There are exceptions to this trend. For example, Klahr and Wallace (1976) and Case (1978a,b) have attempted to lay the groundwork for comprehensive, information-processing theories of cognitive development. These attempts have had some impact, but at present no single theory seems to be widely accepted.

Second, it is usually easier to build reasonable models in domains with a large extant data base than with a small one. Consequently, the information-processing view may be more useful in the later stages of research in a particular area than in the beginning stages. For example, Siegler's (1976) rule system was developed, in part, from careful consideration of existing data from Inhelder and Piaget (1958) and Lee (1971). Does this mean that the information-processing orientation is currently inappropriate for developmental research? Not at all. Most developmentalists would agree that developmental data of interest and import abound; missing are theories of the processes underlying developmental change seen in these data.

Third, no attempt is made, usually, to provide a mechanism of developmental change. That is, while information-processing models may provide quite accurate descriptions of the thought of a 4-year-old contrasted with that of a 10-year-old, there is little effort made to suggest how the 4-year-old's thought comes to resemble that of the 10-year-old. The argument made by most information-processing researchers (e.g., Klahr & Wallace, 1972) is that without detailed models of the states that undergo change, a precise model of transition between states is impossible. Further, this criticism can be applied to the vast majority of developmental research, not just that conducted within the information-processing framework: Most research in developmental psychology deals with developmental *differences* rather than developmental *change*. The principal exception is Piaget's notion of equilibration, which is still primarily a metaphor for developmental change rather than a precise mechanism. Some theorists, such as Klahr and Wallace (1976), Bruner (1970), Pascual-Leone (1970), and Case (1978a) have made hypotheses about the mechanisms and principles that could account for transition and change, but these hypotheses will require additional research and elaboration before they are adopted widely.

PROSPECTUS

What does the future hold for information-processing research on developmental phenomena? We can see some evidence for at least three general trends.

First, information-processing research will almost certainly move beyond purely cognitive aspects of development to include social phenomena as well. In fact, information processing has already been used as a conceptual framework in studying aspects of social development such as moral reasoning (e.g., Feldman, Klosson, Parsons, Rholes, & Ruble, 1976) and children's communication with peers (e.g., Patterson, Massad, & Cosgrove, 1978). It seems reasonable to expect that use of information-processing methods in these areas of research should follow soon.

Second, there seems to be a trend toward the use of information-processing methods to study the relationship between cognition and instruction. For many years educators have argued that instructional goals should be stated in terms of behavioral objectives. We might, for example, establish as a behavioral objective for a first grader the ability to solve simple addition problems of the type $a + b = ?$, where a and b can be integers between 1 and 9. However, in the past few years a growing number of educators and psychologists (e.g., Glaser, 1976) have argued that these behavioral objectives are likely to be achieved only if we identify the cognitive processes necessary for the behaviors of interest. These processes would then constitute the *cognitive objectives* of instruction (Greeno, 1976). Of course, information-processing methods are designed explicitly for the purpose of identifying cognitive skills underlying performance. Thus, it should not be surprising that there are now several successful cases in which information-processing methods were used to identify the specific processes in which individuals should receive instruction, with improved performance being the typical result (e.g., Butterfield, Wambold, & Belmont, 1973; Holzman, Glaser, & Pellegrino, 1976; Siegler, 1976).

Finally, we noted in our Summary and Evaluation section that, while information-processing research often seems narrow in focus, several comprehensive information-processing descriptions of cognitive development have emerged recently. Such integrative efforts almost certainly will become more frequent in years to come. Thus we anticipate that future information-processing theories will combine the breadth and scope of Piagetian theory with the precision and specificity of current information-processing models.

REFERENCES

Anderson, J. R. *Language, memory, and thought.* Hillsdale, N. J.: Lawrence Erlbaum Associates, 1976.

Baylor, G. W., Gascon, J., Lemoyne, G., & Pothier, N. An information processing model of some seriation tasks. *Canadian Psychologist,* 1973, *14,* 167–196.

Baylor, G. W., & Gascon, J. An information processing theory of aspects of the development of weight seriation in children. *Cognitive Psychology,* 1974, *6,* 1-40.

Baylor, G. W., & Lemoyne, G. Experiments in seriation with children. Towards an information processing explanation of the horizontal decalage. *Canadian Journal of Behavioural Science,* 1975, *7,* 4-29.

Bruner, J. S. The growth and structure of skill. In K. J. Connolly (Ed.), *Mechanisms of motor skill development.* London: Academic Press, 1970.

Butterfield, E. C., Wambold, C., & Belmont, J. M. On the theory and practice of improving short-term memory. *American Journal of Mental Deficiency,* 1973, *77,* 654-669.

Case, R. Intellectual development from birth to adulthood: A neo-Piagetian interpretation. In R. S. Siegler (Ed.), *Children's thinking: What develops?* Hillsdale, N. J.: Lawrence Erlbaum Associates, 1978. (a)

Case, R. Piaget and beyond: Toward a developmentally based theory and technology of instruction. In R. Glaser (Ed.), *Advances in instructional psychology* (Vol. 1). Hillsdale, N. J.: Lawrence Erlbaum Associates, 1978. (b)

Day, M. C. Developmental trends in visual scanning. In H. W. Reese (Ed.), *Advances in child development and behavior* (Vol. 10). New York: Academic Press, 1975.

Feldman, N. S., Klosson, E. C., Parsons, J. E., Rholes, W. S., & Ruble, D. N. Order of information presentation and children's moral judgments. *Child Development,* 1976, *47,* 556-559.

Flavell, J. H. *The developmental psychology of Jean Piaget.* Princeton, N. J.: Von Nostrand, 1963.

Flavell, J. H. Stage-related properties of cognitive development. *Cognitive Psychology,* 1971, *2,* 421-453.

Flavell, J. H., & Wohlwill, J. F. Formal and functional aspects of cognitive development. In D. Elkind and J. H. Flavell (Eds.), *Studies in cognitive development: Essays in honor of Jean Piaget.* New York: Oxford University Press, 1969.

Gagné, R. M. Contributions of learning to human development. *Psychological Review,* 1968, *75,* 177-191.

Gelman, R. Cognitive development. *Annual Review of Psychology,* 1978, *29,* 297-332.

Glaser, R. Components of a psychology of instruction: Toward a science of design. *Review of Educational Research,* 1976, *46,* 1-24.

Greeno, J. G. Cognitive objectives of instruction: Theory of knowledge for solving problems and answering questions. In D. Klahr (Ed.), *Cognition and instruction.* Hillsdale, N. J.: Lawrence Erlbaum Associates, 1976.

Greeno, J. G. A study of problem solving. In R. Glaser (Ed.), *Advances in instructional psychology* (Vol. 1). Hillsdale, N. J.: Lawrence Erlbaum Associates, 1978.

Groen, G. J., & Parkman, J. M. A chronometric analysis of simple addition. *Psychological Review,* 1972, *79,* 329-343.

Holzman, T. G., Glaser, R., & Pellegrino, J. W. Process training derived from a computer simulation theory. *Memory & Cognition,* 1976, *4,* 349-356.

Hunt, E. Quote the raven? Nevermore! In L. W. Gregg (Ed.), *Knowledge and Cognition.* Potomac, Md.: Lawrence Erlbaum Associates, 1974.

Hunt, E. Varieties of cognitive power. In L. B. Resnick (Ed.), *The nature of intelligence.* Hillsdale, N. J.: Lawrence Erlbaum Associates, 1976.

Inhelder, B., & Piaget, J. *The growth of logical thinking from childhood to adolescence.* New York: Basic Books, 1958.

Kail, R. V., & Siegel, A. W. The development of mnemonic encoding in children: From perception to abstraction. In R. V. Kail & J. W. Hagen (Eds.), *Perspectives on the development of memory and cognition.* Hillsdale, N. J.: Lawrence Erlbaum Associates, 1977.

Klahr, D., & Siegler, R. S. The representation of children's knowledge. In H. W. Reese (Ed.), *Advances in child development and behavior* (Vol. 12). New York: Academic Press, 1978.

Klahr, D., & Wallace, J. G. Class inclusion processes. In S. Farnham-Diggory (Ed.), *Information processing in children.* New York: Academic Press, 1972.

Klahr, D., & Wallace, J. G. *Cognitive development: An information-processing view.* Hillsdale, N. J.: Lawrence Erlbaum Associates, 1976.

Lee, L. C. The concomitant development of cognitive and moral modes of thought. A test of selected deductions from Piaget's theory. *Genetic Psychology Monographs,* 1971, *85,* 93–146.

Lindsay, P. H., & Norman, D. A. *Human information processing* (2nd ed.). New York: Academic Press, 1977.

Newell, A. You can't play 20 questions with nature and win: Projective comments on the papers of this symposium. In W. G. Chase (Ed.), *Visual information processing.* New York: Academic Press, 1973.

Newell, A., & Simon, H. A. *Human problem solving.* Englewood Cliffs, N. J.: Prentice-Hall, 1972.

Pachella, R. G. The interpretation of reaction time in information processing research. In B. Kantowitz (Ed.), *Human information processing: Tutorials in performance and cognition.* Hillsdale, N. J.: Lawrence Erlbaum Associates, 1974.

Pascual-Leone, J. A mathematical model for the transition rule in Piaget's developmental stages. *Acta Psychologica,* 1970, *32,* 301–345.

Patterson, C. J., Massad, C. M., & Cosgrove, J. M. Children's referential communication: Components of plans for effective listening. *Developmental Psychology,* 1978, *14,* 401–406.

Reese, H. W., & Overton, W. F. Models of development and theories of development. In L. R. Goulet & P. B. Baltes (Eds.), *Lifespan developmental psychology: Research and theory.* New York: Academic Press, 1970.

Resnick, L. B. Task analysis in instructional design: Some cases from mathematics. In D. Klahr (Ed.), *Cognition and instruction.* Hillsdale, N. J.: Lawrence Erlbaum Associates, 1976.

Siegel, A. W., Kirasic, K. C., & Kail, R. V. Stalking the elusive cognitive map: The development of children's representations of geographic space. In I. Altman and J. F. Wohlwill (Eds.), *Human behavior and environment* (Vol. 3). New York: Plenum, 1978.

Siegler, R. S. Three aspects of cognitive development. *Cognitive Psychology,* 1976, *8,* 481–520.

Siegler, R. S. The origins of scientific reasoning. In R. S. Siegler (Ed.), *Children's thinking: What develops?* Hillsdale, N. J.: Lawrence Erlbaum Associates, 1978.

Simon, H. A. On the development of the processor. In S. Farnham-Diggory (Ed.), *Information processing in children.* New York: Academic Press, 1972.

Stanovich, K. E. Information processing in mentally retarded individuals. In N. R. Ellis (Ed.), *International review of research in mental retardation* (Vol. 9). New York: Academic Press, 1978.

Sternberg, R. J. *Intelligence, information processing and analogical reasoning: The componential analysis of human abilities.* Hillsdale, N. J.: Lawrence Erlbaum Associates, 1977.

Sternberg, R. J., & Rifkin, B. The development of analogical reasoning processes. *Journal of Experimental Child Psychology,* 1979, *27,* 195–232.

Terman, L. M., & Merrill, M. A. *Measuring intelligence.* Boston: Houghton Mifflin, 1960.

Trabasso, T. The role of memory as a system in making transitive inferences. In R. V. Kail & J. W. Hagen (Eds.), *Perspectives on the development of memory and cognition*. Hillsdale, N. J.: Lawrence Erlbaum Associates, 1977.

Wickelgren, W. A. Speed–accuracy tradeoff and information processing dynamics. *Acta Psychologica,* 1977, *41,* 67–85.

Woods, S. S., Resnick, L. B., & Groen, G. J. An experimental test of five process models for subtraction. *Journal of Educational Psychology,* 1975, *67,* 17–21.

8 Prosocial Behavior and Self-Control

JOAN E. GRUSEC

Traditionally, psychologists have viewed the young child as amoral or even immoral, a creature deficient in the ability to resist temptation, delay gratification, or show concern for the needs of others. If this picture is an accurate one, a major research problem becomes that of understanding how children achieve a state of morality—how they develop the ability to inhibit impulse expression and to behave in a selfless manner.

Different theoretical approaches to the acquisition of morality have emphasized different parts of the process, or suggested the operation of different mechanisms. Psychoanalytic theorists, for example, see the origin of morality in identification with the same-sexed parent. Social learning theorists have argued for the importance of reinforcement, punishment, and modeling, while cognitive developmentalists have proposed that human beings are naturally impelled toward a state of moral maturity and that, given reasonably adequate environmental experiences, such an end state will be achieved. These three approaches have also focused on different aspects of morality—psychoanalytic on the emotional (e.g., guilt after transgression), social learning on the behavioral (e.g., resistance to transgression), and cognitive developmental on the cognitive (e.g., the reasons children give for moral actions, and their ability to understand how the world is perceived by others). Regardless of theoretical underpinnings, however, the research generated by various viewpoints yields information about the process of socialization for morality. It is this research—or rather, methodological approaches to this research—that will provide the focus for this chapter.

Scientific investigation begins with a decision about what one is going to study and a definition of one's subject matter. Psychologists must be especially sensitive in this regard, for they are dealing with phenomena—

245

the behavior of human beings—about which everyone is an expert at some level and about which everyone is highly likely to have preconceived notions. One researcher's idea of what moral behavior is, for example, may be quite different from another's, even though they both use the same label. Therefore one investigator might conclude one thing about morality, while another might conclude the opposite: Their state of confusion could be resolved once they realized they were actually talking about different events.

Even at the level of definition problems arise in the study of moral behavior. What, for example, *is* a moral act? One is talking, of course, about the distinction between right and wrong. But is this distinction innate in the act or is it imposed by society? Are there some absolute moral values accepted by all of human society and other values considered important only by certain groups within society? Do "Thou shalt not kill" and "Keep off the grass" belong to the same class of behaviors or should the one be considered a moral command and the other a social convention? If they are seen as equivalent acts, then the study of one should yield information about the other. If, however, they are seen to be different, then understanding how children learn that it is wrong to disobey signs or requests directing them to stay off the grass should not be particularly helpful in understanding how they learn that it is wrong to kill.

To date most psychological researchers have considered various behaviors that must be learned in the course of socialization to be equivalent. Given that there appear to be very few universal taboos in human society—one culture, for example, considers premarital sex a sin while another considers it perfectly normal—this appears to be a reasonable approach. Thus, knowing the effective techniques for eliciting conformity to a "No smoking" sign should help one know how best to teach people not to steal.

Lately, however, some investigators (e.g., Turiel, 1978) have suggested that much information about the acquisition of morality is limited because researchers have failed to distinguish between moral norms and social conventions, that is, between rules that involve harming or benefiting others and rules that help to maintain social order and regularity. Turiel argues that the antecedents of the two are very different. Knowledge of moral norms stems directly from the events themselves—there is a natural connection between the event and the negative result it produces, such as when one child hits another. Knowledge of social conventions, on the other hand, must be transmitted by agents of socialization since social conventions are arbitrary—alternative courses of action could serve the same function of regulating behavior. If this is so, then, no active measures need be taken to help children conform to moral norms, but such measures *would* be necessary for them to conform to social conventions.

Problems of equivalence arise not only in the study of moral norms and social conventions, but in other areas as well. Consider the following. People are enjoined not to engage in a variety of behaviors. But the passive individual who never lies or cheats or harms others is not highly morally developed. It is the individual who, in addition, *does* engage in prosocial activities, who sacrifices his or her own interests for those of others, who is considered to have attained true morality. Different emphases have been placed on these two aspects of morality—that which *is not* to be done and that which *is* to be done—by different writers. Freud, for example, underlined the self-centered aspect of human nature and the necessity for society to suppress id-driven and selfish desires. More recent theoretical formulations have opened the way for a concern with the positive side of morality —the expression of altruism or concern for others. Nevertheless, the suppression of unwanted behavior was the major concern of psychological researchers for many years: With a few noteable exceptions (e.g., Murphy, 1937) the intensive study of altruism has only begun in the last 15–20 years.

If there are these two parts—the prescriptive and the proscriptive—to morality, then one can ask the same question that was asked about moral norms and social conventions. Are their antecedents the same? Generally the answer has been assumed to be affirmative. For those who emphasize the role of identification or imitation, of course, the specific behaviors and values exhibited by a parent would be of crucial importance. A parent who displayed little antisocial behavior, but little prosocial behavior as well, would have a child who showed little antisocial and little prosocial behavior. Others have seen an even closer link, however, between that which is prescribed and that which is proscribed, finding the roots of both in parental discipline. Hoffman (1970a, 1975) reported that parents who attempted to arouse their children's empathic capacities by pointing out the consequences of their misbehavior for others were successful in producing both altriusm as well as guilt after deviation. Zahn-Waxler, Radke-Yarrow, and King (1979) found that mothers who explained how their children's misbehavior distressed others, and who did so in an affectively-toned way, had children who were altruistic and who also made reparation when they deviated. They also found that mothers who were sensitive and responsive to their children's needs had children who were rated high in altruism and reparation after deviation.

It may be premature to conclude, however, that the inhibition of undesirable behavior and the expression of concern for others are opposite sides of the same coin: Prescriptive parents who emphasize being good have children who are more generous than do proscriptive parents who emphasize not being bad (Olejnik & McKinney, 1973). And while altruism and reparation after deviation may be related, does that necessarily mean that altruism and resistance to deviation are also related? In the case of reparation after deviation, interest is focused on how children help others after they have directed antisocial behavior against them. But in the case of resistance to deviation interest is focused on how successfully antisocial behaviors are suppressed in the first place.

It may be that moral conventions and social norms, and prescribed and proscribed behaviors are, indeed, equivalent members of the class of moral behaviors and that research will eventually show this to be the case. On the other hand, failure to make appropriate distinctions may make inferences about the acquisition of morality more ambiguous than they ought to be. This is a question which can only be settled by more research. And it is a question which highlights the importance of definition in psychological research.

RESEARCH ISSUES AND PROBLEMS

The aim of socialization in the moral domain is seen by most to be the internalization of societal values, beliefs, and attitudes. Thus children must come to adopt adult values as their own, and to conform to them independent of the hope of external reward or fear of external punishment. Society's agents begin by imposing values, by controlling children from without. They end by having transferred that control so that external control becomes self-control and other people's beliefs become the child's own beliefs. Internalization may not really be a viable goal. Perhaps children who comply with society's dictates do so only because of conditioned anxiety—basically a fear of punishment. But the aim of research in the area is fairly clear-cut, that is, to determine which events come nearest to producing a child who appears to genuinely believe that his or her morality is self-caused.

This conceptualization of morality produces an immediate problem for anyone wishing to study it. How can one be sure that a given behavior is really a reflection of some internalized value, and that it is not being done in order to gain social approval, material benefit, or to avoid some externally-imposed negative outcome that is either real or imagined? Is such a distinction even possible? Some researchers have placed children alone in a room and observed their behavior (unbeknownst to them) through a one-way mirror, assuming that any apparently moral act must be truly self-motivated under those conditions. But how can an investigator be certain that a seemingly moral act is not motivated by anticipation of some external consequence when it occurs under more normal circumstances? The answer to this question is far from self-evident, and so researchers have coped with the problem only by discounting obvious instances where "moral" appearing behavior is clearly self-serving. Because it is so difficult to infer the meaning of a given act to the actor, then, it is difficult to know whether that act in reality represents an underlying moral disposition.

Other issues arise in considering the acquisition of morality. Most research on the development of morality has been directed toward assessment of the role of parental discipline and childrearing techniques. Yet it must be realized that there are other major influences on socialization as well. The media, particularly television, have been recognized as important agents of socialization, and much research has been directed toward the delineation of television's role in teaching children about societal values and in providing models for both antisocial and altruistic behavior. In addition, the importance of the peer group in teaching the child about moral notions such as justice and fairness has long been recognized (Piaget, 1932), and it cannot be denied that age mates play an important role in the acquisition of morality.

Additional questions have been addressed. To what extent is socialization affected by characteristics and responses of children themselves? Do temperamental differences, for example, in the ease with which children can be controlled determine the techniques of discipline used by their parents (Bell, 1968)? Must children really be trained to conform with society's values, or are they basically compliant because compliance with the demands of the group ensures survival and hence contribution to the gene pool? Is noncompliance, in fact, induced by harmful parental discipline practices (Stayton, Ainsworth, & Hogan, 1971)? Is there a general disposition toward morality such that people who are moral in one area of behavior tend to be moral in others? Or is morality specific to the situation in which it occurs (Hartshorne & May, 1928; Mischel, 1968)? Are some people more likely to be consistently moral than others (Bem & Allen, 1974)? What parental disciplinary practices might lead to more consistent morality?

A HISTORICAL SURVEY

Adherence to various methodologies has altered in psychology over its recent history, and the area of moral development reflects these alterations as well as any. At no point in time has one approach been universally considered substantially better than another, although various approaches have waxed and waned in their popularity. What follows is a historical survey of the field over the past 25 years, based on a selective survey of some studies of moral development chosen to represent examples of different methodological approaches. In this way, the reader may come to understand the strengths of various approaches, as well as the limitations which have led researchers to favor one methodology at one time and another at a different time. With technological advances (e.g., videotape recording), thoughtful insights on the part of sometimes disillusioned investigators, and new statistical techniques for analyzing previously unanalyzable data, abandonned methodological approaches reappear in improved form and once again are used in answering the question of how prosocial behavior and self-control emerge in the human organism.

Correlational Studies of Discipline and Moral Development

If parents are so important in the growth of morality, then the task of the investigator could be one of comparing the approach to socialization used by a successful parent with that used by an unsuccessful parent. Although the data so collected would be correlational in nature, the approach would at least make possible some tentative conclusions about the most effective approach to childrearing.

But how do we find out how parents handle discipline in the privacy of their own homes? A major breakthrough in socialization research came in the late 1950s when investigators from Harvard University published the results of a large-scale study of the childrearing practices of 379 mothers of kindergarten-aged children (Sears, Maccoby, & Levin, 1957). Mothers were asked open-ended questions about their childrearing practices in the areas of feeding, toilet-training, sex, and aggression, and about how restrictive and demanding they were of their children. As well, they were asked questions about their child's typical behavior in these various areas. Specifically the mothers were asked 72 open-ended questions, but with suggested probes for each question that an interviewer could ask or not, depending on the original answer. In this way Sears *et al.* were able to learn *how* mothers raise their children: As well, they could gain some idea of the most effective childrearing techniques by correlating maternal usage with child behavior.

A number of relationships emerged from this study. Perhaps the best known in the area of moral development is that mothers who disciplined by withdrawing their love, rather than by physical punishment or withdrawal of material rewards, had children who showed the greatest signs of conscience development. These were mothers, however, who were also relatively warm. Cold, rejecting mothers were not very effective in their use of withdrawal of love. Sears *et al.* defined conscience as any evidence of confession, apology, or attempts at restitution after deviation. Although they felt that resistance to temptation and acting the parental role (imitating parental prohibitions) were indices of conscience development as well, they were unable to measure these behaviors from their interviews. Nevertheless, even with this incomplete assessment of conscience, they argued that their results supported a theory of moral development that states that children identify with their parents, taking on their various behaviors and attitudes including those in the moral domain. Mothers who withdraw love after deviation—assuming they are warm and therefore have love to withdraw—are effective because they make it necessary for their children to imitate them in order to ensure themselves of their mother's love, to avoid her withdrawal of love, and even to provide lost love for themselves.

Sears *et al.* (1957) included reasoning in their category of love withdrawal techniques because they found it was generally associated with praise, isolation, and withdrawal of love. They suggested that the use of reasoning—explanation, guidance, verbal assistance—facilitates morality because children imitate this aspect of maternal behavior and in so doing display a more moral approach to the solution of problems.

While making an important start on the assessment of parent socialization practices, the Sears *et al.* study was not without its methodological problems. First of all, information about child rearing practices and the child's behavior were both obtained from the same source—the mother. Sears *et al.* themselves pointed out that certain temporary or enduring attitudes could color a mother's reports. A mother who was cold and restrictive, for example, might tend to define anything her child did as negative, whereas the child's behavior might appear much more positive in another observer's eyes. A preferable approach might be to obtain separate ratings of children's behavior either from teachers or from independent observations of their behavior in natural or controlled test situations. Such changes were made in subsequent studies of child-rearing practices (e.g., Sears, Rau, & Alpert, 1965).

The mother interview, although valuable in identifying interesting areas for future investigation, presented further methodological problems for investigators of moral development. We know that people's impressions (e.g., "What do you usually do when your child misbehaves?") are generally not accurate indicators of their true behavior. A mother who reports the use of physical punishment, for example, may actually use reasoning much more: It is the more salient physical punishment, however, which assumes prominence in her mind. Moreover, mothers do not usually think of their disciplinary behavior in the abstract terms investigators ask them to use, so one cannot be sure that they can adopt such an outlook quickly, easily, or accurately. No matter how honest one encourages a parent to be, the problem of positive self-presentation cannot be overlooked. Parents do have some idea of how they are supposed to discipline children—they read columns by childrearing experts in magazines and newspapers and listen to these same experts dispense advice over radio and television. Given that they have even some minimal desire to impress an interviewer they cannot help but present their approach to discipline in the most socially desirable way. Finally, parental discipline changes over time. It may begin with reasoning, escalate to physical punishment, and subside to withdrawal of love as a child learns to inhibit a specific behavior. It is unclear how a parent interview can capture the nuances of these changes.

After the ground-breaking work of Sears, Maccoby, and Levin, investigators developed an active interest in the disciplinary antecedents of morality. They began, as well, to modify their methodological approaches in an attempt to gather data less subject to criticism on methodological grounds. One major study, described here in some detail, was reported by Hoffman and Saltzstein (1967). In this study of a large sample of seventh graders they employed a variety of techniques for measuring children's morality and parental reactions to deviation. Clearly, if each of these techniques yielded similar results, these investigators were on a surer footing when it came to drawing conclusions about their findings. On the other hand, since their measures represented different levels of morality, and different aspects (prosocial behavior versus suppression of antisocial behavior), and there is no reason to believe that these different levels and aspects are correlated, lack of consistency in findings need not be surprising.

Hoffman and Saltzstein's first measure of guilt was a projective one in which subjects were asked to complete a story about a child who had transgressed (in one story a child's negligence had contributed to the death of a younger child and in the second story a child cheated in a swimming race and won), telling what the central character felt and thought and what happened afterward. Stories were coded for guilt (extreme guilt, for example, was coded if the hero underwent a personality change or committed suicide). Second, children were asked to make judgments about several hypothetical transgressions and their judgments were coded as having an orientation toward control by fear ("You can go to jail for that") or control by internal means ("It's wrong to violate someone's trust in you"). Overt reactions to deviation were also obtained by asking teachers and mothers to describe how the child typically reacted after wrongdoing. A fourth measure assessed concern for others using a sociometric technique—each child nominated three of his or her classmates who were most likely to care about others' feelings and to defend someone who was being made fun of. Finally, Hoffman and Saltzstein measured the child's parent identification by asking whom the child most admired, wanted to be like, and was most similar to.

Measures of parental practice were obtained in a more structured way than that used by Sears, Maccoby, and Levin. Both mothers and fathers were asked to imagine four concrete situations involving a child who misbehaved—delayed compliance with a parent's request, careless destruction, talking back, and academic failure. They were then given a list of possible disciplinary actions and asked to indicate which they would use at present and those they had used when their child was 5 years old. As well, the children themselves were asked to describe how their parents would discipline them in each of these four situations, although they were not asked to recall what their parents had done several years earlier. Finally, parents were also asked their reaction to a child's deviation toward his or her peers.

Hoffman and Saltzstein found that frequent use of power assertion by the mother (physical punishment, deprivation of material objects or privileges, application of force, or the threat of any of these things) was consistently associated with weak moral development, whereas the use of induction by the mother (appeals to the child's potential for guilt by referring to the consequences of his or her action for the parent) was consistently associated with advanced moral development. Love withdrawal on the part of the mother (ignoring, isolating, indicating dislike) related infrequently to moral development. For fathers no consistent set of relationships emerged.

Unlike Sears, Maccoby, and Levin, then, Hoffman and Saltzstein separated reasoning and withdrawal of love in their analyses, finding that the one, but not the other, contributed to the growth of morality. Indeed, Hoffman (1970a) reanalyzed the data from a number of studies of parental discipline where a distinction between reasoning and love withdrawal had not been made. Overall, he found that frequent use of power assertion was associated with weak moral development, induction was associated with advanced moral development, and love withdrawal did not correlate at all with moral development. This pattern was strongest for guilt and attempts at reparation and less strong for resistance to temptation and confession.

While Sears *et al.* had explained their findings in terms of identification theory, Hoffman's approach was rather different. He suggested that what he termed "other-oriented induction"—making children aware of the effect of their misdemeanor on others—arouses empathic guilt, an awareness of one's own inescapable role in causing distress to others. Power assertion, on the other hand, arouses anger and hostility in children and thereby makes them unwilling to comply with parental dictates. As well, it provides a model of aggressive behavior. Love withdrawal, while not arousing hostility, does not employ the child's empathic capabilities and therefore does not motivate the child to show great concern for the needs and desires of others.

Hoffman and Saltzstein's methodology represented a substantial improvement on earlier approaches to the development of morality. It was still, however, correlational in nature, necessitating a leap of inference from parental child-rearing style to offspring behavior. Although Hoffman's interpretation of the relationship between other-oriented induction and morality was highly plausible, other equally plausible explanations exist. Perhaps parents who control through reason and logic, placing great emphasis on concern and consideration for others, are also people who display prosocial behaviors in all areas of their lives. They thereby provide a multitude of examples of moral behavior for their children to follow, and the fact that they discipline by induction is only one of many demonstrations they provide of positive social behavior. Parents who report the use of power assertion may make frequent threats, some of which are not carried through. Thus children may learn that they can often deviate and not really experience negative consequences. Bell (1968), as was noted earlier, has argued that differences in children's temperament may have a substantial impact on the discipline their parents employ. Parents of children who are compliant and eager to please need only reason in order to gain their compliance. Children who are temperamentally difficult, however, will require that their parents use strong methods of control—power assertion—in order to gain compliance. In both cases, however, it is the child's behavior which dictates parental practice, rather than the practice which dictates the behavior. Some recent evidence (Grusec & Kuczynski, 1980) indicates that parents are not, in fact, at all consistent in the type of discipline they use, and that they adjust their discipline to the particular misdemeanor they are attempting to suppress. This might mean that the kinds of misdemeanors typically displayed by a child are one of the major determinants of parental discipline: Possibly less severe misdeeds elicit reasoning, and more severe ones elicit power assertion.

Aside from the variety of alternative explanations which could be offered for the findings of childrearing studies, the strength of the correlations they produced was not impressive. While there seemed some consistency in the nature of the relationships uncovered, the time was ripe for a more controlled approach to the study of conscience and morality.

Experimental Studies of Discipline
and Moral Development

In the early 1960s a new approach to the problems of socialization was formalized by Bandura and Walters (1963). They argued that principles of learning—reinforcement, extinction, and punishment—could be reliably used to explain the growth of socially acceptable behavior. In addition, however, Bandura and Walters maintained that another powerful determinant of social learning is imitation—children use the behaviors of those around as models for their own behavior. Among these are the moral attitudes and values of society. While researchers had earlier advocated the importance of learning principles in socialization their formulations had been somewhat affected by the concepts of psychoanalytic theory. Bandura and Walters, however, presented a form of socialization theory that completely rejected more psychodynamic interpretations of behavior.

From a methodological standpoint, as well, Bandura and Walters made a substantial contribution to the area of social development. They were instrumental in introducing the control and experimental rigor of the psychological laboratory into studies of the socialization process. Most of their studies were of the modeling process: Aside from their pertinence to questions of moral development they provided the prototype for a different way of conducting socialization research. Essentially they involved the reproduction of family and other constellations and interactions into the laboratory (nursery school "surprise room" or research trailer) where events could be telescoped in time, variables manipulated, and conclusions about cause and effect clearly drawn.

In one classic study, for example, Bandura, Ross, and Ross (1963) demonstrated how the consequences a model receives for aggression affect the willingness of observers to imitate the model's aggressive behavior. Children viewed a film of an adult model who exhibited considerable physical and verbal aggression in the course of taking the possessions of another adult. Half the children saw the model succeed in his aggression while the other half saw him severely punished. Other children were assigned to one of two control groups—either a group that had no exposure to the model or a group that observed a highly expressive but nonaggressive model (the latter a control for the model's high activity level). After they had seen the film the children were left alone in a different experimental setting, and the amount of aggression they displayed was observed through a one-way mirror. Those who had seen the model succeed at aggression imitated him more (even though they expressed disapproval of his behavior in postexperimental interviews) than those in the control groups or the group where the model had been punished.

Many investigations of the imitation process were carried out during the 1960s. In a typical experiment Mischel and Grusec (1966) set out to show how the often-unpleasant disciplinary restrictions parents impose on children are not only incorporated into their children's repertoires but are, in fact, transmitted by them to the next generation. We reasoned that both the nurturant and loving relationship that exists between parent and child as well as the control the parent exercises over resources important to the child would facilitate the adoption and transmission of parental values. Essentially, within a 45-minute period—the length of time it took to perform the experimental manipulations and to assess their effects—we hoped to gain some insight into the long-term effects of certain qualities of caretakers—warmth and control of resources—on the acquisition and transmission of moral standards.

Nursery school children were taught a game by an adult who was either warm and rewarding or cool and aloof, and who stated either that she was going to be the child's new teacher (high control) or that she was a visiting teacher who was leaving the school that same day (low control). During the course of the game the adult modeled activities designed to be aversive for the child (criticism and imposed delay of reward), as well as neutral behaviors (distinctive verbalization and marching). The child was then observed as he or she played the game alone and, subsequently, as he or she taught it to another individual. Children rehearsed the neutral and aversive behaviors of the model when they were by themselves, and they also transmitted these behaviors to the experimental confederate (the "next generation"). Neutral behaviors were more likely to be rehearsed when the model was highly rewarding and high in control, whereas aversive ones were rehearsed more when the model was high in control. Aversive behaviors were more likely to be transmitted when the model had been liberal in granting rewards.

These two studies, and many others like them, served to underline the important role played by models in the acquisition of aggressive behavior and of self-control. As well, investigators have demonstrated that children will imitate models who delay, or fail to delay, gratification (Bandura & Mischel, 1965) and who resist or yield to temptation (e.g., Bussey & Perry, 1977; Grusec, Kuczynski, Rushton, & Simutis, 1979).

Models have also been shown to play a significant role in the development of concern for others (e.g., Bryan & Walbek, 1970; Grusec & Skubiski, 1970; Rushton, 1975), particularly if the models have power, or the potential for power, over the children observing them (Grusec, 1971). In studies of altruism children have typically played a miniature bowling game which they are told is a game of skill but for which scores are actually preset by the experimenter. (The bowling game was first introduced by

Bandura and Kupers in 1964 to study the acquisition of standards for self-reward.) On winning trials subjects receive tokens or gift certificates, which can be traded at the end of the experimental session for prizes of varying value. Subjects are also offered the opportunity to share their winnings with needy children (orphans, victims of floods, etc.), and the effects of modeling (and other variables) on their willingness to donate are thereby assessed. Staub (e.g., Staub, 1971) has employed a slightly different situation to study altruism. He left children alone and then played tape-recorded sounds of distress which appeared to come from the next room. By measuring how quickly the children went to offer help he was able to assess the effects of modeling, as well as other experimental manipulations, on willingness to show concern for others.

Other experimental paradigms were developed to study the role of disciplinary techniques in moral development. One, in fact, was borrowed from the animal laboratory where experimental control and rigor had always been a major priority. Solomon, Turner, and Lessac (1968), in research conducted in the late 1950s, had studied resistance to temptation and guilt in dogs. They swatted food-deprived puppies with a rolled-up newspaper either just as the puppies approached a bowl of forbidden horsemeat or several seconds after they had begun to eat it. There was no difference in how quickly the puppies learned not to eat the horsemeat while the experimenter was in the room. But when they were alone—a measure of internalization—the puppies that had been punished early in the eating sequence showed greater suppression of responding, or greater resistance to temptation, than did those who had been punished late. The late-punished puppies, however, appeared more agitated and anxious after they had eaten the forbidden horsemeat—a suggestion that they were experiencing guilt. Solomon *et al.* suggested that anxiety becomes classically conditioned to the proprioceptive stimuli produced by the response that is punished. When punishment is delivered early anxiety occurs as soon as deviation occurs, and the anxiety is reduced by response suppression. When punishment is delivered late, however, anxiety is not produced until the punished behavior is well under way.

The Solomon *et al.* paradigm was translated into the "forbidden toy" paradigm and frequently used to study the effects of punishment on response suppression in children. (Note how the terminology changed from that used by earlier and somewhat more psychodynamically oriented researchers. Conscience, morality, resistance to temptation, and guilt were replaced by response suppression (sometimes response inhibition) and anxiety. Investigators generally believed, however, that they were studying similar phenomena.) The basic procedure used in the forbidden toy paradigm was to ask a child to choose between one of two toys to play with and then to punish the preferred selection, often by sounding a harsh buzzer. The children were then left alone and the amount of time they played with the forbidden toy was recorded.

Using this procedure investigators were able to show that punishment delivered just as children started to touch the forbidden toy produced less subsequent deviation than that delivered after the toy had been touched (Aronfreed & Reber, 1965; Parke & Walters, 1967). This appeared to be true, however, only if the intensity of punishment was low (Cheyne & Walters, 1969; Parke, 1969)—under high intensities of punishment, it was suggested, anxiety was great enough to extend the generalization gradient of suppression to response-produced stimuli accompanying ongoing transgression.

While researchers like Sears et al. and Hoffman had argued against the effectiveness of power assertion as a technique for suppressing undesirable behavior, investigators using the forbidden toy paradigm were finding punishment under laboratory conditions to be an effective deterrent of responding, even when the child was alone. What was to be made of this apparent discrepancy? It should be noted that the effects of punishment were being tested in the laboratory under short-term conditions, whereas correlational studies of childrearing considered the effects of punishment over a considerably longer period of time. Indeed, Cheyne and Walters found that, over time (specifically, three 5-minute periods), children who had been punished with a buzzer began to deviate with everincreasing frequency, whereas those who had been given a reason for not deviating continued to inhibit their responding. Parke (1974) hypothesized that children who have a reason for not deviating can repeat that reason to themselves, thereby reinstating the relevant cues and the anxiety associated with deviation, whereas those who have merely been punished forget the prohibition, or may not remember it is still in effect after some time has elapsed.

While punishment does not appear to be a sufficient condition for moral development, it does appear to be a necessary one. While Hoffman's early correlational studies had suggested that other-oriented induction alone was the effective ingredient in socialization, a later report (Hoffman, 1970b) indicated that mothers who relied on other-oriented reasoning were more inclined to use power assertion when their children refused to obey than were mothers who frequently used withdrawal of love for misbehavior. Similarly, Baumrind (1973), in a study of childrearing practices, found that mothers of children who were socially responsible, independent, and self-controlled tended to rely on reasoning *and* power assertion to gain compliance. And, as has been previously noted, Zahn-Waxler and co-workers (1979) have reported that mothers who provided explanations for why their children should not deviate, and who did so in a strong affective context (conveying intensity of feeling, disappointment, and judgmental reactions) were most successful in facilitating altruism and reparation after deviation.

What appears to emerge from correlational studies, and is corroborated by experimental laboratory studies, is the picture of an effective parent as one who reasons and who backs up his or her reasoning with the threat of unpleasant consequences for lack of conformity. Presumably the unpleasant consequences (provided they are moderate in intensity) provide the motivation or anxiety to resist temptation, while the accompanying reason allows the child to attribute conformity to something other than external pressure, thereby facilitating internalization (Walters & Grusec, 1977). The question of whether this conclusion pertains to the suppression of all unwanted behaviors or only the suppression of some unwanted behaviors is, for the present, left in abeyance.

Criticisms of the Laboratory Paradigm. While the rigor and control offered by the laboratory experiment are unparalleled, this approach has been the object of some harsh criticism in recent years. It has been asserted that the laboratory setting is artificial, and that the kind of behavior elicited by experimental manipulations bears little resemblance to what would be elicited by occurrence in a real-life, or natural, setting. While experimenters may be learning something about immediate situational reactions to a given event, it is argued, one cannot extrapolate from their results to any conclusions about the long-term effects of certain socialization practices. Moreover, it has been maintained, even the immediate situational reactions may be "unnatural," determined by the child's expectations about how he or she ought to act in a strange situation with a strange adult who is often engaging in strange behavior. Finally, the lack of any strong relationship between a concocted laboratory situation and the real life events it is meant to simulate has been pointed out. Is resisting playing with an arbitrarily forbidden toy akin in any way to resisting the temptation to lie or cheat or steal? Is donating tokens just won in a preceding game to unseen poor children at all related to helping a friend who is in real trouble? Is a 15-minute period of pleasant interaction between model and child equivalent to several years of a warm and loving relationship?

It is difficult to say how justified these criticisms are, or whether one should instead simply consider the laboratory paradigm as having its own set of strengths and weaknesses, just as any other research paradigm. Indeed, investigators in the 1970s have revealed a certain schizophrenia in their approach, which reflects some confusion on the topic. On the one hand, it is argued that experimental manipulations have a mild and transitory effect, confined to the specific experimental situation in which they are carried out. On the other hand, it is maintained that children who deviate in the forbidden toy situation may experience guilt, which investigators must dispel before returning those children to their regular classroom settings, or that children who observe aggressive models in the laboratory may continue to show increases in aggression outside the laboratory so that, on ethical grounds, such studies must not continue to be conducted. A given manipulation, of course, cannot be considered to have just transitory effects on the one hand and longer-term effects on the other. Clearly, the issue has not been settled.

Investigators have responded to criticisms of artificiality in a variety of ways. Some have abandonned the experiment, moving to interesting new survey and observational techniques. Some have turned to the field experiment. Others, unwilling to give up the control and rigor that only the laboratory experiment provides, have extended it by assessing the durability and generalizability of findings beyond the situation in which experimental manipulations were actually carried out.

The Field Experiment. In the field experiment independent variables are manipulated and their effects assessed under more natural conditions—in the nursery school itself, on the school playground. With this increase in naturalness may come a decrease in the amount of control that can be exerted over the experimental situation: While an experimenter can ensure that the conditions for experimental and control subjects are identical in the laboratory, he or she has no such control over variables in a natural setting. In an attempt to measure the effects of aggressive and nonaggressive models on children's aggression in the playground, for example, there is no way of ensuring that differences observed are due solely to the experimental manipulation. One child—in the experimental group—may be more aggressive during a recess period because he or she has just been hit by another child who had not been so kind as to hit a child in the control group as well. Nor is a field experiment always *completely* natural. Suppose an investigator is studying the effects of watching television violence. In real life children select the programs they watch themselves (presumably within the limits of parental supervision). In a field experiment their television diet is selected for them arbitrarily, and this may arouse hostility. In one study, for example, (Fesbach & Singer, 1971), male adolescents complained when they were not allowed to watch "Batman," so the experimenters had to allow them to do so. Obviously, however, the conclusions to be drawn from this study were weakened.

Field experiments have yielded some interesting data, often confirming the results of experiments conducted in the laboratory. In one instance, Friedrich and Stein (1973) assessed the amount of aggression, as well as altruism, that children ordinarily displayed in the nursery school. They then assigned children to one of two groups, either a group that watched television programming with prosocial content ("Misterogers' Neighborhood") or a group that watched programming with aggressive content ("Batman"). The children watched these shows three times a week for 4 weeks, and then were observed once more for prosocial and antisocial behavior in their regular nursery school setting. Many laboratory experiments had shown that children would imitate, in the laboratory, adults who directed hostile and aggressive behavior to objects such as inflated plastic dolls and, as we have seen, that they would also imitate in the laboratory, adults who donated tokens to needy children. Friedrich and Stein found that children who watched typical children's television programming would also imitate the altruism and aggression they observed there in the course of their daily interaction with other children. Not all children, in fact, increased in concern for others or in antisocial conduct, an indication that experimental manipulations do not always override the effects of the socialization experiences children bring with them to the laboratory. Interpersonal aggression increased only for children who were initially above the group average in aggression. Prosocial behavior increased only for children from lower socioeconomic status families. Nevertheless, the Friedrich and Stein study served to increase confidence in the interpretation of results from laboratory experiments. While the conditions of the laboratory may have been relatively unnatural, the responses they evoked in children appear to have been comparable to those which would be evoked in more everyday kinds of settings.

Yarrow, Scott, and Waxler (1973) undertook a field experiment to evaluate the effects of modeling on preschoolers' altruism and, more particularly, of the effects of a model's warmth and responsiveness to children on their willingness to imitate her concern for others. Children were assigned to an experimental group in which an adult female teacher was either warm and rewarding (nurturant) or reserved and aloof over a 2-week period. The adult then modeled altruism either by using miniature models of animals and people in distress, or by combining this kind of training with modeling of help-giving in real behavioral situations where concern for others could be expressed. Altruism to real victims increased primarily in the latter condition, and primarily when the teacher was warm and rewarding. Thus Yarrow *et al.* replicated, in the field, the findings of the many laboratory studies that had demonstrated the important role played by models in the acquisition of concern for others.

Durability and Generalizability of Laboratory Findings. One need not make a sharp distinction between field and laboratory experiments. Yarrow *et al.,* for example, did not confine their experimental activities strictly to the "field." Thus, in order to assess the effect of their training conditions on concern for others, they tested children's responses in a highly structured and contrived situation, one in which the children were observed to see whether or not they would pick up a basket of spools and buttons which "accidentally" fell off a table, as well as retrieve for a baby some toys that had fallen out of the playpen.

In the Yarrow et al. study, then, experimental manipulations were conducted in the field, with their effects measured in the laboratory. The reverse—manipulation in the laboratory and measurement in the field—is also possible. If laboratory manipulations can be demonstrated to have durability, that is, their effects can be seen to last for some time beyond their application, and if they can also be seen to affect behaviors related but not identical to those with which they were originally associated (both in the laboratory and outside of it), then the argument that the effects of these manipulations is situation-specific loses its force.

Such an outcome occurred in a study carried out by Grusec and Redler (1980). In this study we investigated the effect of explanations adults provide to children for their behavior on subsequent manifestations of that behavior. It has been demonstrated that, if adults attribute altruism to an inner personality characteristic of the child, the altruism is more likely to continue than if it has been attributed to external pressure (Grusec, Kuczynski, Rushton, & Simutis, 1978). Thus attributions to internal causes appear to promote internalization of value systems. The Grusec and Redler study was designed to compare the effectiveness of attribution to internal causation with social reinforcement. We reasoned that reinforcement for a specific act would increase the probability of occurrence of that particular act but that it would not facilitate the development of other, related, acts of altriusm. On the other hand, we thought that a child who had had a specific act of altriusm attributed to his or her concern for others would subsequently behave altruistically in a variety of situations in order to maintain a perceived self-consistency in behavior.

In order to test this hypothesis, experimental manipulations were carried out in a research laboratory, but the effects of these manipulations, including their durability and generalization, were assessed in other situations, including "more natural" ones. Specifically, children aged 5 and 8 years came individually to a research trailer where it was suggested they might share their winnings from a bowling game with poor children if they wished to, although they did not have to. Such a suggestion was sufficient to ensure donation, at least if an adult was present and watching. The children were thanked for donating and then told that they had done a good thing (social reinforcement) or that they had donated because they were the kind of people who helped others whenever possible (internal attribution). In the control group they were merely thanked. Subsequently the children were left alone to play the bowling game and their donations were observed. They were then given a chance to share some pencils anonymously with other children in their school who would not have the opportunity to come to the research trailer. A few days later the children returned individually to the trailer, but to a different room, where they helped another experimenter they had never seen before. Again, they received either social reinforcement or had their helping attributed to an internal desire to be helpful. Thy were then given the opportunity either to continue helping the experimenter or to play, instead, with an attractive toy. Finally, several days later, the children were visited in their classroom by an adult they had not seen before and were asked by this adult to make drawings and collect craft materials for children who were hospitalized. This latter was an event that frequently occurs in schools in the city where this research was conducted. In these various ways, then, the effects of specific experimental manipulations far beyond the situation in which they had been first employed could be assessed.

The results of this study confirmed our predictions, at least for 8-year-olds. For these children social reinforcement only increased donation of tokens to poor children, and attribution increased generosity in all the tests of altruism. While social reinforcement and attributional statements facilitated donation for 5-year-olds, neither had an effect on tests of generalized altruism. We suspected this may have been due to the fact that 5-year-olds may not yet think of themselves as having enduring dispositional attributes which dictate behavioral consistency across a variety of related situations.

Naturalistic Observation

Increasingly, in recent years, researchers have turned to methodological techniques initially developed and refined by ethologists in their study of animal behavior. Rather than concern themselves primarily with the question of how moral behavior can be manipulated, they have simply observed the occurrence of moral behaviors in naturalistic, field, or real-life settings. Such techniques can be more than descriptive, of course. While an observational study enables one to see what control techniques parents may use, for example, or the nature and extent of children's deviations (e.g., Clifford, 1959) it also allows the researcher to relate usage of different techniques with the nature and extent of deviation. By observing children and parents in their natural habitat, of course, researchers overcome the problems of distortion when parents are asked in an interview setting to report on their own child-rearing techniques.

Observations can be carried out in homes, schools, parks, playgrounds, or any other place where parent–child interactions occur in the course of daily activities. And they can be done by trained observers whose only job is to record ongoing activities, or they can be done by people who are normally participants in the settings as well. The use of such techniques to study behaviors related to moral issues is not a recent innovation. Indeed, Florence Goodenough published the results of one such study (1931). Goodenough was interested in the causes, frequency, and duration of outbursts of anger in young children, as well as the methods parents used to handle such outbursts. Goodenough used mothers as her observers. She provided them with data sheets (see Figure 8.1) on which they were asked to make a record of each of their children's displays of anger, recording its cause, its duration, a description of its behavioral manifestations (did the children stamp, kick, hold their breath, make their bodies limp, cry, argue, etc.), and the technique they used to deal with it. (Mothers were, in fact, given a whole list of possible techniques to make their recording task easier.)

Goodenough's actual results can only be suggestive, in part because the techniques for appropriate statistical analysis were not available at the time. Nevertheles, they do accord with the findings of more recent studies. She found, for example, that reasoning, while it was not effective in producing an immediate cessation to angry outbursts, was effective in reducing the frequency of future outbursts. Praise for engaging in another activity and appeals to the child's self-esteem and sense of humor were effective in terminating outbursts.

Before mothers began to make daily records, Goodenough asked them to answer a questionnaire about the methods they used to control their children's behavior. They were given a list of control techniques and asked to indicate those they used frequently (as often as once a day), moderately frequently, rarely, and those they never used. Goodenough was then able to compare their reported usage with real usage, as reflected in the daily records the mothers kept. Interestingly enough, there was little correlation between actual and reported frequency of use of various control techniques. Moreover, of the 43 mothers who participated in the study, only 9 never, in fact, used a method which they said they did not use on the questionnaire.

Promising though this particular observational technique was, it, too, was not without its problems. Behavioral observers are highly trained individuals and so mothers must also be reasonably well-trained to carry out their observational duties. As people become conscious or aware of specific behaviors, these behaviors may actually change. A mother who is making records of her discipline practices, for example, may begin to give some

INSTITUTE OF CHILD WELFARE   UNIVERSITY OF MINNESOTA

OBSERVATIONAL STUDY OF ANGER
DAILY RECORD SHEET
(Use a fresh sheet every day, even if there are no entries.)

Date ....Hours not included: from........to .... from........ to........

Child's name ....Child in bed previous night at.............asleep at.............

awake at........ up at........ Night sleep: Sound or restless?.............Bed wet?.............Day nap from.......... to...........

Bed wet?.......................

Underline any of the following occurring during the day: adult visitors in home, child visitors in home, child taken visiting or calling, taken shopping, to church or Sunday school, on motor trip, to movies, to doctor or dentist, delayed or irregular meal hours, new toy, new playmate, new food, other unusual circumstances (describe) ....

Physical condition (underline): Normal, slight cold, heavy cold, digestive disturbances, other sicknesses......

Bowel movements at........................... Normal amount?................. Consistency?....................................

Notes:...

List here each instance of anger, rage, or marked irritation displayed by child during the day. See instruction sheet.

TIME	IMMEDIATE CAUSE OR PROVOCATION	BEHAVIOR: Underline appropriate terms. Indicate order of events by numbering in parentheses.	METHODS OF CONTROL: Write either the name or list number of method or methods used in order as tried. Describe any methods that are not listed.
Hour	What was the child doing at the time?....	*Type:* Undirected energy ( ), resistance ( ), retaliation ( )	*Methods used:* ....
Place: Indoors or out-doors?		*Directed toward:*	....
Home, or	....	....	By whom? ....
Duration of outburst	....	*Motor:* Kicking, stamping, jumping, striking, throwing self on floor, holding breath	*Outcome with reference to the point at issue:* Did the child yield?...... Was the issue yielded?
....	What difficulty arose?	....	
Duration of after ef-fects, if any...............	....	*Vocal:* Screaming, threatening, refusing, "calling names," crying	Was a compromise effected? .... How? ....
Recorded by	....	*Behavior following outburst:* Cheerful, sulky, fretful, continued sobbing, resentful........	Was situation left unsettled? ....
....	....	....	....

FIGURE 8.1. Daily record sheets used by mothers. (From *Anger in Young Children,* by F. Goodenough. Copyright © 1931 by the University of Minnesota.)

serious thought to her procedures and even modify them. But researchers want to know what parents really do in the normal course of events, not what they do after a period of consideration of their usual practices.

The problem of observer reliability, as well, is a difficult one. In the typical observational study indices of observer agreement are routinely obtained, in order to ensure that the criteria for identification of specific behaviors are sufficiently clear that they could be used by all observers. In this way one can determine that the data of a study are not the peculiar observations of one individual, but representative of observations attainable by anyone. In many of the experimental paradigms described earlier, observer reliability was not an issue since dependent measures were frequently clear-cut. One can see how many tokens a child places in a bowl for poor children. If something obscures this view, the number can be determined by subtracting the number of tokens the child has at the end of a study from the number the experimenter knows he or she actually won. But how can we be sure that mothers are reliable in the observations they make, particularly when they are describing complex sets of behavioral interactions in which they themselves are often participants and during which they may well be emotionally aroused? Goodenough, in fact, pointed out that some of her mother's records may have been incomplete because they could not reliably observe all aspects of an outburst. In general, she reported, they tended to record the most conspicuous aspects while ignoring the less violent behaviors. There were as well problems of ambiguity about what to classify as an angry outburst. It is quite possible that some mothers may not have reported a particular event that others may well have classified as anger. Such problems can usually be solved relatively easily in a normal observational study. While they are certainly theoretically soluble when mothers are observers, there are practical problems in training large numbers of mothers to attain this degree of precision.

Yet the data obtained in this way are so rich and so close to the problem of interest that it seems a shame to give up on the possibility of using mothers as observers and recorders of mother–child interactions. Indeed, while observers from outside the family may be more objective, and while researchers such as Patterson (e.g., 1974) and Lytton (e.g., 1979) have used them to obtain some extremely interesting data, this latter method of data collection has its own problems. Observers cannot be present for 24 hours a day and for weeks on end. Moreover, their presence may modify family interactions, particularly in situations where emotions may be strong and reactions of the sort that are not generally made public.

Much can be done to improve the quality of the data collected by mothers themselves. Recently, Zahn-Waxler *et al.* (1979) revived Goodenough's procedure in order to study the development of children's altruism. They attempted to solve some of the problems that have just been outlined. Mothers were hired as research assistants and trained for 8 hours in two group sessions and one individual session. They were asked to tape-record a description of any incident in which someone expressed emotional distress in the presence of their children, including the antecedents of the distress situation, the child's reaction, and their own. Every third week the mother was visited by an investigator, who continued to supervise her data collection. During the visit mothers were also required to simulate distress themselves, such as choking or crying: In this way it was possible to obtain estimates of observer reliability by comparing the descriptions of the mother and the investigator. Some of Zahn-Waxler *et al.*'s findings have already been discussed, and it is comforting to note that they accord with findings about altruism that have been obtained with other methodologies.

In our own laboratory we are beginning to use a similar technique to assess children's altruism. However, while Zahn-Waxler *et al.* focused primarily on the child's response to emotional distress in others, our major focus has been on reactions children receive when they show consideration for others. Thus we have looked at a wide variety of situations in which children have helped others, including those in which the individual helped could not really be described as undergoing emotional distress (e.g., a child who gets his or her own breakfast in the morning in order to allow the parents, who were out late the previous evening, to sleep in). As well, we have asked mothers to record their responses to situations in which children should have helped others but failed to do so. Our mothers have had one group training session and a series of individual sessions until they appeared able to make complete records (of a written, rather than tape-recorded, variety). At the first training session we spend some time impressing upon them that their behavior should not change, that we do not know the right way to develop in children a concern for others, that sometimes parents do apparently heinous things to their children and they work, and that they must tell us what they *usually* do. The extent to which this kind of approach is successful in preventing mothers from changing their behavior is, of course, something we cannot assess.

In order to cope with the problem of observer reliability we have established the following procedure. Just before they begin their observations mothers are shown a 20-minute video recording of a typical day in the life of one family. Embedded in this tape are a number of incidents that involve, in some way, concern for others. Mothers view the tape and record each of these incidents as though they were recording the behavior of their own children—they are free to stop the videotape at any point so as to make their record. In this way we can compute an index of observer agreement between the mother's record and our own. To date we have obtained, on the average, agreement in 86% of the videotaped instances relating to altruism. When there is disagreement, or a mother has failed to note a particular sequence, she and the research technician discuss the problem until it is clarified.

Data Analysis. New statistical procedures have been devised in the last few years that increase the range of conclusions that can be drawn from studies such as those just described. It is a truism, for example, that the correlational data provided by naturalistic studies preclude the drawing of causal conclusions. Parents who use explanation delivered in an emotional way may have children who are more altruistic, but the direction of causation is not entirely clear. Indeed, some third variable (e.g., empathic concern for others having a genetic basis, and therefore covarying in mother and child) may be responsible for both outcomes. One statistical technique, called "cross-lagged panel correlation" (Campbell & Stanley, 1963), provides a strategy for implying causation from correlational data (although the approach is not without its critics, e.g., Rogosa, 1980). Figure 8.2 shows a variety of (imaginary) correlations between physical aggression and the use of other-oriented induction, with measures of the two events taken at 4 and 7 years of age. The correlation of .50 between physical aggression and parental usage of other-oriented induction at 7 years of age is not interpretable from the standpoint of causality—perhaps children who display little physical aggression are generally well behaved and require only mild forms of discipline. The correlation of .10, however, between physical aggression and the use of induction at age 4 suggests that a causal relatior.ship may have emerged between the ages of 4 and 7. Moreover, note that there is little stability between aggression displayed at 4 and 7 years, as indicated by the low correlation of .12, whereas parental use of induction was stable ($r = .72$). This is further indication that an event that remained unchanged—parental use of induction—may have been responsible for an event that did change—the child's aggression. The correlation of .65 between induction at age 4 and physical aggression at age 7 maintains the consistency of the picture posed by these relationships. While caution must still be exercised in interpreting these relationships, they are certainly highly suggestive. Taken together with experimental findings, they serve to in-

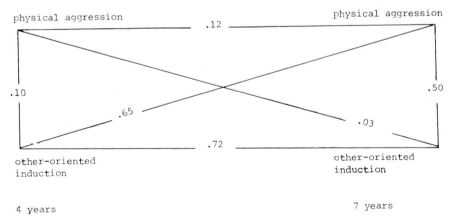

FIGURE 8.2. Hypothetical correlations between physical aggression and parental use of other-oriented induction at 4 and 7 years of age.

crease confidence in the picture we draw of the processes underlying moral development.

Another recently developed technique of anlaysis that has increased the informational yield from naturalistic observational studies involves the analysis of sequences of behavior. This technique helps investigators to organize and describe an ongoing stream of behavior in a social interaction. Patterns in the data are described by conditional probabilities, so that events more likely to co-occur, or events more likely to follow a given event, can be established. Lytton and Zwirner (1975), for example, attempted to establish what kinds of parental techniques were most likely to elicit compliance in their 2-year-old children. A trained observer visited homes on two afternoons in successive weeks, observing parent–child interactions for the 3 hours before the child's bedtime, and recording parent behaviors such as physical restraint, criticism, hugging, smiling, commands and suggestions, and child behaviors of compliance or noncompliance. By examining the sequential contingencies between child and parent behavior, Lytton and Zwirner established that the probability of compliance was highest after parental suggestion, and that it decreased progressively with commands and reasoning. As well, slaps, physical restraints, threats, and criticism were more likely to lead to compliance than were positive actions such as expressions of love and approval.

By using sequential analysis, then, Lytton and Zwirner could establish how parental acts that immediately precede a child's compliance or noncompliance control that compliance. Sequential analysis, of course, does not show what the long-term effects of parent behaviors are on children's compliance—the question of greater interest to researchers in the past. Nevertheless, a comparison of short- and long-term effects leads to some interesting conclusions. In Lytton and Zwirner's study it was power-assertive techniques—command more than reasoning, threat rather than expressions of love—that facilitated immediate compliance. Long-range effects of parental control techniques, however, were established from the same set of data. Here it was consistency of rule enforcement, amount of play with the child, and use of psychological rewards and reasoning that determined compliance, a finding generally in keeping with other literature on moral development that has been reviewed in this chapter. What works in the short run, then, may not be what is most effective in the long run.

CONCLUSIONS

The methodologies available to investigators of moral development are, as we have seen, diverse. And, as we have seen, each has its advantages and disadvantages. Increasingly, in the last few years, investigators in all areas of psychology have become sensitive to the issue of how meaningful and relevant their findings are for real-life manifestations of the behavior they are interested in. At the same time some (e.g., McCall, 1977) have also argued that psychologists have been so involved in asking how things work that they have ignored the more descriptive approach involved in asking what it is that people do. Debate will no doubt continue about what investigative approaches are most likely to yield ecological validity. In addition, researchers will continue to be concerned about the relative importance of describing how children are actually socialized, as opposed to explaining relationships between different kinds of socialization experiences and the child's level of moral development. The debate is healthy, for it makes researchers sensitive to the assumptions they automatically make when they set out to study a particular problem. No doubt, different individuals will continue to use different (although presumably increasingly refined) approaches to the study of the same problem. In this diversity, however, lies strength. For if the picture that emerges about the origins of moral development is consistent no matter what methodological technique is employed, our faith in the reliability and validity of findings can only be strengthened.

REFERENCES

Aronfreed, J., & Reber, A. Internalized behavioral suppression and the timing of social punishment. *Journal of Personality and Social Psychology*, 1965, *1*, 3–16.

Bandura, A., & Kupers, C. J. The transmission of patterns of self-reinforcement through modeling. *Journal of Abnormal and Social Psychology*, 1964, *69*, 1–9.

Bandura, A., & Mischel, W. Modification of self-imposed delay of reward through exposure to live and symbolic models. *Journal of Personality and Social Psychology*, 1965, *2*, 698–705.

Bandura, A., Ross, D., & Ross, S. A. Vicarious reinforcement and imitative learning. *Journal of Abnormal and Social Psychology*, 1963, *67*, 601–607.

Bandura, A., & Walters, R. H. *Social learning and personality development*. New York: Holt, Rinehart and Winston, 1963.

Baumrind, D. The development of instrumental competence through socialization. In A. D. Pick (Ed.), *Minnesota symposia on motivation* (Vol. 7). Minneapolis: University of Minnesota Press, 1973.

Bell, R. Q. A reinterpretation of the direction of effects of socialization. *Psychological Review*, 1968, *75*, 81–95.

Bem, D. J., & Allen, A. On predicting some of the people some of the time: The search for cross-situational consistencies in behavior. *Psychological Review*, 1974, *81*, 506–520.

Bryan, J. H., & Walbek, N. Preaching and practicing generosity: Children's actions and reactions. *Child Development*, 1970, *41*, 329–353.

Bussey, K., & Perry, D. G. The imitation of resistance to deviation: Conclusive evidence for an elusive effect. *Developmental Psychology*, 1977, *13*, 438–443.

Campbell, D. T., & Stanley, J. C. *Experimental and quasi-experimental designs for research.* Chicago: Rand McNally, 1963.

Cheyne, J. A., & Walters, R. H. Intensity of punishment, timing of punishment, and cognitive structure as determinants of response inhibition. *Journal of Experimental Child Psychology,* 1969, *7,* 231–244.

Clifford, E. Discipline in the home: A controlled observational study of parental practices. *Journal of Genetic Psychology,* 1959, *95,* 45–82.

Feshbach, S., & Singer, R. D. *Television and aggression.* San Francisco: Jossey-Bass, 1971.

Friedrich, L. K., & Stein, A. H. Aggressive and prosocial television programs and the natural behavior of preschool children. *Monographs of the Society for Research in Child Development,* 1973, *38* (4, Serial No. 151).

Goodenough, F. *Anger in young children.* Minneapolis: University of Minnesota Press, 1931.

Grusec, J. E. Power and the internalization of aversive behaviors. *Child Development,* 1971, *42,* 93–105.

Grusec, J. E., Kuczynski, L., Rushton, J. P., & Simutis, Z. Modeling, direct instruction, and attributions: Effects on altruism. *Developmental Psychology,* 1978, *14,* 51–57.

Grusec, J. E., Kuczynski, L., Rushton, J. P., & Simutis, Z. M. Learning resistance to temptation through observation. *Developmental Psychology,* 1979, *15,* 233–240.

Grusec, J. E., & Kuczynski, L. Direction of effect in socialization: A comparison of the parent vs. the child's behavior as determinants of disciplinary techniques. *Developmental Psychology,* 1980, *6,* 1–9.

Grusec, J. E., & Redler, E. Attribution, reinforcement, and altruism. *Developmental Psychology,* 1980, *16,* 525–534.

Grusec, J. E., & Skubiski, S. L. Model nurturance, demand characteristics of the modeling experiment, and altruism. *Journal of Personality and Social Psychology,* 1970, *14,* 352–359.

Hartshorne, H., & May, M. A. *Studies in the nature of character,* Vol. 1: *Studies in deceit.* New York: Macmillan, 1928.

Hoffman, M. L. Moral development. In P. H. Mussen (Ed.), *Manual of child psychology,* New York: Wiley, 1970. (a)

Hoffman, M. L. Conscience, personality, and socialization techniques. *Human Development,* 1970, *13,* 90–126. (b)

Hoffman, M. L. Altruistic behavior and the parent–child relationship. *Journal of Personality and Social Psychology,* 1975, *31,* 937–943.

Hoffman, M. L., & Saltzstein, H. D. Parent discipline and the child's moral development. *Journal of Personality and Social Psychology,* 1967, *5,* 45–57.

Lytton, H. Disciplinary encounters between young boys and their mothers and fathers: Is there a contingency system? *Developmental Psychology,* 1979, 256–269.

Lytton, H., & Zwirner, W. Compliance and its controlling stimuli observed in a natural setting. *Developmental Psychology,* 1975, *11,* 769–779.

McCall, R. B. Challenges to a science of developmental psychology. *Child Development,* 1977, *48,* 333–344.

Mischel, W. *Personality assessment.* New York: Wiley, 1968.

Mischel, W., & Grusec, J. Determinants of the rehearsal and transmission of neutral and aversive behaviors. *Journal of Personality and Social Psychology,* 1966, *3,* 197–205.

Murphy, L. *Social behavior and child personality: An exploratory study of some roots of sympathy.* New York: Columbia University Press, 1937.

Olejnik, A. B., & McKinney, J. P. Parental value orientation and generosity in children. *Developmental Psychology,* 1973, *8,* 311.

Parke, R. D. Effectiveness of punishment as an interaction of intensity, timing, agent nurturance, and cognitive structuring. *Child Development,* 1969, *40,* 213–235.

Parke, R. D. Rules, roles, and resistance to deviation: Recent advances in punishment, discipline, and self-control. In A. Pick (Ed.), *Minnesota Symposia on Child Psychology* (Vol. 8). Minneapolis: University of Minnesota Press, 1974.

Parke, R. D., & Walters, R. H. Some factors determining the efficiency of punishment for inducing response inhibition. *Monograph of the Society for Research in Child Development*, 1967, *32*, No. 109.

Patterson, G. R. A basis for identifying stimuli which control behaviors in natural settings. *Child Development*, 1974, *45*, 900–911.

Piaget, J. *The moral judgment of the child*. London: Routledge & Kegan Paul, 1932.

Rogosa, D. A critique of cross-lagged correlation. *Psychological Bulletin*, 1980, *88*, 245–258.

Rushton, J. P. Generosity in children: Immediate and long-term effects of modeling, preaching, and moral judgment. *Journal of Personality and Social Psychology*, 1975, *31*, 459–466.

Sears, R. R., Maccoby, E. E., & Levin, H. *Patterns of child rearing*. New York: Harper, 1957.

Sears, R. R., Rau, L., & Alpert, R. *Identification and child rearing*. Palo Alto, Calif.: Stanford University Press, 1965.

Solomon, R. L., Turner, L. H., & Lessac, M. S. Some effects of delay of punishment on resistance to temptation in dogs. *Journal of Personality and Social Psychology*, 1968, *8*, 233–238.

Staub, E. A child in distress: The influence of nurturance and modeling on children's attempts to help. *Developmental Psychology*, 1971, *5*, 124–132.

Stayton, D. J., Hogan, R., & Ainsworth, M. D. Infant obedience and maternal behavior: The origins of socialization reconsidered. *Child Development*, 1971, *42*, 1057–1069.

Turiel, E. The development of concepts of social structure: Social convention. In J. Glick & A. Clarke-Stewart (Eds.), *Social and cognitive development* (Vol. 1). New York: Gardner, 1978.

Walters, G. C., & Grusec, J. E. *Punishment*. San Francisco: Freeman, 1977.

Yarrow, M. R., Scott, P. M., & Waxler, C. Z. Learning concern for others. *Developmental Psychology*, 1973, *8*, 240–260.

Zahn-Waxler, C. Z., Radke-Yarrow, M. R., & King, R. A. Child rearing and children's prosocial initiations toward victims of distress. *Child Development*, 1979, *50*, 319–330.

9 Sex Role Development

BEVERLY I. FAGOT

In the 1970s interest in sex differences grew to an all-time high. Psychologists and sociologists influenced by the women's movement have published studies in a variety of journals, and a new journal entitled *Sex Roles: A Journal of Research* was established in the middle of the decade. However, there are some psychologists who continue to argue that the study of sex differences is a waste of time, leading to uninteresting and unimportant results. The research emphasis in the area has shifted from studies designed to demonstrate sex differences to studies designed to illustrate the underlying process of sex role development. This shift has come about partly in response to criticism concerning the lack of theoretical framework in the area, and partly because after a decade we now have enough information to start trying to tie results together. The master lecture at the 1979 APA meeting presented by Block (1979) was the most ambitious attempt to organize the area and point the field in new directions.

The work of the past decade has demonstrated the importance of sex role development at several different levels. First, sex role identification is tied very closely to the discovery of the self, and the process of indentifying oneself as a separate person who is either a boy or girl takes place very young, most likely at the same time language is developing. It seems clear that the study of personality development cannot take place without an understanding of sex role development. Second, boys and girls "live in very different worlds," and the same behaviors have different consequences depending on the sex of the child. Finally, the differing environments of the boy and the girl have long-term consequences for the development of cognitive and social processes. In fact, more than any other area, sex role development cuts across the artificial distinctions between cognitive and social development, and makes it clear that we must study the child as a

273

STRATEGIES AND TECHNIQUES
OF CHILD STUDY

complete organism interacting with the setting in which development takes place.

THEORIES OF SEX ROLE DEVELOPMENT

The study of sex role development or gender differentiation has been likened to the tale of the blind men trying to identify an elephant (Constantinople, 1979), and certainly the attempts to explain the phenomena have resembled the gropings of the blind men feeling different parts of the elephant. Psychological research has been primarily influenced by two major theoretical approaches. Each of these approaches highlights a different aspect of the process of sex role development.

The first approach, the cognitive–developmental, developed by Kohlberg (1966), has focused rather exclusively on gender identity. Kohlberg has maintained that gender development proceeds in a regular progression, or series of stages, as a function of the child's level of cognitive development. Up until this point in the theory, there is little disagreement by others with Kohlberg's view because, indeed, children do appear to learn early in life to label themselves as either male or female (in Kohlberg's terms, to have some form of gender identity). Then, as a second step, children understand that one's sex is stable over the life cycle; that is, little boys become men, not women (gender stability). Finally, in a third step, children come to understand that sex is constant despite perceptual transformations of the self or other person (gender constancy). There is rough agreement as to the correlation between age and stage, with the final step of gender constancy occurring sometime between 5 and 7 years of age for most children. However, Kohlberg speaks of the cognitive structures of the child as the primary organizers of gender role, and this is an area of controversy among people working in the area.

The second approach, social learning, has been most thoroughly outlined by Mischel (1966, 1970). This approach focuses on gender role, rather than gender identity, and emphasizes environmental and social influences on the public expression of behavior. The research based on this approach has sought to reveal the importance of social reinforcement and modeling by the key people in the child's environment (e.g., parents, peers, and teachers) in shaping gender role behaviors.

TERMINOLOGY

The study of sex role development has been hindered by a lack of agreement on appropriate terminology. Unger (1979) suggested that our present terminology is biased toward biological models of sex differences, and suggests that the word "gender" is a better term for the process of development because it carries with it fewer assumptions concerning the orgins of behaviors.

Money and Ehrhardt (1972) have developed a useful terminology for the process of sex role development, or gender differentiation, and the adoption of this terminology for describing the two major outcomes of the process may help to eliminate some confusion.

> *Gender identity* is the sameness, unity and persistence of one's individuality as male, female, or ambivalent, while *gender role* is everything a person says and does to indicate to others or to the self that degree that one is either male, female, or ambivalent . . . Gender identity is the private experience of gender role, while gender role is the public expression of gender identity [Money and Ehrhardt, 1972, p. 4].

While the private expression has been studied within the confines of Kohlberg's theory and terminology, the public expression of gender has been studied in many different ways using a multitude of terms. Actual differences in behaviors or preferences have been referred to in the research literature in several ways: sex preferred (Fagot, 1977), sex-typed behaviors (Lynn, 1969), or sex role adoptions (Fling and Manosevitz, 1972). Although these terms all have slightly different meanings, they are referring to sex differences in behavior. These differences are relative because, in fact, there is always an overlap of behavior between the sexes. The behaviors that show differences will be described as *sex-typical behaviors.* That is, they are more typical of one sex than the other, although not exclusive of one sex (e.g., both boys and girls show aggressive behaviors, but boys typically show more). Such differences can be forms of play activities or broader categories of behaviors such as aggression or dependency.

Another measure of gender role is the individual's attitude concerning the appropriateness of activities or behaviors for males and females. These attitudes are *sex stereotypes,* and it should be clear that both children and adults show sex stereotypes.

In this chapter, sex will be used when discussing actual differences found between males and females or when discussing attitudes concerning males and females. Gender will be used when discussing the process of development.

To summarize, gender differentiation in sex role development is the overall process, both biological and social, of becoming male or female. Gender identity is the internal or private experience, whereas gender role is the public expression of that indentity. Gender indentity has been studied as a cognitive phenomenon by Kohlberg and others, who have charted the stages of development. Gender role has been studied as expressed through sex-typical behaviors and sex stereotypes.

ISSUES DIRECTING RESEARCH

The research results concerning sex differences and gender differentiation often seem to be unplanned, as if the researchers were reporting findings they had not expected. Even studies designed specifically to look for sex differences often lacked good rationale for particular strategies and methods. There are several issues of particular concern for those working in the area that should be considered prior to embarking on a research project. Perhaps the most critical issue in the study of gender differentiation is the question of just how biologically determined are the existing differences. The question is extremely complex and has become more complex as we have come to understand how environmental events have biological consequences. As an example in the study of sexual behavior, numerous studies were conducted looking at the effects of different levels of testosterone on sexual behavior with the assumption that testosterone affected sexual behavior. Recent studies (Rose, Gordon, & Bernstein, 1972) have shown that when male primates are given access to receptive females, or to novel receptive females, the testosterone level rises. A similar kind of feedback was noted in human females. Aging women often complain of a lack of lubrication during sex, but Masters and Johnson report that the aged women in their sample who had frequent sex showed quick lubrication, and to at least a partial extent, it may be infrequent sex rather than aging alone that contributes to loss of lubrication (Masters & Johnson, 1966, p. 234).

It is clear that in doing research in sex role development, it is necessary to explore biological determinants and social determinants and to study their relationships. Another equally important problem is separating the biological consequences of one's sex from the social consequences of being a member of that sex. For instance, menstruation is a biological consequence of being female; having your activity restricted during menstruation is a social consequence of being female. While we are dealing with a biological phenomenon, most consequences of menstruation are social, and when those consequences are removed, menstruation produces rather minor changes in most females' lives (Parlee, 1973). Sex role development is an area in which it is very easy to jump on either the biological or environmental bandwagon, and neither is appropriate.

As mentioned earlier in the chapter, research in the area of sex differences has been very atheoretical. In fact, many of our findings have been serendipitous. Yet there are many theories concerning sex role development, and sex role development is a major portion of most theories of personality. Why then are so few studies designed to test predictions from theories? To understand current reasearch in this area it is necessary to look at research prior to the sixties. If we look at sex role development research in the 1940s and 1950s, we find that most studies were rather directly designed to test theories. At that time, the Freudian theories and their derivatives (Brofenbrenner, 1960) were most popular. Fairly specific predictions were made concerning differences between boys and girls, and between parental treatment of boys and girls. It became apparent that the wrong questions were being asked at the wrong times of the child's development. Freudian-based theories had posed questions derived from theories based upon extrapolation from adults rather than from direct study of children, and attempts to demonstrate that Freudian principles were correct were stymied by the fact that neither the children nor their parents acted as predicted, so that formal testing of the hypotheses did not help us understand sex role development. At that time, it was fortituous that researchers influenced by ethological work, social learning principles, and the cognitive development approaches backed away from the traditional formal testing of hypotheses to an approach aimed at discovering principles. In all three approaches, the first step in trying to understand a problem was to observe the child in a variety of natural settings. Theory building was not to be attempted until the researcher had a good understanding of the capabilities of the child. These approaches freed the researcher from unrealistic theoretical constraints and promoted the collection of information concerning boys' and girls' capabilities and social worlds.

The study of sex role development is an interesting case illustrating Sampson's (1978) different paradigms in science: Paradigm 1—the natural sceince model has been the dominant viewpoint within psychology. The emphasis in on the objective and eliminates the standpoint of the knower from knowledge so that pure facts are achieved, and universal and general principles of abstract functioning are sought. Paradigm 2—the historical model of science recognizes that data are always embedded in context, and part of knowledge is the understanding of that context. Consequently, designs using this paradigm do not call for the elimination of context, but use that context to understand data. Sampson (1978) points out that Type 1 science glorifies the abstract principle over and above specific cases, and that this influences not only methods but interpretation of findings. For instance, dealing with the abstract is more mature than dealing with the concrete and it is more moral (Kohlberg, 1969). Incidentally, as Sampson points out, those abstract qualities are more typical of males than females. Sampson suggests that "the very paradigm of science that we employ, by eliminating the concept of historically generated and rooted knowledge, blinds us to the kind of bias that helps support and affirm a male-dominated world view, while aligning female thought with the thought of children and primitives [1978, p. 1339].'' When studying sex role development, it is important to keep in mind the models from which one is working prior to putting value judgments on different modes of responding to the environment.

However, Sampson's views contribute to the study of sex role development in ways other than suggesting care in the interpretation of findings. Paradigm 1 models suggest that we try to free questions from the context and to control for as many variables as possible. But sex role development is totally confounded with context, and is perhaps a function of context, rather than the organism. In order to understand sex role development, it is necessary to study within the context of that development, and that leads us naturally to a Type 2 approach for we must understand the way that the culture influences sex role development. This leads us to an approach where much of our research is done in a natural environment, because it is in that environment that the context shaping the development exists. It suggests that laboratory findings always should be checked against real-world findings, and if the two disagree, it is the laboratory findings we should suspect and not those of the real world. This is not to suggest that the techniques and controls developed within the Type 1 paradigm are no longer useful, only that such findings can no longer be considered the criterion against which all works are judged.

Another issue that has plagued the research in sex role development has been the lack of relationship between attitude measurements and sex role behaviors. Over and over again, it is found that attitudes concerning sex appropriate behaviors and the performance of sex-typical behaviors show very low correlations. To some extent, the disenchantment with attitudes as predictors of overt behaviors came about because attitude measurement is an outgrowth of Type 1 methodology, an attempt to find objective and abstract "rules" that would hold over a variety of situations and which are centered in the individual's cognitive structure, rather than influenced by changing events. Overt behaviors, however, have always been acknowledged as under both individual and environmental control. This same kind of dilemma has arisen in the field of personality, with the prolonged argument over whether personaility traits reside within the individual or whether personality is situationally specific (Mischel, 1969). Fortunately, in both social and personality psychology, the discussion has passed beyond the stage of arguing for trait and attitude measurements or behavioral and situational assessments to a recognition that we need measurements that allow us to look at the individual variables in relation to the situation in order to predict behavior (Ajzen & Fisbein, 1977; Bem & Funder, 1978). However, although this recognition has taken place in theoretical articles, there appears to be little recognition of the fact in most studies looking at sex role development. Attitudes (usually called sex stereotypes) are collected and used as if they somehow control and guide behaviors, in some studies with the assumption that such attitudes reflect behaviors, or if both behavioral and attitude measures have been made with dismay that there appears to be little relationship between the two. Fortunately, there is at least one project that is attempting to use a variety of measures within the behavioral and cognitive domains (Block & Block, 1979), and this study might be used as a model for others who wish to face the attitude–behavior relationship in designing a project. The Blocks have been concerned with measuring multiple concepts over multiple time periods, using multiple kinds of data with the same subjects. First, there are L-data (life), which are societal, demographic, nonobserver-based. L-data are real, but often have confounded or obscure meanings. Next, there are O-data (observer), which are derived from the observer's evaluation of individuals leading natural lives. O-data allow the observer to integrate significant behaviors but are also open to distortion by the observer. S-data are self-reported and can be attitudes, feelings, etc. S-data are quickly gathered and obviously are a window to the subject's thoughts, but they also are derived through an unknown filter of the subject and can distort in unknown ways. T-data are derived from standardized tests or laboratory situations where the range of responses are preselected by the examiners. T-data are objective, and are not dependent upon the individual making the responses, but they can be pallid and lack relevance or generalizability to natural situations. However, judicious combinations of all forms of data can allow the researcher to balance the strengths and weaknesses of each approach to gain a more complete understanding of the individual within the environment.

Another issue facing the researcher who wishes to study sex role development is one facing all who work in developmental psychology. What accounts for change in the developing organism? Are observed changes due to maturation and development within the organism, to specific environmental variables, or, more likely, to an interaction between the organism and the environment? The difficulty is that we do not yet understand what changes take place in the child, and we are not able to predict individual differences in rate of change. This is further complicated by the problem of measurement over different ages. We do not really know if we are measuring the same basic structures at different ages, because we must change our measures to suit the child's behavioral capabilities. Underlying all this is the broader question of whether the structures are preserved as the child develops. Perhaps sex role behaviors in early childhood bear no relation to sex role adoptions in adolescence. Kagan (1979) suggested that perhaps we place too much faith in continuities across age spans and that in the normal course of development we should be studying change. Perhaps, but the problems of measurement still remain, whether looking for continuities or change.

Some of the issues that make current work in sex role development difficult to interpret have been discussed in this section. Those doing work in the area should take care not to ascribe differences to biological or environmental causes without consideration of the complex interaction between the two. The researcher should be aware that acceptance of particular paradigms actually influences our findings and that questions should be studied with a multimethod approach. Related to the above is the concern with the lack of correlation between our behavioral and attitude measures. The lack of adequate theoretical framework for guiding research in sex role development was discussed. Finally, the problems of measuring the continuity of the gender differentiation process within a still-developing organism were discussed. None of these issues has clear-cut answers, but recognition of their existence should help produce more sophisticated, well-designed studies.

SOCIALIZATION DIFFERENCES OF BOYS AND GIRLS WITHIN THE FAMILY

Theories of sex role development have always assumed that boys and girls are treated differently by their parents and that sex role development is influenced by the different conditions and treatments they receive within the family situation. Yet, after an extensive review of the sex differences literature, Macobby and Jacklin (1974) came to the following conclusions concerning differential shaping of sex typed behaviors: "we have been able to find very little evidence to support it in relation to behaviors other than sex typing as very narrowly defined (e.g., toy preferences). The reinforcement contingencies for the two sexes appear to be remarkably similar [p. 342]." Maccoby and Jacklin did conclude that boys receive more intense socialization pressures than girls, but this conclusion has not been discussed as much as the finding of lack of differential reinforcement. Block (1978) feels that such acceptance of the null hypothesis about differential rearing is premature for several reasons. First, the studies that Maccoby and Jacklin reviewed were primarily concerned with children 6 and under, yet many sex-typical behaviors begin to have salience for parents only when the children enter school or even adolescence. Second, most of the studies reviewed focused on the mother, and yet we have evidence that the father more than the mother feels sex typing is important (Fagot, 1974; Block, vonDerlippe, & Block, 1973). Block also notes that concepts such as dependency have different meanings in different studies and sometimes in the same study. How could we hope to have consistent findings when the constructs themselves are defined differently acccording to each researcher, and the behaviors used to measure the construct show radical changes across studies and across ages of the children? Block also points out that all studies were considered equally by Maccoby and Jacklin, but that the studies differ in size of sample, and the care with which appropriate statistical procedures were used. In fact, in some of these studies, the testing of sex differences appeared to be a post hoc phenomenon and very much unrelated to the purpose of the study. Block feels that the question of sex-determined socialization remains open.

How could highly respected researchers come to such different conclusions concerning the same set of studies? In part because research in this area illustrates all the issues discussed previously in this paper. First, it is necessary to examine why certain variables were chosen for the study of sex role socialization. Some variables were chosen specifically from theoretical predictions; for instance, Freud predicted that girls should show a weaker superego development than boys owing to the incomplete resolution of the Oedipal situation. Therefore, development of conscience was often studied as a function of sex of the child as well as parental values. Differences in aggressiveness and dependency were also predicted from theories of sex role development and from this it was assumed that there would be differences in treatment of children by parents. There were two problems using the broad constructs derived from Freudian theory. In some cases, the predicted sex differences did not exist at the time the child was studied. For instance, in the development of conscience, with young children at least, girls appear to develop a conscience earlier and appear to have more control over their behaviors (Sears, Maccoby, & Levin, 1957). Second, it may be that sex differences exist, but that they are not a result of differential parent attitudes but arise from other causes. Alternatively, it may be that attitudes of parents toward aggression have little to do with the development of aggression, but that the role models parents and others provide to the child have more influence. For whatever reason, the studies derived from theory that examined parental effects on large systems of behaviors have been inconclusive, with the effect that, for a time, attempts to understand how differential socialization might take place were discontinued.

The research in the area of differential socialization has been affected by the problems of relationship between attitudes and behaviors. As early as 1957 Sears, Maccoby, and Levin reported that mothers often felt that they should not treat children differently according to their sex. Sex role socialization is a sensitive area, and parents and teachers tend to give answers that are socially approved. However, the behaviors that are socially approved differ by generation, social class, and educational level, so that parental attitudes are influenced in ways we cannot always specify. For the past 25 years there has been a trend toward egalitarianism in society. This is reflected in attitudes toward child rearing, and if parents are asked how treatment of boys and girls differ, they often respond that they do not. If asked how boys and girls differ, they will give you rather accurate descriptions of observed sex differences, but they cannot or will not give the same accurate descriptions of rearing differences. Most of the studies of rearing examined by Maccoby and Jacklin used attitudes rather than observations of behaviors to look at differential rearing.

My study on toddlers and their parents (Fagot, 1978) illustrates the perils of relying on parent attitudes concerning sex role development or on parents' reports of how they treat children. In this study, I observed toddlers and their parents interacting in their homes, asked the parents to rate behaviors appropriate for boys and girls (sex stereotypes), and interviewed parents on their values and socialization practices concerning sex roles. I also looked at three broad categories of behavior often considered important in the development of sex role by psychologists: aggression, adult dependency, and large motor activities. It was possible from the observations to determine which behaviors were actually more typical of one sex, so that those behaviors for which there were empirical differences were called sex-preferred (although I now use the term sex-typical as it does not have so great a value loading). Parent reactions to the behaviors were classified as positive, negative, or neutral. Parents did not differ in their reactions to sex-stereotyped behaviors (except in the case of doll play, which was also sex-typical), but they did differ in their reactions to sex-typical behaviors. Parents did differ in their reactions to some behaviors in the category of large motor activity and in some of the adult dependency measures. Differences in attitudes toward sex role development as measured in the interview did not appear to influence the parent's responses to sex-typical behaviors. This is not to say that sex stereotypes were unrelated to sex-typical behaviors, for there was a significant correlation of .32 between sex-stereotyped behaviors and sex-typical behaviors. However, this is not an impressive relationship, and leaves more of the variance to be explained that it explains.

The results of this study suggest that parents are not fully aware of their socialization techniques, and that to rely on their values and attitudes gives a false picture of the actual socialization process. The study also suggests that for young children the sex stereotypes held by parents are not yet congruent with their own reactions to behaviors. The behaviors that show parental differences are perhaps precursors to behaviors considered important for sex role development. I suggested that these precursors were simple, but subtle, whereas the behaviors socialized in middle childhood are obvious and complex. The results from this study illustrate how important it is not to rely on one source of information in trying to study a problem for which both the subjects and the context are important. If observation in this study had been done only in areas considered important by parents, the conclusion would have been that differential socialization does not take place in toddler children. It is important to point out that observing the process in a natural environment will not solve every problem if the observation techniques are limited by preconceived constraints of what is important. In designing studies of parent–child interactions, it costs nothing in terms of observation time to do the observation in terms of non-value-laden behaviors rather than more subjective categories. The tests can always then be made on both the broad categories one feels are subjectively important and on the narrow behavior descriptions. I would also like to point out one other finding from this study that suggests why it is so difficult to find consistent results in this area. Male sex role for toddler boys was defined almost entirely in the negative; it was defined in terms of behaviors that boys should avoid rather than behaviors that boys should do. This lack of positive definition makes it very difficult to study continuities, and also makes it difficult to measure the relationship between parental attitudes and behaviors. It may be that the male role is mostly defined by avoidance of the famale in the young child; this at least has been suggested by Chodorow (1978). It also suggests why we may see more continuity in sex role development for boys than for girls. If maleness is defined to a large extent by avoidance of very specific behaviors, then we should see the boys learning appropriate patterns earlier. It is easier to teach a child to aviod a restricted set of activities than adopt an ill-defined set of behaviors.

Block (1979) suggested that socialization becomes more sex-differentiated with increasing age of the child, reaching a maximum during the high school age. This may well be true, of course, but it may be that this is as much a function of changing capabilities of the child and the child's reactions to earlier pressure as it is to the parents' feeling that sex differentiation is more important for the older child. It is probable that parents do have a clearer picture of what they want in terms of sex role development in adolescence, or, if they do not want it, they can still give clearer behavioral descriptions of how adolescents differ. Part of the reason for this is that sex role is clearly tied up with sexual relationships. Prior to adolescence, this is a class of behaviors not applicable to the child. However, once sexual relationships become possible, then all the sex role behaviors become more salient, and there may be many more pressures to conform. As an example, parents are extremely accepting of masculine activity patterns in girls (tomboyishness) until adolescence. Once the possibility of boy–girl dating begins, most parents put great pressure on their daughters to conform and to leave behind the male activities. It is not that the parents' values have changed but that, as the child's capabilities changed, the values are now applicable whereas before they were not.

It is interesting to speculate how early sex-determined socialization practices may actually shape later parent attitudes toward the existence of differences. For instance, parents of grade school children often say that their girls are more socially responsive and that their boys are more active and spend time in active exploration outside the home. They will tell you that these differences are just there, were not encouraged by them, and, in fact, are sometimes causes for concern. Yet it is not surprising that we find these differences in 10-year-old children, considering that from at least year 1, girls were given more positive reactions for social responsiveness and boys for exploration and active behavior (Fagot, 1978). However, as the parents do not recognize their early differential responsiveness, they then see the differences in 10-year-olds as appearing out of nowhere and attribute them to the biological sex of the child rather than to a long pattern of differential treatment.

The problems exhibited in the various interpretations of the research on differential socialization can only be resolved by attending to the issues raised earlier in the chapter. First, that it is impossible to consider socialization of children outside a historical context, for what has gone before influences the type of rearing at any particular time. Second, multiple types of measurement involving multiple types of data need to be taken, because we are not yet at the stage where we can say just exactly in what domain differences will or will not be present. Finally, the influence of the child on the parent as well as of the parent on the child must be taken into account, and ways to study just how child differences influence parent rearing practices must be found. At the present time, all such issues are recognized in articles discussing research in development, but in practice, very few research projects exhibit such principles of design. Too often the study will pay lip service to one or more of the above, then proceed to use a method almost guaranteeing a lack of findings. Unfortunately, findings are sometimes reported as if the issues supposedly directing the research had no part in interpretations. The failure to discuss whether the measurement techniques are appropriate to the questions being asked is of particular concern when examining socialization differences, because age-related measurement problems tend to hinder the study of sex role development at every level.

MEASUREMENT PROBLEMS AT DIFFERENT AGE LEVELS

Measurement problems at different ages can lead to quite different conclusions concerning the capacities of the child. As an example, when the sex role literature prior to 1969 is examined, there is fairly uniform agreement that sex differences in children below the age of 4 are unstable. This, of course, also matched most theoretical predictions, whether Freudian, where the identification process took place somewhere between 4 and 5, or Sears (1965), who used a modified learning approach in which the child matched behaviors with the mother until the father took a more active role with the boy, when the child could start matching behaviors to the father. Kohlberg (1966) in his cognitive development theory also suggested that around 5 was when real sex differences would emerge as a function of the cognitive understanding of gender identity. The technique of measurement used in many studies, the It test (Brown, 1956), suggested that most popular stable estimates were really not obtained until around 5 years of age. Yet today argument over the existence or nonexistence of stable sex differences centers around the first year of life and not around ages 3 and 4. It is now generally accepted that 3 and probably 2-year-old children show well-developed sex differences in their behaviors. So what happened? Did children suddenly become more sophisticated? No, the indication is that children haven't changed much at all. For instance, data collected in 1963 on 3-year-olds are very similar to data collected in the 1970s (Fagot, 1977), but what has changed is the way that data are collected. Basically, what has happened is that, through the influence of two different theories, social learning and ethological, children were observed playing in their natural environments, and the findings from research influenced by both theories is that sex differences are present from age 3 (Clark, Wyon, & Richards, 1969; Fagot & Patterson, 1969). Studies using similar techniques have since found stable sex differences from 18 months (Blurton-Jones, 1972; Etaugh, Collins, & Gerson, 1975). It is now generally accepted that the earlier negative and inconsistent findings were due to the difficulties of obtaining reliable verbal responses to testing rather than lack of differences in children.

At the present time, work with infants below 18 months shows the same pattern of negative and inconsistent findings. Korner (1973) reported finding sex differences in newborn infants. Phillips, King, and DuBois (1978) suggest that such differences are due to the fact that boys are circumcised. However, they use slightly different measures from Korner's so we do not quite know whether they have resolved the question or not. Goldberg and Lewis (1969) found sex differences in the play of 12-month-old children, whereas Jacklin, Maccoby, and Dick (1973) did not. The samples in these studies are small, the conditions vary slightly, and observation periods are always very short. Even more difficult is the measurement of gender identity in the infant, because gender identity seems to carry with it some capability for representation that implies a cognitive skill not present in children of this age. Yet we keep getting anecdotal evidence that suggests that 12-month-olds have some concept of their sex. It is extremely important that this issue be faced directly because, as things are now, both extreme biologists and extreme environmentalists pick out one or another of these studies and report them in professional journals, but more discouragingly in lay journals, as definitive findings. It is also difficult to develop a reasonable theory of sex role development without adequate data during the first 18 months. We need to know the capabilities of young children before we can decide if variations in environmental variables are important. It is critical that normative behavioral studies be conducted with children below the age of 18 months similar to the many studies of 2-and 3-year-olds. Measures of understanding of gender identity appropriate for children from 12 to 18 months must be developed. These measures might call for understanding of verbal descriptions, but should take account of the child's greater capacity to understand than to produce.

Because sex role development is embedded within the individual context of each child, this means we must use longitudinal techniques. However, longitudinal studies often run into difficulties that make the data less than clear-cut. First, subjects tend to drop out, and the subjects who do so are those who are underrepresented in most psychological research: working class subjects, those experiencing difficulties in coping, and those with disinterested parents. However, perhaps even more important is the problem of measurement across ages. If we measure gender identity at 1 year through a picture preference task (i.e., How long does the child look at pictures of boys and of girls?), are we measuring the same thing at 2 or 3 when we expect the child to answer directly whether a picture is of a boy or a girl? If this can be a problem in a period of 2–3 years, it is even a greater problem when we look over the period of 20 years of development. As an example, we might wish to use Bem's (1974) concept of androgyny with the notion of finding out just what is involved in the development of either a masculine, feminine, androgynous, or undifferentiated sex role identity. Bem designed the Bem Sex Role Inventory (BSRI) empirically by having college-age men and women rate how characteristic of themselves were a set of personality characteristics. The test consists of a set of 20 items seen as characteristic of men and 20 of women, plus 20 filler items. Individuals who are high on the male items and low on female are masculine; those high on female and low on male are feminine; those high on both male and female are androgynous; and those low on both are undifferentiated.

Bem's work suggests that the individuals who characterize themselves as androgynous have the needed flexibility to succeed in a variety of situations, for instance, using assertiveness when necessary but also being willing to show nurturance when appropriate (Bem, 1975). The concept has attracted a good deal of attention and, as might be expected, there is interest in looking at these different patterns of sex role development over the lifespan. However, such work has run into problems, for it turns out that the personality traits labeled masculine and feminine for college students do not distinguish between boys and girls below 12. This leaves us with a dilemma. We can choose characteristics (either behaviors or descriptors) that do show differences, that may have face validity as masculine and feminine, and then look at individuals who score in the four types of sex role identifications. But are we really measuring the same concept? Alternatively, we can use the same personality characteristics (even though for younger children, they are not thought of more as characteristic of boys and girls) and to assign children to one of the four categories. But again, what are we measuring? Certainly not sex role identification, and that is supposedly what we are interested in. In a recent study, Hyde and Phillis (1979) found that several of the personality characteristics labeled masculine were not endorsed as such by men over the age of 30, and that they appeared to be specific to the college population used by Bem to standardize the test. Also, many feminine characteristics seem more appropriate for men over 30, indicating that, to a certain extent, it was the stage in life rather than sex role adoption that influenced the college-age male responses. This leaves us with a very narrow test, and it seems that if we are to salvage the interesting notion of masculine and feminine as orthogonal dimensions, and the relations of these dimensions to effective functioning, we are going to have to find measures not so dependent upon the age of the subject.

Such problems must be solved before even beginning a longitudinal study. We must develop measures that fit the definitions of sex role at several age levels. Obviously, the only way this can be done is through cross-sectional pilot work. Then one could proceed with a longitudinal study with the hope that, indeed, one is measuring similar concepts across ages. But what happens if you find little continuity in sex role development? A problem still exists, for you do not know if the lack of continuity is due to measurement problems or a lack of continuity in the development of sex role. This is a particular problem in the study of sex role development, for it appears that the level of cognitive functioning may not be related to gender role adoptions. Instead, once children have reached a level of gender constancy, they may then show less rigidity in gender role adoptions (Marcus and Overton, 1978). Basically, what all this means is that using longitudinal techniques will not automatically help us understand the developmental process, but that prior to beginning a longitudinal study care must be taken to define carefully all aspects of sex role development, and multiple measurements of each aspect must be made. Then at least there is a fighting chance that the study will help to untangle processes of development rather than adding tangled strings to the picture.

When designing a longitudinal study, setting effects must also be sampled over time. Too often in longitudinal studies, the child is seen at infrequent intervals, and only a crude outline of setting effects will be made. How can we hope to understand development without some knowledge of the environmental events? This, of course, means even more time and expense, but to embark on longitudinal studies without some plan for reasonably detailed measurement of the environment as it interacts with each individual child is to waste a good deal of time, effort, and money. This is particularly important for the study of sex role because the demands on the child change both with the age of the child and the attitudes of the culture.

METHODS AND TECHNIQUES

Developmental psychologists make use of a variety of methods for studying children, and those working on sex role development have made use of all of them. Unfortunately, the methods leave us, as Bronfenbrenner (1979) says, "caught between a rock and a soft place, with the rock being rigor and the soft place being relevance [p. 18]." The methods most commonly used are naturalistic studies, laboratory studies, self-report measures, and standardized tests. Each method, as pointed out earlier in this chapter when summarizing the Blocks' work, has both problems and potential. What specifically does each method have to contribute to our understanding of sex role development, and where do the problems arise?

There have recently been several persuasive calls for a return to naturalistic findings (Bronfenbrenner, 1979; McCall, 1977; Tunnell, 1977). The reasoning behind each of these works is that it is not possible to understand development out of context, and the only way we are ever to understand the person is to understand the setting in which that person is living. In the study of sex role development, naturalistic studies have been important in reshaping our thinking about the course of development. Observed sex differences that have occured at younger ages than predicted by psychological theories, and lack of observed differences in newborns as predicted by biological theories, have led us to a rethinking of the whole sex role development process. Studies in the natural environment have shown us the importance of peer reactions (Fagot, 1977), of the physical design of the classroom (Harper & Sanders, 1975), and of teachers (Fagot, 1973, Serbin, O'Leary, Kent, & Tonik, 1973) to the process of sex role development. It is now accepted by most developmental psychologists that naturalistic studies are a powerful tool to discover influences that shape development as well as providing the ultimate testing grounds for theoretical predictions.

However, anyone who conducts studies in the natural environment becomes aware of the limitations of the method. There are excellent discussions available concerning limitations and strengths of observation methods in the natural environment (Johnson & Bolstad, 1973; Sackett, 1978), and anyone planning such a study should read the literature with care. The study of sex role development poses two particular problems. First, we know that individuals use sex as a cue for predicting physical and behavioral differences even when no such differences exist (Rubin, Provenzano, & Luria, 1974), and it is extremely difficult to keep the sex of the subject from the observer. While it is probably impossible to eliminate such observer effects, one can alert observers to this problem and minimize the effect by continuous training to avoid such biases. The other problem with studying sex role development within the natural environment is the type of coding scale to use. If you decide on broad categories in which the observer must make subjective judgments, then the sex of the child very likely will bias their ratings. If, however, you decide to code very narrow behavior categories, you often miss important qualitative differences in behavior. As an example, the 2-year-olds in Figure 9.1a and b are both climbing up a slide. If a behavior code is used, both behaviors are coded as climb, but somehow something important is missed in such a coding. However, when raters are asked to rate Figure 9.1b and are told that the subject is a boy, the rating is caution, whereas the rating for the same picture when they are told the subject is a girl is fearful. Again, the suggestion is that one method cannot be used alone and that converging data on the same hypotheses be collected in as many ways as possible.

Finally, in discussing naturalistic research, the researcher should understand that it is impossible to rule out all confounds totally. Research using this approach asks questions differently, and will always be open to the kind of criticism that proposes alternative explanations for findings, most often on variables beyond the control of naturalistic studies. To give an example, I have done a study on preschool children, in which I looked retrospectively at two different variations in sex role behavior: First, what happens in terms of peer and teacher reactions when a child performs a behavior typical of a child of the opposite sex—for example, a boy plays with dolls. The second variation was to look at children who consistently showed a preference for opposite sex behaviors and compare the reactions

(a)

FIGURE 9.1a and b. Children using the slide.

of peers and teachers to them and to averages of reactions to all children of the same sex in their class. The results were reasonably clear-cut in that boys who engaged in feminine behaviors tended to receive less positive and more negative peer reactions than the average received by all same-sex children in the class. The effects did not hold for girls. In general, the study is accepted as a first step in understanding how the worlds of boys and girls differ, and as adding needed understanding of how adoption of cross-gender behaviors affect the reactions of others in the environment. Certainly it suggests that adoption of cross-sex behaviors has very different

FIGURE 9.1 *(continued)*

consequences for boys and girls. However, for some individuals used to thinking in the Type 1 experimental paradigm, the selection of a variable to study implies much more than it does to those of us used to working in naturalistic studies. To individuals used to working in an experimental paradigm, the selection of the variable implies that the variable is to be used as an explanation of behavior. They quite correctly point out that perhaps cross-gender children differ on other dimensions and that this might explain the different results. In other words, they interpret the cross-gender behavior as *explaining* the negative consequences, whereas in a naturalistic paradigm the most you can say is that cross-gender behavior is followed by negative consequences. This finding opens the way to the next question of exactly how these children differ in their interactions from other children. Fortunately, within developmental psychology, naturalistic methods are becoming accepted as one approach, and the readers are sufficiently sophisticated to understand the difference between variables chosen for study in naturalistic and experimental studies. However, this means that when using naturalistic techniques, authors should take some time to translate findings into the language that those used to experimental paradigms can understand.

Laboratory studies are the traditional tool of American psychologists, and, had this chapter been written 15 years ago, there would have been no question that for many psychologists it would have been considered the only proper method. Studies were not sound unless as many variables as possible were controlled, and the behavior to be predicted defined as completely and narrowly as possible. As Bronfenbrenner so nicely put it, "it can be said that much of developmental psychology as it now exists is the science of the strange behavior of children in strange situations with strange adults for the briefest possible periods of time [1979, p. 19]. McCall (1977) made an important distinction between "can versus does" questions in developmental research, which has important implications for the study of sex role development. He suggests that there are all kinds of behaviors that *can* be manipulated under experimental control, but this does not mean that this necessarily *does* happen in the natural course of development. To some extent it probably will never be possible to predict with certainty what are the causes of development. However, that the task is difficult is not sufficient reason to leave the important questions behind and study only those questions simple enough to control. Too often in the study of sex role development, there has been a tendency to grasp the "can" questions and leave the "does" questions alone. This is not to suggest that developmental psychologists should abandon the laboratory approach, but only that they should understand the constraints imposed on the direction of research by reliance on this method as the only scientific way to study behavior.

Laboratory methods have proved to be particularly suited to the study of cognitive processes, and even with infants, who are notoriously hard to test, techniques have been designed to study the development of perceptual processes, speech perception, and attention and memory processes. One interesting thing to note concerning the study of sex differences and cognitive processes is that laboratory measures elicit few differences between boys and girls. In fact, the cleaner the measure, that is, the more devoid it is of content and of contingencies normally affecting performance, the less likely we are to find differences between the sexes. Fairweather 1976 proposed that most of the differences in performance found in boys and girls do seem to be under the control of environmental events and may be differences in performance and not in basic cognitive competencies. Fairweather's conclusions merely point up what the Blocks said in a different way, that you must use multiple methods and multiple measurements to study the development of each phenomenon.

The laboratory method has been less successfully used in the study of social processes, probably because those processes are so embedded in the context of the child's development. However, laboratory findings have been useful in untangling some social process problems. For instance, one of the more consistent findings in the sex role area is that boys are more aggressive than girls. Yet, in laboratory studies, given the appropriate contingencies, girls can and will perform aggressive acts. It seems clear that girls have learned the forms of aggression, but do not perform them as boys do. It is also clear that feelings of anger are present in girls just as they are in boys, and such feelings can be tapped through tests or through self-report, but still, girls do not show the behavioral manifestations of such anger so readily as boys. The laboratory studies suggest that we must look either outside the organism to find what maintains aggression in boys but not in girls, or look at more molecular levels of maintenance, perhaps hormonal, within the organism to account for performance differences.

Laboratory methods have been important in trying to untangle sex-of-parent by sex-of-child effects. This has been done in several ways, by training children to react in a certain fashion and then looking at the responses of male and female adults. An example of this technique was used by Bates (1976) in an experiment in which boys were trained to respond with minimal positive nonverbal gestures such as smiling or direct eye gaze, or to give many positive gestures. Female adults responded differentially to the low- and high-responding confederates, whereas male adults did not. Another technique is to use a child who is dressed in a neutral manner and whose sex is ambiguous, and have adults rate the child's behavior or interact with them in some way. Using this technique, the child can be presented on videotape so that many adults can react to the same stimuli. Still another technique is to give adults a set script and see if boys and girls attempt to elicit different behaviors from adults. All of these laboratory techniques have been useful in attempting to untangle some of the complicated child–adult interactions we have observed in naturalistic studies.

Perhaps the most widely used method to study sex role development is the use of standardized tests in which the subjects are given some structue to their answers. The data generated from this approach range from very free responses that can contain a great deal of information but are difficult to score, to data that consist of a "yes" or "no" to a question for which quick scores can be generated on a large number of subjects. This technique has obvious advantages for use with children: It is quick and nonintrusive, tests can often be given in groups, all the children are responding to a standard set of questions, and the questions can be directed to the areas in which the experimenter is interested. The procedures involved in using test data can range from open-ended interviews structured by the subjects' responses, to paper and pencil tests, to information obtained through reactions to the computer. It is a truism that test data are only as good as the test questions, but a truism often overlooked when interpreting the data. For instance, Brown's (1956) It scale was a widely used measure of sex role identification. The child is shown a stick figure and is asked a set of questions about It's preferences in terms of toys, activities, etc. The assumption behind the test was that the children would identify with It, and would answer for themselves. Unfortunately, it is clear that the It is perceived as a boy by most children (Fling & Manosevitz, 1972; Thompson & Mc-Candless, 1970) and consequently, boys appear to have achieved sex role identity and girls do not. While it has been possible to correct the problem to some extent either by concealing the figure or having the child imagine the figure, the conclusions from earlier studies, which used the old format, are still quoted in the sex role literature, despite the fact that they appear to be a function of a test flaw rather than a function of any differences in the process of sex role development for boys and girls.

In designing tests, there are many problems that bias the results and, unfortunately, many of these biases appear to be confounded with the sex role process. For instance, items can vary in social desirability, and it appears that men and women are willing to expose different degrees of undesirable traits. There are social class differences in test taking abilities, and there are social class differences in the male and female roles. There are differences in willingness to be tested between young boys and young girls, and their reaction to the test taking itself influences the ways they answer questions. Finally, the tests are always a function of the experimenter's notion of how things are organized, with the answers being analyzed in terms of the experimenter's ideas of what is right and wrong or more mature and less mature. The less cut-and-dried the question being asked, the more open to experimenter bias do the test and its evaluation become. In the area of sex role development this has been a very real problem, because there has been a tendency to define the way males answer as correct, more mature, more competent, etc., but that is only a *matter of the researcher's bias,* not of any higher order truth. Sex role tests are not like mathematical problems with one agreed-upon right solution, but often the resulting scores are used that way.

Despite the fact that testing procedures are so open to biases, because a hard and fast score is obtained, they are likely to be used as quick and simple answers to complex questions. Test data can generate interesting individual comparisions, but they also often tell us as much about the researcher as about the subjects, and should be used with extreme care when asking complex questions. Anyone wishing to measure sex role development who is tempted to use one of the many existing tests should reread the Sears, Rau, and Alpert (1965) book, *Identification and Child Rearing,* and note the lack of correlation between several measures of sex role adoption. The results were discouraging, to say the least, and suggested that the various measures were tapping quite different things.

One technique much used within developmental psychology is the rating method. An individual is asked to rate another individual on some variable such as aggression, or self-esteem. Rating methods generate global impressions about other person's functioning and can be valuable in determining how that individual is perceived. However, rating scales also have many of the same problems as standardized tests. The initial construction is determined by the researcher, and often the individuals doing the ratings do not feel comfortable with the qualities they are being asked to rate. There is also the difficulty of interpretation of the use of rating scales, and in cases where all the subjects are rated by different individuals—for example, parents rating their own children—some portion of the variance will be a function of differences among the raters rather than differences among the subjects. Through good training and careful scale designs, these problems can be minimized, but they always exist. The problems and potentials that reside in each of these techniques confirm that researchers should strive to use multimethods to study developmental processes.

Fortunately for the study of sex role development, techniques are now available that allow us to use naturalistic methods more extensively and to make our laboratory research more realistic. The widespread availability of inexpensive computers allows us to code data in the field more easily and to analyze it in more detail with minimal loss of time between collection and analysis. Computers also allow us to develop laboratory analogues, which should facilitate the study of parent–child interactions. Video equipment, which is portable and inexpensive, should allow us to overcome many of the method problems once associated with field research, and should provide many stimuli for laboratory studies.

Along with changes in technology that have made the actual collecting of data easier within natural settings has come a change in thinking about the use of statistics. Psychologists for years have tended to emphasize statistics in one of two ways: First, to test hypotheses generated through experimental research, in which the treatments or independent variables were under the control of the experimenter, and where experimenters were able to control the sample so that there was assurance that statistical constraints were met. A second major method was, of course, correlational techniques, which allow the researcher to determine if two or more variables vary in some predictable fashion. Those doing research using natural field settings in the absence of strict experimental controls did not have suitable statistical techniques available to analyze the large amounts of data generated by observation studies, and were forced to start applying traditional statistical techniques in somewhat unorthodox fashions. Fortunately for those working with observation data, there has been an excellent statistics reference book published by Cook and Campbell (1979) dealing with problems of research in field settings. Most of the techniques discussed by Cook and Campbell have evolved from research, and their clear-headed and persuasive discussion of why some techniques are valid and some are not should prove extremely helpful to newcomers to the use of observation techniques, but, perhaps more importantly, should blunt some of the criticism leveled by those trained in the strict laboratory tradition. For instance, they make it clear that a researcher interested in, for example, sex differences in aggression, who needs to use several different classrooms to obtain enough subjects, can test for the main effect of sex differences across the classrooms, if they use an analysis that takes into account possible classroom differences such as analysis of covariance. In general, one does acknowledge that there are effects in observation studies that cannot be experimentally controlled, so that you are using your statistical procedures as a control as well as for a test of your hypotheses.

The Cook and Campbell book also discusses in detail the use of correlational techniques to infer causation. In the study of sex role development, we are often interested in knowing just how various environmental consequences are affecting some behavior. For instance, we may be interested in looking at the development of mathematical ability in boys and girls. Mathematical ability is obviously influenced by social and cognitive factors, and, if one wishes to pinpoint why girls appear to develop at a different rate than boys, then one needs some way to specify how each variable influences the path of development. However, if we wish to infer what happens to cause different courses of development for boys and girls, we cannot manipulate the variables, and we must use a technique that allows us to infer cause from passive observation. Cook and Campbell discuss techniques such as path analysis and cross-lag correlations, which allow us to test causation without disrupting the process we are interested in studying. Even more importantly, they discuss the limitations of such techniques; particularly of cross-lag panel correlations, which assume that variables do not change in reliability over time. This is, of course, just what does not happen in developmental research since generally reliability of measurement increases with age. The real difficulty in the use of cross-lags in longitudinal studies is that few variables increase reliability at the same rate, and consequently interpretation becomes extremely difficult. Although correction factors for change in reliability are available, it is not clear that they are adequate, and so it appears that a technique being increasingly used within developmental psychology should be interpreted with extreme care. This is bad news, particularly for those who wish to look at parent–child interactions and try to untangle whether parents or children are controlling the development of certain styles. For instance, we might be interested in looking at mother's verbal instructions to boys and girls at 1 and again at 3 years of age. Unfortunately, while at first thought a cross-lag panel correlation might seem appropriate to determine if the mother or the sex of the child determines amount of interaction, we have to consider that mother's verbal abilities remain stable and that measurements are probably reliable, but that for children, measurements will be very unreliable and unreliable in ways that we cannot really predict.

It is certain that developmental psychologists interested in sex role development will continue to use multimethods to study the process; however, for the first time, we have the technical capacity available to study the process as it occurs in the environment. This should mean that we see fewer conflicts between our psychological theories and what we observe to be happening in the real world. Too often in the past in the area of sex role development, real-life consequences have been ignored because of the difficulty of placing them in testable forms. The time when such arguments can be made is past, because we now have techniques to test laboratory-generated hypotheses in the field and to come to firm conclusions.

PROGRESS IN THE STUDY OF SEX ROLE DEVELOPMENT

Despite all the methodological issues discussed in this chapter, it should be emphasized that the last 10 years have been a fruitful time for the study of sex role development. One issue of importance is the beginning of a reconciliation between the cognitive and behavioral findings. In a broader sense, this means that we are starting to understand the process of formation of gender identity and gender role adoptions. Rather than looking for either behavioral or cognitive explanations for gender differentiation, we are starting to understand that two different processes are at work and to think of ways to study the interaction of the two processes rather than proposing them as alternative explanations. We hope that this reconciliation between alternative methods of testing for and explaining sex role will also help in explaining some of the differences between attitudes and behavior, since attitudes are one type of cognitive measure of sex role.

A second area where we have made real progress is in understanding the social consequences of one's sex. Part of the impetus for such understanding has come out of the feminist movement, with its insistence on recognition for the different experiences a woman has in this society as compared to a man. The study of how children are socialized by adults in the natural environment has led us to understand that society places many constraints on gender role behavior that have real consequences for one's life-style.

Finally, the work in sex role and sex differences is beginning to be influenced by changes in the area of developmental psychology. As Cairns (1979) points out, developmental psychologists who are faced with unique methodological constraints have moved toward particular ways of thinking about development, which he terms the developmental synthesis. Four key themes of this synthesis are identified by Cairns: (*a*) that there is bidirectionality in both structure and function of behaviors, (*b*) that there is an emphasis on the interactive nature of the behaviors to be explained, (*c*) the fact that social activities are organized, and (*d*) the finding that social relationships and social behaviors are malleable and reversible to varying degrees. Each of these themes applies to the work on sex role development and, as we examine what we know concerning the process of sex role development by using the developmental synthesis, we find that many of our findings are placed in a clearer perspective. Sex role development makes more sense when placed in the perspective of recent developmental findings rather than considered as a disconnected group of findings from a variety of studies designed to test some other hypothesis.

DISCUSSION OF REMAINING PROBLEMS IN THE AREA

While progress has been made, there are some areas that still seem to be at a standstill. There is a real need to reconcile the work on the effect of hormones with the results in the psychological literature. Right now, individuals working in the area of hormone influences tend to ignore the effects of social influences on sex differences, and those working on social influences ignore the hormone work. There is not one published study in which the researcher has done a sophisticated job of measuring hormone influences and social influences. It is difficult to be an expert in all things, but there needs to be some collaboration between those sophisticated in hormonal analysis and those sophisticated in studying social development.

Another area in which we must develop new techniques is in work with children below the age of 2. Although we have measures for infants, usually they are in very restricted areas. We have ways to measure the behavior of young children, but we have no way to tap the beginning of the child's cognitive understanding of gender identity. Yet we know that by 2, children understand that they are boys or girls, and attempts to change the sex run into difficulty (Money, 1978). This would seem to me to be a critical area for new research technology.

Finally, in answer to the question posed early in the chapter, do we know enough to start to develop a coherent theory concerning sex role development, I think the answer is yes. We need to start making the attempt to bring together the very diverse findings we have in this area. The first attempts will obviously be unsatisfactory, but the very process of trying to organize and integrate the multitude of facts we now have should help us clarify our thinking about the gender differentiation process.

ETHICAL ISSUES FACING THE AREA

As a final point of discussion for this chapter, the use of findings in the area of sex role development needs to be raised. Appropriate sex role development is a delicate issue for many people, and ideas put forth tentatively in the psychological literature have a way of showing up in treatment programs as absolutes. Freud's theorizing concerning development of the male and female reproductive systems and his categorizations of correct and incorrect types of orgasms (Freud, 1972) have had vicious ramifications for the psychological treatment of women over the years. At the present time, two kinds of intervention programs are developed and used that attempt to make use of the research in sex role development. The programs are those attempting to develop nonsexist rearing in the home and school, and programs designed to change the behaviors of children diagnosed as having gender problems. Both kinds of interventions are controversial, although with different groups of people. The programs make assumptions and argue strongly for the position that the child will be better off adopting appropriate gender behaviors (Rekers, 1979) or being allowed to practice all behaviors freely. I think it is important to note that we know little concerning early adoptions of gender role behaviors, and what we do know suggests that gender role adoptions and gender identity questions are two quite separate issues. The questions concerning the relationship between appropriate sex role behaviors and the mental health of the child are not yet answered. While it would be nonsense to suggest that we do not design treatment programs until we understand the whole process (if we did this, treatment programs of every kind would come to a halt), it does suggest that those using programs designed to change the child's adoption of sex role behaviors need to proceed cautiously. It also suggests that they should use the approach of multimethods, multitime, and multitypes of data suggested by the Blocks to avoid having their own beliefs influence the interpretation of their results.

A final issue is at what point should one report research results. There is a cost to premature reporting of results that are then not replicated, as well as withholding of important results past the point where they add useful information. All the researcher can do is realize that the more important the results, the more sure one should be that they can be replicated. The best technique is often to replicate the results oneself prior to publication. There is also the issue of how and where to report nonsignificant results. As journals are now organized, it is very difficult for results that confirm the null hypothesis to be published. Yet by publishing only articles with significant results, the journals tend to overemphasize the magnitude of sex differences. Authors should argue strongly for full reporting of their findings, rather than summaries of significant findings only.

In summary, the study of sex role development should be embedded in the methodology growing out of the work in developmental psychology. However, those working in the area should take care to remember that they are working in an area that is of interest to those beyond the narrow confines of sophisticated co-workers. The real life applications and interpretations of the sex role development work suggest that researchers in the area should proceed cautiously and avoid overinterpretation of their results. This is a sound prescription for all scientific work, but an imperative for anyone working in an area of concern that extends beyond the walls of the laboratory.

REFERENCES

Ajzen, I., & Fishbein, M. Attitude–behavior relations: A theoretical analysis and review of empirical research. *Psychological Bulletin,* 1977, *84,* 888–918.

Bates, J.E. Effect of children's non-verbal behavior on adults. *Child Development,* 1976, *47,* 1079–1088.

Bem, S.L. The measurement of psychological androgyny. *Journal of Clinical and Consulting Psychology,* 1974, *42,* 155–162.

Bem, S.L. Sex role adaptibility: One consequence of psychological androgyny. *Journal of Personality and Social Psychology,* 1975, *31,* 624–643.

Bem, D.J., & Funder, D.C. Predicting more of the people more of the time: Assessing the personality of situations. *Psychological Review,* 1978, *85,* 485–501.

Block, J.H. Another look at sex differentiation in the socialization behaviors of mothers and fathers. In J. Sherman and F. Denmark (Eds.), *Psychology of women: future directions of research.* New York: Psychological Dimensions, 1978.

Block, J.H. Socialization influences on personality development in males and females. Master Lecture: American Psychological Association, New York, September 1979.

Block, J.H., & Block, J. The Role of ego-control and ego resiliency in the organization of behavior. In W.A. Collins (Ed.), *Minnesota Symposium on Child Psychology* (Vol. 13). New York: Lawrence Erlbaum, 1979.

Block, J., vonDerlippe, A., & Block, J.H. Sex-role and socialization patterns: Some personality concomitants and environmental antecedents. *Journal of Consulting and Clinical Psychology,* 1973, *41,* 321-341.

Blurton-Jones, N. (Ed.). *Ethological studies of child behavior.* Cambridge, England: Cambridge University Press, 1972.

Bronfenbrenner, U. Freudian theories of identification and their derivatives. *Child Development,* 1960, *31,* 15-40.

Bronfenbrenner, U. *The ecology of human development: Experiments by nature and design.* Cambridge, Mass.: Harvard University Press, 1979.

Brown, D.C. Sex role preference in young children. *Psychological Monographs,* 1956, *70,* 14. (Whole No. 421).

Cairns, R.B. *Social Development: The origins and plasticity of interchanges.* San Francisco: W.H. Freeman, 1979.

Chodorow, N. *The reproduction of mothering: Psychoanalysis and the sociology of gender.* Berkeley: University of California Press, 1978.

Clark, A.H., Wyon, S.M., & Richards, M.P.M. Free play in nursery school children. *Journal of Child Psychology and Psychiatry,* 1969, *10,* 205-216.

Constantinople, A. Sex role acquisition: In search of the elephant. *Sex Roles: A Journal of Research,* 1979, *5,* 121-133.

Cook, T.D., & Campbell, D.T. *Quasi-experimentation: Design and analysis issues for field settings.* Chicago: Rand McNally, 1979.

Etaugh, C., Collins, G., & Gerson, A. Reinforcement of sex-typed behaviors of two-year-old children in a nursey school setting. *Developmental Psychology,* 1975, *11,* 255.

Fagot, B.I. Influence of teacher behavior in the preschool. *Developmental Psychology,* 1973, *9,* 198-206.

Fagot, B.I. Sex differences in toddlers' behavior and parental reaction. *Developmental Psychology,* 1974, *10,* 554-558.

Fagot, B.I. consequences of moderate cross-gender behavior in preschool children. *Child Development,* 1977, *48,* 902-907.

Fagot, B.I. The influence of sex of child on parental reactions to toddler children. *Child Development,* 1978, *49,* 459-465.

Fagot, B.I., & Patterson, G.R. An in vivo analysis of reinforcing contingencies for sex-role behaviors in the preschool child. *Developmental Psychology,* 1969, *1,* 563-568.

Fairweather, H. Sex differences in cognition. *Cognition,* 1976, *4,* 231-280.

Fling, S., & Manosevitz, M. Sex typing in nursery school children's play interests. *Developmental Psychology,* 1972, *7,* 146-152.

Freud, S. *Three essays on the theory of sexuality* (J. Strachey, Ed.). New York: Avon Books, 1972. (Originally published, 1905.)

Harper, L.U., & Sanders, K.M. Preschool children's use of space: Sex differences in outdoor play. *Developmental Psychology,* 1975, *11,* 119.

Hyde, J.S., & Phillis, D.E. Androgyny across the lifespan. *Developmental Psychology,* 1979, *15,* 334-336.

Jacklin, C., Maccoby, E., & Dick, A. Barrier behavior and toy preferences: Sex differences (and their absence) in the year-old child. *Child Development,* 1973, *44,* 196-200.

Johnson, S., & Bolstad, O. Methodological issues in naturalistic observation. Some problems and solutions for field research. In L.C. Handy & E.J. Mash (Eds.), *Behavior change: Methodology, concepts, and practice.* Champaign, Ill.: Research Press, 1973, pp. 7-67.

Kagan, J. *Continuity and change in behavioral development in retrospect and prospect.* Invited address to the International Society for the Study of Behavioral Development, June 25–29, 1979, Lund, Sweden.

Kohlberg, L. A cognitive–developmental analysis of children's sex-role concepts and attitudes. In E. Maccoby (Ed.), *The development of sex differences.* Stanford, Calif.: Stanford University Press, 1966.

Kohlberg, L. Stage and sequence: The cognitive–developmental approach to socialization. In D.A. Goslin (Ed.), *Handbook of socialization theory and research.* Chicago: Rand McNally, 1969.

Korner, A.F. Sex differences in newborns with special reference to differences in the organization of oral behavior. *Journal of Child Psychology and Psychiatry,* 1973, *14,* 19–29.

Lynn, D.B. *Parental and sex-role indentification: A theoretical formulation.* Berkeley, Calif.: McCutchan, 1969.

McCall, R.B. Challenges to a science of developmental psychology. *Child Development, 1977, 48,* 333–344.

Maccoby, E.E., & Jacklin, C.N. *The psychology of sex differences.* Stanford, Calif.: Stanford University Press, 1974.

Marcus, D.E., & Overton, W.F. The development of cognitive gender constancy and sex role preferences. *Child Development,* 1978, *49,* 434–444.

Masters, W.H., & Johnson, V.E. *Human sexual response.* Boston: Little, Brown, 1966.

Mischel, W. A social-learning view of sex differences in behavior. In E. Maccoby (Ed.), *The development of sex differences.* Stanford, Calif.: Stanford University Press, 1966.

Mischel, W. Continuity and change in personality. *American Psychologist,* 1969, *24* 1012–1018.

Mischel, W. Sex-typing and socialization. In P.H. Mussen (Ed.), *Carmichael's manual of child psychology.* New York: Wiley, 1970.

Money, J. Sex determination and sex stereotyping: Aristotle to H-Y antigen. Address to the Western Psychological Association, San Francisco, April 19–22, 1978.

Money, J., & Ehrhardt, A.A. *Man & woman, boy & girl.* Baltimore: Johns Hopkins University Press, 1972.

Parlee, M.B. The premenstrual syndrome. *Psychological Bulletin,* 1973, *80,* 454–465.

Phillips, S., King, S., & Dubois, L. Spontaneous activities of female vs. male newborns. *Child Development,* 1978, *49,* 590–597.

Rekers, G. Psychosexual and gender problems. In L. Nash and C. Terdal (Eds.), *Behavioral assessment of childhood disorders.* New York: Guilford Press, 1979.

Rose, R.N., Gordon, T.P., & Bernstein, I.S. Plasma testosterone levels in the male rhesus: Influences of sexual and social stimuli. *Science,* 1972, *178,* 643–645.

Rubin, J.Z., Provenzano, F.J., & Luria, Z. The eye of the beholder: Parent's views on sex of newborns. *American Journal of Orthopsychiatry,* 1974, *44,* 512–519.

Sackett, G.P. (Ed.). *Observing behavior: Data collection and analysis methods* (Vol. 2). Baltimore: University Park Press, 1978.

Sampson, E.F. Scientific paradigms and social values: Wanted—A scientific revolution. *Journal of Personality and Social Psychology,* 1978. *36,* 1332–1343.

Sears, R.R. Development of gender role. In F.A. Beach (Ed.), *Sex and behavior.* New York: Wiley, 1965.

Sears, R.R., Maccoby, E.E., & Levin, H. *Patterns of child rearing.* Evanston, Ill.: Row, Petersen, 1957.

Sears, R.R., Rau, L., & Alper, R. *Identification and child rearing.* Stanford, Calif.: Stanford University Press, 1965.

Serbin, L.A., O'Leary, K.D., Kent, R.N., & Tonik, I.J. A comparison of teacher response to the preacademic and problem behavior of boys and girls. *Child Development,* 1973, *44,* 796–804.

Thompson, N.L., & McCandless, B.R. It score variations by instructional style. *Child Development,* 1970, *41,* 425–436.

Tunnell, G.B. Three dimensions of naturalness: An expanded definition for field research. *Psychological Bulletin,* 1977, *24,* 426–437.

Unger, R.K. Toward a redefinition of sex and gender. *American Psychologist,* 1979, *34,* 1085–1094.

10 Ethics as an Integral Part of Research in Child Development

HARRIET L. RHEINGOLD

The purpose of this chapter is not to present a new code of ethics for the conduct of research with children, but to raise some of the issues investigators face in observing the code. Of codes of ethical standards for the conduct of research there are many; some relate to research with human subjects in general (e.g., *Ethical Principles in the Conduct of Research with Human Participants,* American Psychological Association, 1973), and some to research with children in particular (e.g., *Ethical Standards for Research with Children,* Society for Research in Child Development, 1973, reprinted at the end of this chapter). At the outset let me say that I regard these codes as binding. Yet from personal experience and a long-standing concern for the matter, I know that questions arise in ensuring that not only the letter but the spirit of the codes are observed. There is almost no study that does not call for the strictest scrutiny of its adherence to the rules. Given the variety of questions investigators ask about the development of children, the great number of different behaviors they study, the range of the children's ages, the diverse environments in which the children are studied, and the necessary involvement of parents and other persons, much room remains for aligning one's efforts with ethical principles.

Let us assume that there need be no conflict between, on the one hand, the investigator's attempt to answer scientifically valid questions about human behavior and its development and and, on the other, the observance of the rights of children, their parents, and all other participants. It goes without saying that all persons, regardless of age, have rights. These rights always stand and may not be breached by recourse to any conviction of the ultimate benefit of the research to all persons, now or in the future. In this chapter, then, I shall consider some of the decisions investigators must

305

STRATEGIES AND TECHNIQUES
OF CHILD STUDY

Copyright © 1982 by Academic Press, Inc.
All rights of reproduction in any form reserved.
ISBN 0-12-715080-3 0-12-715082-X (p)

make in designing and conducting their studies so that they not infringe on or dishonor the rights of those they study. As a result, we may become more sensitive to the rights of all participants in the enterprise.

THE RIGHTS OF SUBJECTS AND INVESTIGATORS

The rights of all persons, regardless of age, include the right to be informed about the purpose of the study, the right to privacy, the right to be treated with respect and dignity, the right to be protected from physical and mental harm, the right to choose to participate or to refuse without prejudice or reprisals, the right to anonymity in the reporting of results, and the right to the safeguarding of their records. Nor do the subjects abdicate their rights by consenting to participate in a research project, because they may withdraw from the study at any time. By contrast, the rights of the investigators are far fewer, and may better be labeled as responsibilities. Beyond the obligation to observe the rights of participants, their responsibility lies in contributing to knowledge about human behavior with strict allegiance to the rules of the scientific enterprise.

Ideally, there should be no conflict between the investigators' responsibilities as scientists and the rights of the children and other participants they study. Investigators know that many kinds of experiments that can be performed on nonhuman subjects cannot be performed on human subjects. They must obtain knowledge about the principles of human behavior and human development without depriving children of normal experiences or harming them in any way. Still, beyond these strictures, the potential for conflict between the investigators' responsibilities and the rights of children does exist.

A risk–benefit accounting of the scientific enterprise seems unwarranted to me. As the benefits of research are almost always unknown during its conduct, risks to the participants ought not to be justified by such potential benefits. The investigators should therefore be mindful of the potential conflict between their own convictions of the value of their research and the rights of their subjects. For the investigators, the research they plan constitutes a measure of their own personal worth, as well as of their obligation to contribute to human welfare. They do not plan their research lightly, being mindful of the commitment of time, effort, and money. Beyond that, they are indeed motivated by a conviction that the research will contribute to a better understanding of human behavior. The danger, if danger there is, arises only when investigators leave no room in their convictions for a consideration of the possible effects of the procedures on their subjects.

We cannot then rest content because we experience our motives as pure. These motives confer no license on any operation that may cause harm, embarrassment, or self-devaluation to our subjects. It is not our motives that need scrutiny, but the effect on our subjects of how we propose to obtain answers that requires the most scrupulous attention.

A BRIEF HISTORY

Children have been studied systematically by behavioral scientists for almost a hundred years, but only within the last couple of decades have explicit ethical standards been set for such research. Although the increased awareness of the rights of all persons seems to be a relatively recent achievement, as long ago as 1947 the American Psychological Association began the process of setting ethical standards for the behavior of psychologists. After publishing drafts of sections of the standards in the *American Psychologist,* scheduling panels and symposiums, holding open sessions on the codes at annual meetings, and soliciting the opinions of many individuals and groups, the association published the *Ethical Standards of Psychologists* in 1953. That document, however, devoted only 12 of the 169 pages to ethical standards in research, and only 4 of the 12 to the investigators' relationships to their subjects.

In 1967 the American Psychological Association published the *Casebook on Ethical Standards of Psychologists,* providing illustrative cases of the 19 principles that constituted the society's code, in which only Principle 16 applied to research precautions. In the same year, however, the Office of Science and Technology of the Executive Office of the President published a report entitled *Privacy and Behavioral Research* (1967), the work of a distinguished committee of which Robert Sears was a member. As far as I know, this report was one of the first to deal explicitly with the ethical standards that today govern our behavior. It is an eloquent statement and in my opinion still the best general treatment of the topic. I recommend it to your attention, together with M. Brewster Smith's (1967) more explicit statement on research with children.

To continue this brief historical account, in 1968 the Division of Developmental Psychology of the American Psychological Association published its own standards "to govern investigators who conduct research on the behavior, growth, and development of children" (p. 1). Then, in 1973 the Society for Research in Child Development adopted its *Ethical Standards for Research with Children.* That same year the American Psychological Association published its *Ethical Principles in the Conduct of Research with Human Participants* (1973), a manual of 104 pages devoted to the single topic, in contrast to the 12 pages of the 1953 publication. Also in that year the federal government established the Commission for the Protection of Human Subjects of Biomedical and Behavioral Research. Beginning in November 1973, the *Federal Register* has been publishing a series of regulations on the protection of human subjects, some with special consideration of research with children. A possible easing of standards for simple behavioral studies, a topic of much interest to us, is currently being debated. It behooves us as concerned investigators to keep ourselves informed as new regulations are proposed.

With increasing frequency, conferences and seminars around the country are being held on ethical standards. For example, in March 1979, a conference on "The Role and Function of Institutional Review Boards and the Protection of Human Subjects," sponsored by the Public Responsibility in Medicine and Research Board, was held in conjunction with the Boston University School of Medicine. Furthermore, such organizations as the Hastings Center's Institute of Society, Ethics, and the Life Sciences, and the Joseph and Rose Kennedy Center for Bioethics at Georgetown University have been established.

Lest this brief account suggest that only psychologists have established codes of ethical standards for the conduct of research with human subjects, I point out that the Society for Research in Child Development is a multidisciplinary society, and that societies of other disciplines (e.g., American Anthropological Association, American Association on Mental Deficiency, and American Sociological Association) have also established such codes.

NATURE OF RESEARCH ON CHILD DEVELOPMENT

Myriad indeed are the forms of research on child development, as this book illustrates. The range of the children's ages extends from the newborn to the adolescent. The children are studied in nurseries, homes, day care centers, and schools and playgroups of many kinds, as well as in laboratories. In some studies they are seen by themselves—each alone—and in others they are observed interacting with other persons—their parents, teachers, friends, or just peers. As varied are the types of behavior studied. They range from relatively free and unrestrained behavior observed in both natural and laboratory settings to studies designed to measure, for example, perceptual abilities, memory, language, academic skills, and moral judgment.

Beyond the diversity of ages, settings, and behaviors, research on child development also includes studies of children of varying abilities, in particular those with sensory, motor, or intellectual handicaps, and of children growing up in different socioeconomic environments. And in many studies the behavior of adults in relation to the children constitutes an integral part of the study of the children's development, including, for example, studies of the interaction of parent or teacher or other adult and the child, as well as ratings of the children by parents and teachers. Furthermore, in some studies the children are studied only once in cross-sectional designs, and in others many times over a span of years in longitudinal designs.

This summary has been presented for its relevance to ethical considerations. It shows that psychological research is not of the so-called "invasive" type, not prescribing drugs and not physically harmful. Many studies entail only simple observation as the children go about their usual business, as they talk, play, or interact with other persons. Many other studies closely resemble educational operations routinely carried out in school settings.

The apparently harmless nature of all these types of studies would seem to require no special code of ethical standards. Yet as I shall show, there probably is no study, free of moral issues as it may seem, that does not present dilemmas for the investigators to ensure adherence to the ethical standards.

WHY A SPECIAL CODE FOR RESEARCH WITH CHILDREN?

Several reasons are proposed for a special consideration of the ethical standards to be observed in conducting research on children, beyond those to be observed in conducting research on persons of any age. In the first instance, a cardinal principle of conducting research with human beings states that they consent to being studied with full knowledge of what their participation entails. This principle cannot be honored in the case of infants and very young children, who cannot give consent; this is also true of the mentally retarded. Even in the case of older normal children, one can often question their ability to comprehend what participation entails, although age 12 is usually accepted as an age by which they can.

Another cardinal principle states that no harm, physical or mental, results from the subject's participation in the research. Although one might propose that children are more resilient in recovering from distress or embarrassment, we nevertheless are constrained by the possibility that any unhappy experience may have a harmful effect, children having fewer ego defenses and rationalizations. And, as children (probably under the age of 12) cannot give formal consent, the investigator must obtain the consent of the children's parent or parents, as well as of those responsible for the children at the time of the study, including school officials and teachers, superintendents of institutions, and directors of day care centers, nursery schools, and research institutes.

Even when consent of the parent and others has been obtained, one must still obtain the child's consent to participate. The child must be given the right to refuse, without prejudice, and to withdraw even in the midst of a study. Fortunately, in well-designed and well-run studies the investigator's greater problem is how to limit the number of children to those required, so often are children eager to be studied, regarding participation as a special privilege.

Children then are not to be coerced by the power that resides in adults. They are not to be treated as a captive population, but should be accorded all the rights to which persons of any age are entitled. Because of their special susceptibility to the authority of adults, investigators should exercise an extra measure of caution that they not infringe on the children's rights.

OBTAINING INSTITUTIONAL APPROVAL

To ensure that ethical standards are honored, almost all proposals for research with children today are examined by formally constituted review boards. Of consequence in that statement are, first, that the proposal must be reviewed before the research can be begun; then, that approval of the board must be obtained; and further, that often the approval of several boards is required.

Many investigators today are supported by funds from federal, state, and private agencies. To obtain such financial support, the proposal for a study is judged first on its scientific merit, and then approval is granted only if it complies with the established ethical practices of that agency. For the latter purpose, to use the National Institutes of Health as an example, the home institution of the investigator must provide written assurance that it will abide by the policy of the Public Health Service (U.S. Department of Health, Education and Welfare, 1969) for all research involving human subjects that it supports. This assurance consists of a written statement of compliance with the requirements regarding initial and continuing review of research involving human subjects, as well as a description of the institution's review committee structure, its review procedures, and the facilities and personnel available to protect the health and safety of human subjects. In addition to providing the assurance, the institution must also certify to the Public Health Service for each proposal involving human subjects that its committee has reviewed and approved the proposed research before an award may be granted. Even though previously approved by both the institution and the Public Health Service, the institution should be prepared at all times to question the conduct of the research, because "the safety and welfare of the subject are paramount [p. 2]."

The necessity of obtaining approval today extends beyond research funded by governmental and other agencies. Not only must any plan for research with human subjects be approved by the home institution of the investigator (be the investigator a student or research scientist or professor), but also by the school or institution where the research will be conducted. After obtaining approval from these authorities, the consent of parents or legal guardian must also be solicited.

This series of procedures is illustrated by recent efforts of a graduate student who planned to study memory in children 3–5 years of age. First, the student presented the plan to the department's Ethics Committee. For this review the student presented information on the purpose of the study; where the study would be conducted; the ages and number of children required; what operations the children would be asked to perform; the possibility of risk (defined as physical, mental, or social discomfort, harm, or danger) and the steps taken to minimize risk, if any; how informed consent would be obtained from the subjects, parents, and others, together with copies of the consent form; the use of any deception and how it would be explained to the participants; and the procedures for assuring the subjects' privacy and the confidentiality of the data. Finally, the student signed the following statement: "I have read Principle 9 of the American Psychological Association's Ethical Standards for Psychologists (1977 revision and its subsequent revision of 1979) concerning the use of human subjects in psychological research and agree to abide by it. I also agree to report any significant and relevant changes in the procedures and instruments to the committee for additional review."

After the department's committee approved the proposal, the student approached the directors of the town's nursery schools. For each meeting with a director, she presented a statement giving the purpose of the study, the number of children needed, the tasks they would perform, the length of each session, and the contribution to knowledge the study might make. The director also approved the consent form to be signed by the parent. Before the day of testing, the student visited each center to meet the teachers and children.

Similar procedures are followed to obtain approval to study children in schools, proceeding from superintendent to principal to teacher to parent, as well as in such other settings as hospitals and research institutes.

If investigators wish to conduct research in a setting not requiring formal review, I recommend that they constitute their own review bodies. We must always entertain the possibility that our enthusiasm and convictions about the value of our research may blind us to the rights of our subjects. Here I can mention a preference for including in any review body a parent of the sample of children to be studied. I may also suggest that in each instance we ask ourselves if we would agree to serving as subject or to having our own child so serve. Although investigators naturally fret during what is often a time-consuming process, we have no choice, and must take as much comfort as we can in finally winning approval for our dearly held idea.

More and more often review boards are basing approval not only on the researcher's strict observance of the rights of subjects but also on the scientific merit of the proposal. Resentful as investigators may be of such an infringement on the right of scientific inquiry, still the invasion of another human being's right to privacy must be justified by its worth, that is, by the likelihood of its contributing to knowledge of consequence. Especially in schools, officials and teachers are now questioning the value of the research in terms of the students' time away from classroom instruction.

OBTAINING INFORMED CONSENT

People are not to be subjected to study without their consent, a rule that applies to all except the very young, for whom the consent of the parent is substituted. With today's one-way windows, inconspicuous microphones, and closed-circuit TV cameras, subjects could well be under surveillance without their knowledge. Yet these powerful tools cannot be used to betray our subjects' trust; their presence and use must be explicitly remarked.

Investigators have every advantage in securing subjects and therefore must be especially sensitive to the rights of their subjects and of all others whose consent they must obtain. First, they have behind them the power conferred by years of formal education. They also have the status conferred by the academic or research institution where they work or study. Furthermore, children, and older people as well, generally find it easier to acquiesce with requests than to refuse them. It often requires a special measure of independence for children and of conviction for adults to say no, because no one likes to risk the disapproval of an apparently important person. Certainly a relationship of power must be avoided, and we should strive to enlist the cooperation of children and adults as partners working together to increase knowledge. In any case, whatever the population from which one samples, in securing the cooperation of children and their parents, the request should be framed so that it is as easy to refuse as to accept participation. It is natural enough for us to be so convinced of the importance of the research that a measure of coercion may unwittingly come through in our voice and manner. It is this possibility that we must guard against.

Next I treat two related issues: (a) from whom consent should be obtained; and (b) what constitutes informed consent. Consent is not enough; it must be informed consent.

Infants and very young children, of course, cannot give their consent. Nevertheless, the rule should be that no child should be studied who objects; children should not be coerced but should participate willingly and agreeably, after first being told in words they can understand what they will be asked to do. Given that there are many ways for the investigator to describe participation that make it attractive, it still behooves the investigator to remove any self-devaluation from a child's reluctance to participate.

With older children, and especially with parents and all others responsible for them, informed consent must be obtained. Informed consent consists of voluntarily agreeing to participate after being given the credentials of the investigator, a full statement of the purpose of the study, the potential value of the knowledge to be gained, the exact operations the child or adult will be asked to perform, how long the study will take, and how frequently the subject will be expected to participate if the study is longitudinal. It goes without saying that all questions should be answered. Although the principle governs our behavior, many questions arise in the course of its observance. These concern especially how the purpose will be presented and how much information about the operations will be given, topics to be treated as I proceed.

Effect of Labeling Groups

Under the topic of informed consent I now raise the problems associated with studies that call for the formation of groups for comparative purposes. At issue is the extent to which parents, teachers, or children should be informed of the group to which they are assigned. Let us consider the kinds of groupings an investigator of children's behavior might employ, how these groups might be labeled, and then the ethical problems that might arise if persons, children and adults, were informed of the labels. Grouping by age presents no problem, age being obvious and carrying no pejorative implications. Also, no problem need arise in studies in which the effect of different directions on the behavior of interest is measured. Grouping into experimental and control conditions would appear to carry no pejorative implication if determined at random, but might well prove disturbing to parents if they thought some characteristic of the child determined the assigning. Here the investigator must weigh the advantages and disadvantages of disclosing not only the assignment but the basis for it.

A more serious problem arises, however, in studies in which the groupings are based on some apparently less than desirable characteristics of the subjects or their parents. Even if the investigator is careful not to affect the dignity and self-worth of the parent or child by labeling the groups in their presence, must the investigator here divulge the purpose of the study? There is, of course, no problem when the child has physical, mental, or behavioral problems that the parent recognizes. Still, the requirement for full disclosure places the burden on the investigator of presenting the information without embarrassing the participants.

Explaining the Purpose of the Study

We usually encounter no difficulty in telling our subjects what they will be asked to do. To children we can say that they are to play as they usually do, or that they will be asked to memorize lists or solve problems, or make up stories, and so on. To parents we can say they are to care for the baby as they usually do, or to teach the child how to solve a puzzle, or to fill out rating scales or questionnaires. Presenting the purpose of the study, however, does deserve special consideration. Obviously it must be framed in terms the participant, child or adult, can understand, and not in the special vocabulary of our science. But the very real possibility exists that, however framed, divulging the purpose may well reduce the representativeness of the behavior under study. It is then that the investigator often frames the purpose very generally to draw attention from what is specifically under study. And it is just here that investigators struggle with their consciences, and ask themselves whether presenting the explicit purpose at the end of the study (and offering the participants the opportunity to have their data withdrawn) meets the requirement of informed consent. A still more serious dilemma faces the investigator who, for example, looks for differences in performance by socioeconomic class. How can the purpose of such a study be presented without impairing the participants' self-esteem? Confronted with such a dilemma, investigators may nevertheless discover that they can indeed, as in fact they must, explain the purpose honestly and openly.

These considerations lead to the thorny question of deception. On principle we must be opposed to deceiving subjects about the true purpose of a study. Having said that, I know there is room for judgment on what constitutes deception, for deception comes in many forms.

Deceiving subjects as to the purpose of a study has become a matter of serious concern among behavioral scientists. All recognize that deception should be avoided. All accept on principle that deception is not fair to subjects and may even damage the experimenter's own self-image. Yet how is the investigator to obtain a representative record of, for example, how parents *usually* behave with their children? It remains an indisputable fact, however, that there are some instances in which, were subjects aware of the exact purpose of the study, they might well behave in quite different ways than they normally would. Fortunate indeed are the investigators who can state openly to their subjects exactly what they are studying and why these behaviors are of interest. Nevertheless, the safest and most desirable course recommends that no deception be practiced. It is just here that investigators must consult their peers.

Troublesome also are those frequent and almost inevitable instances in which new questions, beyond those of the stated original purpose, arise in the minds of investigators as they analyze their data. A kind of deception is being practiced, and yet no easy solution comes to mind. The best advice recommends that we recognize the problem and be mindful of how we ourselves would feel were we the participants.

The practice of "debriefing," that is, disclosing the true purpose of a study entailing a fairly serious deception at its conclusion, can also be questioned. Can debriefing remove the possible embarrassment of a person's having been led to behave in a fashion antithetical to that person's own system of values? Can debriefing (and the deception practiced) enhance the faith we wish our subjects to have in the scientific enterprise? Such questions deserve serious thought.

CONDUCT DURING THE STUDY

All participants, children and adults alike, should be accorded every courtesy during the study. A consideration of the invasion of their privacy certainly recommends such behavior. We must be especially careful, then, that not only are the participants assured of our gratitude for their cooperation, but that none be allowed to think that they have failed. In work with parents and young children, we can make it a point to comment favorably on some behavior, even if in other ways the children or the parents do not (as why should they?) conform to expectations. Investigators must also consider how to give children who are performing tasks a sense of satisfaction and achievement regardless of the quality of their performance. Praise too easily dispensed may be suspect, but some is always warranted.

A special case for consideration arises when some children in a group or classroom are not included in the study because they do not satisfy some requirement of the investigator's (for example, as a result of random selection, or inappropriate age or sex) or because the parent did not return a consent form. Investigators should devise some techniques to preserve these children's sense of personal worth and somehow convey to them that their omission from the study was not their fault. Sometimes the problem can be solved by calling these children from class and allowing them to see or examine the test materials. So simple a solution may not be appropriate in many studies; still, investigators are urged to give the matter careful thought.

As we should provide some positive statements to the participants, so should we also guard against an evaluative remark about some personal characteristic that seems innocent enough to us, and even complimentary, but that may be otherwise interpreted by the recipient. As each of us knows from personal experience, a careless remark can have a lasting damaging effect. Investigators should also be careful not to slip into the role of counselor (a role they may, of course, play in other contexts), but keep the purpose of their research activities sharply in focus. In certain instances the effects of counseling may be the purpose of the study, but in others gratuitous advice should be eschewed. Requests for advice should be referred to other trained persons (e.g., the family physician). And, as stated in the Society for Research on Child Development's code, "When, in the course of research, information comes to the investigator's attention that may seriously affect the child's well-being, the investigator has a responsibility to discuss the information with those expert in the field in order that the parents may arrange the necessary assistance for their child [1973, p. 4]."

The investigator also has the responsibility to convey the general findings of the study to participants. If the investigator does not, the participant—child, parent, or other adult—is left with a feeling of uncertainty. Of course much of the uncertainty concerning the purpose of the study and the value of the participant's cooperation should have been removed in the process of obtaining informed consent. It is understandable, however, that participants, excepting only very young children, want to know how well they have performed. If participants should ask, investigators should take the asking as a warning that they have been remiss in not having fully informed them about the questioning nature of research at the beginning of the study, or sufficiently reassured them at its conclusion. If the investigators recognize their responsibility to make every research experience rewarding for their subjects, as I think they should, subjects will not ask how well they have done. The issue then is how to make the experience rewarding over and beyond the satisfaction participants frequently experience by just cooperating. For example, parents present during observations of their young children often find satisfying just the opportunity to watch them in a setting removed from their everyday cares and distractions. Before the study, parents can be reassured that if anything is at test it is not the child but our own theories. Furthermore, in every instance some behavior of every child is worthy of comment and can be called to the parents' attention. Finally, parents are often gratified by discovering an achievement they did not know their child was capable of until the experimenter brought it to their attention.

How should this matter be handled in the case of other types of studies? Even if outcomes are not so salutary, certainly no subject should leave the study with a sense of failure or a loss of dignity. Let us remember that we are conducting research, that the participants are volunteering an invasion of their privacy. There must be some dignified avenue between foolishly praising a very poor performance and genuine appreciation of the participant's ability. Let us remember that, although we judge a performance as good or bad by the extent to which it justifies the hypothesis we have in mind, there is no sound reason why our subjects should be evaluated by the same criterion.

Finally, providing a written statement of the main findings to parents, teachers, and other persons whose approval was sought not only shows appreciation but also furthers their understanding of the scientific enterprise.

MAINTAINING CONFIDENTIALITY

All information obtained in any study of children must be kept confidential. The identity of the child or parent or other adult is concealed once the data are obtained. Anonymity is best preserved by assigning a number to the subject, so that the record thereafter is identifiable only by that number. Parents, and children if they are old enough to understand, should be informed of this rule as part of obtaining informed consent.

The rule of confidentiality applies not only to all reports of the findings of the study, whether written or oral, but also to all informal discussions with students and colleagues. The more formal reporting of results presents few problems because the data are almost always summed over a number of subjects and presented in statements of central tendency or entered into statistical tests of significance. This practice also can be easily explained to participants. It is rather the humanly understandable but unethical practice of chatting about one's findings to which we must be ever on our guard. Not only must a name never be linked to the data, but neither should any other attribute that could identify that person.

CONSULTING ONE'S PEERS

Whenever a doubt arises in the minds of investigators about their observance of ethical standards, they should consult their peers and probably other persons as well. I take it for granted that doubts will arise in the designing of almost every study as we become ever more sensitive to the rights of our subjects. At such times investigators should first consult one or two of their colleagues who have much experience in the general area of the research and who can be counted on to be sympathetic with the investigator's purpose. Much can be learned from such an informed and partisan source. The consulting should not end there, however, but the design as now redefined and altered should be presented to other colleagues less familiar with the topic and the usual procedure. And often just obtaining the approval of the institution's review board may not be sufficient for the concerned investigator aware of niceties of procedure and possible dilemmas beyond the more general cognizance of the reviewing group. Therefore, investigators should seriously consider the desirability of presenting the procedure to a representative or two of those very populations to be studied. What is needed is a fresh eye as well as the test of asking oneself if in that study one would serve or have one's own child serve as a subject.

THE RESPONSIBILITY OF EDITORS OF JOURNALS

To assist in the observance of ethical practices, editors of journals reporting research on children carry a measure of responsibility. Beyond asking investigators for clarification of questionable procedures (see Principle 21 of the Ethical Standards of the Society for Research in Child Development), they should consider the wisdom of requiring authors to include in the method section an explicit discussion of the ethical considerations that entered into the design and conduct of their research, and that manuscripts be accompanied by the formal signed approval of the institutional review board (Sieber, 1979). If these requirements are not met, should the paper be published in a psychological journal? Inasmuch as investigators must anyway satisfy both requirements, and bear full responsibility for meeting the ethical requirements of scientific research, what exactly should be the responsibility of editors?

Two matters may be considered. Should space in journal articles be allowed for a statement of the procedures for meeting ethical standards? In these days when editors must always advise authors to reduce their manuscripts, can additional space be allocated to an account of the steps taken to assure ethical practices or even just to report approval by review boards, of which there often may be several? The second matter concerns the wisdom of adding to the already heavy responsibility of editors for ensuring scientific merit, clear exposition, and so on, requiring them also to assume responsibility for the ethical procedures of the investigator.

A review of the articles published in *Child Development* in 1979 showed that in none of 20 reporting on audio- and videotape recordings of the behaviors of children or of children and their parents was it explicitly stated that the subjects were informed of the recorders—although of course they may have been. In one of these, the children were led to believe that they could not be seen but later were so told. Four articles reported studies that evoked distress in infants. And in five others, deceptions of various kinds were employed, and the children or adults were informed of the deception at the conclusion of the study, in one of which the participants were given the option of having their data deleted. In still another three studies, the children's self-esteem would seem to have been adversely affected. Of the 173 articles published in that year, these 32 do not constitute a large fraction; nevertheless, each would place a measure of responsibility on the editor.

In contrast to these possibly questionable procedures, seven articles explicitly reported that parental consent was obtained, and three of these stated that the children's consent was also obtained. Two articles reported that the investigators were careful to safeguard the self-esteem of the children by ensuring that all were successful or thought they were. The confidentiality of the data was assured the participants in two studies. In 11 articles, then, journal space was granted for the reporting of ethical procedures. The question remains, then, whether the practice should become more general. Or can it be assumed, whether stated or not, that the research operations did in fact satisfy the ethical standards for the conduct of research on human subjects?

CHARGE FOR THE FUTURE

What does the future hold? We will never return to the easy days when scientists thought only of the problem they wished to investigate. Today they must give deep thought to the matter of consent as well as to every operation they plan to carry out, from the beginning to the end of the study. Yet today's code of ethics cannot stand for all time. To this end, every professional society of behavioral scientists should have a standing committee to oversee the ethical practices of its members, with staggered terms to ensure fresh interpretation. New research questions will require new research procedures, and their answers will be pursued with ever-increasing awareness of the rights of children and all other participants.

A statement of ethical standards must of necessity be broad and general.

No statement could cover every possible instance, and even if such a document could be drafted, it might well prove too restrictive. We need instead a series of positive statements that express the spirit of ethical behavior and not the minutiae of observance. Despite the fallibility of human judgment, it will always have to enter into our adherence to standards.

The ultimate goal is policing ourselves so that we need never be policed by society. We should set our standards so high that we easily meet the regulations of any federal, state, or other agency, and we should set the standards before they are set for us, while reserving the right to protest any foolish or irrelevant regulations.

We must of course be careful of the possibility of overweening pride in ourselves as scientists. To be sure, we are each convinced that our motives are to increase knowledge and so serve humankind. But we cannot do so at the expense of others. Thus we have an obligation to both our science and our fellow human beings. Our subjects, children and adults alike, are generally willing and trusting, but when we necessarily invade their privacy, we must do so with the same courtesies we would expect were others to invade ours. With the most sensitive attention to the dignity of our subjects, we can continue to enjoy the blessings and freedom that are now ours. Let us then behave in such a manner that we may continue to add knowledge while at the same time holding society's respect for our efforts.

APPENDIX: ETHICAL STANDARDS FOR RESEARCH WITH CHILDREN (SOCIETY FOR RESEARCH IN CHILD DEVELOPMENT)

Children as research subjects present ethical problems for the investigator different from those presented by adult subjects. Not only are children often viewed as more vulnerable to stress but, having less knowledge and experience, they are less able to evaluate what participation in research may mean. Consent of the parent for the study of his child, moreover, must be obtained in addition to the child's consent. These are some of the major differences between research with children and research with adults.

1. No matter how young the child, he has rights that supersede the rights of the investigator. The investigator should measure each operation he proposes in terms of the child's rights, and before proceeding he should obtain the approval of a committee of peers. Institutional peer review committees should be established in any setting where children are the subjects of the study.
2. The final responsibility to establish and maintain ethical practices in research remains with the individual investigator. He is also respon-

sible for the ethical practices of collaborators, assistants, students, and employees, all of whom, however, incur parallel obligations.

3. Any deviation from the following principles demands that the investigator seek consultation on the ethical issues in order to protect the rights of the research participants.

4. The investigator should inform the child of all features of the research that may affect his willingness to participate and he should answer the child's questions in terms appropriate to the child's comprehension.

5. The investigator should respect the child's freedom to choose to participate in research or not, as well as to discontinue participation at any time. The greater the power of the investigator with respect to the participant, the greater is the obligation to protect the child's freedom.

6. The informed consent of parents or of those who act *in loco parentis* (e.g., teachers, superintendents of institutions) similarly should be obtained, preferably in writing. Informed consent requires that the parent or other responsible adult be told all features of the research that may affect his willingness to allow the child to participate. This information should include the profession and institutional affiliation of the investigator. Not only should the right of the responsible adult to refuse consent be respected, but he should be given the opportunity to refuse without penalty.

7. The informed consent of any person whose interaction with the child is the subject of the study should also be obtained. As with the child and responsible adult, informed consent requires that the person be informed of all features of the research that may affect his willingness to participate; his questions should be answered; and he should be free to choose to participate or not, and to discontinue participation at any time.

8. From the beginning of each research investigation, there should be a clear agreement between the investigator and the research participant that defines the responsibilities of each. The investigator has the obligation to honor all promises and commitments of the agreement.

9. The investigator uses no research operation that may harm the child either physically or psychologically. Psychological harm, to be sure, is difficult to define; nevertheless, its definition remains the responsibility of the investigator. When the investigator is in doubt about the possible harmful effects of the research operations, he seeks consultation from others. When harm seems possible, he is obligated to find other means of obtaining the information or to abandon the research.

10. Although we accept the ethical ideal of full disclosure of information, a particular study may necessitate concealment or deception. Whenever concealment or deception is thought to be essential to the conduct of the study, the investigator should satisfy a committee of his peers that his judgment is correct. If concealment or deception is practiced, adequate measures should be taken after the study to ensure the participant's understanding of the reasons for the concealment or deception.
11. The investigator should keep in confidence all information obtained about research participants. The participant's identity should be concealed in written and verbal reports of the results, as well as in informal discussions with students and colleagues. When a possibility exists that others may gain access to such information, this possibility, together with the plans for protecting confidentiality, should be explained to the participants as a part of the procedure for obtaining informed consent.
12. To gain access to institutional records the investigator should obtain permission from responsible individuals or authorities in charge of records. He should preserve the anonymity of the information and extract no information other than that for which permission was obtained. It is the investigator's responsibility to insure that these authorities do, in fact, have the confidence of the subject and that they bear some degree of responsibility in giving such permission.
13. Immediately after the data are collected, the investigator should clarify for the research participant any misconceptions that may have arisen. The investigator also recognizes a duty to report general findings to participants in terms appropriate to their understanding. Where scientific or humane values may justify withholding information, every effort should be made so that withholding the information has no damaging consequences for the participant.
14. Because the investigator's words may carry unintended weight with parents and children, caution should be exercised in reporting results, making evaluative statements, or giving advice.
15. When, in the course of research, information comes to the investigator's attention that may seriously affect the child's well-being, the investigator has a responsibility to discuss the information with those expert in the field in order that the parents may arrange the necessary assistance for their child.
16. When research procedures may result in undesirable consequences for the participant that were previously unforeseen, the investigator should employ appropriate measures to correct these consequences, and should consider redesigning the procedures.

17. The investigator should be mindful of the social, political, and human implications of his research and should be especially careful in the presentation of his findings. This standard, however, in no way denies the investigator the right to pursue any area of research or the right to observe proper standards of scientific reporting.
18. When an experimental treatment under investigation is believed to be of benefit to children, control groups should be offered other beneficial alternative treatments, if available, instead of no treatment.
19. Teachers of courses related to children should demonstrate their concern for the rights of research participants by presenting these ethical standards to their students so that from the outset of training the participants' rights are regarded as important as substantive findings and experimental design.
20. Every investigator has a responsibility to maintain not only his own ethical standards but also those of his colleagues.
21. Editors of journals reporting investigations of children have certain responsibilities to the authors of studies they review: they should provide space where necessary for the investigator to justify his procedures and to report the precautions he has taken. When the procedures seem questionable, editors should ask for such information.
22. The Society and its members have a continuing responsibility to question, amend, and revise these standards.

Submitted by
Leon Eisenberg
Frank Falkner
Frank A. Pedersen
Phil H. Schoggen
Harriet L. Rheingold, Chairman
14 September 1972

ACKNOWLEDGMENTS

I thank Lynne Baker-Ward, Julie A. Robinson, and especially Sara P. Sparrow for help in writing this chapter.

REFERENCES

American Psychological Association. *Ethical standards of psychologists.* Washington, D. C., 1953.
American Psychological Association. *Casebook on ethical standards of psychologists.* Washington, D. C., 1967.

American Psychological Association. *Ethical principles in the conduct of research with human participants.* Washington, D. C., 1973.

American Psychological Association. *Ethical standards of psychologists (1977 revision).* Washington, D. C., 1977.

American Psychological Association. Latest changes in the ethics code. *APA Monitor,* November 1979, 16–17.

Division of Developmental Psychology, American Psychological Association. Ethical standards in psychological research. *Newsletter,* Spring 1968, 1–3.

Office of Science and Technology. *Privacy and behavioral research.* Washington, D. C.: U. S. Government Printing Office, 1967.

Sieber, J. Working on ethics. *APA Monitor,* January 1979, 3.

Smith, M. B. Conflicting values affecting behavioral research with children. *American Psychologist,* 1967, *22,* 377–382.

Society for Research in Child Development. Ethical standards for research with children. *Newsletter,* Winter 1973, 3–5.

U. S. Department of Health, Education and Welfare. *Protection of the individual as a research subject.* Washington, D. C.: U. S. Government Printing Office, 1969.

11 Working with Children[1]

PENELOPE H. BROOKS AND EARLINE D. KENDALL

Researchers using observational procedures to study children in naturalistic settings encounter a predictable host of practical, technical, and interpretational difficulties. But the psychologist who studies children in an experimental–laboratory setting has one of the greatest challenges of the profession—that of trying to get children to do (and not do) what you want them to in a research session. The present chapter examines some of the typical problems and possible solutions in working with children in a structured, laboratory type of environment.

Children of any age bring experimenters unique problems. The difficulties in working with young infants, who are engaged in an endless succession of sleeping, crying, eating, and eliminating, are legend. As the infant nears 1 year of age, there are longer periods of alertness to the external world and also greater interest in the experimental apparatus—the experimenter's glasses, jewelry, and hair. The babe-in-arms is replaced by the toddling, walking, running child whose exuberance for any new situation often taxes the experimenter's ability to control the child. Only with school age does some docility occur. Even then the scientific road to truth is booby-trapped by the characteristics of the very children under study. These booby traps are not inevitable, but appear most often when the experimenter is not well acquainted with the subject population.

There is frequently an egocentrism in experimenters exceeding even that attributed to his young subjects by Piaget (1965). This egocentrism sometimes takes the form of assuming that the children come into the experimental situation programmed to do the same task that the experimenter

[1] Preparation of this manuscript was supported, in part, by PSH Grants HD–07045 and HD–04510 from the National Institute of Child Health and Human Development.

has planned for them. As will be seen in the following pages, this is seldom the case. Another form of egocentrism occurs when experimenters assume the abilities of the experimental subjects to be comparable to their own abilities. A classic example of this problem occurred in a study a graduate student was conducting concerning the recall of simple sentences varying in the subject–verb–object relationship. The subjects were children 5, 7, and 9 years old. The results showed an incredible difference in recall scores between the 5- and 7-year-olds in favor of the latter group. The advisor and student thought they had uncovered a period of enormous gains in memory. Upon reading the manuscript, the advisor was embarrassed to find that the student had presented the material *printed* on index cards. Is it any wonder that 5-year-olds who could not read could not recall what they had not read?

Those who conduct experimental research with children know that a well-executed experimental session is only half the battle. The other half consists of ethical considerations, maintaining good public relations with schools and parents, and adapting a study to the accommodations provided by the settings. These considerations, too, can be undermined by the egocentrism of the experimenter. This egocentrism may take the form of assuming that the setting's personnel attribute the degree of importance to the research that the experimenter does, or that the purpose, procedure, and results of the study are understood by the school or hospital personnel and parents because the experimenter understands these factors. This assumption may result in failure to communicate purpose, procedure, or results to the persons cooperating in the study.

The purpose of this chapter is to discuss some of the pitfalls on the way to sound and productive experimental research with children. Some sections are concerned with the actual collection of data on children, and some are concerned with the context of the study—parents, schools, teachers, etc. The observations are not only those of the authors, but represent the collective wisdom of a number of colleagues who have been involved with research and children for several years.

RECRUITING SUBJECTS

In working with children in research projects, a first step is to find appropriate populations and gain access to specific subjects. Because children are not able to discern appropriately concerning their participation in research projects, their parents must be approached and informed about the data collection and the activities that will involve their children. Often children in group settings are needed for study. In addition to gaining parental permission, teachers, care givers, or other responsible adults must be approached and informed. These are the "gatekeepers" (Bogden & Taylor, 1975) who can give the experimenter access to parents, as well as children. How, then, does a researcher conducting a study involving children find the children needed and gain access to them?

Locating Appropriate Populations

Usually, the proposed study calls for children of a particular age range, perhaps SES level, and with or without other specific characteristics. Even the first item on this list, age, is deceptively complicated when doing studies with children. Their ages are constantly (and obviously) changing. This period of rapid change is particularly difficult to manage in younger children when even slight age differences are more apt to be one of the strongest indications of developmental variation. "Catching" individual children during specific periods of a few weeks, or even a few hours, as in the case of testing neonates, may call for a large continuing population available to the experimenter. Preschool and school age children are often in group settings where a pool of subjects is available. In addition to their greater availability, older children's ages are not so critically calculated. An age range of a year or more may be sufficient pinpointing for many studies.

Factors other than age are quite specific to individual projects. These additional factors will tend to make it both harder and easier to find particular subjects. The precise variable sought may be the very thing that will enable the researcher to gain access to a particular child. One of the authors studied only newborns whose mothers had an electronic fetal heart monitor during labor and delivery. Although such a factor narrows the available population of subjects, it also very clearly defines the population and sometimes facilitates their participation.

Finding the particular pool of subjects that is needed for a study depends on the formal and informal contacts of the researchers and the institutions from which they come. If prior contact with the experimenter or others doing similar studies has been positive, continuing access is generally possible. Once trust breaks down with a school, hospital, day care center, or other contact, it may be difficult to reopen that site to research. It makes sense, therefore, to maintain relationships between individuals and institutions to allow for later studies by these or other researchers.

Gaining Access to Individual Children

Some studies may lend themselves to making contact with individual families and getting parents' permission for studying their children; however, most projects rely on finding children by contacting an agency or person providing a service to children of the age and with the characteristics needed. In these instances, the parents will be reached through the agency or person serving the family. Many such institutions that provide for the needs of children have policies and human subject committees defining research constraints. In the past, it was common practice to have parents sign research release forms or "blanket permissions" at the time of admission to the program. This is no longer considered sufficient ethical or legal protection for children and their families, the experimenter, or the agency caring for the child. Many programs have routine procedures for experimenters who wish to test, observe, or study the children in their care. If such procedures are not a part of the institution's policy, some other form of gaining informed consent is necessary.

Providing information to parents to gain informed consent and obtaining signed permission forms will have to be worked out with the gatekeeper of the school, day care center, hospital, or other agency. Contacting this person or committee and convincing him or her of the study's worth and of the ability and integrity of the researcher must come first. Prior to approaching parents, a number of details should be discussed: the study's needs must be explained; the researcher's contact and activity with the children must be specified; and the "match" between what the researcher needs and what the agency can provide must be determined. Full endorsement from the school or agency is essential. If the staff does not trust or have rapport with the researcher, they find subtle and not-so-subtle ways to delay or interfere with the research. Parents will be looking for cues from the persons who work regularly with the children to know whether or not they will allow their child's participation in the study. If the child's teacher, doctor, or care giver (who supposedly knows about the request and those making the request) supports the researcher's project, then the parents usually agree readily. If parents sense hesitancy from those they know and who know their children, they may deny permission.

The agency who is approached for participation in a research project will be looking for several things:

1. Is this participation going to be "good" for this school (center, institution, agency) in relations to the community, services exchanged, favors given? Negotiation for in-service training or other professional services may occur.
2. Is participation and cooperation in the study going to interfere with the usual routine?
3. Has participation in similar studies been inconvenient or annoying, in any way, to children, staff, or parents?

4. Is the researcher perceived by staff and parents as competent, cooperative, and responsible?
5. Is the experimenter's work going to take precedent over the reason the child is in the program? (Any teacher knows that what he or she does in the classroom with the child is more "important" than any possible research activity.)

If satisfactory answers to such questions are found, the researcher is usually given the opportunity to approach parents, or the agency offers to explain the project to parents and get their signed permission statements. Often the way to gain the confidence of the parents most easily is for the researcher and someone familiar to the parents from the agency to approach the parents together. In this way, parents' questions are most readily answered, and their feelings of trust are greater than if either the researcher or someone from the agency approaches them independently.

Parents' Informed Consent

Once parents sense the confidence agency officials have in the researcher, they are ready to receive information about the study, its purpose, and the role their children will have in the study. Parents vary a great deal in how much information they want, ask for, or are interested in obtaining. Regardless of the interest they exhibit, or questions they ask, they must be given sufficient information to make "informed consent" possible. Specific guidelines and regulations for informed consent are discussed in Chapter 10.

Approaching Parents. In assuring that parents are given adequate information, care must be used in how parents are approached and how such information is presented. The agency's representatives, through whom the researcher has sought consent, will have vested interest in the way in which parents are approached and how and what they are told about the study. These representatives have as their primary concern their ongoing relationship with the parents and children who are served by their program. They have little, if any, interest in the research and its outcome. They will be eager to make sure the project will in no way cast doubt on their program, staff, and services. They will want to have input, and perhaps participate or be present, when parents are approached. This is usually advantageous to the researcher as it serves as a means of entry and as reassurance to the parents, who may otherwise have some reluctance about allowing strangers to interact, observe, test, or train their children.

Parents, or the agency, may request that someone who knows the child be present during the child's participation if the children in the study are quite young or vulnerable in some other way. Once the staff who works with the children on a day-to-day basis become familiar with the examiner and the routine of the data collection, they usually relax their initial caution, unless there is a continuing lack of trust. In that event, the project may be terminated at the first possible opportunity. Those who work with infants, very young children, and even older children take the responsibility for the children's safety and well-being seriously. They may appear to be overly concerned and hovering to some scientists who have encountered large numbers of children in similar settings. This may be a first, or unusual situation, for the particular teacher, nurse, counselor, or care giver. From a novice's perspective, there may be problems of lack of understanding of research and its usefulness, or lack of appreciation for the particular research or person conducting it. Any of these factors could jeopardize the project.

Even in settings that often are used as sites for the study of young children, staff will find many ways to slow down a project, or discontinue their children's participation if it is a study that they do not like. If the researcher is not liked or trusted, the slowdown increases. Remarks will be made indicating the following: "She *can't* go during snack (or nap, or group time, etc.)." "Johnny, did you finish making cookies (going to the potty, putting away your toys, etc.)?"

Comments to parents may have negative connotations: "Debbie seemed reluctant to go with the examiner." "I don't understand why they want to study such a silly (trivial) thing." As such comments are made in front of children or parents, the researcher's work may be made difficult or impossible. It is essential to gain full support before data collection begins.

Signed Permission. Once full cooperation and understanding have been established, some form for written consent must be presented. If the children are over 7, two permission forms are needed—one to be sent home and signed by parents, and one to be signed by the child. If the agency has a form that parents are accustomed to signing for research participation of their children, this form may serve the situation best. If there is some circumstance of the study that makes the usual form inappropriate, the researcher may need to suggest another form. If the agency is unaccustomed to having research projects, the researcher needs to be prepared to suggest and provide a suitable form.

A copy of the signed and dated form for the specific project under consideration should be kept on file by the researcher, and another copy should be given to the agency for its files. In some instances the parents may also be given a copy of the form.

Approaching Schools, Hospitals, and Day Care Centers

To reach groups of children with similar characteristics and conditions for study, researchers often go to schools, hospitals, and day care centers to conduct their studies. Unless the facility is one whose purpose is research, the children will have been brought there for educational, medical, or family needs. Other activities must "fit in" with the primary concerns of the agency for the family. In approaching any care-giving agency, its primary focus must be understood, acknowledged, and protected if the study is to be considered and approved.

Ongoing relationships between institutions usually exist on several levels. Some agencies establish reputations for cooperation and availability to the broader community. These institutions are more easily approached than those that see themselves as too busy with their own work to accommodate outsiders; however, these more cooperative agencies may be "over-researched" because of ease of access.

Scheduling Research Activities

There are several major hindrances to completing research within a planned time. Too often, researchers new to the enterprise plan too closely in terms of time and subjects. On paper, there may be a perfect match between the sample characteristics and the experimenter's needs. It is easy to ignore the reality of two of the major problems—permission letter attrition and absenteeism on the part of the subjects. Permission letter attrition is a condition attributed to permission letters that do not get signed and returned for whatever reasons. This is a common problem in schools and may have a prevalence of 25–50%. Absenteeism may also be quite high, especially during the winter, and especially among very young, poor, or handicapped children. Most experienced researchers try to plan for twice the number of subjects they need and commit themselves to an aggressive plan of getting permission slips returned. Even after compensating for the inevitable factors of absenteeism and disappearing permission slips, there are other eventualities in scheduling for which plans must be made:

1. If there is going to be a fire drill, it may occur at a critical time during the research study. The consequences of such an occurrence must be weighed by individual researchers. If the consequences are dire, the possibility of such an event might best be discussed in advance with the person who schedules fire drills.
2. The visiting speech therapist, for example, may need the room in which the researcher has equipment set up. Full and uninterrupted use of space at a school is rare. Sharing a room with others may in-

crease the possibility of interruptions and should be arranged ahead of time. PLEASE DO NOT DISTURB, RESEARCH IN PROGRESS signs may be helpful.

3. The room assigned to the investigator may be adjacent to a distracting setting, such as the band room. This occurrence should be foreseen if it is remotely possible that the school's fight song played at 100 decibels by trumpets, trombones, and tubas will interfere with the research.

4. There may either be a flu epidemic or a long siege of school-closing-due-to-snow during the researcher's tenure at a school. A rule of thumb based on the experience of many missed deadlines is to plan a research study to take three times longer than it would under ideal conditions. Sometimes even that rule is idealistic.

Other events occur periodically at schools, and the staff may forget to warn the researcher of these. Pep rallies, field trips, and school picnics are notorious for disrupting research schedules. The researcher who wants to avoid such surprises will consult the school calendar on a regular basis.

The experimenter's desires to the contrary, the school's schedule is a necessary factor in implementing a research plan. Needless to say, students who have to miss part of lunch, PE, a pep rally, or the home-bound school bus to be in a study are not going to give the experimental task their undivided attention or enthusiasm. Similarly, school personnel who have to insist that a math test has priority over an experimental session are not going to be supportive of the research enterprise.

Teachers and Parents

Many parents like having their children participate in research studies. They feel satisfaction in learning their children are desired for such participation. Many will have some feelings of awe of the researcher, the study, and the research setting. Even those who are not in awe may view the experimenter as the "expert." This does not mean that parents want to be treated as knowing less than the expert. In fact, it is the parents who are the experts about their child. Letting parents know that they have valued information, understanding, techniques, and knowledge is important. Teachers need to be given the same courtesy. In either case the scientist is allowed access to the children as subjects by the parents and the teachers. It pays to treat both with respect.

Sometimes parents or teachers may ask for information about a child who is not theirs. They may ask for information that is not to be released. One of the most common requests made by staff members is to know how particular children did on a test. This information should not be a part of the child's record, either on paper or in the staff member's mind, unless explicitly allowed on the permission form. Researchers may refuse graciously on the basis of the permission letters or on the basis of their own qualifications. Unless the researcher is a licensed psychologist, test results from the experimental context may not be used to evaluate the child.

Another frequent request comes from teachers who may want help with a particular child who behaves peculiarly or seems to be depressed or has "perceptual" problems. Unless the researcher is qualified by training to give this kind of advice, abstinence is the recommended response. The most helpful contribution a researcher can make is to suggest ways or places a parent or teacher could get advice about a particular child. One of the authors had a situation arise with a parent who began to relate difficulties with breast feeding when her newborn was being tested. Even though the question being asked was one that could have been easily answered, the mother was told to talk with her physician. To have advised her concerning anything other than her infant's responses to the testing situation would have been inappropriate. Often, larger cities and school systems will have needed services available, in which case the researcher may remind the parent or teacher of their availability. In any event, data collectors will need to know how to respond appropriately to such requests.

It is particularly difficult to deny information to someone with whom the researchers have become friendly during the study or to whom they are indebted for cooperation. These situations can be overcome by setting a tone that is professional from the start of the project. If the role of the researcher is clearly defined prior to the start of the project, then inappropriate requests will be few. From the beginning, clear signals can be given that the researcher is there to do a job. These signals include the way project members dress, stay on task, and treat those at the site. Dress that is similar to those who work there makes the researcher less conspicuous and more easily accepted. Jeans are appropriate if others in that setting wear them; the same is true of beards, dress length, and lab coats.

Even when parents and teachers are not asking for information or help that does not fall under the purview of the experimenter, they may still thwart the research efforts. Preventing their interference is a necessary part of the research plan when working with children. Some parents and teachers intervene with good intentions, giving the children too much information or too many instructions, in the hope that their children will perform better. Others may step in and "side" with the child who is asked to do something that seems too difficult for the child to do. Others may coach the child, invalidating the child's responses. Some of these difficulties are most easily avoided by examining the child when the adult is not present. If the adult is to be present, clearly describing the purpose of the study and the role of the child and the adult will help.

Reports and Organizations

Organizations or settings that cooperate with a research endeavor deserve a footnote of appreciation in the resulting research report. A politically astute researcher sends the organization copies of articles or papers in which that organization is recognized for its contribution. The researcher includes in the acknowledgment names of individuals who were especially instrumental in the completion of the study—teachers, nurses, principals, day care directors, social workers—and also sends them individual copies of the research reports. An offer to talk about the outcome of the study with interested staff or teachers and to discuss with them implications for the setting's mission is appropriate. Occasionally the investigator may even offer to conduct a workshop or in-service training module on a topic that is relevant to the staff's needs. Failure of the investigator to complete the research project with these types of gestures makes collaborators feel like they have been used. Staff are not so enamored of research that just being a part of it is reward enough. Some school administrators have the attitude that allowing the researcher access to the children is a favor that demands repayment. On the positive side, such gestures help ensure a future welcome for that particular investigator and also for researchers yet to come. These gestures are not merely for public relations, however. Subjects, their parents, and those who provide access to subjects have a right to know what has been done with the data that were collected. Did the researcher use them for the purposes initially proposed? Was confidentiality of the subjects' names maintained? Did the study embarrass the setting in any way? In short, reports to the settings and to parents or guardians serve as an indirect, albeit belated, check on the reliability of the researcher. They are necessary ethical procedures.

THE EXPERIMENTAL SESSION

Covarying with the development of children's cognitive and social processes is an interesting change in the nature of research on children. Studying very young children frequently is an observation of what children *will* do in a particular stimulus context. Studying older children is often an attempt to also study what they *can* do. The transition in research questions corresponds with an increase in children's ability to understand and enter into social agreements (Piaget, 1965; Kohlberg, 1976). With older children, the experimental situation takes place in what Orne (1962) terms "a context of explicit agreement of the subject to participate in a special form of social interaction known as 'taking part in an experiment' [p. 777]." This agreement carries with it a well-understood role of subject as under the control of the experimenter, as implicitly agreeing to perform a wide range of actions upon request without inquiring as to their purpose or duration. This socialization process is reflected in a methodology that expects subjects to follow instructions, to accept the experimenter's explanation of the purpose of the study, and to perform their best. The researchers' savvy is demonstrated by the degree to which they understand where subjects are on the continuum from self-determined to passively obedient and adjust the experimental expectations accordingly.

Building Rapport

As initial contact is made with the children who are to be studied, every effort should be made to assure that their first impressions are positive. The adults in the setting will be assessing the researchers' efforts; young children will be watching the adults they know for clues indicating what is expected of them in the new situation.

Briefing the adults prior to working with the children will help establish a natural climate for the study. Most researchers want to study children under normal circumstances, where their reactions are as much like their usual responses as possible. In order to accomplish this, care must be taken with the details of the setting, timing of the sessions, and anything else that detracts from an unobtrusive entry into the children's environment. Bronfenbrenner (1979) notes that American research in child development is based on the study of children by strangers in strange situations. In most situations, children's responses can best be studied when the "strange" element is diminished. Because children do not know what a Ph.D. is, the title of "Dr." has only one kind of reference—the person who gives shots. For the peace of mind of especially the preschool and younger school-age subjects, it is not a good idea for them to be invited to "go play a game with Dr. Doe." The experimental room and the apparatus should have no resemblance to a doctor's office.

One major factor in children's performance is that they may adopt a standard of excellence that is not the same as the experimenter's. In a long-term (50 sessions) study of recall in four kindergartners (Baumeister & Luszcz, 1976), the subjects' day-to-day variability was quite large, indicating that they were not consistently achieving their optimal level of performance. Upon querying the children as to why they did not always recall all the items on the list, they defensively replied "I told you three or four of them." The authors of the study speculated that for the subjects, successful recall of only some of the items constituted acceptable performance. They further speculated that, as children get older, this criterion of acceptability may get more stringent. These authors are thus proposing not an age-related ability but an age-related performance criterion. Investigators should be wary of such a phenomenon because it means that, for younger children, instructions should contain a specification of the appropriate criterion. In the absence of such specification, what is being measured is not the subjects' abilities but their criteria for what is an adequate performance.

Some general directions given by the teacher, nurse, or care giver before the children enter the testing session may help set the tone of cooperation the examiner wishes to achieve. A friendly, but businesslike approach by the researcher, including a manner that is unhurried but clearly indicates purpose, will often help set this tone.

If the children are to be tested or questioned in a separate room, the examiner will do well to have that area ready before bringing children into it. Any materials and equipment that are a part of the study should be checked before bringing the child to the session. Any superfluous objects or distractions need to be eliminated prior to beginning work. Sounds, objects, and other sources of possible stimulation that would be readily ignored by adult subjects may hold undue fascination for children of various ages. Children will need time to examine the environment, the situation, and even the examiner before attending to the research task; however, the researcher who is wise in the ways of children will not delay long. Children lose interest abruptly; the child who was attending and participating with enthusiasm may suddenly turn away, need to potty, go to sleep, become fearful, or otherwise terminate the session.

It can be predicted that many testing and observation efforts will cause adverse reactions in young children. (Actually, even among adults there is some anxiety related to being tested and observed.) Strangers, strange environments, and strange situations will cause some children to cry, try to run away, tense up, or otherwise avoid the experience. In addition to the child's own fears and reactions, there is the added input of the parent or care giver in the situation. Often both the child and adult have a nonspecific fear. Either of them may desire to please or "score" well without knowing exactly what constitutes "good" in the experiment. This implicit pressure adds a degree of uncertainty that increases the negative feelings; these feelings of anxiety and tension affect the results of the study and may change the reactions of the subjects in the study.

Whenever children show signs of fear or begin to cry, most adults hasten to reassure them and ease the tension. Some adults respond with efforts to control the situation and the child by being firm, or even harsh. Generally this tactic adds to the child's fear and crying. Most human-subjects committees require assurance that subjects may withdraw at any time during a research project. This applies to young subjects as well. While agreeing with this in principle, some testing, such as the Brazelton Neonatal Behavioral Assessment Scale, could not be used if this criterion is strictly followed.

If a child is disruptive or is having a tantrum, an investigator can respond by withdrawing attention until the child is again cooperative. These are rare instances if the study has been designed to appeal to children's interests. When interest is low, the children in the study may try to resist the experimenter. If efforts fail to elicit the child's cooperation, then the child should not be forced to continue.

Children's awareness of the investigator's presence can be easily underestimated by researchers. Data collectors observing children are not so unobtrusive as they might think. Stories of children leaving their "stream of behavior," marching over to the observer, pulling down the clipboard, and asking, "Why are you *always* watching *me*? It's not nice," are not rare. Orders to "stop following me!" may be heard from targeted children running on the playground.

Using Appropriate Language with Children

Problems can occur in working with children when the words used do not mean anything to the children or they mean something different to the children than they do to adults. As we saw in Chapter 5, some of the tasks Piaget presented to young children to determine their ability to conserve may fall in this category. When a young child is asked which is more, the ball of clay or the ball that has been divided into pieces, there may be a language difference rather than a lack of conservation when the child replies, "The pieces are more."

Complex instructions with conditional such as, "If the red light goes on, press this button; but if the blue light goes on, press this button," are not appropriate for younger children. The children may not understand conditional phrases or the instructions may be so long as to tax the child's attention or memory. Many experienced child researchers find it useful after giving instructions to the child to have the child explain to them what the task is. To make sure the child understands, a short, simple practice session is often in order. With younger children, however, one must be careful that these practice sessions do not exhaust their ability to be interested in the task. Employing such practice tasks has an additional benefit, that of ensuring that any resulting developmental differences are not due to age-related abilities to participate in the task.

If practice trials are inappropriate, tasks should be constructed so as to be sensitive to three types of response sets that children are prone to exhibit (Achenbach, 1978). The *social desirability* set predisposes children to respond according to how they think they should answer, that is, conform to conventional standards of behavior. An example of this occurred when a student was trying to construct a pictorially depicted scale of children's perception of the home. The task was to pick which of two pictures of each pair was most like the way things were at the child's home. One item showed a father reading the paper with the son playing quietly nearby. Its contrast was a father and son romping together playfully in the back yard. One of the subjects in the study chose the picture of the father reading the paper as most like what happened at his house. When probed, he explained that he was a good boy and never interrupted his father while he was reading the paper. It is unlikely that, for this child, the pair of items was a contrast; he chose the one that showed him being polite.

A second response set that young children demonstrate is yea saying, or saying "yes" to questions regardless of their content. An example is quoted by Achenbach (from Yarrow, 1960, pp. 659–660).

> The child built an enclosure out of large blocks. The examiner asked, "Would you like to be in this all by yourself?" "Yes," replied the child. "Would you like your daddy with you?" "Yes." "Would you like your mommy in there with you?" "Yes." "Would you like to be in this all alone?" "Yes," this time with emphatic agreement.

A third response set is "nay-saying" which occurs less frequently, but its possibility also constrains the design of interviews in such a way that they are sensitive to this tendency. There are no simple ways of keeping children from answering questions according to a response set. As Piaget has so convincingly demonstrated, confronting them with logic will not necessarily work. The only certain option is to design the task so that it detects these response sets, and the protocols of children who are victims can be discarded from the study.

Lest the researcher be tempted to use multiple choice or forced choice techniques to get around these difficulties, there is also a response set endemic to them. Younger children tend to choose the second of two alternatives, regardless of their content, a tendency that has plagued early Piaget studies and personality scale development (Michel, Zeiss, & Zeiss, 1974).

Children may present problems related to language use by being shy and restrained when an adult asks them questions. Even answers they know may not be communicated because of shyness or fear of failure.

When the words used seem too easy to the child, hesitancy may result. If the task or language used is too simple for the developmental level of the child, the child may feel there is a trick. At best, there is the uneasy feeling that this adult does not know very much about the task presented or about children. Either makes the child cautious.

Children are all too accustomed to being ignored or deliberately left out of adult conversations. They are often told to "go play" or some other version of "don't bother me now." Their questions often do not receive serious replies. Therefore, most children are delighted when an adult shows interest in what they are doing and has questions for them. They usually want to cooperate and "do their best." Showing them courtesy, answering their questions about apparatus and equipment, and making sure that genuine communication occurs is something that the adults must do. Too often children recieve less.

Children who are bilingual or who are of a culture other than the examiner's pose special communication problems. An examiner who is of the same culture, or subculture, as the children will be able to comprehend the children's responses more completely. In such a case, the children are likely to understand and to trust an adult who is like them more than an adult of another race, language, or ethnic group.

Materials and Apparatus

This would be the place to advise the novice experimenter to use materials that are appropriate for the age of the children being studied. This advice could mean colorful interesting pictures and words in big print (for younger school-age children). Actually, keeping children's interest in the study is rarely a serious problem. Baumeister and Luszcz (1976) had no trouble keeping three of their four subjects returning for 50 sessions to participate in a boring repetitive task. While their kindergartners had been preselected for cooperativeness and were rewarded for coming (not for performance), they participated far longer than most of us would have predicted. The authors noted that "in the end ironically it was the experimenter who expressed the greatest relief [p. 736]." There is, however, some wisdom concerning materials and apparatus that is offered for the benefit of the experimenter, that is, that (a) all paper materials be laminated or enclosed in plastic to avoid becoming a permanent record of the smudged fingerprints of children in the study, and (b) automated apparatus be inoperable until the experimenter is ready for the subject to respond. Buttons, levers, and push keys are attractive to children of any age. Advice concerning the subject's welfare would consist of a reminder that any object will be orally explored by every child between 3 months and 18 months. About half the time objects will also be thrown. It is usually a reasonable strategy to make such objects digestible, light weight, unbreakable, or anchored to a surface. Sterilizing these objects between uses would help the care giver's peace of mind and the child's health.

Getting Subjects to and from the Research Site. In most cases, the research will be conducted in the same general area as the subjects are located, but escort requirements vary from site to site. Some schools will require the children to be accompanied by someone on their journey from class to lab. Others may require signed permits for the children to be out of class or in the corridor, and still others may be so casual as not to want any kind of formal arrangement. Because the coming and going of subjects can be a real headache at some sites, especially those where institutional escorts are necessary (e.g., juvenile correctional facilities or developmental centers), the arrangements need to be made in advance of a research study. Usually, the personnel at the research site would probably rather not have to cope with the additional management necessary to accommodate the research study. If at all possible, the researchers should provide for this function.

Sometimes subjects must be transported by vehicle to the research site. If so, appropriate permissions from parents and insurance companies should be obtained. Occasionally a researcher needs to transport subjects a very short distance but has difficulty because the subjects cannot walk by themselves. One student had such a problem in needing to get four handicapped toddlers from one place in a large building to another. She could carry two at a time but she could not leave those two alone while she went after the other two. She came up with the solution of putting them all in a grocery cart and pushing them back and forth from the experimental room. She had other problems when one of them had to go to the bathroom in the middle of a session, but the transportation problem was solved very cleverly. Foresight and planning on the part of the researcher will eliminate most transportation problems.

Rewards. There is general agreement that children will work harder and even perform more accurately for rewards. Often rewards are used contingent upon participation (but not performance) in order to ensure that the subjects will come willingly, if not eagerly, to the experimental session. Such rewards may be advantageous to both subject and experimenter but may not be so to staff or parents. Neither parents nor teachers like for great quantities of M&Ms to be given children right before the officially ordained nutritious lunch. Many parents do not like for their children to have extra money with which they can buy things without the parents' knowledge. Many teachers do not like rewards of trinkets or food that are so attractive as to disrupt the classroom.

Children are likely to compare rewards and even engage in some under-the-desk trading. It may be wise to provide every subject the same amount of the reward or the same item. If rewards are to be given, the kind and amount should be revealed to parents in the permission letter and should be agreed to by staff who are in charge of the children.

Intersubject Communication

Experimenters are deluding themselves if they expect children not to talk about a particular study to their friends, especially if the children have been admonished "not to discuss the experiment with anyone." Horka and Farrow (1970) documented the extent of intersubject communication in a study on embedded figures identification. They switched the order of the figures at noon during an experimental day and then simply counted the number of afternoon subjects who gave the morning's correct response order (which was now incorrect). They found that twice as many of their afternoon subjects gave the morning's correct response as gave the afternoon's correct response. The damage this kind of communication can do to research findings is mind boggling. There are several ways that such communication could interfere with the validity of research findings:

1. Group performance could be elevated if the "correct" response was communicated.
2. Group performance could be depressed if the information interfered with correct performance.
3. Combinations of facilitation and interference could occur when information comes from various sources to everyone or only to a few.

There are some obvious precautions that an experimenter can take to avoid damage by intersubject communication: drawing one's subjects from several classes in several schools, telling subjects that their friends will have a different task and that it would only confuse their friends to be told the correct answers, and arranging to complete the experiment before subjects have an opportunity (e.g., lunch, PE) to discuss their experiences.

Intersubject communication may occur for various reasons:

1. The study may appear to be such a novel experience that the students talk about it.
2. If only a few students are selected, they may gain peer status by talking about it.
3. Peers who have not yet participated may be apprehensive and ask a student who has participated what happened.

One way to handle some of these problems is to talk to the class as a whole before a study begins, explaining what will happen, mentioning that they could confuse each other by talking about it, and to allow every child who can get permission to participate, regardless of whether their data are needed. An even more elaborate precaution would be to have three tasks for each subject, with the middle one being the task of experimental interest. That way, if the primacy and recency effects can be counted on, only the irrelevant information from the first and third tasks will be passed along. If there is some danger of contamination because of intersubject communication, the experimenter is advised to compare the performance of the first subjects in the study with those of later ones. Significantly different performance or greater variability may indicate that the later subjects have had different life experiences, namely, that they were told what to do by a fellow student. This statistical comparison, however, does not prevent such communication; it merely examines the data for evidence that it had an effect.

CONCLUSION

There are a number of challenges associated with studying children, several of which have been mentioned in this chapter, along with what we hope are some workable solutions. There is obviously much to gain by careful preparation and pilot work before beginning a study. Understanding the perspective of the cooperating staff and the children whose behavior is to be observed is a prerequisite to a successful research study. There is one further responsibility of the researcher we have not mentioned. This is a subtle responsibility incurred because, for one short period of time, children's self-esteem and knowledge about themselves are entrusted to the judgment of the experimenter. It is easy for feelings of inadequacy, incompetence, or inferiority to result from the researcher's insensitivity to the children's concern for their performance. Perhaps, overall, the remainder of the researcher's ingenuity should be used to ensure that these children, who have been generous in helping us, may in turn profit in some small way from the experience.

REFERENCES

Achenbach, T. *Research in developmental psychology: Concepts, strategies, methods.* New York: Free Press, 1978.

Baumeister, A., & Lusczc, M. A within-subjects analysis of free recall with preschool children. *Child Development,* 1976, *47,* 729–736.

Bogden, R., & Taylor, S. *Introduction to qualitative research methods: A phenomenological approach to the social sciences.* New York: Wiley, 1975.

Bronfenbrenner, U. *The ecology of human development: Experiments by nature and design.* Cambridge, Mass.: Harvard University Press, 1979.

Horka, S., & Farrow, B. A methodological note on intersubject communication as a contaminating factor in psychological experiments. *Journal of Experimental Child Psychology,* 1970, *10,* 363–366.

Kohlberg, L. Moral stages and moralization: The cognitive–developmental approach. In T. Lickona (Ed.), *Moral development and behavior: Theory, research, and social issues,* New York: Holt, Rinehart & Winston, 1976.

Michel, W., Zeiss, R., & Zeiss, A. Internal–external control and persistence: Validation and implications of the Stanford Preschool Internal-External Scale. *Journal of Personality & Social Psychology,* 1974, *29,* 265–278.

Orne, M. On the social psychology of the psychological experiment: With particular reference to the demand characteristics and their implications. *American Psychologist,* 1962, *17,* 776–783.

Piaget, J. *The moral judgment of the child.* New York: Free Press, 1965.

Yarrow, M. The measurement of children's attitudes and values. In P. H. Mussen (Ed.), *Handbook of research methods in child development.* New York: Wiley, 1960.

Author Index

Subject Index